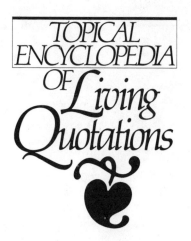

TOPICAL
ENCYCLOPEDIA
OF Living
Quotations

*Erma
God bless you
Sherwood Wirt*

Edited by

SHERWOOD ELIOT WIRT
•KERSTEN BECKSTROM•

TOPICAL ENCYCLOPEDIA
OF *Living*
Quotations

BETHANY HOUSE PUBLISHERS
MINNEAPOLIS, MINNESOTA 55438
A Division of Bethany Fellowship, Inc.

Originally published under the title, *Living Quotations for Christians* by Harper
& Row, Publishers, Inc.

Published by Bethany House Publishers
A Division of Bethany Fellowship, Inc.
6820 Auto Club Road, Minneapolis, Minnesota 55438

Printed in the United States of America

Library of Congress Cataloging in Publication Data
Main entry under title:

Topical encyclopedia of living quotations.

   Rev. ed. of: Living quotations for
Christians.   1st ed. 1974.
   Includes index.
   1. Quotations, English.   2. Religion—   Quotations,
maxims, etc.   I. Wirt, Sherwood Eliot.   II. Beckstrom, Kersten.
III. Living quotations for Christians.
PN6084.R3T6   1982   808.88'2   82-4503
ISBN 0-87123-574-9   AACR2

Acknowledgments

Acknowledgment is made to the following for permission to reprint copyrighted material:

ABINGDON PRESS: *What Are You Living For?* by John Sutherland Bonnell, copyright 1950 by Abingdon Press; *The Interpreter's Bible,* volume 8, copyright 1952 by Pierce and Smith; *Abundant Living* by E. Stanley Jones, copyright 1942 by Whitmore & Stone; *Mastery: The Art of Mastering Life* by E. Stanley Jones, copyright © 1955 by Abingdon Press; *The East Window* by Halford E. Luccock, copyright 1925 by Halford E. Luccock; *The Christlike God* by Francis J. McConnell, copyright 1929 by Abingdon Press; *The Art of Counseling* by Rollo May, copyright 1939 by Abingdon Press; *Take a Second Look at Yourself* by John Homer Miller, copyright 1950 by Pierce and Smith; *Include Me Out* by Colin Morris, copyright © 1968 by Abingdon Press; *The Secret of Radiant Life* by W. E. Sangster, copyright © 1957 by Abingdon Press; *Stewardship Studies* by Roy L. Smith, copyright 1954 by Pierce and Washabauth; *The Church and Psychotherapy* by Karl Ruf Stolz.

ALL-CHURCH PRESS: extracts from the Fort Worth *Tribune.*

GEORGE ALLEN & UNWIN LTD.: *Christianity and Fear,* tr. by W. H. Johnston (1948).

THE ALLIANCE WITNESS: quotation by V. Raymond Edman, March 27, 1968.

NORMA ALLOWAY: greeting card, copyright © 1972 by FTF Press, Toronto.

AMS PRESS, INC.: *The Anatomy of Melancholy* by Robert Burton, ed. by A. R. Shilleto.

AMERICAN BIBLE SOCIETY: *Good News for Modern Man,* from the *Today's English Version of the New Testament,* copyright © American Bible Society 1966, 1971.

APPLETON-CENTURY-CROFTS: *Reason and Emotion* by John Macmurray (1935); *The Philosophy of Religion* by Fulton J. Sheen (1948).

ARNOLDO MONDADORI EDITORE: *Shadow and Substance* by Paul Vincent Carroll.

ASSOCIATED BOOK PUBLISHERS LTD.: *Revelations of Divine Love,* recorded by Lady Julian of Norwich, ed. by Grace Warwick (1958); *Evolutionary Theory and Christian Belief* by David Lack, Methuen & Co. (1957); *The Open Way: A Study in Acceptance* by E. Graham Howe and L. Le Mesurier, Methuen & Co. (1939).

ASSOCIATED CHURCH PRESS: "Reforming the Reformation" by Karl A. Olsson.

ASSOCIATION PRESS: *Sex and Religion Today* by Peter A. Bertocci, ed. by Simon Doniger (1953); *Jesus in the Experience of Men* by T. R. Glover, copyright 1921 by T. R. Glover.

ASTOR-HONOR, INC.: *Up from Liberalism* by William F. Buckley, Jr., copyright © 1959, 1968 by William F. Buckley, Jr.

ATHENEUM PUBLISHERS: *The Making of the President—1960* by Theodore H. White, copyright © 1961 by Theodore H. White.

AUGSBURG PUBLISHING HOUSE: *In the Rustling Grass* by Herbert F. Brokering, copyright © 1964 by Augsburg Publishing House; *Infant Baptism and Adult Conversion* by Ole Hallesby, copyright 1924 by Augsburg Publishing House; *Prayer* by Ole Hallesby, copyright 1931, 1959 by Augsburg Publishing House.

BABSON'S REPORTS, INC.: for quotation by the late Roger W. Babson.

BACK TO THE BIBLE BROADCAST: from song "Nothing Is Impossible" by Eugene Clark, copyright © 1966 by the Good News

Broadcasting Association Inc.

BAKER BOOK HOUSE: *Baker's Dictionary of Practical Theology*, ed. by Ralph G. Turnbull, copyright © 1967 by Baker Book House; *Baker's Dictionary of Theology*, ed. by Everett F. Harrison and Geoffrey W. Bromiley, copyright © 1960 by Baker Book House; *In Christ's Stead* by Arthur John Gossip, copyright 1925 by Baker Book House; *Good Morning, Lord* by Charles R. Hembree, copyright © 1971 by Baker Book House; *Pocket of Pebbles* by Charles R. Hembree, copyright © 1969 by Baker Book House; *Voice of the Turtledove* by Charles R. Hembree, copyright © 1971 by Baker Book House; *Christianity and Liberalism* by J. Gresham Machen, copyright 1923 by Macmillan Company; *Ecumenics: The Science of the Church Universal* by John A. Mackay, copyright © 1964 by Prentice-Hall; *When You Get to the End of Yourself* by W. T. Purkiser (1970); *Textbook of the History of Doctrines* by Reinhold Seeberg, tr. by Charles E. Hay, volume 2 (1952); *The Supernaturalness of Christ: Can We Still Believe in It?* by Wilbur M. Smith, copyright 1940 by W. A. Wilde Company; *Heralds of God* by James S. Stewart (1946); "Patristic Ethics" by Paul Woolley, in *Baker's Dictionary of Christian Ethics*, ed. by Carl F. H. Henry, copyright © 1973 by Baker Book House.

THE BANNER OF TRUTH TRUST PUBLISHERS: *George Whitefield* by Arnold A. Dallimore, volume 1, copyright © 1970 by Arnold A. Dallimore; *The Puritan Hope* by Iain H. Murray, copyright © 1971 by Iain H. Murray.

BASIL BLACKWELL PUBLISHER: *Preaching in England in the Late Fifteenth and Sixteenth Centuries* by J. W. Blench, copyright © 1964 by Basil Blackwell.

BEACON HILL PRESS OF KANSAS CITY: *Christ's Parables Today* by George K. Bowers, copyright © 1966 by Beacon Hill Press; *Personal Renewal Through Christian Conversion* by W. Curry Mavis, copyright © 1969 by Beacon Hill Press; *Interpreting Christian Holiness* by W. T. Purkiser, copyright © 1971 by Beacon Hill Press.

BILLY GRAHAM EVANGELISTIC ASSOCIATION: *Decision* magazine, copyright © 1962, 1963, 1964, 1965, 1966, 1967, 1968, 1969, 1970, 1971, 1972, 1973 by the Billy Graham Evangelistic Association; *Great Preaching*, ed. by Sherwood E. Wirt and Viola Blake, copyright © 1970 by the Billy Graham Evangelistic Association.

BENZIGER BRUCE & GLENCOE, INC.: *Perfection Is for You* by Thomas J. Higgins, copyright 1953 by The Bruce Publishing Company.

BLOCH PUBLISHING COMPANY: *Dreamers of the Ghetto* by Israel Zangwill, copyright 1923 by Bloch Publishing Company.

THE BOBBS-MERRILL COMPANY, INC.: *Pathways of the Inner Life*, ed. by Georges A. Barrois, copyright © 1956 by The Bobbs-Merrill Company; *Did You Ever See a Dream Walking?* ed. by William F. Buckley, Jr., copyright © 1970 by The Bobbs-Merrill Company; *The Dawn of Personality* by Emile Cailliet, copyright © 1955 by The Bobbs-Merrill Company; *Christianity and Modern Man* by Albert T. Mollegen, copyright © 1961 by The Bobbs-Merrill Company.

BOOKSTORE JOURNAL: excerpt by Francis A. Schaeffer, copyright © Bookstore Journal magazine, September 1972.

BROADMAN PRESS: *Hastings' Illustrations* by Robert J. Hastings, copyright © 1971 by Broadman Press; *A Word Fitly Spoken*, ed. by Robert J. Hastings, copyright © 1962 by Broadman Press; *From a Black Brother* by Manuel Lee Scott, copyright © 1971 by Broadman Press.

CURTIS BROWN, LTD.: *Poems, 1902–1919* by John Drinkwater, Houghton Mifflin Company, copyright © 1919 by John Drinkwater.

BURNS & OATES LTD.: *The Law of Love* by Francis Devas.

ROBERT CALHOUN: *God and the Common Life* by Robert L. Calhoun, Chas. Scribner's Sons.

CAMBRIDGE UNIVERSITY PRESS: *The Expanding Universe* by A. S. Eddington, copyright 1933 by Cambridge University Press; *The Mysterious Universe* by James H. Jeans, copyright 1930, 1932 The Macmillan Company; *Dr. Johnson and Others* by S. C. Roberts, copyright © 1958 by Cambridge University Press; *Mind and Matter* by Erwin Schrodinger, copyright © 1958 by Cambridge University Press; *Christian Doctrine* by John S. Whale, copyright 1942 The Macmillan Company.

CANADA MONTH: quotation by Charlotte Whitton, June 1963.

CEYLON CHURCHMAN: quotations by the Rt. Revd. Mark R. Carpenter-Garnier and by E. B. Pusey.

CHOSEN BOOKS: *The Hiding Place* by Corrie ten Boom with John and Elizabeth Sherrill, copyright © 1971 by Corrie ten Boom with John and Elizabeth Sherrill, distributed by Fleming H. Revell.

CHRISTIAN ATHLETE: quotation by William Inge, March 1968.

THE CHRISTIAN CENTURY FOUNDATION: *The Christian Century*, January 12, 1972, and August 2, 1972, copyright © 1972 Christian Century Foundation.

CHRISTIAN HERALD: "The Love Chapter Revised" by Margaret Anderson, copyright © 1961.

THE CHRISTIAN INDEX: quotation by John Quincy Adams, October 1968.

ACKNOWLEDGMENTS

CHRISTIAN LIFE PUBLICATIONS: *Christian Life* magazine, July, copyright © 1969 Christian Life Publications, Inc.

CHRISTIAN LITERATURE CRUSADE INC.: *The Way to Pentecost* by Samuel Chadwick (1932); *We Would See Jesus* by Roy and Revel Hession, copyright © 1958 by Christian Literature Crusade, London and Fort Washington, Pa.; *Rees Howells, Intercessor* by Norman Grubb (1952); *The Deep Things of God* by Norman Grubb, copyright © 1958 by Norman P. Grubb; *In the Day of Thy Power: The Scriptural Principles of Revival* by Arthur Wallis, copyright © 1956 by Christian Literature Crusade, London and Fort Washington, Pa.; *Oswald Chambers: An Unbribed Soul* by D. W. Lambert (1968); *The Normal Christian Life* by Watchman Nee, copyright © 1958 Witness & Testimony Publishers; *Show Me Thy Way* by Wesley W. Nelson (1954); *There Is an Answer* by Leith Samuel, copyright © 1966 by Christian Literature Crusade, Fort Washington, Pa.; *The Check Book of the Bank of Faith* by C. H. Spurgeon (1957); *Not Good If Detached* by Corrie ten Boom, copyright © 1957 by Christian Literature Crusade, London; *Pray in the Spirit* by Arthur Wallis, copyright © 1970 by Arthur Wallis; *Ploughed Under* by Amy Carmichael (1932).

CHRISTIAN WITNESS PRODUCTS, INC.: *The Simplicity of the Spirit-filled Life* by L. L. Legters, copyright © 1968 by Christian Witness Products, Inc.; *Victory: The Will of God for Me* by L. L. Legters, copyright 1932 by Christian Life Literature Fund.

CHRISTIANITY TODAY: quotations from issues dated January 20, 1958; July 4, 1960; November 8, 1963; July 18, 1969; January 2, 1970; March 13, 1970; March 27, 1970; March 12, 1971; March 31, 1972.

THE CHURCH HERALD: quotation by Robert D. DeHaan, February 28, 1969.

THE CHURCH HERALD AND HOLINESS BANNER: quotation, January 4, 1968.

THE CLARENDON PRESS (Oxford): *The Oxford English Dictionary*, 1933, volume 12; *Miracles & the New Psychology* by E. R. Micklem, first published 1922 by Oxford University Press.

JAMES CLARKE & COMPANY LTD.: *Institutes of the Christian Religion* by John Calvin, tr. by Henry Beveridge, volume 2 (1953); *Commentary on Galatians* by Martin Luther (1953); *The Quiet Heart* by Alistair MacLean, Allenson & Company Ltd. (1940); *Radiant Certainty* by Alistair MacLean, Allenson & Company Ltd.

WM. COLLINS SONS & CO. LTD.: *The Imitation of Christ* by Thomas à Kempis (1957); *The Destiny of Man* by Nicolas Berdyaev, copyright 1937 by Geoffrey Bles Ltd.; *A Mind Awake: An Anthology of C. S. Lewis*, ed. by Clyde S. Kilby, copyright © 1968 by Executors of the Estate of C. S. Lewis; *Christian Behaviour* by C. S. Lewis, copyright 1943 by Geoffrey Bles Ltd.; *Christian Reflections* by C. S. Lewis, copyright © 1967 by Executors of the Estate of C. S. Lewis; *Letters to Malcolm: Chiefly on Prayer* by C. S. Lewis, copyright © 1963, 1964 by C. S. Lewis; *Mere Christianity* by C. S. Lewis, copyright © 1958; *The Problem of Pain* by C. S. Lewis (1940); *The Screwtape Letters* by C. S. Lewis, copyright 1942 by C. S. Lewis; *The Weight of Glory* by C. S. Lewis, copyright 1949 by Macmillan Publishing Co.; *True Humanism* by Jacques Maritain, copyright 1936 by Geoffrey Bles Ltd.; *Freedom and the Spirit* by Jacques Maritain, copyright 1935 by Geoffrey Bles Ltd.

DAVID C. COOK PUBLISHING COMPANY: *The View from a Hearse* by Joseph Bayly, copyright © 1969 by David C. Cook Publishing Company.

COVENANT PRESS: quotation by E. James Kennedy in *The Covenant Companion*, copyright Covenant Press; *A Burning Heart* by Erik Dahlhielm, copyright 1951 by Covenant Press.

CREATION HOUSE: *Our Society in Turmoil*, ed. by Gary Collins, copyright © 1970 by Creation House; *Be All You Can Be* by David Augsburger, copyright © 1970 by Creation House.

THOMAS Y. CROWELL COMPANY, INC.: *Contemporary Quotations*, comp. by James Simpson, copyright © 1964 by James B. Simpson; *The International Thesaurus of Quotations*, comp. by Rhoda Thomas Tripp, copyright © 1970 by Thomas Y. Crowell Company, Inc.; *The Cross on the Mountain* by Sherwood Eliot Wirt, copyright © 1959 by Sherwood Eliot Wirt; *A Message to Garcia* by Elbert Hubbard.

WALTER DE GRUYTER INC.: *Meister Eckhart*, tr. by R. B. Blakney.

T. S. DENISON & COMPANY: *We Believe in Prayer*, ed. by Lawrence M. Brings, copyright © 1958 by T. S. Denison & Company.

J. M. DENT & SONS LTD.: *Under Western Eyes* by Joseph Conrad, copyright 1911 by George H. Doran Company, by permission of the Trustees of the Joseph Conrad Estate; *Youth* by Joseph Conrad, copyright © 1958 by permission of the Trustees of the Joseph Conrad Estate; *The Diary of a Nobody* by George and Weedon Grossmith; *Searchlights and Nightingales* by Robert Lynd (1939); *Essays and Addresses on the Philosophy of Religion* by Baron Friedrich von Hügel.

DETROIT NEWS: quotation by Richard Emrich, *Detroit News*, June 25, 1961.

LESTER E. DENONN: *Wit and Wisdom of Oliver Wen-*

dell Holmes, ed. by Lester E. Denonn, Beacon Press.

DIVINE WORD PUBLICATIONS: *Meditations for the Layman,* copyright 1951 by J. S. Paluch Co. Inc.

DODD, MEAD & COMPANY: *The Place of Help* by Oswald Chambers, copyright 1936 by Dodd, Mead & Company; *My Utmost for His Highest* by Oswald Chambers, copyright 1935 by Dodd, Mead & Company, renewed 1962.

DOHNAVUR FELLOWSHIP: *If* by Amy Carmichael, Christian Literature Crusade, distributor.

DOUBLEDAY & COMPANY, INC.: *Calm Delight* by Elsie Chamberlain, copyright © 1960 by Elsie D. Garrington; *The New Testament in the Light of Modern Research* by Adolf Deissmann, copyright 1929 by George H. Doran Company; *The Challenge* by Billy Graham, copyright © 1969 by Billy Graham; *Peace with God* by Billy Graham, copyright 1953 by Billy Graham; *World Aflame* by Billy Graham, copyright © 1965 by Billy Graham; *Adventures in Friendship* by David Grayson, copyright 1910 by Doubleday & Company; *For Instance* by Donald T. Kauffman, copyright © 1970 by Donald T. Kauffman; *The Responsibility of Power,* ed. by Krieger & Stern; *The Greatest Story Ever Told* by Fulton Oursler, copyright 1949 by Fulton Oursler, published 1950; *The Outline of History: The Whole Story of Man* by H. G. Wells; *Thinking Through the Scripture* by William Parker White, copyright 1927 by George H. Doran Company; *A. L. Alexander's Treasurehouse of Inspirational Poetry & Prose,* copyright © 1966 by A. L. Alexander; *A History of Preaching* by E. C. Dargan, copyright 1912 by George H. Doran Company; *I Believe: Sermons on the Apostles' Creed* by G. A. Studdert Kennedy, George H. Doran Company (1911); *Expositions of Holy Scripture* by Alexander Maclaren, volume 2, George H. Doran Company.

DROKE HOUSE/HALLUX, INC.: *Fountains of Faith* by William Arthur Ward, used by permission; *The Independent Magazine,* December 27, 1970.

E. P. DUTTON & COMPANY, INC.: *A Chain of Prayer Across the Ages* by Selina F. Fox (1964); *Man and Society in Calamity* by Pitirim A. Sorokin, copyright 1942 by E. P. Dutton & Co., Inc., renewed 1970 by Helen P. Sorokin.

WM. B. EERDMANS PUBLISHING COMPANY: *Convictions to Live By* by L. Nelson Bell, copyright © 1966 by Wm. B. Eerdmans; *Systematic Theology* by L. Berkhof, copyright 1939, 1941 by L. Berkhof; *When Jesus Came* by Handel H. Brown, copyright © 1963 by Wm. B. Eerd-

mans; *Enter into Life* by William Fitch, copyright © 1961 by Wm. B. Eerdmans; *Remaking the Modern Mind* by Carl F. H. Henry, copyright 1946 by Wm. B. Eerdmans; *Christian Personal Ethics* by Carl F. H. Henry, copyright © 1957 by Wm. B. Eerdmans; *The Uneasy Conscience of Modern Fundamentalism* by Carl F. H. Henry, copyright 1947 by Wm. B. Eerdmans; *Crucial Questions about the Kingdom of God* by George E. Ladd, copyright 1952 by Wm. B. Eerdmans; *God in the Dock* by C. S. Lewis, copyright © 1970 by Wm. B. Eerdmans; *Letters to an American Lady* by C. S. Lewis, ed. by Clyde S. Kilby, copyright © 1967 by Wm. B. Eerdmans; *The Ante-Nicene Fathers,* ed. by Allan Menzies, volume 10; *The Creative Theology of P. T. Forsyth,* ed. by Samuel J. Mikolaski, copyright © 1969 by Wm. B. Eerdmans; *The Quest for Serenity* by G. H. Morling, copyright © 1955 by Wm. B. Eerdmans; *The New Bible Dictionary,* ed. by J. D. Douglas, copyright © 1962 by Inter-Varsity Fellowship; *Do Not Sin Against the Cross* by S. J. Reid, copyright 1940 by Wm. B. Eerdmans; *The Witness of the Spirit* by Bernard Ramm, copyright © 1959 by Wm. B. Eerdmans; *Christian Letters to a Post-Christian World: A Selection of Essays* by Dorothy L. Sayers, copyright © 1969 by Wm. B. Eerdmans; *Out of the Depths* by Helmut Thielicke, copyright © 1962 by Wm. B. Eerdmans; *The Kingdom and the Church* by Geerhardus Vos, copyright 1951 by Wm. B. Eerdmans; *Miracles: Yesterday and Today* by Benjamin B. Warfield, copyright 1954 by Wm. B. Eerdmans.

DWIGHT D. EISENHOWER LIBRARY: quotation by General Dwight Eisenhower.

THE EPISCOPALIAN: quotation by Louis Cassels, copyright © 1972 by The Episcopalian, Inc.

EPWORTH PRESS: *Peter Taylor Forsyth: Director of Souls* by Peter Taylor Forsyth; *Hope of Immortality* by W. R. Matthews (1966).

ETERNITY: quotation by Edward John Carnell, copyright The Evangelical Foundation, Philadelphia.

EVANGELICAL LITERATURE SERVICE: *The High Calling of God* by Jordan C. Khan, copyright © 1968 by Evangelical Literature Service.

FABER AND FABER LTD.: *The Theology of the Sacraments* by Donald M. Baillie (1957); *The Idea of a Christian Society* by T. S. Eliot, copyright 1939 by Faber and Faber Ltd.; *Return to Philosophy* by C. E. M. Joad (1936).

FARM JOURNAL, INC.: *My Last Wonderful Days* by Hazel Beck André, July 1956.

JOHN FARQUHARSON LTD.: *Time and Time Again* by James Hilton.

F. E. L. PUBLICATIONS, LTD.: for song "They'll Know

We Are Christians by Our Love" by Peter Scholtes, copyright © 1966 by F. E. L. Publications, Ltd.

FORTRESS PRESS: *Christian Woman* by R. Y. Nelson; *How the World Began* by Helmut Thielicke, tr. by J. W. Doberstein, copyright © 1961 by Muhlenberg Press.

SAMUEL FRENCH, INC.: *The Terrible Meek* by Charles Rann Kennedy, copyright 1912, 1933 by Charles Rann Kennedy, copyright 1939 (in renewal) by Charles Rann Kennedy, copyright © 1961 (in renewal) by Harold J. Gorst. All rights reserved. Used by permission of the owners and Samuel French, Inc.

SIGMUND FREUD COPYRIGHTS, LTD.: *The Problem of Anxiety* by Sigmund Freud, W. W. Norton & Company, Inc. (1936).

LESLIE FREWIN PUBLISHERS LTD.: *The Wit of Prince Philip*, ed. by Peter Butler.

FRIENDSHIP PRESS: *The Household of God* by Lesslie Newbigin, copyright 1954 by Friendship Press.

FUNK & WAGNALLS PUBLISHING COMPANY, INC.: *Why England Slept* by John F. Kennedy, copyright © 1960 by Wilfred Funk, Inc. With permission of Funk & Wagnalls.

H. L. GEE: *Briefly*, comp. by H. L. Gee, copyright © 1964 The Epworth Press, London.

GIRARD BANK: *The Testimony of the Soul* by Rufus M. Jones, copyright 1936; Rufus M. Jones Trust Under Deed 5784.

GOOD NEWS PUBLISHERS: *In the Beloved* by Norman F. Douty.

GOSPEL LIGHT PUBLICATIONS: *Don't Look Now* by Ethel Barrett, copyright © 1968 by Gospel Light Publications, Regal Book Division; *How to Be a Christian Without Being Religious* by Fritz Ridenour, copyright © 1967 by Gospel Light Publications, Regal Book Division; *431 Quotes from the Notes of Henrietta C. Mears*, comp. by Eleanor L. Doan, copyright © 1970 by Gospel Light Publications, Regal Book Division.

HARCOURT BRACE JOVANOVICH, INC.: *Power* by Adolf A. Berle, copyright © 1969 by Adolf A. Berle; *The Idea of a Christian Society* by T. S. Eliot (1939); *Modern Man in Search of a Soul* by Carl Gustav Jung, Kegan Paul, Trench, Trubner & Co. (1947); *The General Theory of Employment, Interest and Money* by J. M. Keynes, copyright 1936 by Harcourt Brace Jovanovich, Inc.; *Surprised by Joy* by C. S. Lewis, copyright © 1955 by C. S. Lewis; *No Man Is an Island* by Thomas Merton, copyright © 1955 by Harcourt Brace Jovanovich, Inc.; *Flight to Arras* by Antoine de Saint-Exupéry (1942).

HARPER & ROW, PUBLISHERS: *Heirlooms*, ed. by Margaret T. Applegarth, copyright © 1967 by

Margaret T. Applegarth; *Life Together* by Dietrich Bonhoeffer, copyright 1954 by Harper & Brothers; *No Escape from Life* by John Sutherland Bonnell, copyright © 1958 by Harper & Row; *Christian Manifesto* by Ernest T. Campbell, copyright © 1970 by Ernest T. Campbell; *The Impact of American Religious Liberalism* by Kenneth Cauthen (1962); *Civilisation: A Personal View* by Kenneth Clark, copyright © 1969 by Kenneth Clark; *Quotation Finder* by Everett McKinley Dirksen and Herbert V. Prochnow, copyright © 1971 by Louella Dirksen and Herbert V. Prochnow; *Faith and Reason* by Nels F. S. Ferre (1946); *White House Sermons*, ed. by Ben Hibbs, copyright © 1972 by Harper & Row; *My Life's History* by Anna Mary Moses (1951); *The Racial Problem in Christian Perspective* by Kyle Haselden (1959); *The Passionate State of Mind* by Eric Hoffer, copyright © 1955 by Harper & Row; *Christian Theology* by Walter Horton, copyright © 1955; *The Great Tradition of the American Churches* by W. S. Hudson (1953); *From Victory to Peace* by Paul Hutchinson, copyright 1943, Willett, Clark & Company; *Clear Thinking* by R. W. Jepson; *Artemus Ward's Best Stories*, ed. by Clifton Johnson, copyright 1912 by Harper & Brothers; *A Calvin Treasury*, ed. by William F. Keesecker, copyright © 1961 by William F. Keesecker; *A Testament of Devotion* by Thomas R. Kelly, copyright 1941 by Harper & Row; *Have This Mind* by Gerald Kennedy (1948); *The Acts of the Apostles in Present-Day Preaching* by Halford E. Luccock, copyright 1942 by Willett, Clark & Company; *The Virgin Birth of Christ* by J. Gresham Machen, copyright 1930 by Harper & Brothers; *Great Preaching Today*, ed. by Alton M. Motter, copyright © 1955 by Harper & Brothers; *Something Beautiful for God* by Malcolm Muggeridge, copyright © 1971 by The Mother Teresa Committee; *Treasury of the Christian World*, ed. by A. Gordon Nasby, copyright 1953 by Harper & Brothers; *God's Good News* by Gerald Kennedy, copyright © 1955 by Gerald Kennedy; *Thanks Be to God* by Robert N. Rodenmayer (1960); *Love Is a Spendthrift* by Paul Scherer (1961); *With the Holy Spirit and with Fire* by Samuel M. Shoemaker (1960); *The Nobel Lecture on Literature* by Aleksandr I. Solzhenitsyn, tr. by Thomas P. Whitney, copyright © 1972 by The Nobel Foundation, English tr. copyright © 1972 by Thomas P. Whitney; *The Rule and Exercises of Holy Living* by Jeremy Taylor, copyright © 1970 by Kenneth Langford and Ronald Goff; *Our Heavenly Father* by Helmut Thielicke, tr. by John W. Doberstein, copyright © 1960 by

ACKNOWLEDGMENTS

John W. Doberstein; *The Adventure of Living* by Paul Tournier, copyright © *1965 by Paul Tournier; The Knowledge of the Holy* by A. W. Tozer, copyright © 1961 by Aiden Wilson Tozer; *The Logic of Belief* by D. Elton Trueblood, copyright 1942; *Have Faith Without Fear* by Kenneth L. Wilson, copyright © 1970 by Kenneth L. Wilson; *Jesus Power* by Sherwood E. Wirt, copyright © 1972 by Sherwood E. Wirt; *Love Song: Augustine's Confessions for Modern Man* by Sherwood E. Wirt, copyright © 1971 by Sherwood E. Wirt; *The Social Conscience of the Evangelical* by Sherwood E. Wirt, copyright © 1968 by Sherwood E. Wirt.

GEORGE G. HARRAP & COMPANY LTD.: *Benham's Book of Quotations,* comp. by Sir Gurney Benham, copyright 1948 by George G. Harrap & Company Ltd.

EUGENE M. HARRISON: *How to Win Souls* by Eugene M. Harrison, Scripture Press (1952).

PAUL HARVEY NEWS: "The Mystery in the Mirror" in *These Times,* May 1971.

ELOISE HATFIELD: quotation from *Decision* magazine, copyright © 1971 by Eloise Hatfield.

HAWTHORN BOOKS, INC.: *Reflections on Life* by Alexis Carrel, copyright 1952 by Hawthorn Books, Inc.; *Three to Get Married* by Fulton J. Sheen; *Reason and Emotion* by John Macmurray, copyright 1935, Appleton-Century, Publishers; *The Philosophy of Religion* by Fulton J. Sheen, Appleton-Century, Publishers (1948).

DAVID HIGHAM ASSOCIATES, LTD.: *Creed or Chaos* by Dorothy L. Sayers, Methuen & Co. Ltd. (1947).

THE HIGHWAY EVANGELIST: quotation by Bill Frye, April 1971.

HILLARY HOUSE PUBLISHERS, LTD.: *Return to Philosophy* by C. E. M. Joad (1936).

HIS INTERNATIONAL SERVICE: *His Comfort* by Norman B. Harrison, copyright © 1964 by Christian Service Fellowship Publications.

HODDER & STOUGHTON LIMITED: *Christ in the Silence* by C. F. Andrews (1933); *The Way to Pentecost* by Samuel Chadwick (1932); *Smoke on the Mountain* by Joy Davidman (1955); *The Social Hope of the Church* by Stanley G. Evans (1965); *Studies in the Life of Christ* by A. M. Fairbairn (1881); *Uncommon Prayers* by Cecil Hunt (1948); *Mary Slessor of Calabar: Pioneer Missionary* by W. P. Livingstone (1915); *The Secret of Serenity* by Gordon Powell (1957); *In Christ's Stead* by John Gossip (1925); *The Power of Prayer* by Dora Greenwell and P. T. Forsyth; *Heralds of God* by James S. Stewart (1949); *The New Testament in Life and Literature* by Jane T. Stoddart; *New Testament Christianity* by J. B. Phillips,

copyright © 1956 by J. B. Phillips.

HOLT, RINEHART AND WINSTON, INC.: *Secrets of Self-Mastery* by L. R. Ditzen, copyright © 1958 by Holt, Rinehart and Winston, Inc.; *The Sane Society* by Erich Fromm, copyright © 1955 by Erich Fromm; *Living Joyously* by Kirby Page, copyright 1950; *The Comments of Bagshot* by J. A. Spender, copyright 1912 by Henry Holt and Company; *Personality: A Psychological Interpretation* by Gordon W. Allport, copyright 1937 by Holt, Rinehart and Winston, Inc.

JOHNS HOPKINS PRESS: *From the Stone Age to Christianity* by William Foxwell Albright, copyright © 1957 by Anchor Books; *Proc. of the Second Colloquium on Personality Investigation,* Johns Hopkins University Press (1930).

HOUGHTON MIFFLIN COMPANY: *Strange Fruit* by Phyllis Bottome (1928); *Silent Spring* by Rachel Carson, copyright © 1962 by Rachel L. Carson; *The Gathering Storm* by Winston S. Churchill (1948); *Autobiography* by Will Rogers, ed. by Donald Day (1949); *Letters, Lectures, Addresses, 1909* by Charles E. Garman; *Parkinson's Law and Other Studies in Administration* by C. Northcote Parkinson (1957); *Counseling and Psychotherapy* by Carl R. Rogers, copyright 1942 by Carl R. Rogers; *The Vital Center* by Arthur M. Schlesinger, copyright 1949 by Houghton Mifflin Company.

KATHARINE HOWARD: *New Every Morning* by Philip E. Howard, Jr., copyright © 1969 by Philip Howard, published by Zondervan Publishing House.

HUMANITIES PRESS INC.: *Tractatus Logico-Philosophicus* by Ludwig Wittgenstein.

HUTCHINSON & COMPANY, LTD.: *The Act of Creation* by Arthur Koestler, copyright © 1964, 1969 by Arthur Koestler.

THE INTERNATIONAL FELLOWSHIP OF EVANGELICAL STUDENTS: quotation from *IFES Journal,* volume 18, #2, 1965.

INTER-VARSITY PRESS (Downers Grove, Ill.): *The Dust of Death* by Os Guinness, copyright © 1973 by Inter-Varsity Christian Fellowship, used by permission of Inter-Varsity Press; *Back to Freedom and Dignity* by Francis A. Schaeffer, copyright © 1972 by L'Abri Fellowship; *The Church at the End of the 20th Century* by Francis A. Schaeffer, copyright © 1970 by L'Abri Fellowship; *Death in the City* by Francis A. Schaeffer, copyright © 1969 by L'Abri Fellowship.

INTEXT PRESS: *Adlai's Almanac,* ed. by Bessie R. James and Mary Waterstreet, copyright 1952 by Henry Schuman, Inc., published by Abelard-Schuman, Ltd.

THE IONA COMMUNITY (Publishing): *Only One Way Left* by George F. MacLeod (1954); *We Shall*

ACKNOWLEDGMENTS

Re-Build by George F. MacLeod (1947).

THE KANSAS CITY STAR: quotation by Bill Vaughan.

P. J. KENEDY & SONS: *Faith, Reason and Modern Psychiatry* by Francis J. Braceland, copyright © 1955 by P. J. Kenedy & Sons; *The Spiritual Writings of Father Francis Devas, S. J.,* ed. by Philip Jeanaman, S. J., copyright 1954 by P. J. Kenedy & Sons; *All You Who Are Burdened* by Martin J. Scott, copyright 1946 by P. J. Kenedy & Sons.

ALFRED K. KNOPF, INC.: *Markings* by Dag Hammarskjöld, tr. by Leif Sjöberg and W. H. Auden, copyright © 1964 by Alfred K. Knopf, Inc.; *A Mencken Chrestomathy* by H. L. Mencken, copyright 1949 by Alfred K. Knopf, Inc.

JOHN KNOX PRESS: *Secrets* by Paul Tournier, copyright © M. E. Bratcher 1965, used by permission of John Knox Press.

LANCASTER THEOLOGICAL SEMINARY: *The Latin Works of Huldreich Zwingli,* ed. by William John Hinke, copyright 1922 by the American Society of Church History.

BRUCE LARSON: *Setting Men Free* by Bruce Larson, copyright © 1967 by Bruce Larson, Zondervan Publishing House.

LIFE OF FAITH: quotation by Lane Adams, September 1971.

LIGHT AND LIFE: quotation from *The Free Methodist* (now *Light and Life*), March 15, 1966.

ERNEST M. LIGON: *The Psychology of Christian Personality* by Ernest Ligon, The Macmillan Company (1935).

J. B. LIPPINCOTT COMPANY: *Revolution and the Christian Faith* by Vernon C. Grounds, copyright © 1971 by J. B. Lippincott Company; *Notes for Living* by Raymond Irving Lindquist, copyright © 1968; *The Great Reversal: Evangelism Versus Social Concern* by David O. Moberg, copyright © 1972 by David O. Moberg; *John Mistletoe* by Christopher Morley, copyright 1929, renewed 1958 by Christopher Morley. All selections reprinted by permission of J. B. Lippincott Company.

LITTLE, BROWN AND COMPANY: *Christmas in Our Town* by Alice Carrick; *Mr. Dooley Remembers* by Finley Peter Dunne, copyright © 1963 by Little, Brown and Company; *Time and Time Again* by James Hilton; *My Ideas of God* by Joseph Fort Newton, copyright 1927 by Little, Brown and Company; *The Optimist's Good Morning,* comp. by Florence Hobart Perin, copyright 1907 by Little, Brown and Company; *Daily Strength for Daily Needs,* selected by Mary W. Tileston, copyright 1912 by Little, Brown and Company; *Joy and Strength* by Mary Wilder Tileston, copyright 1901, 1929 by Mary Wilder Tileston.

LIVERIGHT PUBLISHING CORPORATION: *The Conquest of Happiness* by Bertrand Russell, copyright © 1958 by Bertrand Russell. By permission of Liveright, Publishers.

LOGOS INTERNATIONAL: *These Are Not Drunken As Ye Suppose* by Howard M. Ervin, copyright © 1968 Logos International; *Take Another Look at Guidance* by Bob Mumford, copyright © 1971 Logos International.

LOIZEAUX BROTHERS, INC: *Lectures on the Levitical Offerings* by H. A. Ironside; *Notes on Philippians* by H. A. Ironside, copyright 1922 by Loizeaux Brothers, Inc.; *The New Life* by Captain Reginald Wallis, copyright 1932 by Loizeaux Brothers, Inc.

LONGMAN GROUP LTD.: *Outspoken Essays: Second Series* by William R. Inge (1922); *The Vision of God* by Kenneth E. Kirk, abridged edition 1934.

LUTTERWORTH PRESS (Guildford and London): *The Divine Imperative* by Emil Brunner, tr. by Olive Wyon, English trans. first published 1937 by Lutterworth Press; *Christian Vocation* by W. R. Forrester (1951); *The Deep Things of God* by Norman P. Grubb, copyright © 1958 by Norman P. Grubb; *Rees Howells, Intercessor* by Norman P. Grubb (1952).

LUZAC & COMPANY LTD.: *Readings from the Mystics of Islam,* ed. by Margaret Smith (1950).

MCGRAW-HILL BOOK COMPANY: *A Man Called Peter* by Catherine Marshall, copyright © 1951 by Catherine Marshall; *The First Easter* by Peter Marshall, copyright © 1959 by McGraw-Hill Book Co.; *Lift Up Your Heart* by Fulton J. Sheen, copyright 1950 by McGraw-Hill Book Co.; *Peace of Soul* by Fulton J. Sheen, copyright 1949 by McGraw-Hill Book Co.

DAVID MCKAY COMPANY, INC.: *The Life and Times of Jesus the Messiah* by Alfred Edersheim, volume 1 (1915); *Human Destiny* by Pierre LeComte du Nouy; *The Fruits of the Spirit* by Evelyn Underhill, copyright 1942 by David McKay Co.

MACMILLAN PUBLISHING COMPANY, INC.: *The Individual and His Religion* by Gordon W. Allport, copyright 1950 by Macmillan Publishing Co.; *The Cost of Discipleship* by Dietrich Bonhoeffer (1948); *Ethics* by Dietrich Bonhoeffer, copyright © 1955 by Macmillan Publishing Co.; *Minister* by John B. Coburn, copyright © 1963 by John B. Coburn; *The Act of Creation* by Arthur Koestler, copyright © 1964, 1969 by Arthur Koestler; *Mere Christianity* by C. S. Lewis, copyright © 1958 by Macmillan Publishing Co.; *The Great Divorce* by C. S. Lewis, copyright 1946 by Macmillan Publishing Co.; *Miracles* by C. S. Lewis, copyright 1947 by Macmillan Publishing Co.; *The Problem of*

Pain by C. S. Lewis, copyright 1940 by Macmillan Publishing Co.; *The Screwtape Letters* by C. S. Lewis, copyright 1942 by C. S. Lewis; *The Weight of Glory* by C. S. Lewis, copyright 1949 by Macmillan Publishing Co.; "The Everlasting Mercy," in *Poems* by John Masefield, copyright 1912 by Macmillan Publishing Co., renewed 1940 by John Masefield; *Reading the Bible* by William Lyon Phelps, copyright 1919 by Macmillan Publishing Co., renewed 1947 by John J. McKeon; *New Testament Christianity* by J. B. Phillips, copyright © 1956 by J. B. Phillips; *A Theology for the Social Gospel* by Walter Rauschenbusch, copyright 1917 by Macmillan Publishing Co., renewed 1945 by Pauline E. Rauschenbusch; *A Theological Word Book of the Bible,* ed. by Alan Richardson, copyright 1950 by Macmillan Publishing Co.; *The Architecture of the Universe* by William Francis Gray Swann, copyright 1939 by Macmillan Publishing Co., renewed 1962 by W. F. G. Swann; *To the End of the World* by Helen C. White, copyright 1939 by Macmillan Publishing Co., renewed 1967 by Helen C. White.

MACMILLAN (London and Basingstoke): *Life of Florence Nightingale* by Sir E. T. Cook, volume 1; *Emerson* by John Morley (1923); *Christus Veritas* by William Temple; *Mens Creatrix* by William Temple, copyright 1917 by Macmillan, London and Basingstoke; *Nature, Man and God* by William Temple (1934); *The Tragic Sense of Life* by Miguel de Unamuno, tr. by J. E. Crawford Flitch, copyright 1921 Macmillan, London and Basingstoke.

MARSHALL, MORGAN & SCOTT PUBLICATIONS LTD.: *Oswald Chambers: An Unbribed Soul* by D. W. Lambert, copyright © 1968; *The Spirit of Christ* by Andrew Murray, copyright © 1963; *The Passion for Souls* by Oswald J. Smith (1965); *The Check Book of the Bank of Faith* by C. H. Spurgeon (1957); *Parables of the Cross* by I. Lilias Trotter; *The Keswick Week, 1957* by L. F. E. Wilkinson; *The Glory of the Cross* by Samuel M. Zwemer.

THE METHODIST STORY: quotation by Roy L. Smith, published by the Commission on Promotion and Cultivation. Permission granted by Interpretation, Joint Committee on Communications of the United Methodist Church.

MOODY MONTHLY: *Why Does God Not Answer?* by Gordon Chilvers, copyright © September 1970 Moody Bible Institute of Chicago; *Christian Reflections* by Phillip R. Newell, copyright © September 1970 Moody Bible Institute of Chicago; "How to Stop Worrying" by George Sweeting, copyright © October 1972 Moody Bible Institute of Chicago.

MOODY PRESS: *Witness Is Withness* by David Augsburger, copyright © 1971 by the Moody Bible Institute of Chicago; *The Life and Diary of David Brainerd,* ed. by Philip E. Howard, Jr., copyright 1949 by Moody Bible Institute; *The Cream Book,* comp. by Keith L. Brooks (1938); *The Christ We Know* by Arno C. Gaebelein, copyright 1927 by The Bible Institute Colportage Ass'n; *Full Assurance* by H. A. Ironside, copyright 1937 by Moody Bible Institute; *Lights from the Chapel Window,* comp. by Mary Jess, copyright © 1972 by Moody Bible Institute; *The Suffering Saviour* by F. W. Krummacher, copyright 1947 by Moody Bible Institute; *Personal Evangelism* by J. C. Macaulay and Robert H. Belton, copyright © 1956 by Moody Bible Institute; *Born Crucified* by L. E. Maxwell, copyright 1945 by Moody Bible Institute; *The Inspiration and Authority of Scripture* by René Pache, copyright © 1969 by Moody Bible Institute; *Life on the Highest Plane* by Ruth Paxson, volume 1, copyright 1928 by Moody Bible Institute; *Rivers of Living Water* by Ruth Paxson, copyright 1941; *My Pursuit of Peace* by Dorothy H. Pentecost, copyright © 1962 by Moody Bible Institute; *Set Forth Your Case* by Clark H. Pinnock, copyright © 1967 by Craig Press; *Spiritual Problems* by J. Oswald Sanders, copyright 1944 by Moody Bible Institute; *On to Maturity* by J. Oswald Sanders, copyright © 1962 by Moody Bible Institute; *The Biblical Doctrine of Heaven* by Wilbur M. Smith, copyright © 1968 Moody Bible Institute; *Unger's Bible Dictionary* by Merrill F. Unger, copyright © 1961 by Moody Bible Institute.

THE THOMAS MORE ASSOCIATION: quotation reprinted from *The Critic,* copyright © 1962 by the Thomas More Association, Chicago.

WILLIAM MORROW & CO., INC.: *Venture to the Interior* by Laurens van der Post (1951).

A. R. MOWBRAY & CO. LTD.: *Life and Letters of Father Andrew,* ed. by Kathleen E. Burne (1961); *Christian Healing* by Evelyn Frost (1940, 1949).

JOHN MURRAY LTD.: *A Chain of Prayer Across the Ages* by Selina F. Fox (1956).

NATIONAL COUNCIL OF THE CHURCHES OF CHRIST: The verses marked (RSV) are from the Revised Standard Version Bible and used by permission.

THE NATIONAL OBSERVER: quotation by Malcolm Muggeridge from July 20, 1970, *National Observer,* copyright © Dow Jones & Company, Inc. 1973.

THE NEW AMERICAN LIBRARY, INC.: *Gandhi, His Life and Message for the World* by Louis

ACKNOWLEDGMENTS

Fischer, Mentor Books (1960); *The Action Approach* by George Weinberg (1969).

THE NEW YORK TIMES: quotations by Mary Ellen Chase, William Jennings Bryan, Arthur H. Compton, Eric Hoffer, Thomas Beecham, Eddie Rickenbacker, copyright 1922, 1931, 1959, 1961, 1963 by The New York Times Company.

JAMES NISBET & COMPANY LTD.: *God's Order* by John A. Mackay (1953); *A Preface to Christian Theology* by John A. Mackay (1942); *The Nature and Destiny of Man* by Reinhold Niebuhr, volume 1 (1941).

W. W. NORTON & COMPANY, INC.: *The Rescue* by Joseph Conrad, reprint of 1919 edition; *Love and Will* by Rollo May, copyright © 1969 by W. W. Norton & Company; *The Mature Mind* by Harry Allen Overstreet (1949).

CECIL G. OSBORNE: *The Art of Understanding Your Mate* by Cecil G. Osborne, copyright © 1970 by Zondervan Publishing House.

OXFORD UNIVERSITY PRESS, INC.: *And the Life Everlasting* by John Baillie (1934, 1948); *A Diary of Readings* by John Baillie (1955); *The Sense of the Presence of God* by John Baillie, copyright © 1962 by F. Jewel Baillie; *The Epistle to the Romans* by Karl Barth, tr. by Edwyn C. Hoskyns (1933); *Oxford Dictionary of the Christian Church*, ed. by F. L. Cross, copyright © 1958 by Oxford University Press; *The Oxford Dictionary of Quotations* (1941); *A Study of History* by Arnold J. Toynbee, copyright 1946 by Oxford University Press, New York (1947); *The New English Bible*, copyright © The Delegates of the Oxford University Press and The Syndics of the Cambridge University Press, 1961, 1970.

PANTHEON BOOKS, INC.: *Pilgrim of the Absolute—Selections from Writings of Leon Bloy*, ed. by Raissa Maritain, tr. by John Coleman and Harry L. Binsse, copyright 1947 by Pantheon Books, a Division of Random House, Inc.

THE PATERNOSTER PRESS LTD.: *Darwin: Before and After* by Robert E. D. Clark (1948); *The Universe: Plan or Accident* by Robert E. D. Clark, copyright © 1961 by Paternoster Press.

PENGUIN BOOKS LTD.: *Christianity and Social Order* by William Temple, copyright 1942 by William Temple.

A. D. PETERS & COMPANY: *The Noble Castle* by Christopher Hollis (1941).

PHILADELPHIA COLLEGE OF BIBLE: *Simple Studies in Romans* by William L. Pettingill, copyright 1915 Fred Kelker, Philadelphia School of Bible, Inc.

MCCANDLISH PHILLIPS: *The Bible, the Supernatural and the Jews* by John McCandlish Phillips, copyright © 1970 by McCandlish Phillips.

S. G. PHILLIPS, INC.: *Exploring English Character* by Geoffrey Gorer, Criterion Books, New York (1955).

PHILOSOPHICAL LIBRARY PUBLISHERS: *The Quiet Way: Selections from the Letters of Gerhart Tersteegen*, tr. by Emily Chisholm, copyright 1950 by the Philosophical Library.

THE PLOUGH PUBLISHING HOUSE: *Action in Waiting* by Karl Barth, copyright © 1966 by Plough Publishing House; *Christoph Blumhardt and His Message* by R. Lejeune (1963).

PRENTICE-HALL, INC.: *The Small Needle of Doctor Large* by John E. Large, copyright © 1962 by John Ellis Large; *Distilled Wisdom* by Alfred Armand Montapert, copyright © 1964 by Alfred A. Montapert; *The Power of Positive Thinking* by Norman Vincent Peale, copyright © 1956 by Prentice-Hall, Inc.

PRESBYTERIAN AND REFORMED PUBLISHING COMPANY: *The Inspiration and Authority of the Bible* by Benjamin B. Warfield, copyright © 1948 by the Presbyterian and Reformed Publishing Company.

THE PRESBYTERIAN JOURNAL: quotation by James E. Coulter, March 15, 1972.

THE PRESBYTERIAN OUTLOOK: quotation by John A. Mackay, December 13, 1965.

PRESBYTERIAN SURVEY: quotations from December 1965, and March 3, 1967, issues.

GORDON C. PRINCE: *The Unconscious* by Morton Prince, Macmillan Publishing Company (1914).

PRINCETON UNIVERSITY PRESS: *The Collected Works of C. G. Jung*, ed. by G. Adler, M. Fordham, and H. Read, tr. by R. F. C. Hull, Bollingen Series XX, volume 7, "Two Essays on Analytical Psychology," copyright 1953 and 1966 by Bollingen Foundation; *Dostoevsky: His Life and Work* by Konstantin Mochulsky, tr. by Michael A. Minihan, copyright © 1967 by Princeton University Press.

G. P. PUTNAM'S SONS: *A Rustic Moralist* by William Ralph Inge (1937); *Science and Religion*, ed. by J. C. Monsma (1962).

RADIO BIBLE CLASS: quotations from *Our Daily Bread*, copyright © 1973 Radio Bible Class.

RAND MCNALLY & COMPANY: *Left, Right and Center*, ed. by Robert A. Goldwin, copyright © 1965, 1967 by the Public Affairs Conference Center, Kenyon College. Reprinted by permission of Rand McNally College Publishing Co.

HENRY REGNERY COMPANY: *The Man in the Mirror: Studies in the Christian Understanding of Selfhood* by Alexander Miller, copyright © 1958.

REINER PUBLICATIONS: *The Sovereignty of God* by Arthur W. Pink, copyright 1930 by I. C. Herendeen.

FLEMING H. REVELL COMPANY: *One Divine Mo-*

ment: The Asbury Revival, ed. by Robert E. Coleman, copyright © 1970 by Fleming H. Revell Co.; *God's Turf* by Bob Combs, copyright © 1969 by Fleming H. Revell Co.; *The Psychology of Christian Conversion* by Robert O. Ferm, copyright © 1959 by Fleming H. Revell Co.; *Ride the Wild Horses!* by J. Wallace Hamilton, copyright 1952 by Fleming H. Revell Co.; *Repent or Else* by Vance Havner, copyright © 1960 by Fleming H. Revell Co.; *Truth for Each Day* by Vance Havner, copyright © 1960 by Fleming H. Revell Co.; *The Practice of the Presence of God* by Nicolas Herman, copyright © 1958 by Fleming H. Revell Co.; *The Passion for Souls* by John Henry Jowett, copyright 1905 by Fleming H. Revell Co.; *The Morning Altar* by Harold Lindsell, copyright © 1956 by Fleming H. Revell Co.; *The Spirit of God* by G. Campbell Morgan, copyright 1900 by Fleming H. Revell Co.; *Victorious Christian Living* by Alan Redpath, copyright © 1955 by Fleming H. Revell Co.; *Christian: Commit Yourself* by Paul S. Rees, copyright © 1957 by Fleming H. Revell Co.; *Candle, Star and Christmas Tree* by Charles L. Allen and Charles L. Wallis, copyright © 1959 by Fleming H. Revell Co.

THE RONALD PRESS COMPANY: *The Meaning of Anxiety* by Rollo May, copyright 1950 by The Ronald Press Company.

ROUTLEDGE & KEGAN PAUL LTD.: *Modern Man in Search of a Soul* by C. G. Jung (1933); *Technics and Civilization* by Lewis Mumford (1946); *Tractatus Logico-Philosophicus* by Ludwig Wittgenstein.

ST. ANDREW PRESS: *The Scots Confession: 1560,* rendered into modern English by James Bulloch, The Saint Andrew Press, Edinburgh (1960).

SCHOLARLY PRESS: *South Wind* by Norman Douglas, reprint of 1925 edition.

SCM PRESS LTD.: *The Cost of Discipleship* by Dietrich Bonhoeffer (1948); *Ethics* by Dietrich Bonhoeffer (1955); *The Faith That Rebels* by D. S. Cairns (1928); *Baptism in the New Testament* by Oscar Cullmann, tr. by J. K. S. Reid (1951); *The Clue to History* by John Macmurray (1939); *Christian Vocation in the Contemporary World* by Alexander Miller (1946); *The Crisis in the University* by Sir Walter Moberly (1951); *Christian Faith and Life* by William Temple (1931).

CHARLES SCRIBNER'S SONS: *The Record of America* by James Truslow Adams; *The Sense of the Presence of God* by John Baillie, copyright © 1962 by F. Jewel Baillie; *The Little Minister, III* by James M. Barrie; *Slavery and Freedom* by Nicolas Berdyaev, copyright 1944 by Nicolas Berdyaev; *The Inescapable Christ* by Walter Russell Bowie (1925); *The Theology of Crisis* by H. Emil Brunner, copyright 1929 by Charles Scribner's Sons; *I and Thou* by Martin Buber (1958); *The Practice of Evangelism* by Bryan Green (1951); *The Children of Light and the Children of Darkness* by Reinhold Niebuhr (1945); *Christianity and Power Politics* by Reinhold Niebuhr (1940); *Discerning the Signs of the Times* by Reinhold Niebuhr (1946); *The Nature and Destiny of Man* by Reinhold Niebuhr, copyright 1943 by Charles Scribner's Sons; *Cry, the Beloved Country* by Alan Paton, copyright 1948 by Alan Paton; *Philosophy and Religion: Six Lectures Delivered at Cambridge* by Hastings Rashdall (1909); *A Faith to Proclaim* by James S. Stewart, copyright 1953 by Charles Scribner's Sons; *Thine Is the Kingdom* by James S. Stewart, copyright © 1956 by Charles Scribner's Sons; *A History of the Christian Church* by Williston Walker (1942).

SCRIPTURE PRESS PUBLICATION, INC.: *The Disciplines of Life* by V. Raymond Edman, copyright 1948 by Scripture Press Foundation; *Storms and Starlight* by V. Raymond Edman, copyright 1951 by Scripture Press Foundation.

THE SEABURY PRESS: *Suffering* by Louis Evely, copyright © 1967 by Herder & Herder, Inc.; *We Dare to Say Our Father* by Louis Evely, copyright © 1965 by Herder KG, Germany; *The Miracle of Dialogue* by Reuel Howe (1963); *Apron Pocket Book of Meditation,* comp. by M. Benson and H. Smith, copyright © 1958 by Seabury Press.

THE SEATTLE TIMES: quotation by Ethel Waters, May 19, 1967.

SHEED & WARD, INC.: *The Kingdom of God and History* by Christopher Dawson, copyright 1937; *Stimuli* by Ronald A. Knox, copyright 1951 by Sheed & Ward, Inc.; *For Goodness Sake* by William Lawson, copyright 1951 by Sheed & Ward, Inc.; *We Die Standing Up* by Dom Hubert Van Zeller, O.S.B., copyright 1949 by Sheed & Ward, Inc.; *Pardon and Peace* by Alfred Wilson, C.P., copyright 1947 by Sheed & Ward, Inc.; *The Splendor of the Liturgy* by Maurice Zundel, copyright 1934.

SIMON & SCHUSTER, INC.: *How to Win Friends and Influence People* by Dale Carnegie, copyright 1936; *The Story of Philosophy* by Will Durant, copyright 1926 by Simon & Schuster, Inc., and Julius E. Haldeman; *The Business of Life* by William Feather; *Release from Nervous Tension* by David Harold Fink, copyright 1943; *Peace of Mind* by Joshua Loth Liebman, copyright 1946; *A New Treasury of Words to Live By,* ed. by William Nichols, copyright 1947-1959 by United Newspapers Magazine Corporation;

The Chosen by Chaim Potok, copyright © 1967; *Pacem in Terris*, ed. by Edward Reed, Pocket Books (1965); *Courage Is . . .*, comp. by Ralph L. Woods, copyright © 1968.

SINGER FEATURES: *God Knows No Colorline* by Billy Graham, as told to Kurt Singer.

PETER SMITH PUBLISHER, INC.: *The Good Society* by Walter Lippmann (1937).

THE SOCIETY OF AUTHORS: quotations by permission of The Society of Authors on behalf of the Bernard Shaw Estate and on behalf of the John Masefield Estate; *Pygmalion* by George Bernard Shaw, by permission of The Society of Authors on behalf of the Bernard Shaw Estate.

SOVEREIGN GRACE PUBLISHERS: *The Holy Spirit* by John Owen (1954); *Trapp's Commentary on the New Testament* by John Trapp (1958).

SPCK: *Christus Victor* by Gustaf Aulén, tr. by A. G. Herbert (1940); *Edges of His Ways* by Amy Carmichael (1955); *Ploughed Under* by Amy Carmichael, (1932); *Real Life Is Meeting* by J. H. Oldham (1942).

GERALD STEARN: "Conversations with McLuhan" in *Encounter* magazine, June 1967.

THE SUNDAY ORGANIZATION: *Billy Sunday, the Man and His Message* by William T. Ellis, copyright 1914 by L. T. Myers.

SWORD OF THE LORD PUBLISHERS: *The Birth of the Savior* by John R. Rice, copyright © 1955 by Sword of the Lord Publishers.

T. & T. CLARK: *The Hero in Thy Soul* by Arthur John Gossip, copyright 1928 by T. & T. Clark.

THEOLOGY TODAY: extracts from *Theology Today*, October 1966 and January 1967.

TIDINGS: *Spiritual Life Through Tithing* by G. Ernest Thomas, copyright 1953 by Tidings.

TIME INC.: quotation from *Life*, October 16, 1950, copyright 1950 Time Inc.; "View from the Bridge" by Clark Kerr, reprinted from *Time*, The Weekly Newsmagazine, copyright Time Inc.

TYNDALE HOUSE PUBLISHERS: *Life Is Tremendous!* by Charles E. Jones, copyright © 1968 by Charles E. Jones; *High on the Campus* by Gordon R. McLean and Haskell Bowen, copyright © 1970 by Tyndale House Publishers; *The Marriage Affair*, ed. by J. Allan Petersen, copyright © 1971 by Tyndale House Publishers; *Words of Wisdom*, comp. by George M. Wilson, copyright © 1967 by Tyndale House Publishers, World Wide Publications; *Is God Dead?* by Richard Wolff, copyright © 1966 by Tyndale House Publishers; Scripture passages from *The Living Bible* by Kenneth Taylor, copyright © 1971 by Tyndale House Publishers.

TYNDALE PRESS: *Morality, Law and Grace* by J. N. D. Anderson, copyright © 1972 The Tyndale Press; *The Tyndale New Testament Commentaries, The Epistles of Paul to the Colossians and Philemon* by Herbert M. Carson, copyright © 1960 The Tyndale Press; *The Death of Christ* by James Denney, copyright © 1961 The Tyndale Press; *Sacrifice: A Challenge to Christian Youth* by Howard W. Guinness, published by The Inter-Varsity Fellowship; *The New Bible Commentary Revised*, ed. by D. Guthrie and J. A. Motyer, copyright © 1970 by Inter-Varsity Press, London; *In Understanding Be Men* by T. C. Hammond, copyright © 1956 by Inter-Varsity Press, London; *The Scientific Enterprise and Christian Faith* by Malcolm A. Jeeves, copyright © 1969 The Tyndale Press.

UNITED CHURCH PRESS: *The Heidelberg Catechism*, tr. by Allen O. Miller and M. Eugene Osterhaven, copyright © 1962 United Church Press.

UNITED FEATURE SYNDICATE: quotation from *Peanuts* by Charles M. Schulz, copyright © 1959 United Feature Syndicate, Inc.

THE UNITED PRESBYTERIAN CHURCH: Westminster Larger Catechism, copyright © 1966, 1967 by the General Assembly of the United Presbyterian Church in the USA.

THE UNITED REFORMED CHURCH: *Christian Freedom* by Albert Peel, Independent Press Ltd., London (1932); *The Soul of Prayer* by Peter Taylor Forsyth, Epworth Press (1948).

UNIVERSITY OF CHICAGO PRESS: *The Wisdom of Ben Sirach* in *The Apocrypha: An American Translation*, copyright 1938 by Edgar J. Goodspeed, Random House (1959), reprinted with permission of UC Press.

UNIVERSITY OF NORTH CAROLINA PRESS: *Notes on the State of Virginia*, ed. by William Peden (1955).

THE UPPER ROOM: *The Last Supper: The Story of the Leonardo da Vinci Masterpiece* by Howard W. Ellis, copyright © 1963 by The Upper Room.

VANGUARD PRESS, INC.: *Days with Bernard Shaw* by Stephen Winsten by permission of the publisher, The Vanguard Press, Inc., copyright 1949 by The Vanguard Press, Inc.

VICTORY PRESS: *The Normal Christian Life* by Watchman Nee, copyright © Angus I. Kinnear 1961; *There Is an Answer* by Leith Samuel, copyright © 1966 by Leith Samuel; *Pray in the Spirit* by Arthur Wallis, copyright © 1970 by Arthur Wallis.

THE VIKING PRESS, INC.: *Skyline* by Gene Fowler, copyright © 1961 by Agnes Fowler, by permission of The Viking Press; *The Province of the Heart* by Phyllis McGinley, copyright 1954 by Phyllis McGinley.

ACKNOWLEDGMENTS

VITAL SPEECHES: speech by Fred Smith in *Vital Speeches of the Day*, May 1, 1970.

VOICE PUBLICATIONS: *Come Away My Beloved* by Frances J. Roberts, copyright © 1967 by Frances J. Roberts; *Face Up with a Miracle* by Don Basham, copyright © 1967 by Voice Publications.

HENRY E. WALTER LTD.: *Discipleship* by G. Campbell Morgan (1961).

WASHINGTON STAR SYNDICATE, INC.: *Way to Happiness* by Fulton J. Sheen, George Mathew Adams Service, Inc.

A. WATKINS, INC.: *The Mind of the Maker* by Dorothy L. Sayers (1941).

A. P. WATT & SON: *Mr. Britling Sees It Through* by H. G. Wells (1917), by permission of the Estate of the late H. G. Wells; *A Short History of the World* by H. G. Wells (revised edition 1965), by permission of Professor G. P. Wells.

WESLEYAN METHODIST (The Wesleyan Advocate): quotation by George L. Ford.

THE WESTMINSTER PRESS: adaptation from *Meditations from Kierkegaard*, tr. and ed. by T. H. Croxall, copyright © 1955 by W. L. Jenkins; *Christ and Time* by Oscar Cullmann, tr. by Floyd V. Filson, copyright © 1964, W. L. Jenkins; *Design for Christian Living* by Hugh Thomson Kerr, ed. by Donald C. Kerr, copyright 1953 by W. L. Jenkins; *Honest to God* by John A. T. Robinson, copyright © 1963 by SCM Press Ltd.; quotation by William C. Skeath in *Today*, November 1942; *The Strong and the Weak* by Paul Tournier, tr. by Edwin Hudson (1963).

THE H. W. WILSON COMPANY: *Quotations for Special Occasions*, comp. by Maud van Buren, copyright 1938 by The H. W. Wilson Company.

THE WITTENBURG DOOR: "My Worst Christmas" by Craig Wilson, *The Wittenburg Door*, December 1972.

WORD BOOKS: *No Longer Strangers* by Bruce Larson, copyright © 1971 by Word, Inc.; *The Church's Worldwide Mission*, ed. by Harold Lindsell (1966); *Habitation of Dragons* by Keith Miller, copyright © 1970 by Keith Miller; *A Second Touch* by Keith Miller, copyright © 1967 by Keith Miller; *Don't Sleep Through the Revolution* by Paul S. Rees, copyright © 1969 by World Vision, Inc.

THE WORLD PUBLISHING COMPANY: *Mr. Kennedy and the Negroes* by Harry Golden, copyright © 1964 by Harry Golden; *Religion in America*, ed. by John Cogley, copyright © 1958 by Fund for the Republic, Inc.; Reprinted by permission of The World Publishing Company from *The Holy Bible*, King James Version, all rights reserved.

WORLD VISION INTERNATIONAL: "John G. Paton: South Seas Pioneer" by Paul S. Rees, *World Vision* magazine, September 1972.

WORLD WIDE PUBLICATIONS: *One Race, One Gospel, One Task*, ed. by Carl F. H. Henry and W. Stanley Mooneyham, volume 1, copyright © 1967 by World Wide Publications; *Evangelism Now*, ed. by George M. Wilson, copyright © 1969, 1970 by World Wide Publications.

ZONDERVAN PUBLISHING HOUSE: *Witness and Revelation in the Gospel of John* by James M. Boice, copyright © 1970 by Zondervan Publishing Co.; *The Holy Spirit in Today's World* by W. A. Criswell (1966); *Steps to Crucifixion* by Paul P. Fryhling, copyright © 1961 by Zondervan Publishing House; *The Jesus Generation* by Billy Graham, copyright © 1971 by Billy Graham; *Complete Worship Services for College Age*, comp. by Kay Gudnason (1956); *Christian Maturity* by Richard C. Halverson, copyright © Cowman 1956; *The Nine-to-Five Complex* by James L. Johnson, copyright © 1972 by Zondervan Publishing House; *Harper Study Bible* by Harold Lindsell, copyright © 1962 by Zondervan Publishing House; *The Resurrection of Jesus* by James Orr (1965); *Share My Pleasant Stones* by Eugenia Price, copyright © 1957 by Zondervan Publishing House; *Discoveries: Made from Living My New Life* by Eugenia Price, copyright 1953 by Zondervan Publishing House; *The Holy Spirit and His Gifts* by J. Oswald Sanders (1970); *Day-by-Day with Andrew Murray*, comp. by M. J. Shepperson, copyright © 1961 by Zondervan Publishing House; *Words of Revolution* by Tom Skinner, copyright © 1970 by Tom Skinner; *Re-entry* by John Wesley White, copyright © 1970 by Zondervan Publishing House; *The Modern Language Bible*, The Berkeley Version, copyright 1945, 1959, 1969 by Zondervan Publishing House.

TOPICAL ENCYCLOPEDIA
OF *Living*
Quotations

Preface

This book aims to provide quick access to some of the more fascinating thoughts expressed in human language. Some sayings are ancient; some are modern; some are by the great and near-great; some are by people no one ever heard of. If a quotation seems to the editors to be interesting and relevant, and carries the ring of truth, it is included. Because the editors are active in Christian circles, it is expected that the selections will represent that interest.

Three indexes are provided so that the user can find easily what he or she wants. The book itself is the primary index. Its 350 categories are arranged alphabetically, while an individual number is given to each of the 3,500 quotations. At the rear of the book may be found both an author index and a topical index. The latter provides extensive cross references to related quotations available in these pages.

Where the author of a quotation is unknown, no identification appears. Those quotations which carry no identification, but are marked with an asterisk, are from the writings of co-editor Sherwood Wirt. Diligent effort has been made to trace the quotations to their sources and to receive copyright permissions where required. The editors wish to thank Charlene M. Anderson for assistance in the obtaining of permissions; and Clayton E. Carlson and Eleanor Jordan of Harper & Row for their help in preparing the text for publication.

We hope and pray that these Living Quotations will be a source of help to people everywhere.

S.E.W.
K.B.

Introduction

Man's accumulated wisdom seems to be as dependent for its endurance on the invention of memorable phrasing as on giving birth to the original thought. No civilization can exist without a substantial word hoard, for in a way no philosopher or specialist in linguistics can unravel, words are what we know. Arranged with clarity and felicity, words compose the only heritage of man largely immune to the erosion of time's tooth.

If, therefore, the selection be judicious and purposeful, it is practically impossible to compose a volume of quotations which does not contribute to the continuation of civilization and to the well-being of the individual reader. This is such a collection, valuable because its subject is large and vital, and its selection careful and knowledgeable. One may thumb through it at random, having his attention fixed by memorable, and often unexpected, expressions of important ideas; or one may study it systematically, by topic, to the expansion of one's general understanding.

Memorability of phrasing does more than aid in one's personal possession of a thought. It shapes and controls the thought itself, making form as well as content part of that which we know. The richness of a language and the flexibility of its structure are therefore essential to the exactness and subtlety of the thoughts expressed in it. Certain ideas cannot be rendered in certain languages. We are fortunate to have inherited a language with the variety and precision of English, for its resources are practically inexhaustible.

These resources are wonderfully used in the quotations given in this volume. Not to know the thoughts spread out on the following pages is to deprive our intellect of its cultural and spiritual heritage. To absorb them in all the power and clarity of the English language is at once to inform our minds, to sensitize our capability for thought, to lift our vision, and to enlarge our capacity for faith.

CALVIN D. LINTON
Professor of English Literature
Dean, Columbian College of Arts and Sciences
The George Washington University

ACCEPTANCE

[1]
I threw myself down under a fig tree and let the tears gush freely. These were the streams that proved a sacrifice acceptable to You, my Lord.

AUGUSTINE OF HIPPO

[2]
I accepted the One who alone had dared to make a claim so seemingly preposterous—so defiantly out of harmony with the mundaneness of human affairs—as to match the scale of the universe itself and, for that reason, to be an entertainable explanation of the purpose underlying it.

JIM CAMERON

[3]
To accept the will of God never leads to the miserable feeling that it is useless to strive any more. God does not ask for the dull, weak, sleepy acquiescence of indolence. He asks for something vivid and strong. He asks us to cooperate with him, actively willing what he wills, our only aim his glory.

AMY CARMICHAEL

[4]
To live by the law of Christ and accept him in our hearts is to turn a giant floodlight of hope into our valleys of trouble.

CHARLES R. HEMBREE

[5]
A man can accept what Christ has done without knowing how it works; indeed, he certainly won't know how it works *until* he's accepted it.

C. S. LEWIS

[6]
The saying is sure and worthy of full acceptance, that Christ Jesus came into the world to save sinners.

1 TIMOTHY 1:15 (RSV)

[7]
Accepting one's life means also accepting the sin of others which causes us suffering, accepting their nerves, their reactions, their enthusiasms, and even the talents and qualities by means of which they outshine us.

PAUL TOURNIER

ACHIEVEMENT

[8]
One small step for a man, one giant leap for mankind.

NEIL A. ARMSTRONG
(first words spoken on the moon)

[9]
Whatever you do, do all to the glory of God.

1 CORINTHIANS 10:31 (RSV)

[10]
To God be the glory, great things he hath done.

FANNY CROSBY

[11]
Nothing great was ever achieved without enthusiasm.
RALPH WALDO EMERSON

[12]
A man's life does not consist in the abundance of his possessions.
LUKE 12:15 (RSV)

[13]
Today's Christians are too often like deep-sea divers encased in suits designed for many fathoms deep, marching bravely forth to pull plugs out of bathtubs.
PETER MARSHALL

[14]
Whenever you hear of a man doing a great thing, you may be sure that behind it somewhere is a great background. It may be a mother's training, a father's example, a teacher's influence, or an intense experience of his own, but it has to be there or else the great achievement does not come, no matter how favorable the opportunity.
CATHERINE MILES

[15]
The squares of Europe are littered with the statues of generals, admirals and statesmen whose titles and deeds we have forgotten. But still alive in memory are the men and women who attempted more than they could carry out and left unfinished work that their successors completed.
ALEC WAUGH

[16]
The world is divided into men who accomplish things and those who get all the credit.

[17]
There is no limit to the good a man can do if he doesn't care who gets the credit.

[18]
Yesterday's hits won't win today's ball game.

ACTION

[19]
Happy persons seldom think of happiness. They are too busy losing their lives in the meaningful sacrifices of service.
DAVID AUGSBURGER

[20]
To solve the human equation, we need to add love, subtract hate, multiply good, and divide between truth and error.
JANET T. COLEMAN

[21]
Whatever your hand finds to do, do it with your might.
ECCLESIASTES 9:10 (RSV)

[22]
Love's secret is always to be doing things for God, and not to mind because they are such very little ones.
FREDERICK W. FABER

[23]
It is possible to be so active in the service of Christ as to forget to love him.
P. T. FORSYTH

[24]
Since my heart was touched at seventeen, I believe I have never awakened from sleep, in sickness or in health, by day or by night, without my first waking thought being how best I might serve my Lord.
ELIZABETH FRY

[25]
Jesus Christ didn't come into my heart to sit down; he started moving around.
ANDY HAMILTON

[26]
A Christian should always remember that the value of his good works is not based on their number and excellence, but on the love of God which prompts him to do these things.
JUAN DE LA CRUZ

[27]
The Christian who tugs on the oars hasn't time to rock the boat.
AUSTIN ALEXANDER LEWIS

[28]
I am prepared to go anywhere, provided it be forward.
DAVID LIVINGSTONE

[29]
I have always thought the actions of men the best interpreters of their thoughts.
JOHN LOCKE

[30]
Every man feels instinctively that all the beautiful sentiments in the world weigh less than a single lovely action.
JAMES RUSSELL LOWELL

[31]
I have never heard anything about the resolutions of the apostles, but a great deal about their acts.
HORACE MANN

[32]
Not everyone who says to me, "Lord, Lord," shall enter the kingdom of heaven, but he who does the will of my Father who is in heaven.
MATTHEW 7:21 (RSV)

[33]
There are always twenty excellent reasons for doing nothing for every one reason for starting anything—especially if it has never been done before.
PHILIP, DUKE OF EDINBURGH

[34]
We have a shortage of effective Christian action at the real centers of national influence because of misplaced Christian energy and misplaced Christian money—and misplaced Christians.
MCCANDLISH PHILLIPS

[35]
The faith that does not act, is it truly faith?
JEAN BAPTISTE RACINE

[36]
To live is not merely to breathe; it is to act.
JEAN JACQUES ROUSSEAU

[37]
I seldom made an errand to God for another, but I got something for myself.
SAMUEL RUTHERFORD

[38]
Suit the action to the word, the word to the action.
SHAKESPEARE
Hamlet, III, ii

[39]
In the Psalms the Christian is found on his knees. In the book of Proverbs the Christian is on his feet doing things.
GEORGE M. WILSON

[40]
The princes among us are those who forget themselves and serve mankind.
WOODROW WILSON

[41]
Too many churchgoers are singing "Standing on the Promises" while they are just sitting on the premises.

[42]
When something goes wrong, it is important to talk not about who is to blame, but about who is going to fix it.

ADVERSITY

[43]
Prosperity is not without many fears and distastes; and adversity is not without comforts and hopes. The virtue of prosperity is temperance, but the virtue of adversity is fortitude, which in morals is the more heroical virtue. Prosperity is the blessing of the Old Testament, adversity is the blessing of the New, which carrieth the greater benediction, and the clearer revelation of God's favor.

FRANCIS BACON

[44]
The soul would have no rainbow had the eyes no tears.

JOHN VANCE CHENEY

[45]
Though God take the sun out of heaven, yet we must have patience.

GEORGE HERBERT

[46]
The measure of passing adversity which has come upon us should deepen the spiritual life of the people, quicken their sympathies and spirit of sacrifice for others, and strengthen their courage.

HERBERT HOOVER

[47]
If anyone would tell you the shortest, surest way to happiness and all perfection, he must tell you to make it a rule to yourself to thank and praise God for everything that happens to you. For it is certain that whatever seeming calamity happens to you, if you thank and praise God for it, you turn it into a blessing.

WILLIAM LAW

[48]
The hardness of God is kinder than the softness of men, and his compulsion is our liberation.

C. S. LEWIS

[49]
A Christian should never let adversity get him down except on his knees.

MAE NICHOLSON

[50]
Grace grows best in the winter.

SAMUEL RUTHERFORD

[51]
As sure as ever God puts his children in the furnace he will be in the furnace with them.

CHARLES H. SPURGEON

[52]
If a bird is flying for pleasure it flies with the wind, but if it meets danger it turns and faces the wind, in order that it may rise higher.

CORRIE TEN BOOM

[53]
Adversity causes some men to break; others to break records.

WILLIAM A. WARD

[54]
Too much sunshine in life makes a desert.

J. GUSTAV WHITE

[55]
In order to realize the worth of the anchor, we need to feel the stress of the storm.

[56]
The Christian may be knocked down, but not knocked out.

AFFLICTION

[57]
If you would not have affliction visit you twice, listen at once to what it teaches.

JAMES BURGH

[58]
Not until we have passed through the furnace are we made to know how much dross there is in our composition.

CHARLES C. COLTON

[59]
This slight momentary affliction is preparing for us an eternal weight of glory beyond all comparison.

2 CORINTHIANS 4:17 (RSV)

[60]
It is in the furnace of affliction that our Savior watches for Christlikeness to be brought out in us. He is pictured as a purifier and refiner of silver, and we are told that he counts the process complete only when he can see his likeness in the molten metal.

NORMAN B. HARRISON

[61]
Strength is born in the deep silence of long-suffering hearts, not amid joy.

FELICIA HEMANS

[62]
Sanctified afflictions are spiritual promotions.

MATTHEW HENRY

[63]
Afflictions are but the shadow of God's wings.

GEORGE MACDONALD

[64]
Many are the afflictions of the righteous; but the Lord delivers him out of them all.

PSALM 34:19 (RSV)

[65]
The Lord gets his best soldiers out of the highlands of affliction.

CHARLES H. SPURGEON

[66]
Come then, affliction, if my Father wills, and be my frowning friend. A friend that frowns is better than a smiling enemy.

AGE

[67]
It is not how many years we live, but what we do with them.

EVANGELINE BOOTH

[68]
I prefer old age to the alternative.

MAURICE CHEVALIER

[69]
It is better to wear out than to rust out.

RICHARD CUMBERLAND

[70]
The older the fiddle the sweeter the tune.

ENGLISH PROVERB

[71]
The evening of a well-spent life brings its lamps with it.

JOSEPH JOUBERT

[72]
Age is not all decay; it is the ripening, the swelling, of the fresh life within, that withers and bursts the husk.

GEORGE MACDONALD

[73]
The beauty of old men is their gray hair.

PROVERBS 20:29 (RSV)

[74]
To be interested in the changing seasons is a happier state of mind than to be hopelessly in love with spring.

GEORGE SANTAYANA

[75]
I have taken much pains to know everything that is esteemed worth knowing among men; but with all my reading, nothing now remains to comfort me at the close of this life but this passage of the Apostle Paul: "It is a faithful saying, and worthy of all acceptation, that Jesus Christ came into this world to save sinners." To this I cleave, and herein do I find rest.

JOHN SELDEN

[76]
Let us respect gray hairs, especially our own.

J. P. SENN

[77]
Age cannot wither her, nor custom stale her infinite variety.

SHAKESPEARE
Antony & Cleopatra, II, ii

[78]
When men grow virtuous only in old age, they are making a sacrifice to God of the devil's leavings.

JONATHAN SWIFT

[79]
The greatest need of youth is money; of middle age is time; of old age is energy.

[80]
When saving for old age, be sure to put away a few pleasant thoughts.

AIM

[81]
There will be the works of God manifested through us, people will get blessed, and one or two will show gratitude and the rest will show gross ingratitude, but nothing must deflect us from going up to our Jerusalem.

OSWALD CHAMBERS

[82]
The man who shoots above the target does not prove thereby that he has superior ammunition. He just proves that he cannot shoot.

JAMES DENNEY

[83]
To aim is not enough; we must hit.

GERMAN PROVERB

[84]
Not failure, but low aim, is crime.

JAMES RUSSELL LOWELL

[85]
Aim high. It is no harder on your gun to shoot the feathers off an eagle than to shoot the fur off a skunk.

TROY MOORE

ALIENATION

[86]
Man's sin problem is never cured until his alienation from God is overcome, until the rebellion of the human against the divine is ended, until God and man are brought back together.

MYRON S. AUGSBURGER

[87]
They are darkened in their understanding, alienated from the life of God because of the ignorance that is in them, due to their hardness of heart.

EPHESIANS 4:18 (RSV)

[88]
By alienation is meant a mode of experience in which the person experiences himself as an alien. He has become, one might say, estranged from himself. He does not experience himself as the center of his world, as the creator of his own acts—but his acts and their consequences have become his masters, whom he obeys, or whom he may even worship.

ERICH FROMM

[89]
The more affluent a society is, the more pronounced is the sense of ultimate emptiness and alienation on the part of its members.

BILLY GRAHAM

[90]
Whenever a man is not fulfilled by his own view of himself, his society or his environment, then he is at odds with himself and feels estranged, alienated and called in question.

OS GUINNESS

[91]
It is not surprising that the young men in the streets, who are only anonymous digits in their society, should gang together in violent attacks to make sure their assertion is felt. Loneliness and its stepchild, alienation, can become forms of demon possession.

ROLLO MAY

[92]
Students today live in a generation of alienation. Alienation in the ghettos, alienation in the university, alienation from parents, alienation on every side. Sometimes [they] forget that the basic alienation with which they are faced is a cosmic alienation. . . . [They feel] there is nobody home in the universe.

FRANCIS A. SCHAEFFER

ANGER

[93]
Be not quick to anger, for anger lodges in the bosom of fools.

ECCLESIASTES 7:9 (RSV)

[94]
For many years I have observed that the moralist typically substitutes anger for perception. He hopes that many people will mistake his irritation for insight.

MARSHALL MCLUHAN

[95]
All anger is not sinful, because some degree of it, and on some occasions, is inevitable. But it becomes sinful and contradicts the rule of Scripture when it is conceived upon slight and inadequate provocation, and when it continues long.

WILLIAM PALEY

[96]
A soft answer turns away wrath.

PROVERBS 15:1 (RSV)

[97]
The continuance of anger is hatred.

FRANCES QUARLES

[98]
He that would be angry and sin not must not be angry with anything but sin.

THOMAS SECKER

[99]
The greatest remedy for anger is delay.

SENECA

ANXIETY

[100]
God never built a Christian strong enough to carry today's duties and tomorrow's anxieties piled on the top of them.

THEODORE L. CUYLER

[101]
Anxiety is the fundamental phenomenon and the central problem of neurosis.

SIGMUND FREUD

[102]
Anxiety is the natural result when our hopes are centered in anything short of God and his will for us.

BILLY GRAHAM

[103]
Anxiety is the psychological condition which precedes sin. It is so near, so fearfully near to sin, and yet it is not the explanation of sin.

SØREN KIERKEGAARD

[104]
Anxiety is not only a pain which we must ask God to assuage but also a weakness we must ask him to pardon—for he's told us to take no care for the morrow.

C. S. LEWIS

[105]
We often hear of people breaking down from overwork, but in nine cases out of ten they are really suffering from worry or anxiety.

JOHN LUBBOCK

[106]
You must not set your heart on what you eat or drink, nor must you live in a state of anxiety. The whole heathen world is busy about getting food and drink, and your Father knows well enough that you need such things. No, set your heart on his kingdom, and your food and drink will come as a matter of course.

LUKE 12:29–31
(Phillips)

[107]
Anxiety is the apprehension cued off by a threat to some value which the individual holds essential to his existence as a personality. . . . Man's creative abilities and his susceptibility to anxiety are two sides of the same capacity. . . . Man's power to resolve the conflict between expectation and reality—his creative power—is at the same time his power to overcome neurotic anxiety.

ROLLO MAY

[108]
Anxiety is the internal precondition of sin.

REINHOLD NIEBUHR

[109]
Have no anxiety about anything, but in everything by prayer and supplication with thanksgiving let your requests be made known to God.

PHILIPPIANS 4:6 (RSV)

[110]
Anxiety does not empty tomorrow of its sorrows, but only empties today of its strength.

CHARLES H. SPURGEON

APPEARANCE

[111]
Half the work that is done in this world is to make things appear what they are not.

E. R. BEADLE

[112]
Handsome is that handsome does.

HENRY FIELDING

[113]
Cf.: Handsome is that handsome doesn't.

WINOLA WELLS WIRT

[114]
All is not gold that glitters.

DAVID GARRICK

[115]
Men in general judge more from appearances than from reality.

NICCOLÒ MACHIAVELLI

[116]
Cure yourself of the inclination to bother about how you look to other people. Be concerned only with the idea God has of you.

MIGUEL DE UNAMUNO

APPRECIATION

[117]
The deepest principle in human nature is the craving to be appreciated.

WILLIAM JAMES

[118]
Be humble, thinking of others as better than yourself.

PHILIPPIANS 2:3
(*The Living Bible*)

[119]
The best things in life are appreciated most after they have been lost.

ROY L. SMITH

[120]
Carnal-minded men see no more grace in a church than in a tavern, and no more delight in a Christian than in a ruffian; nor esteem any whit better of a preacher than a craftsman; nor find any more sweetness in a sermon than a play; nor take any more delight in the Gospel than in a little peddler's French.

EDWARD TOPSELL

ASSURANCE

[121]
One who knows by the assurance of the witnessing Spirit that he is born of God knows he must be free.

WARREN A. CANDLER

[122]
Let us draw near with a true heart in full assurance of faith, with our hearts sprinkled clean from an evil conscience and our bodies washed with pure water.

HEBREWS 10:22 (RSV)

[123]
Faith rests on the naked Word of God; that Word believed gives full assurance.

H. A. IRONSIDE

[124]
Suppose a man made me a hundred promises, and he had ten years to fulfil them, and the next month the ten years will expire. He has fulfilled 99 of the promises and is able to fulfil the other. Would not I have good reason to trust him that he would fulfil it?

DWIGHT L. MOODY

[125]
I have learned to place myself before God every day as a vessel to be filled with his Holy Spirit. He has filled me with the blessed assurance that he, as the everlasting God, has guaranteed his own work in me.
ANDREW MURRAY

[126]
Purchase gives title, but only delivery gives possession.
RUTH PAXSON

[127]
Our gospel came to you not only in word, but also in power and in the Holy Spirit and with full conviction.
1 THESSALONIANS 1:5 (RSV)

ATHEISM

[128]
A little philosophy inclineth men's minds to atheism; but depth in philosophy bringeth men's minds about to religion.
FRANCIS BACON

[129]
An atheist is a man without any invisible means of support.
JOHN BUCHAN

[130]
If God doesn't exist, then I am God.
FYODOR DOSTOEVSKY
Kirilov, in *The Devils*

[131]
It takes more credulity to accept the atheistic position than most men can muster.
GERALD KENNEDY

[132]
Every effort to prove there is no God is in itself an effort to reach for God.
CHARLES EDWARD LOCKE

[133]
The nature of man is correlative to the nature of God; if there is no God, there is also no man.
KONSTANTIN MOCHULSKY

[134]
There are more atheists in lip than in life.
CLARK H. PINNOCK

[135]
Few men are so obstinate in their atheism that a pressing danger will not compel them to the acknowledgment of a divine power.
PLATO

[136]
That man is a fool who says to himself, "There is no God!"
PSALM 14:1
(*The Living Bible*)

[137]
The atheist is always alone.
IGNAZIO SILONE

ATONEMENT

[138]
For the sake of each of us he laid down his life—worth no less than the universe. He demands of us in return our lives for the sake of each other.
CLEMENT OF ALEXANDRIA

[139]
You can trust the man who died for you.
LETTIE COWMAN

[140]
The simplest word of faith is the deepest word of theology: Christ died for our sins.
JAMES DENNEY

[141]
With reason and truth scholars keep pointing out that when the Scriptures tell us that Christ died for us, the preposition used is "on behalf of," and not "in the place of." For Barabbas there was no distinction. And it is never clean cut. "On behalf of" keeps merging into "in the place of," do what you may. The men who faced the hardships of the front . . . bore and died not merely upon our behalf but literally in our stead.

ARTHUR JOHN GOSSIP
The Interpreter's Bible

[142]
We are told that Christ was killed for us, that his death has washed out our sins, and that by dying he disabled death itself. Any theories we build up as to how Christ's death did all this are, in my view, quite secondary.

C. S. LEWIS

[143]
It is not enough to want to get rid of one's sins. We also need to believe in the One who saves us from our sins. Because we know that we are sinners, it does not follow that we are saved.

C. S. LEWIS

[144]
While the substitutionary death of Christ is not everything in redemption, nothing else is enough without it.

LEWIS B. SMEDES

[145]
The real teaching of the Bible is that in the atoning death of his Son, instead of laying the punishment of guilty man upon an innocent third person, God took the shame and suffering due to man upon himself; and so far from that being unjust and cruel, it is amazing grace!

R. A. TORREY

[146]
The Old Testament Hebrew word that we translate "atonement" means literally "to cover up." The animal sacrifices were intended to "cover" a man's sins. In the New Testament, however, the meaning of atoning sacrifice is conveyed by the word "expiate," which means "to put away." The blood that Jesus shed in our behalf on the cross at Calvary does not merely cover up our sin, it puts away our sin as though it had never been committed.

T. W. WILSON

ATTITUDES

[147]
The best thing to give to your enemy is forgiveness; to an opponent, tolerance; to a friend, your heart; to your child, a good example; to your father, deference; to your mother, conduct that will make her proud of you; to yourself, respect; to all men, charity.

ARTHUR JAMES BALFOUR

[148]
Love means to love that which is unlovable, or it is no virtue at all; forgiving means to pardon that which is unpardonable, or it is no virtue at all—and to hope means hoping when things are hopeless, or it is no virtue at all.

G. K. CHESTERTON

[149]
Events are less important than our responses to them.

JOHN HERSEY

[150]
Be careful for nothing, prayerful for everything, thankful for anything.

DWIGHT L. MOODY

[151]
All looks yellow to the jaundiced eye.
ALEXANDER POPE

[152]
It is only by thinking about great and good things that we come to love them, and it is only by loving them that we come to long for them, and it is only by longing for them that we are impelled to seek after them; and it is only by seeking after them that they become ours.
HENRY VAN DYKE

[153]
To be glad of life because it gives you the chance to love and to work and to play and to look up at the stars; to be satisfied with your possessions, but not contented with yourself until you have made the best of them; to despise nothing in the world except falsehood and meanness, and to fear nothing except cowardice; to be governed by your admirations rather than your dislikes; to covet nothing that is your neighbor's except his kindness of heart and gentleness of manner; to think seldom of your enemies, often of your friends, and every day of Christ.
HENRY VAN DYKE

[154]
If a man has limburger cheese on his upper lip he thinks the whole world smells.

[155]
If you don't get everything you want, think of the things you don't get that you *don't* want.

AUTHORITY

[156]
The historicity of Christ is as axiomatic for an unbiased historian as the historicity of Julius Caesar.
F. F. BRUCE

[157]
I am convinced that people are open to the Christian message if it is seasoned with authority and proclaimed as God's own Word.
BILLY GRAHAM

[158]
Both the authenticity and the general integrity of the books of the New Testament may be regarded as finally established.
FREDERIC KENYON

[159]
All authority ultimately comes from God and is rooted in God himself. But how are we to handle it? What is the norm? For the Christian there is only one answer: the norm is found in Scripture. Being the Word of God, Scripture is the highest norm for all authority, because it deals with the basic questions of life.
KLAAS RUNIA

BAPTISM

[160]
In the thought of the early church . . . we find Christian baptism closely connected with the death and resurrection of Christ as a solemn rite in which the individual becomes so united with Christ that he dies to sin and rises with a new life.
DONALD M. BAILLIE

[161]
According to the New Testament, all men have in principle received baptism long ago, namely on Golgotha, at Good Friday and Easter.

OSCAR CULLMANN

[162]
The promises of God are never spoken to the individual alone, but to all at one time. Baptism, on the contrary, is something that God does to the individual.

OLE HALLESBY

[163]
[Baptism] signifies that the old Adam in us is to be drowned by daily sorrow and repentance, and perish with all sins and evil lusts; and that the new man should daily come forth again and rise, who shall live before God in righteousness and purity forever.

MARTIN LUTHER

[164]
The baptism of the Holy Spirit, or regeneration, occurs when the sinner abandons himself wholly to Christ, in mind, heart, will, thus appropriating Christ's imputed righteousness, and when, upon that surrender of the sinner to him, Christ imparts to the sinner the life of God, changing him from a carnal to a spiritual creature.

J. C. MASSEE

[165]
The baptism of the Spirit is the primary blessing; it is, in short, the blessing of regeneration. When a man is baptized with the Spirit, he is born again.

G. CAMPBELL MORGAN

[166]
Baptism points back to the work of God, and forward to the life of faith.

J. A. MOTYER

[167]
In baptism, the direction is indicated rather than the arrival.

FRIEDRICH REST

[168]
Baptism symbolizes the Savior's death and his resurrection; it symbolizes the believer's death to sin and his resurrection to righteousness; it apparently symbolizes the mystery of the new birth, or regeneration; it symbolizes the fact of the believer's union and identification with Christ; it symbolizes the fact of the believer's incorporation into one body with his brethren; it symbolizes the idea of the believer's purification from sin.

WILLIAM CLEAVER WILKINSON

BEAUTY

[169]
Beauty is a gift of God.

ARISTOTLE

[170]
Spring is God thinking in gold, laughing in blue, and speaking in green.

FRANK JOHNSON

[171]
A thing of beauty is a joy for ever.

JOHN KEATS

[172]
God's fingers can touch nothing but to mold it into loveliness.

GEORGE MACDONALD

[173]
If you have never heard the mountains singing, or seen the trees of the field clapping their hands, do not think because of that that they don't. Ask God to open your ears so you may hear it, and your eyes so you may see it, because, though few men ever know it, they do, my friend, they do.

McCandlish Phillips

[174]
Worship the Lord in the beauty of holiness.

Psalm 29:2 (kjv)

[175]
Who is this that looks forth like the dawn, fair as the moon, bright as the sun?

Song of Solomon 6:10 (rsv)

BEHAVIOR

[176]
A good example is the tallest kind of preaching.

African Chief

[177]
Walk softly, speak tenderly, pray fervently, do not run up stairs, do not run down God's people.

T. J. Bach

[178]
There ain't much fun in medicine, but there's a good deal of medicine in fun.

Josh Billings

[179]
You have not fulfilled every duty, unless you have fulfilled that of being pleasant.

Charles Buxton

[180]
Distinction between virtuous and vicious actions has been engraven by the Lord in the heart of every man.

John Calvin

[181]
Resolved, never to do anything which I should be afraid to do if it were the last hour of my life.

Jonathan Edwards

[182]
If one fights for good behavior, God makes one a present of the good feelings.

Juliana H. Ewing

[183]
We are turning out machines that act like men, and men that act like machines.

Erich Fromm

[184]
We talk a great deal of religion in this country, but we need to stop long enough to let our feet catch up with our mouths.

Billy Graham

[185]
The wheel was man's greatest invention until he got behind it.

Ford Jarrell

[186]
It would scarcely be necessary to expound doctrine if our lives were radiant enough. If we behaved like true Christians, there would be no pagans.

Pope John XXIII

[187]
We have missed the full impact of the Gospel if we have not discovered what it is to be ourselves, loved by God, irreplaceable in his sight, unique among our fellow men.

Bruce Larson

[188]
If you read history you will find that the Christians who did most for the present world were precisely those who thought most of the next. It is since Christians have largely ceased to think of the other world that they have become so ineffective in this.

C. S. LEWIS

[189]
Jesus taught, first, that a man's business is to do the will of God; second, that God takes upon himself the care of that man; third, therefore, that a man must never be afraid of anything; and so, fourth, be left free to love God with all his heart, and his neighbor as himself.

GEORGE MACDONALD

[190]
If you want to become the perfect guest, then try to make your host feel at home.

W. A. "DUB" NANCE

[191]
Strive to be like a well-regulated watch, of pure gold, with open face, busy hands, and full of good works.

DAVID C. NEWQUIST

[192]
Christianity does not consist in abstaining from doing things no gentleman would think of doing, but in doing things that are unlikely to occur to anyone who is not in touch with the Spirit of Christ.

R. H. L. (DICK) SHEPPARD

[193]
You should be able to tell a Christian by looking at him.

STEVE SLOAN

[194]
A smile takes but a moment, but its effects sometimes last forever.

J. E. SMITH

[195]
Blessed is he who has learned to admire but not envy, to follow but not imitate, to praise but not flatter, and to lead but not manipulate.

WILLIAM A. WARD

[196]
There are two things to do about the Gospel—believe it and behave it.

SUSANNAH WESLEY

[197]
Never look back unless you want to go that way.

[198]
The mark of a man is how he treats a person who can be of no possible use to him.

[199]
All people smile in the same language.

BELIEF

[200]
If you believe what you like in the Gospel, and reject what you like, it is not the Gospel you believe, but yourself.

AUGUSTINE OF HIPPO

[201]
To believe is to commit. . . . In particular belief I commit myself spiritually to Jesus Christ, and determine in that thing to be dominated by the Lord alone. When I stand face to face with Jesus Christ and he says to me, "Believest thou this?" I find that faith is as natural as breathing, and I am staggered that I was so stupid as not to trust him before.

OSWALD CHAMBERS

[202]
The point of having an open mind, like having an open mouth, is to close it on something solid.

G. K. CHESTERTON

[203]
The greatest proof of Christianity for others is not how far a man can logically analyze his reasons for believing, but how far in practice he will stake his life on his belief.

T. S. ELIOT

[204]
If you don't believe in God, you aren't a whole man; you are just a number in a book. A lot of smart people claim they don't believe anything unless they can see it. Look, friend, you can't see electricity in that high-tension wire up yonder, but I dare you to touch it. No, you can't see that electricity, but you can see the light.

J. J. JOHNSON

[205]
If you think strongly enough you will be forced by science to the belief in God, which is the foundation of all religion.

LORD KELVIN

[206]
Believing in God means getting down on your knees.

MARTIN LUTHER

[207]
If I believed the Gospel, I would crawl across England on broken glass on my hands and knees to tell men it was true!

CHARLES PEACE

[208]
If you believe that God is calling you, he will take care of every need.

JOY RIDDERHOF

[209]
I did not believe the story of Daniel in the lions' den until I had to take some of these awful marches [through the leopard forests of Nigeria]. Then I knew it was true, and that it was written for my comfort.

MARY SLESSOR

[210]
If life is a comedy to him who thinks and a tragedy to him who feels, it is a victory to him who believes.

BIBLE

[211]
Apply yourself to the whole text, and apply the whole text to yourself.

JOHANNES ALBRECHT BENGEL

[212]
Any individual or institution that could take the Bible to every home in this country would do more for the country than all the armies from the beginning of our history to the present time.

DAVID J. BREWER

[213]
The Bible was never intended to be a book for scholars and specialists only. From the very beginning it was intended to be everybody's book, and that is what it continues to be.

F. F. BRUCE

[214]
The English Bible is the first of our national treasures.

KING GEORGE V

[215]
The Bible is the sheet anchor of our liberties. Write its principles upon your heart and practice them in your lives.

ULYSSES S. GRANT

[216]
It is impossible mentally or socially to enslave a Bible-reading people.

HORACE GREELEY

[217]
All human discoveries seem to be made only for the purpose of confirming more and more strongly the truths contained in the Holy Scriptures.

JOHN HERSCHEL

[218]
The Bible is a postgraduate course in the richest library of human experience.

HERBERT HOOVER

[219]
Lay hold on the Bible until the Bible lays hold on you.

WILL H. HOUGHTON

[220]
England has two books: the Bible and Shakespeare. England made Shakespeare but the Bible made England.

VICTOR HUGO

[221]
If God is a reality, and the soul is a reality, and you are an immortal being, what are you doing with your Bible shut?

HERRICK JOHNSON

[222]
The Bible is an inexhaustible fountain of all truths. The existence of the Bible is the greatest blessing which humanity ever experienced.

IMMANUEL KANT

[223]
The Bible is a book in comparison with which all others in my eyes are of minor importance, and which in all my perplexities and distresses has never failed to give me light and strength.

ROBERT E. LEE

[224]
All the good from the Savior of the world is communicated through this Book. All the things desirable to man are contained in it.

ABRAHAM LINCOLN

[225]
I consider an intimate knowledge of the Bible an indispensable qualification of a well-educated man.

ROBERT A. MILLIKAN

[226]
There are no songs comparable to the songs of Zion; no orations equal to those of the prophets; no politics like those which the Scriptures teach.

JOHN MILTON

[227]
[Jesus Christ] absolutely trusted the Bible, and though there are in it things inexplicable and intricate that have puzzled me much, I am going to trust the Book, not in a blind sense, but reverently, because of him.

H. C. G. MOULE

[228]
I believe today's young people will discover that people, even the best people, are not gods. They will then recover the Bible. They will see it as a book which, far from merely supporting the "establishment," brings all human contrivance under judgment. They will see it as a book whose author loves people enough to tell the truth about them. They may even, as the book begins to speak to them, hear a word from beyond the book and a voice they did not expect to hear.

KARL A. OLSSON

[229]
I thoroughly believe in a university education for both men and women; but I believe a knowledge of the Bible without a college course is more valuable than a college course without the Bible.

WILLIAM LYON PHELPS

[230]
The Bible is the Book that holds hearts up to the light as if held against the sun.

WILLIAM A. QUAYLE

[231]
If a man is not familiar with the Bible, he has suffered a loss which he had better make all possible haste to correct.

THEODORE ROOSEVELT

[232]
The Christian feels that the tooth of time gnaws all books but the Bible. It has a pertinent relevance to every age. It has worked miracles by itself alone. It has made its way where no missionary had gone and has done the missionary's work. . . . Nineteen centuries of experience have tested the Book. It has passed through critical fires no other volume has suffered, and its spiritual truth has endured the flames and come out without so much as the *smell* of burning.

W. E. SANGSTER

[233]
The whole Bible, from cover to cover, is concerned with this riddle . . . whether or not the universe at its center is or ever was intelligent and purposeful and kind; if it means something still, and means that something intensely; if, as someone has put it, there is a great yawning hole in the middle of things, through which all energy and vision, all lives and prayers and sacrifice, shall be poured at the last and lost—or if God is there! These [sixty-six] books gather all their things together, fill their lungs, and with a mighty shout proclaim that he is!

PAUL E. SCHERER

[234]
The truly wise man is he who believes the Bible against the opinions of any man. If the Bible says one thing, and any body of men says another, the wise man will decide, "This book is the Word of him who cannot lie."

R. A. TORREY

[235]
I did not go through the Book. The Book went through me.

A. W. TOZER

[236]
The Bible is a harp with a thousand strings. Play on one to the exclusion of its relationship to the others, and you will develop discord. Play on all of them, keeping them in their places in the divine scale, and you will hear heavenly music all the time.

WILLIAM P. WHITE

[237]
Man has deprived himself of the best there is in the world who has deprived himself of this: a knowledge of the Bible. . . . This book is the one supreme source of revelation, the revelation of the meaning of life, the nature of God, and the spiritual nature and need of men. It is a book which reveals every man to himself as a distinct moral agent, responsible not to men, not even to those men whom he has put over him in authority, but responsible through his own conscience to his Lord and Maker. Whenever a man sees this vision, he stands up a free man whatever may be the circumstances of his life.

WOODROW WILSON

[238]
Read the Bible. Free gift inside.

BITTERNESS

[239]
I realize that patriotism is not enough. I must have no hatred or bitterness toward anyone.

EDITH CAVELL
(last words)

[240]
Let all bitterness . . . be put away from you, with all malice, and be kind to one another, tenderhearted, forgiving one another, as God in Christ forgave you.

EPHESIANS 4:31–32 (RSV)

[241]
All my sleep has fled because of the bitterness of my soul. O Lord . . . restore me to health and make me live!

ISAIAH 38:15–16 (RSV)

[242]
The Lord is telling us to be honest about our sins, to put away bitterness, criticism, and dishonesty from among us. Christ must have first place in our lives. We need to give him the key to every secret closet in our hearts, and help him to clean out all the junk we have allowed to accumulate there.

CAROL MYERS

[243]
God came in and healed. He took his solvent and dissolved all that bitterness and resentment in my heart so thoroughly that you wouldn't believe I ever had it. . . . What is our home like now? Well, it's a beautiful place.

EVELYN A. THIESSEN

BLESSING

[244]
Prosperity is the blessing of the Old Testament; adversity is the blessing of the New.

FRANCIS BACON

[245]
Taken separately, the experiences of life can work harm and not good. Taken together, they make a pattern of blessing and strength the like of which the world does not know.

V. RAYMOND EDMAN

[246]
How little do my countrymen know what precious blessings they are in possession of, and which no other people on earth enjoy.

THOMAS JEFFERSON

[247]
Never undertake anything for which you wouldn't have the courage to ask the blessings of heaven.

G. C. LICHTENBERG

[248]
We have forgotten the gracious Hand
which has preserved us in peace and
multiplied and enriched and strengthened us, and have vainly imagined in
the deceitfulness of our hearts that all
these blessings were produced by some
superior wisdom and virtue of our
own.

ABRAHAM LINCOLN

[249]
Have you ever thought that in every
action of grace in your heart you have
the whole omnipotence of God engaged to bless you?

ANDREW MURRAY

[250]
I have come upon the happy discovery
that this life hid with Christ in God is a
continuous unfolding.

EUGENIA PRICE

[251]
The Lord commanded the blessing,
life for evermore.

PSALM 133:3 (KJV)

[252]
There is no blessing until we look deep
down in our own soul and see our
spiritual life as it really is.

ALAN REDPATH

[253]
The best things are nearest: breath in
your nostrils, light in your eyes, flowers
at your feet, duties at your hand, the
path of God just before you.

ROBERT LOUIS STEVENSON

[254]
The heavenly Father welcomes us with
open arms and imparts to us blessing
upon blessing—not because we are up-
right but because Jesus Christ has
clothed us with his own virtue.*

BOREDOM

[255]
When people are bored, it is primarily
with their own selves that they are
bored.

ERIC HOFFER

[256]
Your new moons and your appointed
feasts my soul hates; they have become
a burden to me. I am weary of bearing
them.

ISAIAH 1:14 (RSV)

[257]
One cure for boredom is to forget
yourself through activities which bring
you in touch with people and ideas outside yourself.

BLANCHE McKEOWN

[258]
The basic fact about human existence
is not that it is a tragedy, but that it is
a bore.

H. L. MENCKEN

[259]
The backslider gets bored with himself;
the godly man's life is exciting.

PROVERBS 14:14
(The Living Bible)

[260]
At least half the sins of mankind are
caused by the fear of boredom.

BERTRAND RUSSELL

[261]
Somehow or other, and with the best
intentions, we have shown the world
the typical Christian in the likeness of
a crashing and rather ill-natured bore
—and this in the Name of One who
assuredly never bored a soul in those
thirty-three years during which he
passed through the world like a flame.

DOROTHY L. SAYERS

BROKENNESS

[262]
God can never make us wine if we object to the fingers he uses to crush us with. If God would only use his own fingers, and make us broken bread and poured-out wine in a special way! But when he uses someone whom we dislike, or some set of circumstances to which we said we would never submit, and makes those the crushers, we object. We must never choose the scene of our own martyrdom.

OSWALD CHAMBERS

[263]
The body of Jesus was broken for us, crucified, dead, buried and risen, that we might be one bread and one body with him, broken by repentance, crucified by faith, dead unto sin, buried and raised to newness of life in him.

NORMAN P. GRUBB

[264]
If I am not finding Jesus a real Savior, who brings me fully out of darkness and defeat into light and liberty, it is because at one point or another I am not willing to be broken, and see myself as a sinner.

ROY HESSION

[265.]
The Lord fishes on the bottom, and if you want to get to his bait and hook, brother, you've got to get right down on the bottom.

SAM JONES

[266]
Through circumstances, often very humdrum conditions, and sometimes through disagreeable people, God seeks to prepare his servants that they may be for him "broken bread and poured-out wine."

D. W. LAMBERT

[267]
Every story of conversion is the story of a blessed defeat.

C. S. LEWIS

[268]
If you're dead to self you can't hurt any more.

KAY LONG

[269]
God creates out of nothing. Therefore until a man is nothing, God can make nothing out of him.

MARTIN LUTHER

[270]
Do you want to enter what people call "the higher life"? Then go a step lower down.

ANDREW MURRAY

[271]
The sacrifice acceptable to God is a broken spirit; a broken and contrite heart, O God, thou wilt not despise.

PSALM 51:17 (RSV)

[272]
God will never plant the seed of his life upon the soil of a hard, unbroken spirit. He will only plant that seed where the conviction of his Spirit has brought brokenness, where the soil has been watered with the tears of repentance as well as the tears of joy.

ALAN REDPATH

[273]
It is when a man strikes rock-bottom in his sense of nothingness that he suddenly finds he has struck the Rock of Ages.

JAMES S. STEWART

[974]
Brokenness is not revival; it is a vital and indispensable step toward it.

ARTHUR WALLIS

[275]
How else but through a broken heart
may Lord Christ enter in?
                        OSCAR WILDE

[276]
The only things that are improved by
breaking are the hearts of sinners.

CALLING

[277]
We still speak of our daily pursuits as
vocations and callings, bearing unconscious witness to the permeation of ordinary speech by a once novel and daring theological usage. But the words
have gone stale.
                        ROBERT L. CALHOUN

[278]
There is a universal call by which God,
through the external preaching of the
Word, invites all men alike. . . . Besides
this there is a special call which, for the
most part, God bestows on believers
only.
                        JOHN CALVIN

[279]
Let every man abide in the same calling
wherein he was called.
                1 CORINTHIANS 7:20 (KJV)

[280]
No other organization on the face of
the earth is charged with the high calling to which the church is summoned:
to confront men with Jesus Christ.
                        J. W. HYDE

[281]
How is it possible that you have not
been called? You are already a married
man or wife or child or daughter or
servant or maid. . . . Nobody is without
command and calling. . . . God's eyes
look not upon the works, but on the
obedience in the work.
                        MARTIN LUTHER

[282]
The awareness of a need and the capacity to meet that need: this constitutes a
call.
                        JOHN R. MOTT

[283]
The gifts and the call of God are irrevo-
cable.
                ROMANS 11:29 (RSV)

[284]
God's favorite word is—come!
                        ROBERT L. STERNER

[285]
Jesus Christ opens wide the doors of
the treasure-house of God's promises,
and bids us go in and take with boldness the riches that are ours.
                        CORRIE TEN BOOM

[286]
Effectual calling is the work of God's
Spirit, whereby, convincing us of our
sin and misery, enlightening our minds
in the knowledge of Christ, and renewing our wills, he doth persuade and enable us to embrace Jesus Christ freely
offered to us in the Gospel.
                WESTMINSTER SHORTER CATECHISM

[287]
Effectual calling is the work of God's
almighty power and grace, whereby
. . . he doth in his accepted time invite
and draw them to Jesus Christ, by his
word and Spirit.
                WESTMINSTER LARGER CATECHISM

[288]
If God has called you, don't spend time looking over your shoulder to see who is following.

CHALLENGE

[289]
Do not pray for easy lives. Pray to be stronger men. Do not pray for tasks equal to your powers. Pray for powers equal to your tasks.

PHILLIPS BROOKS

[290]
On Mount Moriah it was not Isaac God wanted. It was Abraham.

ROY GUSTAFSON

[291]
Evil in all its concreteness and personal reality challenged Christ and what he stood for, consummating the historic tragedy of the cross. This challenge was of the nature of an "everlasting nay" hurled at God himself. To this challenge God in Christ responded with an "everlasting yea" . . . making an end of sin and its power over man, and, in the resurrection, triumphing.

JOHN A. MACKAY

[292]
God save us from hotheads who would lead us foolishly, and from cold feet that would keep us from adventuring at all.

PETER MARSHALL

[293]
Civilizations come to birth in environments that are unusually difficult and not unusually easy, and this has led us to inquire whether or not this is an instance of some social law which may be expressed in the formula: "The greater the challenge, the greater the stimulus."

ARNOLD J. TOYNBEE

CHANGE

[294]
Great changes do not begin on the surface of society, but in prepared hearts: in men who, by communion with God, rise above the apathy of the age, and speak with living vital energy, and give life to the community and tone to the public mind.

EDWARD BEECHER

[295]
He has changed all our sunsets to sunrise.

CLEMENT OF ALEXANDRIA

[296]
He who shall introduce into public affairs the principles of primitive Christianity will change the face of the world.

BENJAMIN FRANKLIN

[297]
The more it changes, the more it is the same thing.

FRENCH PROVERB

[298]
The prodigal son's father did not say to him, "You stay in the pigpen—we're going to make it a better pigpen."

BILLY GRAHAM

[299]
There is nothing permanent except change.

HERACLITUS

[300]
There is a certain relief in change, even though it be from bad to worse; as I have found in traveling in a stagecoach, it is often a comfort to shift one's position and be bruised in a new place.

WASHINGTON IRVING

[301]
The psychology of the individual is reflected in the psychology of the nation. What the nation does is done also by each individual, and so long as the individual continues to do it, the nation will do likewise. Only a change in the attitude of the individual can initiate a change in the psychology of the nation.

CARL GUSTAV JUNG

[302]
Psychotherapy will put a bandaid on the gash; but for healing, men's lives must be changed from within.

RAYMOND J. LARSON

[303]
It is best not to swap horses while crossing the river.

ABRAHAM LINCOLN

[304]
I am the Lord, I change not.

MALACHI 3:6 (KJV)

[305]
Those who cannot change their minds cannot change anything.

GEORGE BERNARD SHAW

[306]
You can't change circumstances and you can't change other people, but God can change you.

EVELYN A. THIESSEN

[307]
When I came to believe in Christ's teaching, I ceased desiring what I had wished for before. The direction of my life, my desires, became different. What was good and bad changed places.

LEO TOLSTOY

CHARACTER

[308]
Few persons are made of such strong fiber that they will make a costly outlay when surface work will pass as well in the market.

E. M. BOUNDS

[309]
A man is what he thinks about all day long.

RALPH WALDO EMERSON

[310]
The character of Jesus was a manifestation, not an effort.

JOHN BENJAMIN FIGGIS

[311]
It is a peculiarity of the bore that he is the last person to find himself out.

OLIVER WENDELL HOLMES

[312]
The character of Jesus has not only been the highest pattern of virtue, but the strongest incentive to its practice, and has exerted so deep an influence that it may be truly said that the simple record of his three short years of active life has done more to regenerate and soften mankind than all the disquisitions of philosophers and the exhortations of moralists.

WILLIAM LECKY

[313]
I have never felt that football built character. That is done by parents and church. You give us a boy with character and we will give you back a man. You give us a character—and we will give him right back to you.

JOHN MCKAY

[314]
Personal soundness is not an absence of problems but a way of reacting to them.

DONALD W. MACKINNON

[315]
Character is what you are in the dark.

DWIGHT L. MOODY

[316]
Every time a Christian cheats on his income tax, he perverts and obscures the Gospel.

JOHN SANDERSON

[317]
See thou character. Give thy thoughts no tongue,/ Nor any unproportion'd thought his act./ Be thou familiar, but by no means vulgar./ Those friends thou hast, and their adoption tried,/ Grapple them to thy soul with hoops of steel . . .

SHAKESPEARE
Hamlet, I, iii

[318]
Character is not in the mind. It is in the will.

FULTON J. SHEEN

[319]
What you dislike in another, take care to correct in yourself.

THOMAS SPRAT

[320]
He is as big as a church.

ROBERT LOUIS STEVENSON
(of South Seas missionary James
Chalmers)

[321]
Merely going to church doesn't make you a Christian any more than going to a garage makes you an automobile.

BILLY SUNDAY

[322]
If your absence doesn't make any difference, your presence won't either.

[323]
When God measures a man, he puts the tape around the heart, not around the head.

CHOICE

[324]
As sure as I lived, I knew that I possessed a will, and that when I willed to do something or willed not to do something, nobody else was making the decision.

AUGUSTINE OF HIPPO

[325]
No matter how strongly we feel about foreordination, we face today some very real choices regarding the immediate future.

STEPHEN BAYNE

[326]
To be a Christian, or not to be, is not a matter of being a somewhat better man, or a man perhaps not quite so good. It is a matter of life or death.

JAMES DENNEY

[327]
If you intend to accomplish anything, if you mean not to labor in vain or spend your strength for nothing, you must take your side. There can be no halting between two opinions. You must coolly, firmly and irrevocably make your determination and resolve that the Lord is your God, and that you will serve him only.

TIMOTHY DWIGHT

[328]
In darkness there is no choice. It is light that enables us to see the differences between things; and it is Christ who gives us light.

A. W. HARE

[329]
When you have to make a choice and don't make it, that is in itself a choice.

WILLIAM JAMES

[330]
Choose this day whom you will serve . . . as for me and my house, we will serve the Lord.

JOSHUA 24:15 (RSV)

[331]
I would say that the most deeply compelled action is also the freest action. By that I mean, no part of you is outside the action. It is a paradox.

C. S. LEWIS

[332]
In *Surprised by Joy* I wrote that "before God closed in on me, I was offered what now appears a moment of wholly free choice." But I feel my decision was not so important. I was the object rather than the subject in this affair. I was decided upon.

C. S. LEWIS

[333]
Mary has chosen the good portion, which shall not be taken away from her.

LUKE 10:42 (RSV)

[334]
Where there is no choice, we do well to make no difficulty.

GEORGE MACDONALD

[335]
God has no need of marionettes. He pays men the compliment of allowing them to live without him if they choose. But if they live without him in this life, they must also live without him in the next.

LEON MORRIS

[336]
He that is choice of his time will also be choice of his company and choice of his actions, lest he be throwing his time and himself away.

JEREMY TAYLOR

[337]
It is possible for a man to run against the wrong object and bend his lance for good.

A. W. TOZER

[338]
Let it be known on whose side you are. If there is any doubt about it, something is wrong.

[339]
Tomorrow has two handles: the handle of fear and the handle of faith. You can take hold of it by either handle.

[340]
We can take our choice: dancing in the dark or walking in the Light.*

CHRISTIAN

[341]
When a Christian is in the wrong place, his right place is empty.

T. J. BACH

[342]
Some Christians are not only like salt that has lost its savor, but like pepper that has lost its pep.

ALBERT GEORGE BUTZER
The Interpreter's Bible

[343]
Anything that dims my vision of Christ, or takes away my taste for Bible study, or cramps my prayer life, or makes Christian work difficult, is wrong for me, and I must, as a Christian, turn away from it.

J. WILBUR CHAPMAN

[344]
Remember that you are nothing and nobody except Christians, and on the day you cease to provide an available amount of communion for every recognized believer in the Lord Jesus, you will become sectarian, and merely add, by your meetings, to the disorder and ruin of Christendom.

JOHN NELSON DARBY

[345]
If you were arrested for being a Christian, would there be enough evidence to convict you?

DAVID OTIS FULLER

[346]
Collapse in the Christian life is seldom a blowout; it is usually a slow leak.

PAUL E. LITTLE

[347]
I am to become a Christ to my neighbor and be for him what Christ is for me.

MARTIN LUTHER

[348]
There are three distinctive marks of the man who has been influenced by Jesus Christ: poise, simplicity, peace.

FRANCIS GREENWOOD PEABODY

[349]
A good Christian is a velvet-covered brick.

FRED SMITH

[350]
We are not the architects of destiny. We are not the creators or redeemers of the world. We are God's raw materials.

JAMES S. STEWART

[351]
There is nothing so refreshing as to watch a new Christian before he has heard too many sermons and watched too many Christians.

A. W. TOZER

[352]
Whatever makes men good Christians makes them good citizens.

DANIEL WEBSTER

[353]
Faith makes a Christian. Life proves a Christian. Trial confirms a Christian. Death crowns a Christian.

[354]
The Christian life doesn't get easier; it gets better.

CHRISTIANITY

[355]
Christianity is the land of beginning again.

W. A. CRISWELL

[356]
It is unnatural for Christianity to be popular.

BILLY GRAHAM

[357]
If your Christianity isn't contagious, it
may be contaminated.
                    CHESTER H. JOHNSON

[358]
Christianity, if false, is of no importance, and, if true, of infinite importance. The one thing it cannot be is
moderately important.
                              C. S. LEWIS

[359]
Whenever the pillars of Christianity
shall be overthrown, our present
republican forms of government, and
all the blessings which flow from them,
must fall with them.
                         JEDIDIAH MORSE

[360]
Christianity is not a system of doctrine,
but a new creature.
                            JOHN NEWTON

[361]
Christianity is intellectually defensible,
but such intellectual apologetics do not
make Christians. Christians are made
by the Holy Spirit.
                      HAROLD J. OCKENGA

[362]
The primary declaration of Christianity
is not "This do!" but "This happened!"
                      EVELYN UNDERHILL

[363]
Christianity can be condensed into
four words: admit, submit, commit,
and transmit.
                    SAMUEL WILBERFORCE

CHRISTLIKENESS

[364]
The gentleness of Christ is the comeli-
est ornament that a Christian can wear.
                          WILLIAM ARNOT

[365]
He became what we are that he might
make us what he is.
                            ATHANASIUS

[366]
To become Christlike is the only thing
in the whole world worth caring for,
the thing before which every ambition
of man is folly and all lower achievement vain.
                       HENRY DRUMMOND

[367]
Being a Christian is more than just an
instantaneous conversion—it is a daily
process whereby you grow to be more
and more like Christ. Jesus Christ is the
man God wants every man to be like.
                          BILLY GRAHAM

[368]
The Christian goal is not the outward
and literal imitation of Jesus, but the
living out of the Christ life implanted
within by the Holy Spirit.
                          D. W. LAMBERT

[369]
If when you do right and suffer for it
you take it patiently, you have God's
approval. For to this you have been
called, because Christ also suffered for
you, leaving you an example, that you
should follow in his steps.
                    1 PETER 2:20–21 (RSV)

[370]
A cross Christian, an anxious Christian, a discouraged, gloomy Christian, a doubting Christian, a complaining Christian, an exacting Christian, a selfish Christian, a cruel, hard-hearted Christian, a self-indulgent Christian, a Christian with a sharp tongue or bitter spirit—all these may be very earnest in their work, and may have honorable places in the church; but they are not Christlike Christians.

HANNAH WHITALL SMITH

CHRISTMAS

[371]
Christmas is a Son away from home.

NORMA ALLOWAY

[372]
The fact of Jesus' coming is the final and unanswerable proof that God cares.

WILLIAM BARCLAY

[373]
There has been only one Christmas (the rest are anniversaries), and it is not over yet.

W. J. CAMERON

[374]
The cross always stands near the manger.

AMY CARMICHAEL

[375]
Christmas is always a blessed bother and bustle.

ALICE CARRICK

[376]
Christmas is not a date. It is a state of mind.

MARY ELLEN CHASE

[377]
It is Christmas in the heart that puts Christmas in the air.

W. T. ELLIS

[378]
God grant you the light in Christmas, which is faith; the warmth of Christmas, which is love; the radiance of Christmas, which is purity; the righteousness of Christmas, which is justice; the belief in Christmas, which is truth; the all of Christmas, which is Christ.

WILDA ENGLISH

[379]
Instead of being a time of unusual behavior, Christmas is about the only chance a man has to be himself.

FRANCIS C. FARLEY

[380]
I sometimes think we expect too much of Christmas Day. We try to crowd into it the long arrears of kindliness and humanity of the whole year. As for me, I like to take my Christmas a little at a time, all through the year.

DAVID GRAYSON

[381]
Christmas is based on an exchange of gifts: the gift of God to man—his unspeakable gift of his Son; and the gift of man to God—when we present our bodies as a living sacrifice and, like the Macedonians (2 Corinthians 8:5), first give ourselves to God. No one has kept or can keep Christmas until he has had a part in this two-way transaction.

VANCE HAVNER

[382]
Let this Christmas season be a renewing of the mind of Christ in our thinking, and a cleansing of our lives by his pure presence. Let his joy come to our weary world through us.

GERALD KENNEDY

[383]
Christmas is too large to be tucked away in the toe of a child's stocking.

GERALD STANLEY LEE

[384]
I wish we could put some of the Christmas spirit in jars and open a jar of it every month.

HARLAN MILLER

[385]
Men and women everywhere sigh on December 26 and say they're glad Christmas is all over for another year. But it isn't over. "Unto you is born . . . a Savior." It's just beginning! And it will go on forever.

EUGENIA PRICE

[386]
I am wishing for you this day a happy Christmas. I would send you those gifts which are beyond price, outlast time, and bridge all space. I wish you all laughter and pure joy, a merry heart and a clear conscience, and love which thinks no evil, is not easily provoked, and seeks not its own; the fragrance of flowers, the sweet associations of holly and mistletoe and fir, the memory of deep woods, of peaceful hills, and of the mantling snow, which guards the sleep of all God's creatures. I wish that the spirit of Christmastide may draw you into companionship with him who giveth all. Come, let us adore him.

BISHOP REMINGTON

[387]
You can never truly enjoy Christmas until you can look up into the Father's face and tell him you have received his Christmas Gift.

JOHN R. RICE

[388]
The simple shepherds heard the voice of an angel and found their Lamb; the wise men saw the light of a star and found their Wisdom.

FULTON J. SHEEN

[389]
Christmas is the day that holds all time together.

ALEXANDER SMITH

[390]
Christmas is a gift from God that a man cannot keep until he gives it to someone else.

DOROTHY CAMERON SMITH

[391]
The hinge of history is on the door of a Bethlehem stable.

RALPH W. SOCKMAN

[392]
Are you willing to believe that love is the strongest thing in the world— stronger than hate, stronger than evil, stronger than death—and that the blessed life which began in Bethlehem two thousand years ago is the image and brightness of the Eternal Love? Then you can keep Christmas.

HENRY VAN DYKE

[393]
To tidy up the house for Christmas is only a broomstick preparation. Heart preparation sweeps our lives clear.

CHARLES L. WALLIS

[394]
Santa Claus never died for anybody.

CRAIG WILSON

[395]
Deprive the people of the Christmas season and they will find a substitute, and it will not be a spiritual substitute.*

[396]
Christmas is a time for giving, not swapping: giving up sin, giving in to Christ, and giving out to our fellow man that we might meet him in his need.

[397]
Christmas is not just the birth of a baby; it is the heavenly Father saying good-bye to his Son.

[398]
The blessedness of Christmas is all wrapped up in the Person of Jesus. Our relationship determines the measure of the blessing.

[399]
Until one feels the spirit of Christmas, there is no Christmas.

CHURCH

[400]
The Christian church is not a static institution. It is men and women who flesh out in daily life the meaning of faith, the reality of the risen Christ.
MYRON S. AUGSBURGER

[401]
I wish to say one thing as I contemplate the church in the world today: the church needs to be far more clear and sure about its message.
DONALD M. BAILLIE

[402]
The church should be an army on the march; instead, it is a hospital full of wounded soldiers.
STEVEN BARABAS

[403]
Many of today's young people have little difficulty believing that God was in Christ. What they find hard to accept is that Christ is in the church.
ERNEST T. CAMPBELL

[404]
It is common for those that are farthest from God to boast themselves most of their being near to the church.
MATTHEW HENRY

[405]
The church is the only institution in the world that has lower entrance requirements than those for getting on a bus.
WILBUR LAROE

[406]
God never intended his church to be a refrigerator in which to preserve perishable piety. He intended it to be an incubator in which to hatch converts.
F. LINCICOME

[407]
Some people in church look like guests at a royal banquet, who couldn't afford to be left out, but have been forbidden by their doctor to eat anything.
W. R. MALTBIE

[408]
The Christian church belongs to God and not to man; the church cannot become a tool of any social order.
SAMUEL MOFFETT

[409]
The Christian church is the only society in the world in which membership is based upon the qualification that the candidate shall be unworthy of membership.
CHARLES CLAYTON MORRISON

[410]
The holiest moment of the church service is the moment when God's people —strengthened by preaching and sacrament—go out of the church door into the world to be *the Church*. We don't *go* to church; we *are* the Church.
ERNEST SOUTHCOTT

[411]
The Christian church is the one organization in the world that exists purely for the benefit of nonmembers.
WILLIAM TEMPLE

[412]
A church exists for the double purpose of gathering in and sending out.

CIRCUMSTANCES

[413]
If things go wrong don't go with them.
ROGER W. BABSON

[414]
I endeavor to subdue circumstances to myself, and not myself to circumstances.
HORACE

[415]
It is not circumstances in which we are placed, but the spirit in which we meet them, that constitutes our comfort.
ELIZABETH T. KING

[416]
I have learned, in whatever state I am, to be content.
PHILIPPIANS 4:11 (RSV)

[417]
The Christian sees the chances and accidents of history as the very warp and woof of the fabric of providence which God is ever weaving.
W. G. POLLARD

CIVILIZATION

[418]
You think that a wall as solid as the earth separates civilization from barbarism. I tell you the division is a thread, a sheet of glass. A touch here, a push there, and you bring back the reign of Saturn.
JOHN BUCHAN

[419]
However complex and solid [civilization] seems, it is actually quite fragile. It can be destroyed. What are its enemies? Well, first of all, fear . . .
KENNETH CLARK

[420]
The true test of civilization is not the census, nor the size of cities, nor the crops, but the kind of man that the country turns out.
RALPH WALDO EMERSON

[421]
Men and nations sink or soar, survive or perish, as they choose to be dominated by sin or righteousness.
A. P. GOUTHEY

[422]
Civilization can be saved only by a moral, intellectual, and spiritual revolution to match the scientific, technological, and economic revolution in which we are now living.
ROBERT MAYNARD HUTCHINS

[423]
A decent provision for the poor is the true test of civilization.
SAMUEL JOHNSON

[424]
We may live without friends; we may live without books; but civilized man cannot live without cooks.
EDWARD LYTTON

[425]
The veneer of civilization has proved to be amazingly thin. Beneath it has been revealed, not only the ape and the tiger, but what is far worse—perverted and satanic man.

WALTER MOBERLY

[426]
You can't say civilization don't advance, however, for in every war they kill you a new way.

WILL ROGERS

[427]
We must not stay as we are, doing always what was done last time, or we shall stick in the mud. Yet neither must we undertake a new world as catastrophic Utopians, and wreck our civilization in our hurry to mend it.

GEORGE BERNARD SHAW

[428]
A new civilization is generated through the transition of a society from a static condition to a dynamic activity. It could be described in the phrase of General Smuts: "Mankind is once more on the move."

ARNOLD J. TOYNBEE

[429]
No doubt historians will conclude that we of the twentieth century had intelligence enough to create a great civilization but not the moral wisdom to preserve it.

A. W. TOZER

[430]
All that is best in the civilization of today is the fruit of Christ's appearance among men.

DANIEL WEBSTER

[431]
Frankly, I think this civilization of ours is on the topple.

H. G. WELLS

[432]
Our civilization cannot survive materially unless it be redeemed spiritually with the Spirit of Christ.

WOODROW WILSON

CLEANSING

[433]
What God has cleansed, you must not call common.

ACTS 10:15 (RSV)

[434]
Sleep with clean hands either kept clean all day by integrity or washed clean at night by repentance.

JOHN DONNE

[435]
You can fill a twelve-quart bucket with water and pour it into a wicker basket, fill the bucket again and pour it in again, and keep doing it all day long. You'll never fill the basket; but I'll tell you one thing: at the end of the day you will have a clean basket.

ROY GUSTAFSON

[436]
We do not lose peace with God over another person's sin, but only over our own. Only when we are willing to be cleansed there will we have his peace.

ROY HESSION

[437]
The blood of Jesus his Son cleanses us from all sin.

1 JOHN 1:7 (RSV)

[438]
Whitewashing the pump won't make the water pure.

DWIGHT L. MOODY

[439]
Just as Jesus found it necessary to sweep the money-changers from the Temple porch, so we ourselves need a lot of housecleaning.

DALE EVANS ROGERS

[440]
Jesus washed my life when I couldn't do a thing with it.

LOIS WEST

COMFORT

[441]
When you are in the dark, listen, and God will give you a very precious message for someone else when you get into the light.

OSWALD CHAMBERS

[442]
The comfort derived from the misery of others is slight.

CICERO

[443]
Comfort is better than pride.

FRENCH PROVERB

[444]
Christians are sent into the world to comfort the afflicted and to afflict the comfortable.

BUELL GALLAGHER

[445]
God does not comfort us to make us comfortable, but to make us comforters.

JOHN HENRY JOWETT

[446]
Thy rod and thy staff, they comfort me.

PSALM 23:4 (KJV)

[447]
Of all created comforts, God is the lender; you are the borrower, not the owner.

SAMUEL RUTHERFORD

[448]
Most of our comforts grow up between our crosses.

EDWARD YOUNG

[449]
The word "comfort" is derived from the words "con" and "fort," meaning "with strength." Jesus said that if we mourn, we shall be comforted. Behind the promise of his word lies the resurrection of Jesus Christ, where total defeat was turned into glorious victory.*

COMMITMENT

[450]
God can do wonders with a broken heart if you give him all the pieces.

VICTOR ALFSEN

[451]
When James Calvert went out as a missionary to the cannibals of the Fiji Islands, the captain of the ship sought to turn him back. "You will lose your life and the lives of those with you if you go among such savages," he cried. Calvert only replied, "We died before we came here."

DAVID AUGSBURGER

[452]
God does not want people who come under certain reservations. In battle you need soldiers who fear nothing.

PÈRE DIDON

[453]
I go out to preach with two propositions in mind. First, every person ought to give his life to Christ. Second, whether or not anyone else gives him his life, I will give him mine.

JONATHAN EDWARDS

[454]
Learn to commit your soul and the building of it to One who can keep it and build it as you never can.

P. T. FORSYTH

[455]
I laid at Christ's feet a self of which I was shamed, couldn't control, and couldn't live with; and to my glad astonishment he took that self, remade it, consecrated it to Kingdom purposes, and gave it back to me, a self I can now live with gladly and joyously and comfortably.

E. STANLEY JONES

[456]
If you knew that there was One greater than yourself, who knows you better than you know yourself, and loves you better than you can love yourself; One who gathered into himself all great and good things and causes, blending in his beauty all the enduring color of life, who could turn your dreams into visions, and make real the things you hoped were true; and if that One had done one unmistakable thing to prove, even at the price of blood—his own blood—that you could come to him, would you not fall at his feet with the treasure of your years, your powers, your love? And is there not One such?

A. E. WHITHAM

COMMUNICATION

[457]
Put the hay down where the sheep can reach it.

CLOVIS CHAPPELL

[458]
Strides in communication now permit us to talk with people around the globe, but cannot bridge the ever-widening gaps within our own families.

GLORIA FRANCE

[459]
The way from God to a human heart is through a human heart.

S. D. GORDON

[460]
Jesus is God spelling himself out in language that man can understand.

S. D. GORDON

[461]
Good words quench more than a bucket of water.

GEORGE HERBERT

[462]
There is a time to say nothing, and a time to say something, but there is not time to say everything.

HUGO OF FLEURY

[463]
Sometimes we forget to turn off the sound when our mind goes blank.

W. A. "DUB" NANCE

[464]
When a good man speaks, he is worth listening to, but the words of fools are a dime a dozen.

PROVERBS 10:20
(The Living Bible)

[465]
Reliable communication permits progress.

PROVERBS 13:17
(*The Living Bible*)

[466]
We never go all to pieces at once. God talks always about little things and tells us when we are in danger. It pays to mind God.

PAUL RADER

[467]
If we are going to have answers for the twentieth-century world, we must not only have a God who exists, but we must have a God who has spoken!

FRANCIS A. SCHAEFFER

COMPANIONSHIP

[468]
I loved the talk, the laughter, the courteous little gestures toward one another, the sharing of the study of books of eloquence, the companionship that was sometimes serious and sometimes hilariously nonsensical, the differences of opinion that left no more bad feeling than if a man were disagreeing with his own self, the rare disputes that simply seasoned the normal consensus of agreement.

AUGUSTINE OF HIPPO

[469]
In misery it is great comfort to have a companion.

JOHN LYLY

[470]
Fellowship is heaven, and lack of fellowship is hell.

WILLIAM MORRIS

[471]
He who walks with wise men becomes wise, but the companion of fools will suffer harm.

PROVERBS 13:20 (RSV)

[472]
I never found the companion that was so companionable as solitude.

HENRY DAVID THOREAU

[473]
It is possible to be still enough to enjoy companionship with God.

J. GUSTAV WHITE

[474]
Bad company is the devil's net.

COMPASSION

[475]
If you quit loving the moment it becomes difficult, you never discover compassion.

DAVID AUGSBURGER

[476]
Man may dismiss compassion from his heart, but God will never.

WILLIAM COWPER

[477]
The Lord your God will . . . have compassion upon you.

DEUTERONOMY 30:3 (RSV)

[478]
Constitutionality is no match for compassion.

EVERETT McKINLEY DIRKSEN

[479]
The Lord is merciful and has pity, and forgives sin and delivers in times of affliction.

ECCLESIASTICUS 2:11
(Goodspeed)

[480]
God tempers the wind to the shorn lamb.

HENRI ESTIENNE

[481]
Should we feel at times disheartened and discouraged, a simple movement of heart toward God will renew our powers. Whatever he may demand of us, he will give us at the moment the strength and the courage that we need.

FRANÇOIS DE LA MOTHE FÉNELON

[482]
The existence of compassion in man proves the existence of compassion in God.

CHRISTOPHER HOLLIS

[483]
There is no exercise better for the heart than reaching down and lifting people up.

JOHN ANDREW HOLMER

[484]
If someone who is supposed to be a Christian has money enough to live well, and sees a brother in need, and won't help him—how can God's love be within him?

1 JOHN 3:17
(The Living Bible)

[485]
His compassions fail not. They are new every morning.

LAMENTATIONS 3:22–23 (KJV)

[486]
If we could read the secret history of our enemies, we should find in each man's life sorrow and suffering enough to disarm all hostility.

HENRY WADSWORTH LONGFELLOW

[487]
Though our Savior's Passion is over, his compassion is not.

WILLIAM PENN

[488]
Cleverness will enable a man to make a sermon, but only compassion for lost men will make him a soul winner.

LEONARD RAVENHILL

[489]
Biblical orthodoxy without compassion is surely the ugliest thing in the world.

FRANCIS A. SCHAEFFER

[490]
Compassion is the basis of all morality.

ARTHUR SCHOPENHAUER

[491]
Not a sigh is breathed, not a pain felt, not a grief pierces the soul, but the throb vibrates to the Father's heart.

COMPLETION

[492]
Christ was a complete man.

AUGUSTINE OF HIPPO

[493]
The fall of man has led to a condition of incompleteness. Unregenerate man is spiritually incomplete, for he is out of touch with God. He is morally incomplete, for he lacks both the final standard of conduct which is the will of God, and the dynamic which is the indwelling of God's Spirit. He is mentally incomplete, for sin has vitiated even his reasoning power, and he cannot understand spiritual truths. Only through the miracle of regeneration in which, through union with Christ, he partakes of the life of God, does he reach his completeness.

HERBERT M. CARSON

[494]
In him you have been brought to completion.

COLOSSIANS 2:10 (NEB)

[495]
I have never found any way to undo
what Christ has done.

BEN HADEN

[496]
Of one thing I am certain: the One who
started the good work in you will bring
it to completion by the Day of Christ
Jesus.

PHILIPPIANS 1:6 (NEB)

[497]
The knowledge of God is not a completed state, but a perpetual and difficult discovery. God has a plan for us,
for each of us at every moment. What
is this plan? That is his secret. We
strive laboriously to decipher it. . . .
[But] at the time of the coming of the
Master . . . there will no longer be any
secret.

PAUL TOURNIER

CONFESSION

[498]
The confession of evil works is the first
beginning of good works.

AUGUSTINE OF HIPPO

[499]
I have handed Jesus the key to my secret hideout.

PADDY BAKER

[500]
Matthew Henry said that he would not
huddle up his praises in a corner. His
sins had been open, God's mercy had
been open, and he would make open
profession and open payment.

JAMES BARR

[501]
When you get into the book of James
you get the impression that the Apostle
has been reading your mail.

HOWARD G. HENDRICKS

[502]
Confess your sins to one another, and
pray for one another, that you may be
healed.

JAMES 5:16 (RSV)

[503]
For him who confesses, shams are over
and realities have begun.

WILLIAM JAMES

[504]
A fault confessed is a new virtue added
to a man.

JAMES S. KNOWLES

[505]
It is the duty of nations as well as of
men to confess their sins and trans-
gressions in humble sorrow, yet with
assured hope that genuine repentance
will lead to mercy and pardon.

ABRAHAM LINCOLN

[506]
The first step to a believer's personal
renewal is total and full confession of
sin and a willingness to make restitution where God indicates this should
be done. The restitution should be as
wide as the offense was. The Christian
is to get rid of all the garbage and have
an absolutely clean slate with God.

WILBERT L. MCLEOD

[507]
A generous and free-minded confession disables a reproach and disarms
an injury.

MICHEL DE MONTAIGNE

[508]
If you confess with your lips that Jesus
is Lord and believe in your heart that
God raised him from the dead, you will
be saved. For man believes with his
heart and so is justified, and he confesses with his lips and so is saved.

ROMANS 10:9–10 (RSV)

[509]
Confession at once decreases and de-values anxiety and tension.
EDWARD S. STRECKER

[510]
Jesus obliged us to confess our sins for our own sake rather than for his. . . . If you harm a friend, it is not enough to apologize to God—you must apologize to your friend as well.
ALFRED WILSON

[511]
A fault confessed is more than half amended.

CONFIDENCE

[512]
It is on the unshakable fact of the resurrection of Christ from the dead that I base my faith in God's utter integrity and faithfulness. He let Jesus die—but only because he would raise him again. You can count on him! You can stake your faith on God—the God of Jesus Christ. He will keep his word.
LEIGHTON FORD

[513]
We share in Christ, if only we hold our first confidence firm to the end.
HEBREWS 3:14 (RSV)

[514]
This is the confidence which we have in him, that if we ask anything according to his will he hears us.
1 JOHN 5:14 (RSV)

[515]
It is difficult to make a man miserable while he feels he is worthy of himself and claims kindred to the great God who made him.
ABRAHAM LINCOLN

[516]
Confidence in others' honesty is no light testimony to one's own integrity.
MICHEL DE MONTAIGNE

[517]
What have we to expect? Anything. What have we to hope for? Everything. What have we to fear? Nothing.
EDWARD B. PUSEY

[518]
Be courteous to all, but intimate with few; and let those few be well tried before you give them your confidence.
GEORGE WASHINGTON

[519]
I have loved the stars too fondly to be fearful of the night.
SARAH WILLIAMS

[520]
Our confidence in Christ does not make us lazy, negligent or careless, but on the contrary it awakens us, urges us on, and makes us active in living righteous lives and doing good. There is no self-confidence to compare with this.
ULRICH ZWINGLI

CONFLICT

[521]
There is a doctrine of atonement [in the New Testament] . . . whose central theme . . . is divine conflict and victory: Jesus Christ—Christus Victor—fights against and triumphs over the evil powers of the world, the "tyrants" under which mankind is in bondage and suffering, and in him God reconciles the world to himself. . . . Sovereign divine love has taken the initiative, broken through the order of justice and merit . . . and created a new relation between the world and God.
GUSTAF AULÉN

[522]
In battle those who are most afraid are always in most danger.

CATILINE

[523]
It is through [struggle] the lion has gained its strength, the deer its speed, the dog its sagacity. The suffering which the conflict involved may indicate that God has made even animals for some higher end. . . . The ends are eminently worthy of a Divine Intelligence.

ROBERT FLINT

[524]
I am sure that most of us, looking back, would admit that whatever we have achieved in character we have achieved through conflict; it has come to us through powers hidden deep within us, so deep that we didn't know we had them, called into action by the challenge of opposition and frustration. The weights of life keep us going.

J. WALLACE HAMILTON

[525]
I don't accomplish the good that I set out to do, and the evil I don't really want to do I find I am always doing.

ROMANS 7:19
(Phillips)

CONFORMITY

[526]
The virtue in most requests is conformity. Whoso would be a man must be a nonconformist.

RALPH WALDO EMERSON

[527]
To deny self is to become a nonconformist. The Bible tells us not to be conformed to this world either physically or intellectually or spiritually.

BILLY GRAHAM

[528]
The essence of true holiness consists in conformity to the nature and will of God.

SAMUEL LUCAS

[529]
While we were talking came by several poor creatures carried by constables, for being at a conventicle [evangelical worship service]. I would to God they would either conform, or be more wise and be not catched.

SAMUEL PEPYS

[530]
To be conformed to this age is to yield oneself to it, following the line of least resistance, as jelly in a mold, until one gives up the good fight of faith.

WILLIAM L. PETTINGILL

[531]
Do not be conformed to this world but be transformed by the renewal of your mind.

ROMANS 12:2 (RSV)

CONSCIENCE

[532]
A good conscience is a continual feast.

FRANCIS BACON

[533]
He that loses his conscience has nothing left that is worth keeping.

NICOLAS CAUSSIN

[534]
A guilty conscience needs no accuser.

ENGLISH PROVERB

[535]
To have a guilty conscience is a feeling. Psychologists may define it as a guilt complex, and may seek to rationalize away the sense of guilt, but once it has been awakened through the application of the law of God, no explanation will quiet the insistent voice of conscience.

BILLY GRAHAM

[536]
My conscience is captive to the Word of God.

MARTIN LUTHER

[537]
Labor to keep alive in your breast that little spark of celestial fire called conscience.

GEORGE WASHINGTON

[538]
A good conscience is a soft pillow.

CONSERVATISM

[539]
The reason why Christian conservatives can associate with atheists is that we hold that above all faith is a gift and that, therefore, there is no accounting for the bad fortune that has beset those who do not believe or the good fortune that has befallen those who do.

WILLIAM F. BUCKLEY, JR.

[540]
The healthy stomach is nothing if not conservative. Few radicals have good digestions.

SAMUEL BUTLER

[541]
In a world which exists by the balance of antagonisms, the respective merit of the conservator or the innovator must ever remain debatable.

THOMAS CARLYLE

[542]
What is conservatism? Is it not adherence to the old and tried against the new and untried?

ABRAHAM LINCOLN

[543]
The problem of conservatism is to find the way to restore the tradition of the civilization and apply it in a new situation. . . . It is a vindication and renewal of the civilization tradition as the fundament upon which reason must build to solve the problems of the present.

FRANK S. MEYER

[544]
The true conservative is the man who has a real concern for injustices and takes thought against the day of reckoning.

FRANKLIN D. ROOSEVELT

CONSISTENCY

[545]
It is one thing to go through a crisis grandly, but another thing to go through every day glorifying God when there is no witness, no limelight, no one paying the remotest attention to us.

OSWALD CHAMBERS

[546]
A consistent man believes in destiny, a capricious man in chance.

BENJAMIN DISRAELI

[547]
Do not say things. What you are stands over you the while, and thunders so that I cannot hear what you say to the contrary.

RALPH WALDO EMERSON

[548]
He does not believe who does not live
according to his belief.

THOMAS FULLER

[549]
From the darkness round the cross
there rings out this voice so sure that
God is love. In him there is no caprice
and no changeableness. Do what you
will to him, however you may hurt and
disappoint him and break his heart,
you cannot alter his essential nature.

ARTHUR JOHN GOSSIP

[550]
A double-minded man is unstable in all
his ways.

JAMES 1:8 (KJV)

[551]
Purity of heart is to will one thing.

SØREN KIERKEGAARD

[552]
No one who puts his hand to the plow
and looks back is fit for the kingdom of
God.

LUKE 9:62 (RSV)

CONTENTMENT

[553]
No form of society can be reasonably
stable in which the majority of the people are not fairly content. People cannot be content if they feel that the
foundations of their lives are wholly
unstable.

JAMES TRUSLOW ADAMS

[554]
The utmost we can hope for in this
world is contentment.

JOSEPH ADDISON

[555]
Who lives content with little possesses
everything.

NICOLAS BOILEAU-DESPREAUX

[556]
True contentment is a real, even an active, virtue—not only affirmative but
creative. It is the power of getting out
of any situation all there is in it.

G. K. CHESTERTON

[557]
Fortify yourself with contentment, for
this is an impregnable fortress.

EPICTETUS

[558]
Contentment consists not in adding
more fuel, but in taking away some fire;
not in multiplying of wealth, but in sub-
tracting men's desires.

THOMAS FULLER

[559]
When we cannot find contentment in
ourselves it is useless to seek it elsewhere.

FRANÇOIS DE LA ROCHEFOUCAULD

[560]
My God, give me neither poverty nor
riches, but whatsoever it may be Thy
will to give, give me with it a heart that
knows humbly to acquiesce in what is
Thy will.

GOTTHOLD EPHRAIM LESSING

[561]
It is right to be contented with what we
have, never with what we are.

JAMES MACKINTOSH

[562]
I have learned, in whatever state I am,
to be content.

PHILIPPIANS 4:11 (RSV)

[563]
Better is a dry morsel with quiet than a house full of feasting with strife.

PROVERBS 17:1 (RSV)

[564]
Contentment with the divine will is the best remedy we can apply to misfortune.

WILLIAM TEMPLE

CONVERSION

[565]
My life collided with me. Christ, the master Adjuster, investigated and cancelled my policy. Then he gave me his.

MARILYNN BARTLETT

[566]
Conversion is the end of the Christian life—but it's the front end!

J. B. GAMBRELL

[567]
Every time well-meaning souls insist on cheapening his message, lowering the standard, explaining away the cost and agreeing to accept him upon easier terms than those he states, Christ openly repudiates them and will have none of their advice.

ARTHUR JOHN GOSSIP

[568]
Jesus Christ burst from the grave and exploded in my heart.

DONNA HOSFORD

[569]
When one life is changed, the world is changed.

THOMAS L. JOHNS

[570]
No inferior form of energy can be simply converted into a superior form unless at the same time a source of higher value lends it support.

CARL GUSTAV JUNG

[571]
Jesus Christ the transformer took my bundle of spiritual barbed-wire and electrified it into a high-voltage power line.

YVONNE LEHMAN

[572]
It has been said that the true account of what happened to Saul of Tarsus was that he had an epileptic seizure in a thunderstorm. Then men ought always to pray for a multiplication of thunderstorms and an epidemic of epilepsy!

G. CAMPBELL MORGAN

[573]
I cast off the mooring lines at a decaying wharf and pointed the bow toward the open sea of life, trusting my new Captain to take me safely to his heavenly haven.

ROY C. NADEN

[574]
I went to Africa that I might be able to sin to my heart's content. I was a wild beast on the coast of Africa till the Lord caught and tamed me.

JOHN NEWTON

[575]
My dark soul lived at the bottom of a lake; then Jesus walked upon the waters.

RACHEL RICE

[576]
Since the will to war is latent in human nature, only a conversion based on spiritual renewal can lead men to a new concept of living.

RALPH G. TURNBULL

[577]
Let a man go to the grammar school of
faith and repentance before he goes to
the university of election and predesti-
nation.

GEORGE WHITEFIELD

[578]
Jesus Christ will never strong-arm his
way into your life.

GRADY B. WILSON

[579]
The torn garments of our world can be
rewoven only through the expert invisible mending of the greatest Tailor of
all time, Jesus Christ.

BONNIE ZANDT

[580]
Jesus gave me the passport to life.

[581]
My life made a U-turn, and after Christ
removed the roadblocks, I watched my
old ways disappear into the infinity of
the rear-view mirror.

[582]
When I recognized the Master as my
guide, he steered me across a threshold
into unventured expanses, all charted,
as I discovered, in his Word.

CONVICTION

[583]
Conviction, were it never so excellent,
is worthless till it convert itself into
conduct.

THOMAS CARLYLE

[584]
Convictions are the mainsprings of action, the driving powers of life. What a
man lives are his convictions.

FRANCIS C. KELLEY

[585]
I can only say that I have acted upon
my best convictions, without selfishness or malice, and by the help of God
I shall continue to do so.

ABRAHAM LINCOLN

[586]
I heard that if you take a bit of phosphorus and put it upon a slip of wood
and ignite the phosphorus, bright as
the blaze is, there drops from it a white
ash that coats the wood and makes it
almost impossible to kindle the wood.
And so when the flaming conviction
laid upon your heart has burnt itself
out, it has coated the heart and it will
be very difficult to kindle the light there
again.

ALEXANDER MACLAREN

[587]
Trying to live without money is easier
than trying to live without convictions.

ROY L. SMITH

COURAGE

[588]
Courage is fear that has said its prayers.

KARLE WILSON BAKER

[589]
On many of the great issues of our
time, men have lacked wisdom because
they have lacked courage.

WILLIAM BENTON

[590]
In sport, in courage, and the sight of
heaven, all men meet on equal terms.

WINSTON S. CHURCHILL

[591]
Conscience is the root of all true courage; if a man would be brave let him
obey his conscience.

J. F. CLARKE

[592]
Fear can keep a man out of danger, but courage can support him in it.

THOMAS FULLER

[593]
It is better to live one day as a lion than a hundred years as a sheep.

ITALIAN PROVERB

[594]
Only be strong and very courageous, being careful to do according to all the law which Moses my servant commanded you; turn not from it to the right hand or to the left, that you may have good success wherever you go.

JOSHUA 1:7 (RSV)

[595]
Courage consists not in hazarding without fear, but being resolutely minded in a just cause.

PLUTARCH

[596]
Courage consists not in blindly overlooking danger, but in seeing it and conquering it.

JEAN PAUL RICHTER

[597]
Courage is doing what you're afraid to do. There can be no courage unless you're scared.

EDDIE RICKENBACKER

[598]
If God is on our side, who can ever be against us?

ROMANS 8:31
(The Living Bible)

[599]
Whenever Christians start thanking God in tight situations, look for courage to be shown.*

CREATION

[600]
No rain, no mushrooms. No God, no world.

AN AFRICAN CHIEF

[601]
The man makes the preacher. God must make the man.

E. M. BOUNDS

[602]
God created the world for reasons that are sufficient unto himself. It is not necessary that we be told these reasons. As long as we know that God loves us, we have a base for hope. And when we have hope, all else can be borne in patience.

EDWARD JOHN CARNELL

[603]
The probability of life originating from accident is comparable to the probability of the unabridged dictionary resulting from an explosion in a printing shop.

EDWIN CONKLIN

[604]
Love all God's creation, the whole and every grain of sand in it. Love every leaf, every ray of God's light.

FYODOR DOSTOEVSKY
Fr. Zossima, in The Brothers Karamazov

[605]
God is that creative force who made the universe by the power of his speech.

LEONARD MITCHELL

[606]
Posterity will some day laugh at the foolishness of modern materialistic philosophy. The more I study nature, the more I am amazed at the Creator.

LOUIS PASTEUR

CREATIVITY

[607]
The greatest mystery of life is that satisfaction is felt not by those who take and make demands but by those who give and make sacrifices. In them alone the energy of life does not fail, and this is precisely what is meant by creativity.
NICOLAS BERDYAEV

[608]
If you would create something, you must be something.
JOHANN WOLFGANG VON GOETHE

[609]
Language can become a screen which stands between the thinker and reality. This is the reason why true creativity often starts where language ends.
ARTHUR KOESTLER

[610]
Since there is nothing new under the sun, creativity means simply putting old things together in a fresh way.*

CREATOR

[611]
Thus does the world forget You, its Creator, and falls in love with what You have created instead of with You.
AUGUSTINE OF HIPPO

[612]
A dead God is the creation of men; a living God is the Creator of men.
DAVID M. BARR

[613]
We ought to beware lest, in our presumption, we imagine that the ends which God proposed to himself in the creation of the world are understood by us.
RENÉ DESCARTES

[614]
The Almighty is working on a great scale, and will not be hustled by our peevish impetuosity.
W. GRAHAM SCROGGIE

[615]
Why did God make the universe? God is Good, and being Good he could not, as it were, contain himself; consequently, he told the secret of his Goodness to nothingness and that was creation.
FULTON J. SHEEN

[616]
The spiritual interest in the doctrine of Creation lies solely in the assertion of the dependence of all existence upon the will of God.
WILLIAM TEMPLE

[617]
To assert that a world as intricate as ours emerged from chaos by chance is about as sensible as to claim that Shakespeare's dramas were composed by rioting monkeys in a print shop.
MERRILL C. TENNEY

CRITICISM

[618]
It is ridiculous for any man to criticize the works of another if he has not distinguished himself by his own performance.
JOSEPH ADDISON

[619]
To speak ill of others is a dishonest way of praising ourselves.
WILL DURANT

[620]
If you are slandered, never mind; it will all come off when it is dry.
CHARLES G. FINNEY

[621]
It is easy to shoot a skylark, but it is not so easy to produce its song.

LIONEL B. FLETCHER

[622]
Unless we are willing to help a person overcome his faults, there is little value in pointing them out.

ROBERT J. HASTINGS

[623]
Resolved, never to reprove another except I experience at the same time a peculiar contrition of heart.

HENRY MARTYN

[624]
See that your public behavior is above criticism.

ROMANS 12:17
(Phillips)

[625]
Let us therefore stop turning critical eyes on one another. If we must be critical, let us be critical of our own conduct and see that we do nothing to make a brother stumble or fall.

ROMANS 14:13
(Phillips)

[626]
You will never be an inwardly religious and devout man unless you pass over in silence the shortcomings of your fellow men, and diligently examine your own weaknesses.

THOMAS À KEMPIS

[627]
Most of us associate being criticized with being punished or told we're unwanted, and often it bears this implication, especially when parents criticize their children. Only by forcing ourselves to listen to criticism can we teach ourselves that it is sometimes well intended, and that we won't fall to pieces no matter what other people say about us.

GEORGE WEINBERG

[628]
Criticism comes easier than craftsmanship.

ZEUXIS

[629]
A critic is one who would have you write it, sign it, paint it, play it, or carve it as *he* would—if he could.

CROSS

[630]
The cross is the only ladder high enough to touch the threshold of heaven.

GEORGE DANA BOARDMAN

[631]
In the cross of Christ excess in men is met by excess in God; excess of evil is mastered by excess of love.

LOUIS BOURDALOUE

[632]
I was made to see, again and again, that God and my soul were friends by his blood; yea, I saw that the justice of God and my sinful soul could embrace and kiss each other, through his blood. This was a good day to me; I hope I shall never forget it.

JOHN BUNYAN

[633]
It was through what his Son did that God cleared a path for everything to come to him—all things in heaven and on earth—for Christ's death on the cross has made peace with God for all by his blood.

COLOSSIANS 1:20
(The Living Bible)

[634]
But far be it from me to glory except in the cross of our Lord Jesus Christ, by which the world has been crucified to me, and I to the world.

GALATIANS 6:14 (RSV)

[635]
Dying believers seem to care comparatively little for hymns descriptive of the joys and glories of heaven, beautiful as many of these are. It is to the cross, not to the crown, that the last look turns, the lingering grasp cleaves.

DORA GREENWELL

[636]
Life doesn't begin at forty, or at twenty, but at Calvary.

ELAINE KILGORE

[637]
From the cross I can see for miles.

GRETCHEN G. MCKEE

[638]
The reason why Christ chose the hard way of the cross was, among other things, that he saw beyond it.

S. J. REID

[639]
If you take that crabbed tree [the cross] and carry it lovingly, it will become to you like wings to a bird and sails to a ship.

SAMUEL RUTHERFORD

[640]
Jesus now has many lovers of his heavenly Kingdom, but few bearers of his cross.

THOMAS À KEMPIS

CRUCIFIXION

[641]
Without a crucifixion there is no resurrection.

STUART BRISCOE

[642]
It is a grave offense even to bind a Roman citizen, a crime to flog him, almost the act of a parricide to put him to death: what shall I then call crucifying him? Language worthy of such an enormity it is impossible to find.

CICERO

[643]
To preach in the power of the crucified Savior, you have to be a crucified preacher.

JAMES E. COULTER

[644]
Certain it is that we are saved not by one cross but by two—Christ's and our own. We must be crucified with Christ, must die with him, and rise with him into a new way of life and being.

ARTHUR JOHN GOSSIP
The Interpreter's Bible

[645]
I have been crucified with Christ: the life I now live is not my life, but the life which Christ lives in me; and my present bodily life is lived by faith in the Son of God, who loved me and gave himself up for me.

GALATIANS 2:20 (NEB)

[646]
Jesus was crucified not in a cathedral between two candles, but on a cross between two thieves.
GEORGE F. MACLEOD

[647]
Jesus cannot forget us; we have been graven on the palms of his hands.
LOIS PICILLO

[648]
There are some sciences that may be learned by the head, but the science of Christ crucified can only be learned by the heart.
CHARLES H. SPURGEON

[649]
To be crucified means, first, the man on the cross is facing only one direction; second, he is not going back; and third, he has no further plans of his own.
A. W. TOZER

DEATH

[650]
I think of death as a glad awakening from this troubled sleep which we call life; as an emancipation from a world which, beautiful though it be, is still a land of captivity.
LYMAN ABBOTT

[651]
How much more Christian love there would be if we didn't wait for death to release our reserves!
HAZEL BECK ANDRÉ

[652]
The Bible tells us, and tells us clearly, that by the death of Jesus Christ on a cross, death itself has been conquered, its bitter sting has been removed, and in a day yet to be, it will be destroyed.
JOSEPH BAYLY

[653]
The waters are rising but I am not sinking.
CATHERINE BOOTH
(last words)

[654]
I have been dying for twenty years. Now I am going to live.
JAMES BURNS
(last words)

[655]
Death was not God's original purpose for man.
EVELYN FROST

[656]
But we see Jesus, who for a little while was made lower than the angels, crowned with glory and honor because of the suffering of death, so that by the grace of God he might taste death for every one.
HEBREWS 2:9 (RSV)

[657]
I came from God, and I'm going back to God, and I won't have any gaps of death in the middle of my life.
GEORGE MACDONALD

[658]
God will wipe away every tear from their eyes, and death shall be no more, neither shall there be mourning nor crying nor pain any more.
REVELATION 21:4 (RSV)

"DEATH OF GOD"

[659]
Some people are saying God is dead, but it is not the scientists who are saying it.
WALTER F. BURKE

[660]
The difference between the unbelieving fool described by the Psalmist
(Psalm 14:1) and the "God is dead"
theologian is that the Old Testament
fool said *in his heart* there was no God;
the modern fool brays it all over the
countryside.

MARTIN P. DAVIS

[661]
The ages assure us that God does not
die by pronouncement, denial or assas-
sination—and already the "God is
dead" cult is passé while it is aborning.

EDWARD L. R. ELSON

[662]
The Carpenter of Nazareth is not dead;
he is busy building a temple from the
rough lumber of my soul.

ELOISE HATFIELD

[663]
It's a case of mistaken identity; God
isn't dead, some of the theologians are.

BYRON S. LAMSON

[664]
Sartre speaks of the silence of God,
Heidegger of the absence of God, Jas-
pers of the concealment of God, Bult-
mann of the hiddenness of God, Buber
of the eclipse of God, Tillich of the
nonbeing of God, Altizer of the death
of God. And the New Testament? It
speaks of the love of God.

RICHARD WOLFF

DECISION

[665]
The man who insists upon seeing with
perfect clearness before he decides
never decides.

HENRI FRÉDÉRIC AMIEL

[666]
The fine art of executive decision consists in not deciding questions that are
not now pertinent, in not deciding
prematurely, in not making decisions
that cannot be made effective, and in
not making decisions that others
should make.

CHESTER I. BARNARD

[667]
We make our decisions, and then our
decisions turn around and make us.

F. W. BOREHAM

[668]
To see and dare, and decide; to be a
fixed pillar in the welter of uncertainty.
. . .

THOMAS CARLYLE
(of Oliver Cromwell)

[669]
Father, make of me a crisis man. Bring
those I contact to decision. Let me not
be a milepost on a single road; make
me a fork, that men must turn one way
or another on facing Christ in me.

JIM ELLIOT

[670]
Beware of letting slip this note of deci-
siveness, this belief in the definite nature of the passing from "not being a
disciple" to "being a disciple"; from
being "out of Christ," "away," "lost,"
to being "in Christ," "at home,"
"found."

BRYAN GREEN

[671]
I like a person who knows his own mind
and sticks to it; who sees at once what,
in given circumstances, is to be done,
and does it.

WILLIAM HAZLITT

[672]
Multitudes, multitudes, in the valley of decision! For the day of the Lord is near in the valley of decision.

JOEL 3:14 (RSV)

[673]
Your capacity to say No determines your capacity to say Yes to greater things.

E. STANLEY JONES

[674]
How long will you go limping with two different opinions? If the Lord is God, follow him; but if Baal, then follow him.

1 KINGS 18:21 (RSV)

[675]
The man who has not learned to say No will be a weak if not a wretched man as long as he lives.

ALEXANDER MACLAREN

[676]
When he arrived at the banks of the Rubicon, which divides Cisalpine Gaul from the rest of Italy . . . he stopped to deliberate. . . . At last he cried out, "The die is cast!" and immediately passed the river.

PLUTARCH
(of Julius Caesar)

[677]
There is a time when we must firmly choose the course we will follow, or the relentless drift of events will make the decision.

HERBERT V. PROCHNOW

DEMOCRACY

[678]
We are justified, from the point of view of exegesis, in regarding the democratic conception of the State as an expansion of the thought of the New Testament.

KARL BARTH

[679]
The enthronement . . . of the individual . . . rested upon a religious idea which was this—that as an incarnate God, while wearing our flesh, had once died for every man, so no man thus redeemed could, without sacrilege, be abased by any tyranny of prelate or king from his privilege of remaining "a child of God and an inheritor of the kingdom of heaven."

NATHAN H. CHAMBERLAIN

[680]
Democracy is the art of disciplining oneself so that one need not be disciplined by others.

GEORGES CLEMENCEAU

[681]
The choice of public magistrates belongs unto the people by God's own allowance . . . because the foundation of authority is laid, first, in the free consent of the people.

THOMAS HOOKER

[682]
Democracy is the very child of Jesus' teachings of the infinite worth of every personality.

FRANCIS J. MCCONNELL

[683]
Men, as well as women, do not need political rights in order that they may govern, but in order that they may not be misgoverned.

JOHN STUART MILL

[684]
Man's capacity for justice makes
democracy possible. His inclination to
injustice makes democracy necessary.
REINHOLD NIEBUHR

[685]
This democratic idea is founded in human nature, and comes from the nature of God, who made human nature.
To carry it out politically is to execute
justice, which is the will of God.
THEODORE PARKER

[686]
People who want to understand
democracy should spend less time in
the library with Aristotle and more
time on the buses and in the subway.
SIMEON STRUMSKY

[687]
Do you want to be free? Then put your
faith in God, not in man. The people
gave you freedom with a vote and they
can take it away with a vote.
THOMAS V. TOOHER

[688]
Democracy is necessitated by the fact
that all men are sinners; it is made possible by the fact that we know it.
ELTON TRUEBLOOD

[689]
Although Christianity has never been
the guarantee of a democratic state
anywhere in the world, no democracy
has ever thrived successfully for any
period of time outside of Christian influence.
THEODORE H. WHITE

[690]
The Christians of the early church were
keenly alive to a direct clash between
spiritual forces, between the power of
God and evil; they felt psychic forces
opposed to them; they knew of an opposition to God in a spirit world. Thus
Christ proclaimed himself the cham-
pion of the Kingdom of God against
the forces of Satan, and with authority
commanded the demons both to depart from the diseased and to be silent
about his identity.
EVELYN FROST

[691]
The Bible teaches that demons are
real, and are capable of entering and
controlling people. They are spoken of
as unclean, violent and malicious. All
outside of Christ are in danger of demon possession.
BILLY GRAHAM

[692]
It is not more strange that there should
be evil spirits than evil men—evil
unembodied spirits than evil embodied
spirits.
SAMUEL JOHNSON

[693]
Demon possession is presented in
Scripture as a dreadful reality. The
supposition that the demoniacs of the
Gospels were only mentally ill is falla-
cious.
HAROLD LINDSELL

[694]
It is possible for the self to be partly
fulfilled and partly destroyed by its
submission to a power and spirit which
is greater than the self in its empiric
reality but not great enough to do justice to the self in its ultimate freedom.
Such spirit can be most simply defined
as demonic. The most striking contemporary form of it is a religious national-
ism in which race and nation assume
the eminence of God and demand un-
conditioned devotion. This absolute
claim for something which is not absolute identifies the possessing spirit as
demonic.

REINHOLD NIEBUHR

[695]
Jesus' mission can be described as being twofold: it is a battle against the
demons, and it is a battle for men.
. . . Anybody who would understand
history must be in possession of the
category of the demonic.

HELMUT THIELICKE

DEPRAVITY

[696]
Man without God is a beast, and never
more beastly than when he is most intelligent about his beastliness.

WHITTAKER CHAMBERS

[697]
It is not occasionally that the human
soul is under the influence of depravity; but this is its habit and state till the
soul is renewed by grace.

THOMAS DICK

[698]
Men sometimes affect to deny the depravity of our race; but it is as clearly
taught in the lawyer's office and in
courts of justice as in the Bible itself.

TRYON EDWARDS

[699]
The heart is deceitful above all things,
and desperately corrupt; who can understand it?

JEREMIAH 17:9 (RSV)

[700]
We are all quick to copy what is base
and depraved.

JUVENAL

[701]
If our depravity were total we should
not know ourselves to be depraved.

C. S. LEWIS

[702]
The final proof of the sinner is that he
does not know his own sin.

MARTIN LUTHER

[703]
We are not so miserable as we are vile.

MICHEL DE MONTAIGNE

[704]
Depravity of will and corruption of nature are transmitted wherever life itself
is transmitted.

WALTER RAUSCHENBUSCH

[705]
Therefore God gave them up in the
lusts of their hearts to impurity, to the
dishonoring of their bodies among
themselves, because they exchanged
the truth about God for a lie and wor-
shiped and served the creature rather
than the Creator, who is blessed
forever! Amen.

ROMANS 1:24–25 (RSV)

[706]
Man of himself and his own is nothing,
has nothing, can do and is capable of
nothing, but only infirmity, evil and
wickedness.

THEOLOGIA GERMANICA

[707]
Depravity implied that the whole person was tainted by sin and the whole of life was limited in what it could become, apart from the Grace of God.
RALPH G. TURNBULL

[708]
We are utterly indisposed, disabled, and made opposite to all good, and wholly inclined to all evil.
WESTMINSTER CONFESSION OF FAITH

[709]
Christian teaching on total depravity does not mean that man is utterly and completely wicked. It means that in everything man attempts to do, evil is potentially or actively present, since the flaw or bias of sin is in the race.*

DESIRE

[710]
They that desire but a few things can be crossed but in a few.
GERMAN PROVERB

[711]
By annihilating the desires, you annihilate the mind.
CLAUD ADRIEN HELVÉTIUS

[712]
Before we passionately desire anything which another enjoys, we should examine as to the happiness of its possessor.
FRANÇOIS DE LA ROCHEFOUCAULD

[713]
A desire fulfilled is sweet to the soul.
PROVERBS 13:19 (RSV)

[714]
There are two tragedies in life. One is to lose your heart's desire. The other is to gain it.
GEORGE BERNARD SHAW
Man and Superman

[715]
Impossible desires are punished in the desire itself.
PHILIP SIDNEY

[716]
None of us ever desired anything more ardently than God desires to bring men to a knowledge of himself.
JOHANNES TAULER

[717]
Any unmortified desire which a man allows in will effectually drive and keep Christ out of the heart.
CHARLES WESLEY

DESPAIR

[718]
We need not despair of any man as long as he lives.
AUGUSTINE OF HIPPO

[719]
Despair is such a waste of time when there is joy, and lack of faith is such a waste of time when there is God.
LARRY BURNER

[720]
Despair is the offspring of fear, of laziness, and of impatience.
JEREMY COLLIER

[721]
Despair is the conclusion of fools.
BENJAMIN DISRAELI

[722]
I hated all my toil in which I had toiled under the sun, seeing that I must leave it to the man who will come after me; and who knows whether he will be a wise man or a fool? . . . So I turned about and gave my heart up to despair.
ECCLESIASTES 2:18–20 (RSV)

[723]
He that despairs degrades the Deity.
OWEN FELTHAM

[724]
Despair gives courage to a coward.
THOMAS FULLER

[725]
It is impossible for that man to despair who remembers that his helper is omnipotent.
JEREMY TAYLOR

[726]
The mass of men lead lives of quiet desperation.
HENRY DAVID THOREAU

DESTINY

[727]
Life becomes intolerable only to those who feel that there is nothing more for which they can live and to which they can aspire.
GORDON W. ALLPORT

[728]
Man is born to have connection with God.
CLEMENT OF ALEXANDRIA

[729]
Destiny waits in the hand of God, not in the hands of statesmen.
T. S. ELIOT

[730]
As the arrow, loosed from the bow by the hand of the practiced archer, does not rest till it has reached the mark, so men pass from God to God. He is the mark for which they have been created, and they do not rest till they find their rest in him.
SØREN KIERKEGAARD

[731]
Aim at heaven and you will get earth thrown in. Aim at earth and you will get neither.
C. S. LEWIS

[732]
I have a spiritual suitcase and I know where I'm going.
ETHEL WATERS

DIFFERENCES

[733]
[God] made no distinction between them [the Gentiles] and us [the Jews], for he cleansed their lives through faith, just as he did ours.
ACTS 15:9
(*The Living Bible*)

[734]
An unlearned carpenter of my acquaintance once said in my hearing, "There is very little difference between one man and another, but what little there is is very important."
WILLIAM JAMES

[735]
You are to distinguish between the holy and the common, and between the unclean and the clean.
LEVITICUS 10:10 (RSV)

[736]
I can imagine some of you may say, "I am sure I am not as bad as some people." Yonder is an orchard, and in the orchard are two apple trees. They are worthless. Why? Well, one tree has five hundred apples and the other has five. But there is no difference. The fruit is miserable, sour, bitter. One tree may have more fruit than another, but the fruit is still bad.
DWIGHT L. MOODY

DIGNITY

[737]
It is only people of small moral stature
who have to stand on their dignity.

ARNOLD BENNETT

[738]
Dignity is like a perfume: those who
use it are scarcely conscious of it.

QUEEN CHRISTINA OF SWEDEN

[739]
A moral, sensible and well-bred man
will not affront me, and no other can.

WILLIAM COWPER

[740]
Our dignity is not in what we do, but in
what we understand.

GEORGE SANTAYANA

[741]
Jesus consistently lifted the worth of
human life above the minimum levels
to which the ancient world had reduced
it. "Of how much more value," he said,
"is a man than a sheep." He asserted
that men were worth saving, that the
individual member of society had ines-
timable value in God's sight.*

DISAPPOINTMENT

[742]
There are no disappointments to those
whose wills are buried in the will of
God.

FREDERICK W. FABER

[743]
Expectations   improperly   indulged
must end in disappointment.

SAMUEL JOHNSON

[744]
Disappointment is often the salt of life.

THEODORE PARKER

[745]
Disappointments: rivers without water,
clouds without moisture, taxation without representation, business without
profit, roses without fragrance, honey
without sweetness, life without hope,
homes without love.

ERNEST REEVES

[746]
Disappointment is the nurse of wisdom.

BAYLE ROCHE

[747]
Disappointments are to the soul what a
thunderstorm is to the air.

JOHANN FRIEDRICH VON SCHILLER

DISCIPLESHIP

[748]
Happy are they who know that discipleship simply means the life which
springs from grace, and that grace simply means discipleship.

DIETRICH BONHOEFFER

[749]
Discipleship means discipline. The disciple is one who has come with his ignorance, superstition and sin, to find
learning, truth and forgiveness from
the Savior. Without discipline we are
not disciples.

V. RAYMOND EDMAN

[750]
There are stars aplenty today, but have
you seen *His* star and what are you doing about it?

VANCE HAVNER

[751]
By this all men will know that you are
my disciples, if you have love for one
another.

JOHN 13:35 (RSV)

[752]
A disciple is not above his teacher, nor a servant above his master.

MATTHEW 10:24 (RSV)

[753]
God has not promised us an easy journey, but he has promised us a safe journey.

WILLIAM C. MILLER

[754]
The word "disciple" signifies a taught or trained one. Disciples are those who gather around this Teacher [Jesus] and are trained by him. They are seekers after truth, not merely in the abstract, but as a life force. The condition of discipleship was clearly declared by the Lord himself: "If ye abide in my word, then are ye truly my disciples" (John 8:31).

G. CAMPBELL MORGAN

[755]
I have inevitably and increasingly been driven to the conclusion, almost against my own will, that for a West European whose life and background and tradition are in terms of Western European Christian civilization, the only answer lies in the person and life and teaching of Christ.

MALCOLM MUGGERIDGE

[756]
Why should the Queen have good soldiers and not the King of kings?

MARY SLESSOR

[757]
You can't be the salt of the earth without smarting someone.

DISCIPLINE

[758]
The study of God's Word, for the purpose of discovering God's will, is the secret discipline which has formed the greatest characters.

JAMES W. ALEXANDER

[759]
Discipline is demanded of the athlete to win a game. Discipline is required for the captain running his ship. Discipline is needed for the pianist to practice for the concert. Only in the matter of personal conduct is the need for discipline questioned. But if parents believe standards are necessary, then discipline certainly is needed to attain them.

GLADYS BROOKS

[760]
Men are qualified for civic liberties in exact proportion to their disposition to put moral chains upon their appetites.

EDMUND BURKE

[761]
Genius is the capacity for taking infinite pains.

THOMAS CARLYLE

[762]
To live a disciplined life, and to accept the result of that discipline as the will of God—that is the mark of a man.

TOM LANDRY

[763]
Syluer is not syluer tyll it be blowne and purged in the fyre; golde commeth to no honour, till by long hammering and chasing it be forged into a vessell meete for the Kinges seruice.

RICHARD MADDOXE

[764]
I have more trouble with D. L. Moody
than with any other man I ever met.
DWIGHT L. MOODY

[765]
Character is, by its very nature, the
product of probationary discipline.
AUSTIN PHELPS

[766]
Anyone willing to be corrected is on
the pathway to life. Anyone refusing
has lost his chance.
PROVERBS 10:17
(The Living Bible)

[767]
No man is free who cannot command
himself.
PYTHAGORAS

[768]
The highest forms of self-expression
are to be found not in the lotus gardens
of self-gratification but in the gym-
nasium of self-renunciation.
PAUL S. REES

[769]
My father was a Methodist and believed
in the laying on of hands, and believe
me, he really laid them on!
A. W. TOZER

[770]
The cure of crime is not in the *electric*
chair, but in the *high* chair.

DISCOURAGEMENT

[771]
Neither God nor man can use a dis-
couraged person.
MARY McLEOD BETHUNE

[772]
Every thought, word and deed for
Christ carries you away from discour-
agement.
THEODORE L. CUYLER

[773]
Come unto me, all ye that labor and are
heavy laden, and I will give you rest.
MATTHEW 11:28 (KJV)

[774]
Have you ever felt so low that you had
to reach up to touch bottom?

DOUBT

[775]
Every step toward Christ kills a doubt.
THEODORE L. CUYLER

[776]
The doubter's dissatisfaction with his
doubt is as great and widespread as the
doubt itself.
JAN DEWITT

[777]
Never doubt in the dark what God told
you in the light.
V. RAYMOND EDMAN

[778]
There is no moral power in doubt.
TRYON EDWARDS

[779]
There are too many who find, or think
they find, a cheap ticket to scholarship
in parading their doubts. They would
discover that their doubts would die
for want of fresh air if only they would
keep their mouths shut.
ALEXANDER FRAZER

[780]
Give me the benefit of your convictions, if you have any, but keep your
doubts to yourself, for I have enough
of my own.
JOHANN WOLFGANG VON GOETHE

[781]
Test the spirits to see whether they are
of God.
1 JOHN 4:1 (RSV)

[782]
I find that the doing of the will of God
leaves me no time for disputing about
his plans.
GEORGE MACDONALD

[783]
Jesus immediately reached out his
hand and caught him, saying to him,
"O man of little faith, why did you
doubt?"
MATTHEW 14:31 (RSV)

[784]
I've known many who have died of
doubt.
CHARLES MAYO, M.D.

[785]
The Shepherd Psalm has remanded to
their dungeon more felon thoughts,
more black doubts, more thieving sorrows, than there are sands on the sea-
shore.
F. B. MEYER

[786]
Ten thousand difficulties do not make
one doubt.
JOHN HENRY NEWMAN

[787]
Doubt is brother devil to despair.
JOHN BOYLE O'REILLY

[788]
The end of doubt is the beginning of
repose.
PETRARCH

[789]
Doubt makes the mountain which faith
can move.

DRUGS

[790]
All drugs are potentially harmful, in-
cluding aspirin.
F. S. ABUZZAHAB, M.D.

[791]
We live in a drug-oriented society. For
a growing number of adults, drugs are
a way of life.
GORDON R. MCLEAN
AND HASKELL BOWEN

[792]
If alcoholism were a communicable
disease, a national emergency would
be declared.
WILLIAM C. MENNINGER

[793]
It's the biggest fallacy ever to say that
marijuana is no more harmful than al-
cohol. Perhaps you can't get hooked
physically on marijuana, but you can
get hooked on it mentally and emotion-
ally. You get sucked in to marijuana
and then go on to something stronger,
like hashish.
LINDA MYRING

[794]
No one can stay on LSD for any length
of time without encountering demons.
CHRISTOPHER PIKE

[795]
A prudent man won't swallow a potato
bug and then take Paris green to kill it.
BILLY SUNDAY

DUTY

[796]
Our grand business is not to see what lies dimly at a distance, but to do what lies clearly at hand.

THOMAS CARLYLE

[797]
Fear God, and keep his commandments; for this is the whole duty of man.

ECCLESIASTES 12:13 (RSV)

[798]
No personal consideration should stand in the way of performing a public duty.

ULYSSES S. GRANT

[799]
The right, practical divinity is this: Believe in Christ, and do your duty in that state of life to which God has called you.

MARTIN LUTHER

[800]
We have each day to be faithful for the one short day, and long years and a long life will take care of themselves without the sense of their length or their weight ever being a burden.

ANDREW MURRAY

[801]
When praying, do not give God instructions—report for duty!

EASTER

[802]
The great Easter truth is not that we are to live newly after death, but that we are to be new here and now by the power of the resurrection.

PHILLIPS BROOKS

[803]
"Paint Christ," cried Tommaso Campanella to the Italian painters of his day, "not dead but risen, with his foot set in scorn on the split rock with which they sought to hold him down! Paint him the Conqueror of death! Paint him the Lord of life! Paint him as what he is, the irresistible Victor who, tested to the uttermost, has proved himself in very deed mighty to save!"

ARTHUR JOHN GOSSIP

[804]
Easter says you can put truth in a grave, but it won't stay there.

CLARENCE W. HALL

[805]
One trouble with the churches is that too many people want to have Easter without Calvary.

L. P. JACKS

[806]
The story of Easter is the story of God's wonderful window of divine surprise.

CARL KNUDSEN

[807]
Easter is to our faith what water is to the ocean, what stone is to the mountain, what blood is to your body.

RAYMOND I. LINDQUIST

[808]
The stone was rolled away from the door, not to permit Christ to come out, but to enable the disciples to go in.

PETER MARSHALL

[809]
Easter morning is not a mere declaration that we are immortal, but a declaration that we are immortal children of God.

GEORGE MATHESON

[810]
The return of Easter should be to the Christian life the call of a trumpet. It is the news of a great victory. It is the solution of a great perplexity. It is the assurance of a great triumph.

FREDERICK TEMPLE

[811]
The only shadow on the cloudless Easter day of God's victory is the poverty of my own devotion, the memory of ineffective hours of unbelief, and my own stingy response to God's generosity.

A. E. WHITHAM

ECOLOGY

[812]
The land gradually withdraws from the abuse it has received at the hand of man who does not plan or accept responsibility for his own future.

S. P. R. CHARTER

[813]
The Lord will make the pestilence cleave to you until he has consumed you off the land. . . . The Lord will smite you with consumption, and with fever, inflammation, and fiery heat, and with drought, and with blasting, and with mildew. . . . And the heavens over your head shall be brass, and the earth under you shall be iron. The Lord will make the rain of your land powder and dust; from heaven it shall come down upon you until you are destroyed.

DEUTERONOMY 28:21–24 (RSV)

[814]
Littering persons, smoking planes, fuming automobiles, oily motorboat engines and draining sewers threaten the ecological balance of the entire earth.

DAVID O. MOBERG

[815]
Ironically man may be the creature who left as his monument a planet nearly as incapable of sustaining life as its barren neighbors in the dead vacuum of the solar system we are now exploring. . . . Man has an infinite capacity for fouling his environment.

GAYLORD NELSON

[816]
The ground is holy, being even as it came from the Creator. Keep it, guard it, care for it, for it keeps men, guards men, cares for men. Destroy it and man is destroyed.

ALAN PATON

ECUMENISM

[817]
Evangelicals are not the only Christians. There are those who share with us a firm belief in historic, supernatural Christianity, who worship Christ as Lord and Savior, who take a high view of Scripture, yet who may not use all our terminology and who hold a view of the church and the ministry different from ours. They too are Christians; and from some of them we have much to learn.

FRANK E. GAEBELEIN

[818]
I do not want the walls of separation between different orders of Christians to be destroyed, but only lowered, that we may shake hands a little easier over them.

ROWLAND HILL

[819]
It is a matter of experience that the first effect of joining the ecumenical movement is to make everyone more, not less, conscious of his own special loyalties and traditions.
WALTER MARSHALL HORTON

[820]
Putting all the ecclesiastical corpses into one graveyard will not bring about a resurrection.
DAVID MARTYN LLOYD-JONES

[821]
Denominational family relations have still a long way to go before they achieve the oneness that is called for by their common heritage of faith.
JOHN A. MACKAY

[822]
Some of us worked long enough in a shipbuilding district to know that welding is impossible except the materials to be joined are at white heat temperature; and none of our denominational convictions is at white heat. When you try to weld them they only fall apart.
GEORGE F. MACLEOD

[823]
Of what use is it to have many irons in the fire if the fire is going out?
ERIC ROBERTS

[824]
We are one in the Spirit, we are one in the Lord . . . and they'll know we are Christians by our love.
PETER SCHOLTES

[825]
Nothing is so foreign to the spirit of ecumenism as a false irenicism.
SECOND VATICAN COUNCIL

[826]
When pulling together means pulling away from God, a Christian must be willing to stand alone.
MARGARET TROUTT

EDUCATION

[827]
Sunday School teaching is evangelism at its opportune best.
MARGARET ANDERSON

[828]
The roots of education are bitter, but the fruit is sweet.
ARISTOTLE

[829]
A free curiosity is more effective in learning than a rigid discipline.
AUGUSTINE OF HIPPO

[830]
Reading maketh a full man, conference a ready man, and writing an exact man.
FRANCIS BACON

[831]
A good education is not so much one which prepares a man to succeed in the world, as one which enables him to sustain failure.
BERNARD IDDINGS BELL

[832]
If a mule kiks me the sekond time, I allwuss blame miself, and give the mule kredit for it.
JOSH BILLINGS

[833]
There is precious instruction to be got by finding we were wrong.
THOMAS CARLYLE

[834]
Education is the systematic, purposeful reconstruction of experience.
JOHN DEWEY

[835]
Spiritual decay of any Christian college starts in the trustees and administration and not in the student body.

V. RAYMOND EDMAN

[836]
An education isn't how much you have committed to memory, or even how much you know. It's being able to differentiate between what you do know and what you don't. It's knowing where to go to find out what you need to know; and it's knowing how to use the information once you get it.

WILLIAM FEATHER

[837]
You cannot teach a man anything; you can only help him to find it within himself.

GALILEO

[838]
A child's education should begin at least one hundred years before he was born.

OLIVER WENDELL HOLMES

[839]
In training a horse, it is important not to break his spirit because it is his spirit, during and after the training period, which will determine his style and endurance. Does education, we may ask, allow for the expression of the wildness of vitality during the educational process, or does it repress vitality in the interest of form and conformity?

REUEL HOWE

[840]
An education is a conquest, not a bequest; it cannot be given—it must be achieved.

ELBERT HUBBARD

[841]
The problem we face in education is how to produce informed individuals capable of leadership; how to produce people who can think independently, and whose thinking is based on sound knowledge.

ROBERT MAYNARD HUTCHINS

[842]
An educational institution is for the preservation, transmission and advancement of knowledge.

DAVID MCKENNA

[843]
Children should be led into the right paths, not by severity, but by persuasion.

MENANDER

[844]
I call a complete and generous education that which fits a man to perform justly, skilfully, and magnanimously all the offices, both private and public, of peace and war.

JOHN MILTON

[845]
It is a fallacy to suppose that by omitting a subject you teach nothing about it. On the contrary, you teach that it is to be omitted.

WALTER MOBERLY
(on the Bible in the curriculum)

[846]
Every method of education founded, wholly or in part, on the denial or forgetfulness of original sin and grace, and relying solely on the powers of human nature, is unsound.

POPE PIUS XI

[847]
There is nothing so stupid as an educated man, if you get off the thing that he was educated in.

WILL ROGERS

[848]
No man really becomes a fool until he stops asking questions.

CHARLES P. STEINMETZ

[849]
Human history becomes more and more a race between education and catastrophe.

H. G. WELLS

[850]
The only way to keep Christianity out of the school system is to keep Christians out of it.

HAROLD WILTZ

EMOTION

[851]
He that has doctrinal knowledge and speculation only, without holy affection, never is engaged in the business of religion. True religion is a powerful thing . . . a ferment, a vigorous engagedness of the heart.

JONATHAN EDWARDS

[852]
Depth of truth cannot be had apart from a full and free emotional response.

NELS F. S. FERRÉ

[853]
Emotion cannot be cut out of life. No intelligent person would think of say-ing, "Let's do away with all emotion." Some critics are suspicious of any conversion that does not take place in a refrigerator. There are many dangers in false emotionalism, but that does not rule out true emotion and depth of feeling. Emotion may vary in religious experience. Some people are stoical and others are demonstrative, but the feeling will be there. There is going to be a tug at the heart.

BILLY GRAHAM

[854]
There is a universal necessity for the legitimate expression of our feelings in every dimension of life, and the unwise repression of any emotion leads all too frequently to frustration and maladjustments.

JOSHUA LOTH LIEBMAN

[855]
Emotion is not the Cinderella of our inner life, to be kept in her place among the cinders in the kitchen. Our emotional life is *us* in a way our intellectual life cannot be.

JOHN MACMURRAY

[856]
Fervency is not the prairie fire of undisciplined emotionalism; it is the blowtorch of purposeful Christian conviction.

PAUL S. REES

EMPATHY

[857]
It is so much easier to tell a person what to do with his problem than to stand with him in his pain.

DAVID AUGSBURGER

[858]
I prayed to God that he would baptize my heart into the sense of all conditions, so that I might be able to enter into the needs and sorrows of all.
GEORGE FOX

[859]
Empathy is your pain in my heart.
HALFORD E. LUCCOCK

[860]
I praise you when you regard the trouble of your friend as your own.
PLAUTUS

[861]
Great Spirit, help me never to judge another until I have walked two weeks in his moccasins.
SIOUX INDIAN SAYING

ENCOURAGEMENT

[862]
Encouragement is oxygen to the soul.
GEORGE M. ADAMS

[863]
If you want to change people without giving offense or arousing resentment, use encouragement. Make the fault you want to correct seem easy to correct; make the thing you want the other person to do seem easy to do. . . . If you and I will inspire the people with whom we come in contact to a realization of the hidden treasures they possess, we can do far more than change people. We can literally transform them.
DALE CARNEGIE

[864]
Encouragement after censure is as the sun after a shower.
JOHANN WOLFGANG VON GOETHE

[865]
If I cannot give my children a perfect mother I can at least give them more of the one they've got—and make that one more loving. I will be available. I will take time to listen, time to play, time to be home when they arrive from school, time to counsel and encourage.
RUTH BELL GRAHAM

[866]
In quietness and in trust shall be your strength.
ISAIAH 30:15 (RSV)

[867]
The deepest principle in human nature is the craving to be appreciated.
WILLIAM JAMES

[868]
David "encouraged himself in the Lord," and if he had not doggedly set about resisting the pressure of circumstances, and flinging himself as it were, by an effort, into the arms of God, circumstances would have been too strong for him.
ALEXANDER MACLAREN

[869]
I pray you to dig deep. Set a low price upon all things but Christ. Let him have the flower of your heart and your love. Make much of assurance, for it keeps your anchor fixed. Believe me, whoever looks to the white side of Christ's cross, and can take it up handsomely with faith and courage, will find it such a burden as sails are to a ship or wings are to a bird.
SAMUEL RUTHERFORD

[870]
David encouraged himself in the Lord his God.
1 SAMUEL 30:6 (KJV)

[871]
I have never seen a man who could do real work except under the stimulus of encouragement and enthusiasm and the approval of the people for whom he is working.

CHARLES M. SCHWAB

[872]
If God sends us on stony paths, he provides strong shoes.

CORRIE TEN BOOM

ENTHUSIASM

[873]
Men ablaze are invincible. The stronghold of Satan is proof against everything but fire.

SAMUEL CHADWICK

[874]
Enthusiasm is the key not only to the achievement of great things but to the accomplishment of anything that is worth while.

SAMUEL GOLDWYN

[875]
A horse that will pull on a cold collar will do to depend on—and the best Christians are those who never need "warming up."

SAM JONES

[876]
The religion [of some people] is something like the stars, very high, and very clear, but very cold. When they see tears of anxiety, or tears of joy, they cry out critically, "Enthusiasm, enthusiasm!" Well, let us go to the law and to the testimony: "I sat down under his shadow with great delight." Is this enthusiasm? O Lord, evermore give us this enthusiasm!

ROBERT MURRAY MCCHEYNE

[877]
The supreme need of the church is the same in the twentieth century as in the first; it is men on fire for Christ.

JAMES S. STEWART

ENVY

[878]
Envy's a coal comes hissing hot from hell.

PHILIP JAMES BAILEY

[879]
An envious man is a squinty-eyed fool.

H. G. BOHN

[880]
Envy is a sickness that only faith can heal.

MATTHEW A. CASTILLE

[881]
Envy and fear are the only passions to which no pleasure is attached.

JOHN CHURTON COLLINS

[882]
Thou shalt not covet.

EXODUS 20:17 (KJV)

[883]
Envy shooteth at others and woundeth herself.

THOMAS FULLER

[884]
Wherever you find jealousy and rivalry you also find disharmony and all other kinds of evil.

JAMES 3:16
(Phillips)

[885]
Envy is uneasiness of the mind, caused by the consideration of a good we desire, obtained by one we think should not have it before us.

JOHN LOCKE

[886]
Too many Christians envy the sinners
their pleasure and the saints their joy,
because they don't have either one.

MARTIN LUTHER

[887]
The winds howl around the highest
peaks.

OVID

EQUALITY

[888]
The only stable state is the one in
which all men are equal before the law.

ARISTOTLE

[889]
The meanest peasant, once called of
God, felt within him a strength
stronger than the might of kings. In
that mighty elevation of the masses embodied in the Calvinistic doctrines of
election and grace, lay the germs of the
modern principles of human equality.

DOUGLAS CAMPBELL

[890]
In sport, in courage, and the sight of
heaven, all men meet on equal terms.

WINSTON S. CHURCHILL

[891]
Mankind is one in nature and in the
sight of God. No group of men is inherently superior or inferior to any other,
and none is above any other beloved of
God.

The Delaware Conference, 1942

[892]
It is not true that some human beings
are by nature superior and others inferior. All men are equal in their natural dignity.

POPE JOHN XXIII

[893]
I believe in political equality. But there
are two opposite reasons for being a
democrat. You may think all men so
good that they deserve a share in the
government of the commonwealth,
and so wise that the commonwealth
needs their advice. That is, in my opinion, the false, romantic doctrine of
democracy. On the other hand, you
may believe fallen men to be so wicked
that not one of them can be trusted
with any irresponsible power over his
fellows. That I believe to be the true
ground of democracy.

C. S. LEWIS

[894]
Fourscore and seven years ago our fathers brought forth on this continent a
new nation, conceived in liberty, and
dedicated to the proposition that all
men are created equal.

ABRAHAM LINCOLN

[895]
He makes his sun rise on the evil and
on the good, and sends rain on the just
and on the unjust.

MATTHEW 5:45 (RSV)

[896]
All have sinned and fall short of the
glory of God.

ROMANS 3:23 (RSV)

[897]
It was the contemplation of God that
created men who were equal, for it was
in God that they were equal.

ANTOINE DE SAINT EXUPÉRY

[898]
One man is as good as another—and a
great dale better, as the Irish philosopher said.

WILLIAM MAKEPEACE THACKERAY

[899]
The ground is level at the foot of the cross.

ERROR

[900]
Error makes the circuit of the globe while Truth is pulling on her boots.

ORESTES BROWNSON

[901]
It is the nature of every man to err, but only the fool perseveres in error.

CICERO

[902]
An old error is always more popular than a new truth.

GERMAN PROVERB

[903]
If the Spirit of God has really wrought in the production of this Book [the Bible] from start to finish, it is hard to conceive of error save such as may have crept into the text in the course of transmission. . . . We have no reason to conclude from the data of textual criticism that the writers of Scripture were so left to their own devices that error should be expected in the autographs.

EVERETT F. HARRISON

[904]
One must never confuse error and the person who errs.

POPE JOHN XXIII

[905]
We are of God. Whoever knows God listens to us, and he who is not of God does not listen to us. By this we know the spirit of truth and the spirit of error.

1 JOHN 4:6 (RSV)

[906]
It is one thing to show a man that he is in error, and another to put him in possession of truth.

JOHN LOCKE

[907]
Man is a being filled with error. This error is natural and, without grace, ineffaceable.

BLAISE PASCAL

[908]
A man should never be ashamed to own he has been in the wrong, which is but saying, in other words, that he is wiser today than he was yesterday.

JONATHAN SWIFT

ETERNITY

[909]
I thank Thee, O Lord, that Thou hast so set eternity within my heart that no earthly thing can ever satisfy me wholly.

JOHN BAILLIE

[910]
Those who live in the Lord never see each other for the last time.

GERMAN MOTTO

[911]
The choices of time are binding in eternity.

JACK MACARTHUR

[912]
Live near to God, and all things will appear little to you in comparison with eternal realities.

ROBERT MURRAY MCCHEYNE

[913]
We have all eternity to celebrate our victories, but only one short hour before sunset in which to win them.

ROBERT MOFFAT

[914]
I stand on the shores of eternity and cry
out, "Eternity! Eternity! How long art
thou?" Back comes the answer, "How
long?" When ten thousand times ten
thousand times ten thousand years
have passed, eternity will have just
begun. In the great Day of the Lord
some will be stoical, some will whim-
per, some will turn in search of human
sympathy. Let God answer the question, "What shall be the end of them
that obey not the Gospel of God?"
BILLY SUNDAY

ETHICS

[915]
The Bible proclaims that "righteousness exalteth a nation," and through
the centuries the Christian ethic has
made its social impact through the service and leadership of individuals committed to that principle.
JOHN F. BLANCHARD, JR.

[916]
In the Old Testament the service of
God is ethical before it is ceremonial.
STANLEY G. EVANS

[917]
Moral distinctions are [being] simply
drowned in a maudlin emotion in
which we have more feeling for the
murderer than the murdered, for the
adulterer than the betrayed; and in
which we gradually begin to believe
that the really guilty party, the one who
somehow caused it all, is the victim, not
the perpetrator of the crime.
ROBERT E. FITCH

[918]
A man without ethics is a wild beast
loosed upon this world.
MANLY P. HALL

[919]
The failure of the evangelical movement to react favorably on any widespread front to campaigns against social evils has led to a suspicion on the
part of nonevangelicals that there is
something in the very nature of fundamentalism which makes a world ethical
view impossible.
CARL F. H. HENRY

[920]
Two things fill the mind with ever-
increasing wonder and awe, the more
often and the more intensely the mind
of thought is drawn to them: the starry
heavens above me and the moral law
within me.
IMMANUEL KANT

[921]
There can never be a system of Christian ethics, at least if it is true to its
nature.
HENDRIK KRAEMER

[922]
There are no pastel shades in the
Christian ethic.
ARNOLD H. LOWE

[923]
The idea of vocation is the central con-
cept of Christian ethics.
N. H. G. ROBINSON

[924]
Ethical behavior is concerned above all
with human values, not with legalisms.
A. M. SULLIVAN

[925]
The solution of the outstanding problems of ethics is to be sought in terms
neither of utilitarianism, however
ideal, nor of intuitionism, but of vocation.
WILLIAM TEMPLE

[926]
Before Christ, a man loves things and
uses people. After Christ, he loves people and uses things.

HORACE WOOD

[927]
Doctrine and life cannot be separated.
It was the character of the lives of
Christians which brought Christian
teaching to the favorable attention of
their neighbors and friends.

PAUL WOOLLEY

EVANGELISM

[928]
To evangelize is so to present Christ
Jesus in the power of the Holy Spirit
that men shall come to put their trust
in God through him, to accept him as
their Savior, and to serve him as their
King in the fellowship of his church.

The [Anglican] Archbishops'
Committee of Inquiry on the
Evangelistic Work
of the Church, 1918

[929]
Too many clergymen have become
keepers of an aquarium instead of
fishers of men—and often they are just
swiping each other's fish.

MYRON S. AUGSBURGER

[930]
Evangelism is a cross in the heart of
God.

LEIGHTON FORD

[931]
Our business is to get people to close
with Christ. Again and again they come
up to the point of decision, but we
don't push them over—we hardly try.
We work their minds into thorough
agreement that this and that must be
done; but we don't clinch things on the
spot. And so the metal cools again and
nothing happens.

ARTHUR JOHN GOSSIP

[932]
We are involved, not politically but
spiritually, trying to get Jesus Christ
elected.

BILLY GRAHAM

[933]
Evangelism as the New Testament de-
scribes it is not child's play. Evangelism
is work, often hard work. Yet it is not
drudgery. It puts a person in good humor, and makes him truly human.

OSWALD C. J. HOFFMANN

[934]
Evangelism does not primarily aim at
reform, education, cultural development or human betterment, necessary
as these are. They are the by-products
of evangelism after a person is established in a proper relationship with
God through Christ.

HOWARD KEELEY

[935]
These early Christians [in the book of
Acts] were led by the Spirit to the main
task of bringing people to God through
Christ, and were not permitted to en-
joy fascinating sidetracks.

J. B. PHILLIPS

[936]
The church has many tasks but only
one mission.

ARTHUR PRESTON

[937]
Ever since I knew them (which was not in my earliest years) I have loved those who are called "evangelicals." I loved them because they loved our Lord. I loved them for their zeal for souls.
EDWARD B. PUSEY

[938]
The good that has been done in the world, however small, has always been done by evangelical doctrines; and if men who are not called "evangelical" have had successes, they have had them by using evangelical weapons.
J. C. RYLE

[939]
When a Christian is winning souls, he isn't messing around with sin.
GEORGE L. SMITH

[940]
Evangelism stands for a certain interpretation of Christianity emphasizing the objective atonement of Christ, the necessity of a new birth, or conversion, and salvation through faith.
W. W. SWEET

[941]
The church has nothing to do but to save souls; therefore spend and be spent in this work. It is not your business to speak so many times, but to save souls as you can; to bring as many sinners as you possibly can to repentance.
JOHN WESLEY

[942]
Evangelism applies a supernatural remedy for the need of the world.
FARIS WHITESELL

[943]
Evangelism is the proclamation of the Gospel of the crucified and risen Christ, the only Redeemer of men, according to the Scriptures, with the purpose of persuading condemned and lost sinners to put their trust in God by receiving and accepting Christ as Savior through the power of the Holy Spirit, and to serve Christ as Lord in every calling of life and in the fellowship of his church, looking toward the day of his coming in glory.
WORLD CONGRESS ON EVANGELISM
Berlin, 1966

[944]
Evangelism is a sharing of gladness.

[945]
If a man has a soul—and he has—and if that soul can be won or lost for eternity—and it can—then the most important thing in the world is to bring that man to Jesus Christ.

[946]
What a hollow ring there is to evangelism when it does not overflow from a Christ-filled heart.

EVIL

[947]
Tolerance of evil is a dangerous error for no one is free to behave just as he pleases.
ALEXIS CARREL

[948]
When God sends us evil, he sends with it the weapon to conquer it.
PAUL VINCENT CARROLL

[949]
It is easier to denature plutonium than to denature the evil spirit of man.
ALBERT EINSTEIN

[950]
If evil is due to ignorance, then all
professors should be saints.
                    RICHARD S. EMRICH

[951]
Woe to those who call evil good and
good evil.
                    ISAIAH 5:20 (RSV)

[952]
The good man out of his good treasure
brings forth good, and the evil man out
of his evil treasure brings forth evil.
                    MATTHEW 12:35 (RSV)

[953]
Evil communications corrupt good
manners.
                    MENANDER

[954]
Never throw mud. You may miss your
mark; but you must have dirty hands.
                    JOSEPH PARKER

[955]
Fret not thyself because of evil men,
neither be thou envious at the wicked.
                    PROVERBS 24:19 (KJV)

[956]
An evil-speaker differs from an evil-
doer only in the lack of opportunity.
                    MARCUS FABIUS QUINTILIAN

[957]
Evil must not be done that good may
come out of it.
                    SAMUEL SEWALL

[958]
Of two evils, choose neither.
                    CHARLES H. SPURGEON

[959]
There are a thousand hacking at the
branches of evil to one who is striking
at the root.
                    HENRY DAVID THOREAU

EVOLUTION

[960]
Theistic evolution puts God so far
away that he ceases to be a present influence in this life.
                    WILLIAM JENNINGS BRYAN

[961]
The old idea that evolution should be
our guide in sociology has been long
discredited. Its application to numer-
ous sciences other than biology have
all led to false conclusions. The doctrine of the inevitability of progress
. . . has had a sorry set-back. . . . Time
and time again, applications of evolutionary teaching outside biology have
led to muddled thinking and immoral
conduct.
                    ROBERT E. D. CLARK

[962]
There is nothing in science which
teaches the origin of anything at all.
                    LORD KELVIN

[963]
What began with Darwin as evolution
has become *evolutionism*, the effort to
interpret man and his universe in evolutionary concepts.
                    PHILIP SCHARPER

[964]
Evolution is far more a philosophical
concept than a strictly scientific one.
                    ELTON TRUEBLOOD

EXISTENCE

[965]
It would have been easier for me to
doubt my existence than to doubt the
reality of truth.
                    AUGUSTINE OF HIPPO

[966]
The great majority of men exist but do not live.

BENJAMIN DISRAELI

[967]
A living dog is better than a dead lion.

ECCLESIASTES 9:4 (RSV)

[968]
Man can only find meaning for his existence in something outside himself.

VIKTOR FRANKL

[969]
We mostly spend our lives conjugating three verbs: "to want," "to have," and "to do," forgetting that these verbs have no significance except as they are included in the verb "to be."

EVELYN UNDERHILL

EXPERIENCE

[970]
So you think that God does not exist anywhere? You must have a great deal of knowledge about the universe. Apparently you have examined every nook and corner of it. Logically it is impossible to say, "There is no God." All you can say is, "There is no God in my experience." I have found God in Christ. That is my experience. You can have it too. But not your way. You must try God's way.

AKBAR ABDUL-HAQQ

[971]
The reward of suffering is experience.

AESCHYLUS

[972]
The proper name of religious experience is faith.

JOHN BAILLIE

[973]
Experience is the best of schoolmasters, only the school fees are heavy.

THOMAS CARLYLE

[974]
Blacksmiths' children are not afraid of sparks.

DANISH PROVERB

[975]
We need an experience of Christ in which we think everything about the Christ and not about the experience.

P. T. FORSYTH

[976]
I have but one lamp by which my feet are guided, and that is the lamp of experience. I can tell nothing about the future save as I see it written by the finger of the past.

PATRICK HENRY

[977]
Truth divorced from experience will always dwell in the realm of doubt.

HENRY KRAUSE

[978]
He who neglects to drink of the spring of experience is apt to die of thirst in the desert of ignorance.

LING PO

[979]
One thorn of experience is worth a whole wilderness of warning.

JAMES RUSSELL LOWELL

[980]
We are constantly misled by the ease with which our minds fall into the ruts of one or two experiences.

WILLIAM OSLER

[981]
To complain that man measures God by his own experience is a waste of time; he has no other yardstick.

DOROTHY L. SAYERS

[982]
The long experience of the church is more likely to lead to correct answers than is the experience of the lone individual.

ELTON TRUEBLOOD

[983]
The cat, having sat upon a hot stove lid, will not sit upon a hot stove lid again. Nor upon a cold stove lid.

MARK TWAIN

[984]
Experience may not be worth what it costs, but I can't seem to get it for any less.

FAILURE

[985]
Most successes are built on failures.

CHARLES GOW

[986]
It is possible to defeat failure by analyzing its causes and correcting them, not by studying the conditions of success.

HENRY GREBER

[987]
It is not a disgrace to fail. Failing is one of the greatest arts in the world.

CHARLES KETTERING

[988]
It is of the Lord's mercies that we are not consumed, because his compassions fail not. They are new every morning: great is thy faithfulness.

LAMENTATIONS 3:22–23 (KJV)

[989]
Failure is not sin. Faithlessness is.

HENRIETTA MEARS

[990]
If you visualize a failure, you tend to create the conditions that produce failure. Visualize—believe—and thank God in advance.

NORMAN VINCENT PEALE

[991]
All have sinned and fall short of the glory of God.

ROMANS 3:23 (RSV)

[992]
Men do not fail; they give up trying.

ELIHU ROOT

[993]
I cannot give you the formula for success, but I can give you the formula for failure: Try to please everybody.

HERBERT BAYARD SWOPE

[994]
There is no failure so great that a Christian cannot rise from it.

HELEN C. WHITE

[995]
Success has many mothers, but failure is an orphan.

FAITH

[996]
There is a difference between a good, sound reason for our faith, and a reason that sounds good.

MARY ASQUITH

[997]
[Faith is] an inner conviction of being overwhelmed by God.

GUSTAF AULÉN

[998]
Grace means bearing witness to the faithfulness of God which a man has encountered in Christ, and which, when it is encountered and recognized, requires a corresponding fidelity toward God.

KARL BARTH

[999]
Strike from mankind the principle of faith, and men would have no more history than a flock of sheep.

HENRY BULWER

[1000]
Wherever great spiritual personalities endowed with primitive energy of faith have arisen, faith has still been able to move mountains in the world of circumstances as well as in the world of the Spirit.

DAVID S. CAIRNS

[1001]
The life of faith is not a life of mounting up with wings, but a life of walking and not fainting. . . . Faith never knows where it is being led, but it loves and knows the One who is leading.

OSWALD CHAMBERS

[1002]
Faith makes the uplook good, the outlook bright, the inlook favorable, and the future glorious.

V. RAYMOND EDMAN

[1003]
Do not preach the duty of love, but the duty of faith. Do not begin by telling men in God's name that they should love one another. That is no more than an amiable gospel. And it is an impossible gospel till faith gives the power to love. They cannot do it. Tell them God has loved them. . . . Preach faith and the love will grow out of it itself.

P. T. FORSYTH

[1004]
Faith in order, which is the basis of science, cannot reasonably be separated from faith in an Ordainer.

ASA GRAY

[1005]
Faith that is faddish can be as dangerous as faith that is false.

OS GUINNESS

[1006]
My most cherished possession I wish I could leave you is my faith in Jesus Christ, for with him and nothing else you can be happy, but without him and with all else you'll never be happy.

PATRICK HENRY

[1007]
Life has no question that faith cannot answer.

THOMAS L. JOHNS

[1008]
We are wrong when we say that we must verify God and then we will have faith in him. Faith throws a bridge toward God and finds the divine Reality.

HUGH THOMSON KERR

[1009]
We cannot force ourselves to have faith in God. We are as much in need in this respect as in everything else. Faith can only originate in the soul of man by the gift of God.

MARCUS L. LOANE

[1010]
Faith is a living, daring confidence in God's grace. It is so sure and certain that a man could stake his life on it a thousand times.

MARTIN LUTHER

[1011]
This is a wise, sane Christian faith: that a man commit himself, his life and his hopes to God; that God undertakes the special protection of that man; that therefore that man ought not to be afraid of anything!
GEORGE MACDONALD

[1012]
Faith is the sight of the inward eye.
ALEXANDER MACLAREN

[1013]
I prayed for faith and thought that some day faith would come down and strike me like lightning. But faith did not seem to come. One day I read in the tenth chapter of Romans, "Faith cometh by hearing, and hearing by the Word of God." I had [up to this time] closed my Bible and prayed for faith. I now opened my Bible and began to study, and faith has been growing ever since.
DWIGHT L. MOODY

[1014]
Faith is the final triumph over incongruity, the final assertion of the meaningfulness of existence.
REINHOLD NIEBUHR

[1015]
Faith is a resting of the heart in the sufficiency of the evidences.
CLARK H. PINNOCK

[1016]
Most people are brought to faith in Christ not by argument for it but by exposure to it.
SAMUEL M. SHOEMAKER

[1017]
Faith is the subtle chain that binds us to the infinite.
O. E. SMITH

[1018]
Faith is not shelter against difficulties, but belief in the face of all contradictions.
PAUL TOURNIER

[1019]
No Christian has ever been known to recant on his deathbed.
C. M. WARD

[1020]
Faith is not an effort, a striving, a ceaseless seeking, as so many earnest souls suppose, but rather a letting go, an abandonment, an abiding rest in God that nothing, not even the soul's shortcomings, can disturb.

[1021]
Faith makes things possible—it does not make them easy.

FAMILY

[1022]
Everybody believes divorce breaks up families. This is not so. The broken family is not the result of divorce; divorce is the result of the broken family.
PAUL W. ALEXANDER

[1023]
The family that prays together stays together.
AMERICAN PROVERB

[1024]
Wife and children are a kind of discipline of humanity.
FRANCIS BACON

[1025]
A happy family is but an earlier heaven.
JOHN BOWRING

[1026]
And it was a happy day for him [God] when he gave us our new lives, through the truth of his Word, and we became, as it were, the first children in his new family.

JAMES 1:18
(*The Living Bible*)

[1027]
The family, grounded on marriage freely contracted, monogamous and indissoluble, is and must be considered the first and essential cell of human society.

POPE JOHN XXIII

[1028]
The Christian home is the Master's workshop where the processes of character-molding are silently, lovingly, faithfully and successfully carried on.

RICHARD MONCKTON MILNES

[1029]
That man will never be unwelcome to others who makes himself agreeable to his own family.

PLAUTUS

[1030]
Domestic happiness depends upon the ability to overlook.

ROY L. SMITH

[1031]
He that loves not his wife and children feeds a lioness at home and broods a nest of sorrow.

JEREMY TAYLOR

[1032]
If a man does not know how to manage his own household, how can he care for God's church?

1 TIMOTHY 3:5 (RSV)

[1033]
All happy families resemble one another; every unhappy family is unhappy in its own way.

LEO TOLSTOY
Anna Karenina

FANATICISM

[1034]
It is part of the nature of fanaticism that it loses sight of the totality of evil and rushes like a bull at the red cloth instead of at the man who holds it.

DIETRICH BONHOEFFER

[1035]
A fanatic is one who can't change his mind and won't change the subject.

WINSTON S. CHURCHILL

[1036]
Fanaticism is the false fire of an overheated mind.

WILLIAM COWPER

[1037]
There is no strong performance without a little fanaticism in the performer.

RALPH WALDO EMERSON

[1038]
It is easier to tame a fanatic than to put life into a corpse.

WALTER MARSHALL HORTON

[1039]
Fanaticism is an evil, but it is not the greatest of evils.

THOMAS BABINGTON MACAULEY

FEAR

[1040]
If thou hast a fearful thought, share it not with a weakling, whisper it to thy saddle-bow, and ride forth singing.

ALFRED THE GREAT

[1041]
I fear God, yet am not afraid of him.
THOMAS BROWNE

[1042]
There is only one man whom I fear,
and his name is James Garfield.
JAMES A. GARFIELD

[1043]
There is no fear in love, but perfect
love casts out fear.
1 JOHN 4:18 (RSV)

[1044]
God Incarnate is the end of fear; and
the heart that realizes that he is in the
midst, that takes heed to the assurance
of his loving presence, will be quiet in
the midst of alarm. "No weapon that is
formed against thee shall prosper, and
every tongue that shall rise against thee
in judgment thou shalt condemn."
Only be patient and be quiet.
F. B. MEYER

[1045]
According to the first Epistle of John,
fear is caused by disturbances of love.
In most instances these are inhibitions
of love. . . . The two chief causes of fear
are an interference with the impulse toward love in general, and a sense of
guilt in particular.
OSKAR PFISTER

[1046]
The adventurous life is not one exempt
from fear, but on the contrary one that
is lived in full knowledge of fears of all
kinds, one in which we go forward in
spite of our fears.
PAUL TOURNIER

FELLOWSHIP

[1047]
We are all strings in the concert of his
joy.
JACOB BOEHME

[1048]
The grace of the Lord Jesus Christ and
the love of God and the fellowship of
the Holy Spirit be with you all.
2 CORINTHIANS 13:14 (RSV)

[1049]
The only basis for real fellowship with
God and man is to live out in the open
with both.
ROY HESSION

[1050]
To live in prayer together is to walk in
love together.
MARGARET MOORE JACOBS

[1051]
If we live in the light—just as he is in
the light—then we have fellowship one
with another.
1 JOHN 1:7
(*Good News for Modern Man*)

[1052]
The final grounds of holy fellowship
are in God. Persons in the fellowship
are related to one another through
him, as all mountains go down into the
same earth. They get at one another
through him.
THOMAS R. KELLY

[1053]
When the rams are following their
shepherd and looking to him, their
woollies rub each other companion-
ably; but when they look at one another
they see only each other's horns.
Z. A. SALIK

[1054]
To satisfy the burning thirst of tormented souls nothing will do but to take them to the well of living waters, to true fellowship with Christ.

PAUL TOURNIER

[1055]
When I met Christ at the crossroads of life, he showed me which way to go by walking it with me.

FORGIVENESS

[1056]
He who forgives ends the quarrel.

AFRICAN PROVERB

[1057]
"I can forgive, but I cannot forget," is only another way of saying, "I will not forgive."

HENRY WARD BEECHER

[1058]
Nothing in this lost world bears the impress of the Son of God so surely as forgiveness.

ALICE CARY

[1059]
Never build your preaching of forgiveness on the fact that God is our Father and he will forgive us because he loves us. . . . It is shallow nonsense to say that God forgives us because he is love. The only ground on which God can forgive me is through the cross of my Lord.

OSWALD CHAMBERS

[1060]
The noblest vengeance is to forgive.

ENGLISH PROVERB

[1061]
Be kind to one another, tenderhearted, forgiving one another, as God in Christ forgave you.

EPHESIANS 4:32 (RSV)

[1062]
If his conditions are met, God is bound by his Word to forgive any man or any woman of any sin because of Christ.

BILLY GRAHAM

[1063]
If you forgive people enough you belong to them, and they to you, whether either person likes it or not—squatter's rights of the heart.

JAMES HILTON

[1064]
A wise man will make haste to forgive, because he knows the true value of time.

SAMUEL JOHNSON

[1065]
Everyone says forgiveness is a lovely idea, until they have something to forgive.

C. S. LEWIS

[1066]
Dynamic psychology [teaches] that we can achieve inner health only through forgiveness—the forgiveness not only of others but also of ourselves.

JOSHUA LOTH LIEBMAN

[1067]
Forgive us our sins, just as we have forgiven those who have sinned against us.

MATTHEW 6:12
(The Living Bible)

[1068]
A Christian will find it cheaper to pardon than to resent. Forgiveness saves the expense of anger, the cost of hatred, the waste of spirits.

HANNAH MORE

[1069]
If I am even with my enemy, the debt is paid; but if I forgive him, I oblige him for ever.

WILLIAM PENN

[1070]
To err is human, to forgive divine.
ALEXANDER POPE

[1071]
Humanity is never so beautiful as when praying for forgiveness or else forgiving another.
JEAN PAUL RICHTER

[1072]
The really unforgivable sin is the denial of sin, because, by its nature, there is now nothing to be forgiven.
FULTON J. SHEEN

FREEDOM

[1073]
We are subject to the men who rule over us, but subject only in the Lord. If they command anything against him, let us not pay the least regard to it.
JOHN CALVIN

[1074]
If we did not believe in the spiritual character of man, we would be foolish indeed to be supporting the concept of free government in the world.
DWIGHT D. EISENHOWER

[1075]
He is most enslaved when he thinks he is comfortably settled in freedom.
JACQUES ELLUL

[1076]
If you believe in a free society, be worthy of a free society.
JOHN W. GARDNER

[1077]
Where God has spoken absolutely there are absolutes and norms, but where he has not the Christian has the freedom and responsibility to make an existential judgment of the situation within the ultimate framework of God's revelation and under the immediate leadership of the Holy Spirit. . . . A Christian, while he is not open to a vacuum of complete relativism, has a responsible freedom to follow the leading of the Holy Spirit within the norms of revealed Christian morality.
OS GUINNESS

[1078]
The basic test of freedom is perhaps less in what we are free to do than in what we are free not to do.
ERIC HOFFER

[1079]
We find freedom when we find God; we lose it when we lose him.
PAUL E. SCHERER

[1080]
Freedom ranks after life itself as the quintessence of the human experience. Freedom defines the man; it stamps the divine image upon him.*
Sherwood
Wirt

FRIENDSHIP

[1081]
The older I grow in years, the more the wonder and the joy increase when I see the power of these words of Jesus—"I have called you friends"—to move the human heart. That one word "friend" breaks down each barrier of reserve, and we have boldness in his presence. Our hearts go out in love to meet his love.
CHARLES F. ANDREWS

[1082]
How can I lift a struggling soul and guide him if I never take his arm?
VIOLA JACOBSON BERG

[1083]
The firmest friendships have been formed in mutual adversity, as iron is most strongly united by the fiercest flame.
CHARLES C. COLTON

[1084]
The man who throws a stone at the birds scares them away, and the man who abuses a friend destroys a friendship.
ECCLESIASTICUS 22:20
(Goodspeed)

[1085]
Promises may get friends, but it is performance that keeps them.
OWEN FELTHAM

[1086]
If a man does not make new acquaintances as he advances through life, he will soon find himself left alone. A man, sir, should keep his friendship in constant repair.
SAMUEL JOHNSON

[1087]
Jesus' home was the road along which he walked with his friends in search of new friends.
GIOVANNI PAPINI

[1088]
After the friendship of God, a friend's affection is the greatest treasure here below.

FRUIT

[1089]
People throw stones only at trees that have fruit on them.
FRENCH PROVERB

[1090]
When the Holy Spirit controls our lives he will produce this kind of fruit in us: love, joy, peace, patience, kindness, goodness, faithfulness, gentleness and self-control.
GALATIANS 5:22–23
(*The Living Bible*)

[1091]
I do not believe it is possible for the fruits of regeneration to be visible in the unregenerate.
ROSS F. HIDY

[1092]
You did not choose me, but I chose you and appointed you that you should go and bear fruit and that your fruit should abide.
JOHN 15:16 (RSV)

[1093]
The fruits of the Spirit are nothing but the virtues of Christ.
FRIEDRICH SCHLEIERMACHER

FULFILLMENT

[1094]
Throw out the ballast and the balloon will rise.
JAMES BARR

[1095]
Finish your work in time, and in his own time [the Lord] will give you your reward.
ECCLESIASTICUS 51:30
(Goodspeed)

[1096]
It is an infallible rule of prophetic interpretation that the prophecy becomes fully clear only after it has been fulfilled.
WILLIAM SANFORD LASOR

[1097]
The fulfillments [of prophecy] in Israel were only the beginning phase of God's plan. We are still on the road to the final enrichment of that fulfillment, and so can live in trust that God fulfils his promises.
ROBERT B. LAURIN

[1098]
Think not that I am come to destroy the law, or the prophets: I am not come to destroy, but to fulfil.
MATTHEW 5:17 (KJV)

[1099]
Love is the fulfilling of the law.
ROMANS 13:10 (RSV)

[1100]
The dross of my cross gathered a scum of fears in the fire, doubtings, impatience, unbelief, challenging of Providence as sleeping and not regarding my sorrow. But my Goldsmith, Christ, was pleased to take off the scum and burn it in the fire. And blessed be my Refiner, he has made the metal better, and has furnished new supply of grace, to cause me hold out weight; and I hope that he has not lost one grainweight by burning his servant.
SAMUEL RUTHERFORD

[1101]
The old order changeth, yielding place to new,/ And God fulfils himself in many ways.
ALFRED TENNYSON
Idylls of the King

FUTURE

[1102]
Hats off to the past; coats off to the future.
AMERICAN PROVERB

[1103]
The future has a habit of suddenly and dramatically becoming the present.
ROGER W. BABSON

[1104]
Men must pursue things which are just in present, and leave the future to the divine Providence.
FRANCIS BACON

[1105]
You can never plan the future by the past.
EDMUND BURKE

[1106]
Neither a wise man nor a brave man lies down on the tracks of history to wait for the train of the future to run over him.
DWIGHT D. EISENHOWER

[1107]
I said to the man who stood at the gate of the year: Give me a light that I may tread safely into the unknown. And he replied: Go out into the darkness, and put thine hand into the hand of God. That shall be to thee better than light and safer than a known way.
M. LOUISE HASKINS

[1108]
Beloved, we are God's children now; it does not yet appear what we shall be, but we know that when he appears we shall be like him, for we shall see him as he is.
1 JOHN 3:2 (RSV)

[1109]
The future is purchased by the present.
SAMUEL JOHNSON

[1110]
I expect to spend the rest of my life in
the future, so I want to be reasonably
sure of what kind of future it's going to
be. That is my reason for planning.
CHARLES F. KETTERING

[1111]
Has this world been so kind to you that
you should leave it with regret? There
are better things ahead than any we
leave behind.
C. S. LEWIS

[1112]
No man ever sank under the burden of
the day. It is when tomorrow's burden
is added to the burden of today that the
weight is more than a man can bear.
Never load yourself so. If you find
yourself so loaded, at least remember
this: it is your own doing, not God's.
He begs you to leave the future to him,
and mind the present.
GEORGE MACDONALD

[1113]
Don't be anxious about tomorrow.
God will take care of your tomorrow
too. Live one day at a time.
MATTHEW 6:34
(The Living Bible)

[1114]
Every experience God gives us, every
person he puts in our lives, is the perfect preparation for the future that only
he can see.
CORRIE TEN BOOM

[1115]
There are no stains on the pages of
tomorrow.
GRADY B. WILSON

GENEROSITY

[1116]
The quickest generosity is the best.
ARAB PROVERB

[1117]
Do you remember the generosity of
Jesus Christ, the Lord of us all? He was
rich beyond our telling, yet he became
poor for your sakes so that his poverty
might make you rich.
2 CORINTHIANS 8:9
(Phillips)

[1118]
How much easier it is to be generous
than just.
JUNIUS

[1119]
Liberality consists less in giving much
than in giving at the right time.
JEAN DE LA BRUYÈRE

[1120]
Generosity gives help rather than ad-
vice.
LUC DE CLAPIERS VAUVENARGUES

[1121]
Go and sell everything you have and
give the money to the poor, and you
will have treasure in heaven.
MATTHEW 19:21
(The Living Bible)

[1122]
Abstinence from doing is often as gen-
erous as doing, but not so apparent.
MICHEL DE MONTAIGNE

[1123]
A generous action is its own reward.
WILLIAM WALSH

GIFTS, GIVING

[1124]
Silver and gold have I none; but such as I have give I thee.

ACTS 3:6 (KJV)

[1125]
It is possible to give without loving, but it is impossible to love without giving.

RICHARD BRAUNSTEIN

[1126]
God's gifts put man's best dreams to shame.

ELIZABETH BARRETT BROWNING
"Sonnets from the Portuguese"

[1127]
Giving is a joy if we do it in the right spirit. It all depends on whether we think of it as "What can I spare?" or as "What can I share?"

ESTHER YORK BURKHOLDER

[1128]
We make a living by what we get, but we make a life by what we give.

WINSTON S. CHURCHILL

[1129]
Let everyone give as his heart tells him, neither grudgingly nor under compulsion, for God loves the man who gives cheerfully. After all, God can give you everything that you need, so that you may always have sufficient both for yourselves and for giving away to other people.

2 CORINTHIANS 9:7–8
(Phillips)

[1130]
The manner of giving is worth more than the gift.

PIERRE CORNEILLE

[1131]
The Apollo flights are a marvelous proof of the wonderful gifts God has placed in the hands of men. The tragedy is that, given the tools, men can make it to the moon; but given a Savior, they still choose not to make it to God. Yet he is "closer than breathing, nearer than hands and feet."

LEIGHTON FORD

[1132]
God has given us two hands—one for receiving and the other for giving.

BILLY GRAHAM

[1133]
A glad giver takes but little heed of the thing that he gives, but all his desire and intent is to please and solace him to whom he gives it. And if the receiver takes the gift highly and thankfully, then the courteous giver sets at nought all his cost and travail, for joy and delight that he has pleased and solaced him that he loves.

LADY JULIAN OF NORWICH

[1134]
Let us give according to our incomes, lest God make our incomes match our gifts.

PETER MARSHALL

[1135]
He gives twice who gives quickly.

PUBLIUS MIMUS

GLOOM

[1136]
Sadness lies at the heart of every merely positivistic, agnostic or naturalistic scheme of philosophy.

WILLIAM JAMES

[1137]
To see some people you would think
that the essentials of orthodox Christianity is to have a face so long you
could eat oatmeal out of the end of a
gas pipe.

BILLY SUNDAY

[1138]
Is my gloom, after all, / Shade of his
hand, outstretched caressingly?

FRANCIS THOMPSON
"The Hound of Heaven"

[1139]
Your religion is small pertaters, I must
say. You air in a dreary fog all the time,
and you treat the jolly sunshine of life
as tho' it was a thief, drivin' it from your
doors by them pecooler noshuns of
yourn.

ARTEMUS WARD

GLORY

[1140]
I see heaven's glories shine, / And faith
shines equal, arming me from fear.

EMILY BRONTË
"Last Lines"

[1141]
Do everything for the glory of God.

1 CORINTHIANS 10:31
(The Living Bible)

[1142]
We shall see his face, and his name
shall be on our foreheads. We are sons
with him, heirs of God and fellow heirs
with our Lord Jesus Christ. The acquired glory of our Lord is the glory
which every saved sinner will share
with him.

ARNO C. GAEBELEIN

[1143]
The paths of glory lead but to the
grave.

THOMAS GRAY
Elegy Written in a Country Churchyard

[1144]
I am the Lord, that is my name; my
glory I give to no other, nor my praise
to graven images.

ISAIAH 42:8 (RSV)

[1145]
If the glory of God is to break out in
your service, you must be ready to go
out into the night.

M. BASILEA SCHLINK

[1146]
Thus the glory of the world passes
away (sic transit gloria mundi).

THOMAS À KEMPIS

[1147]
If the church could be aroused to a
deeper sense of the glory that awaits
her, she would enter with a warmer
spirit into the struggles that are before
her.

J. H. THORNWELL

[1148]
How many of us go through life as
peasants when we could be walking as
royalty in Christ?

BOB WHEATLEY

GOAL

[1149]
Where do you want to go in life? How do you want to get there? Do the roles you fill contribute to your goal? What is really important that you do? What merely fills up time? In determining your best roles, keep those that advance you toward your goal and eliminate those that are useless and a drag. Your trouble may be too many good roles. You cannot afford to take on more than you can handle well.

HENRY R. BRANDT

[1150]
Perfection of means and confusion of goals characterize our age.

ALBERT EINSTEIN

[1151]
If we make it our first goal always to please God, it solves many problems at once.

PHILIP E. HOWARD, JR.

[1152]
Goals are means to achieving the sub-objectives whereby progress toward objectives can be measured. They should be reasonable, attainable, set in advance for a fixed period, and written.

W. L. HOWSE

[1153]
We can know whether what we are doing is absurd only after we have identified the goals we are trying to achieve.

CHARLES HUGHES

[1154]
This for me will be the goal attained which has been for so long before my soul: I shall be so completely identified with him who has won my heart to himself, that I shall be like him forever, and with him through all the ages to come.

H. A. IRONSIDE

[1155]
Ower box of ruels: Looking unto Jesus. 1. No fiteing. 2. No arging. 3. Be kind. 4. Be cerfull. 5. Be helpfull. 6. Obey. 7. Don't bighte. 8. Love Jesus.

Missionary Children's School,
Tagaytay, Philippines

[1156]
Clear definition of goals is the keynote of success.

EDISON MONTGOMERY

[1157]
All I can say is this: forgetting what is behind me, and reaching out for that which lies ahead, I press toward the goal to win the prize which is God's call to the life above, in Christ Jesus.

PHILIPPIANS 3:13–14 (NEB)

[1158]
[He] set his heart upon the goal, not on the prize.

WILLIAM WATSON

[1159]
The true goal of the Christian life is heaven: nothing more, nothing less, and nothing else.*

GOD

[1160]
God is not in need of anything, but all things are in need of him.

MARCIANUS ARISTIDES

[1161]
God is an infinite circle whose center is everywhere and whose circumference is nowhere.

AUGUSTINE OF HIPPO

[1162]
If the individual can commune with God, then he must matter to God; and if he matters to God, he must share God's eternity.

JOHN BAILLIE

[1163]
When I speak of God, I mean something other than an Identity wherein all differences vanish, or a Unity which includes but does not transcend the differences which it somehow holds in solution. I mean a God whom men can love, a God to whom men can pray, who takes sides, who has purposes and preferences, whose attributes, however conceived, leave unimpaired the possibility of a personal relation between himself and those whom he has created.

ARTHUR JAMES BALFOUR

[1164]
An atheist does not find God for the same reason a thief does not find a policeman. He is not looking for him.

WENDELL BAXTER

[1165]
One of the most convenient Hieroglyphicks of God is a Circle; and a Circle is endlesse; whom God loves, hee loves to the end: and not onely to their own end, to their death, but to his end, and his end is, that he might love them still.

JOHN DONNE

[1166]
We must wait for God, long, meekly, in the wind and wet, in the thunder and lightning, in the cold and the dark. Wait, and he will come. He never comes to those who do not wait. He does not go their road. When he comes, go with him, but go slowly, fall a little behind; when he quickens his pace, be sure of it before you quicken yours. But when he slackens, slacken at once; and do not be slow only, but silent, very silent, for he is God.

FREDERICK W. FABER

[1167]
If you are never alone with God, it is not because you are too busy; it is because you don't care for him, don't like him. And you had better face the facts.

AL-GHAZZALI

[1168]
He who leaves God out of his reasoning does not know how to count.

ITALIAN PROVERB

[1169]
We see God all around us: the mountains are God's thoughts upheaved, the rivers are God's thoughts in motion, the oceans are God's thoughts imbedded, the dewdrops are God's thoughts in pearls.

SAM JONES

[1170]
Some of us believe that God is Almighty and may do all, and that he is All-wisdom and can do all; but that he is All-love and will do all—there we stop short.

LADY JULIAN OF NORWICH

[1171]
How often we look upon God as our last and feeblest resource! We go to him because we have nowhere else to go. And then we learn that the storms of life have driven us, not upon the rocks, but into the desired haven.

GEORGE MACDONALD

[1172]
To see his star is good, but to see his face is better.

DWIGHT L. MOODY

[1173]
Only God is permanently interesting. Other things we may fathom, but he out-tops our thought and can neither be demonstrated nor argued down.

JOSEPH FORT NEWTON

[1174]
The universe is centered on neither the earth nor the sun. It is centered on God.

ALFRED NOYES

[1175]
He who offers to God a second place offers him no place.

JOHN RUSKIN

[1176]
I believe in God as I believe in my friends, because I feel the breath of his affection, feel his invisible and intangible hand, drawing me, leading me, grasping me.

MIGUEL DE UNAMUNO

[1177]
God has two dwellings—one in heaven and the other in a thankful heart.

IZAAK WALTON

[1178]
Until a man has found God and been found by God, he begins at no beginning, he works to no end. He may have his friendships, his partial loyalties, his scraps of honor. But all these things fall into place, and life falls into place, only with God.

H. G. WELLS

[1179]
Does God seem far away? Guess who moved.

God, Action of

[1180]
God is a busy worker, but he loves help.

BASQUE PROVERB

[1181]
We are in danger of forgetting that we cannot do what God can do, and that God will not do what we can do.

OSWALD CHAMBERS

[1182]
There is nothing which God cannot accomplish.

CICERO

[1183]
God is a sure paymaster.

JOHN CLARKE

[1184]
God comes with leaden feet, but strikes with iron hands.

ENGLISH PROVERB

[1185]
God's mills grind slowly but surely.

GREEK PROVERB

[1186]
God strikes with his finger, and not with all his arm.

GEORGE HERBERT

[1187]
God is the sculptor who chisels on the rough block of stone the general outline of what the finished piece will be.

THOMAS J. HIGGINS

[1188]
God never shuts one door but he opens another.

IRISH PROVERB

[1189]
Give me one divine moment when God acts, and I say that moment is far superior to all the human efforts of man throughout the centuries.

DENNIS F. KINLAW

[1190]
There are two kinds of people: those who say to God, "Thy will be done," and those to whom God says, "All right, then, have it your way."

C. S. LEWIS

[1191]
God doesn't always smooth the path, but sometimes he puts springs in the wagon.

MARSHALL LUCAS

[1192]
When God contemplates some great work, he begins it by the hand of some poor, weak, human creature, to whom he afterward gives aid, so that the enemies who seek to obstruct it are overcome.

MARTIN LUTHER

[1193]
Christianity consists supremely in a series of unique events in which the Christian believes that God acted uniquely for the salvation of the world.

DONALD G. MILLER

[1194]
What hath God wrought!

NUMBERS 23:23 (KJV)

[1195]
The heavens are telling the glory of God; and the firmament proclaims his handiwork.

PSALM 19:1 (RSV)

[1196]
Man doeth what he can, and God what he will.

JOHN RAY

[1197]
We know of no effect greater than its corresponding cause, not even atomic chain reaction with its accompanying devastation. On what rational grounds could we assume that an effect such as personality (the supreme distinction of mortal man in the animal world) was produced by a cause which lacked what it somehow managed to produce?

LEITH SAMUEL

[1198]
Man proposes, but God disposes.

THOMAS À KEMPIS

[1199]
Every day God makes silk purses out of sows' ears.

[1200]
The Gospel does not consist of what we can do for ourselves, but of what God stands ready to do for us.

God, Attributes of

[1201]
God does not let out his attributes.

SAMUEL CHADWICK

[1202]
The most perfect idea of God that we can form in this life is that of an independent, unique, infinite, eternal, omnipotent, immutable, intelligent and free First Cause, whose power extends over all things.

E. B. DE CONDILLAC

[1203]
God is indeed merciful and gracious,
but he is also righteous.
THE HEIDELBERG CATECHISM

[1204]
God gives his wrath by weight, and
without weight his mercy.
GEORGE HERBERT

[1205]
God isn't really being slow about his
promised return, even though it sometimes seems that way. But he is waiting,
for the good reason that he is not willing that any should perish, and he is
giving more time for sinners to repent.
2 PETER 3:9
(The Living Bible)

[1206]
God . . . is eternal, infinite, immeasurable, incomprehensible, omnipotent, invisible.
THE SCOTS CONFESSION

[1207]
The quality of mercy is not strain'd,/ It
droppeth as the gentle rain from
heaven / Upon the place beneath./
. . . It is an attribute to God himself.
SHAKESPEARE
The Merchant of Venice, IV, i

[1208]
God is a Spirit, infinite, eternal and unchangeable in his being, wisdom,
power, holiness, justice, goodness and
truth.
WESTMINSTER SHORTER CATECHISM

[1209]
There is but one only living and true
God, who is infinite in being and perfection, a most pure spirit, invisible,
without body, parts, or passions, immutable, immense, eternal, incomprehensible, almighty, most wise, most
holy, most free, most absolute.
WESTMINSTER CONFESSION OF FAITH

God, Children of

[1210]
The Christian faith cannot be inher-
ited; God has no grandchildren.
L. NELSON BELL

[1211]
It is only when we are subject to a common father that we are brothers. To
become brothers we have only to become sons again.
LOUIS EVELY

[1212]
[To the Hebrews] man is created in the
image of God, not begotten; God-son-
ship is a thing not of nature but of
grace.
KENNETH GRAYSTON

[1213]
Children of God are only those who are
regenerated as a result of faith in
Christ. The indwelling Spirit gives to
the child of God the realization of his
sonship. The popular doctrine of the
fatherhood of God and the brother-
hood of man is not taught in Scripture.
Since man is fallen, a person becomes
a child of God only by faith in Christ.
MERRILL F. UNGER

God, Kingdom of

[1214]
A man who is waiting and praying for
the Kingdom of God has to be like a
servant who always watches the hands
of his master.
CHRISTOPH BLUMHARDT

[1215]
The Kingdom of God is not the work of
man. It confounds the work of man.
CHRISTOPHER DAWSON

[1216]
The Kingdom of God is a kingdom of
love.
HENRY W. DuBOSE

[1217]
Jesus' unique vocation was to establish the Kingdom of God.

W. R. FORRESTER

[1218]
The longings and dreams of mankind will be fulfilled as God establishes his glorious Kingdom on earth for the enjoyment of mankind.

BILLY GRAHAM

[1219]
My kingdom is not of this world.

JOHN 18:36 (KJV)

[1220]
While the Kingdom of God as the realm in which God's will is perfectly done continues to be future, the Kingdom as the active saving power of God has come into the world in the person and activity of Christ to redeem men from the kingdom of Satan.

GEORGE E. LADD

[1221]
It is a betrayal at once of man and of God not to understand that history is a movement toward the Kingdom of God. But it is absurd to think that it will come as a part of history. It will come at the end of history.

JACQUES MARITAIN

[1222]
Our Lord's primary interest was not the shoring up of the moral and spiritual values of a sagging social structure, but the ushering in of an altogether new order: the Kingdom of God.

ALEXANDER MILLER

[1223]
There is no escape from the paradoxical relation of history to the Kingdom of God. History moves toward the realization of the Kingdom but yet the judgment of God is upon every new realization.

REINHOLD NIEBUHR

[1224]
There is no structural organization of society which can bring about the coming of the Kingdom of God on earth, since all systems can be perverted by the selfishness of man.

WILLIAM TEMPLE

[1225]
Jesus never speaks of the Kingdom of God as previously existing. To him the Kingdom is throughout something new, now first to be realized.

GEERHARDUS VOS

God, Love of

[1226]
There is no need to plead that the love of God shall fill our heart as though he were unwilling to fill us. He is willing as light is willing to flood a room that is opened to its brightness; willing as water is willing to flow into an emptied channel. Love is pressing round us on all sides like air. Cease to resist, and instantly love takes possession.

AMY CARMICHAEL

[1227]
The same love of God that melted the icy fingers of death now warms my heart.

DAVID CARPENTER

[1228]
The Lord disciplines him whom he loves.

HEBREWS 12:6 (RSV)

[1229]
God loved us before we loved, or could love, him. God's love for us rendered possible and actual our love of God. Hence the most fundamental need, duty, honor and happiness of man is not petition, nor even contrition, nor again even thanksgiving—these three kinds of prayer which, indeed, must never disappear out of our spiritual lives—but adoration.

FRIEDRICH VON HÜGEL

[1230]
The steadfast love of the Lord never ceases, his mercies never come to an end; they are new every morning.

LAMENTATIONS 3:22–23 (RSV)

[1231]
On the whole, God's love for us is a much safer subject to think about than our love for him. Nobody can always have devout feelings; and even if we could, feelings are not what God principally cares about. Christian love, either toward God or toward man, is an affair of the will. But the great thing to remember is that, though our feelings come and go, his love for us does not.

C. S. LEWIS

[1232]
God soon turns from his wrath, but he never turns from his love.

CHARLES H. SPURGEON

[1233]
Love is the greatest thing that God can give us; for himself is love: and it is the greatest thing we can give to God.

JEREMY TAYLOR

God, Power of

[1234]
The greatest undeveloped resource of our country is faith; the greatest unused power is prayer.

ROGER W. BABSON

[1235]
God can strike a powerful blow on a crooked stick.

ANDREW W. BLACKWOOD

[1236]
The sun does not rise because of the rotation of the earth. The sun rises because God says to it, "Get up."

G. K. CHESTERTON

[1237]
I have attempted to cure nervous patients with suggestions of quietness and confidence, but without success until I linked those suggestions to faith in the power of God, as the substance of a Christian's hope.

J. A. HADFIELD, M.D.

[1238]
One on God's side is a majority.

WENDELL PHILLIPS

[1239]
Too often we attempt to work for God to the limit of our incompetency, rather than to the limit of God's omnipotency.

J. HUDSON TAYLOR

[1240]
God is stronger than fire and destruction, and even in the valleys of deepest darkness, rod and staff are put into our hands and bridges are thrown across the abyss.

HELMUT THIELICKE

[1241]
Whatever is to be done at God's command may be accomplished in his strength.

God, Relationship to

[1242]
You have to do a lot of business with God to mellow out in sweetness.

EDWARD JOHN CARNELL

[1243]
Without a hold on Christ there is no
hold on God at all.
THOMAS CHALMERS

[1244]
Lord, send me where Thou wilt, only
go with me; lay on me what Thou wilt,
only sustain me. Cut any cord but the
one that binds me to Thy cause, to Thy
heart.
TITUS COAN

[1245]
You are in the Beloved—his very own,
his member—therefore infinitely dear
to the Father, unspeakably precious to
him. You are never, not for one second, alone; then no reason for loneliness or depression.
NORMAN F. DOUTY

[1246]
The great question of our time is not
Communism versus individualism, not
Europe versus America nor East versus
West; it is whether man can bear to live
without God.
WILL DURANT

[1247]
My understanding of Christianity is
God in search of lost men, not men in
search of a lost God.
RONALD R. HATCH

[1248]
From the day of the Nativity there was
a change in the relations between earth
and heaven. To be one with Christ was
to be one with God; and this union with
God through Christ is the secret and
basis of the new kingdom of souls
which Christ has founded and in which
he reigns.
H. P. LIDDON

[1249]
The Christian who has the smile of
God needs no status symbols.
LEONARD RAVENHILL

[1250]
I do not find God hard to live with.
A. W. TOZER

[1251]
God rules in the realms to which he is
admitted.
MARY WELCH

God, Will of

[1252]
God created this game of life; and only
when we play it his way can we find
meaning, purpose and happiness.
LANE ADAMS

[1253]
The hardness of God is kinder than the
softness of men, and his compulsion is
our liberation.
C. S. LEWIS

[1254]
I find doing the will of God leaves me
no time for disputing about his plans.
GEORGE MACDONALD

[1255]
God's will is not a place, but a condi-
tion; not a when or where, but a how.
FRANCES J. ROBERTS

[1256]
The center of God's will is our only
safety.
BETSIE TEN BOOM

[1257]
To *know* God's will is man's greatest
treasure; to *do* his will is life's greatest
privilege.

GOODNESS

[1258]
It was shown me that things which undergo corruption are in themselves good. If they were supremely good, of course, they could not be corrupted; but neither could they be corrupted if they were no good in the first place. . . . Those things that are divested of goodness cease to exist; but as long as they exist, they are good. Therefore, whatever is, is good.

AUGUSTINE OF HIPPO

[1259]
There was never law, or sect, or opinion, did so magnify goodness as the Christian religion doth.

FRANCIS BACON

[1260]
The Lord's goodness surrounds us at every moment. I walk through it almost with difficulty, as through thick grass and flowers.

R. W. BARBOUR

[1261]
Goodness consists not in the outward things we do, but in the inward thing we are.

EDWIN HUBBELL CHAPIN

[1262]
When good men die their goodness does not perish.

EURIPIDES

[1263]
Goodness is love in action.

JAMES HAMILTON

[1264]
We must first be made good before we can do good; we must first be made just before our works can please God.

HUGH LATIMER

[1265]
Goodness in the church is always individual and personal.

WILLIAM LAWSON

[1266]
We know that all that happens to us is working for our good if we love God and are fitting into his plans.

ROMANS 8:28
(The Living Bible)

[1267]
The cross has revealed to good men that their goodness has not been good enough.

JOHANN HIERONYMUS SCHROEDER

[1268]
There is an idea abroad among moral people that they should make their neighbors good. One person I have to make good: myself.

ROBERT LOUIS STEVENSON

[1269]
Real goodness does not attach itself merely to this life—it points to another world.

DANIEL WEBSTER

GOSPEL

[1270]
That God is more near, more real and mighty, more full of love, and more ready to help every one of us than any one of us realizes, is the undying message [of the Gospels].

DAVID S. CAIRNS

[1271]
It is useless to advertise the banquet if there is nothing to eat.

SAMUEL CHADWICK

[1272]
Woe to me if I do not preach the gospel!

1 CORINTHIANS 9:16 (RSV)

[1273]
Because it was the message of God to humanity, the Gospel could only reveal itself in the simplest of garments.

ADOLF DEISSMANN

[1274]
The glorious Gospel of the grace of God is the profound heritage of the church in its ministry to a lost world.

WILLIAM E. GILROY

[1275]
Talk about the questions of the day; there is but one question, and that is the Gospel. It can and will correct everything needing correction.

WILLIAM E. GLADSTONE

[1276]
Brown bread and the Gospel is good fare.

MATTHEW HENRY

[1277]
There is nothing musty about the Gospel, and nothing misty about it either.

OSWALD C. J. HOFFMANN

[1278]
God writes the Gospel not in the Bible alone, but on trees, and flowers, and clouds, and stars.

MARTIN LUTHER

[1279]
Go into all the world and preach the gospel to the whole creation.

MARK 16:15 (RSV)

[1280]
What mainly confronts us, in the universities as outside, is not reasoned rejection after honest and competent examination. It is a vague impression that belief in God is no longer tenable and that the Christian Gospel is an exploded myth. Those who have made no serious attempt to discover what leading Christian theologians today do really hold and teach are not entitled to make a dogmatic pronouncement, or even to hold a confident opinion, about the Christian claim.

WALTER MOBERLY

[1281]
The music changes, but the message never does.

DUANE PEDERSON

[1282]
How petty are the books of the philosophers with all their pomp, compared with the Gospels!

JEAN JACQUES ROUSSEAU

[1283]
The Gospel is a declaration, not a debate.

JAMES S. STEWART

[1284]
I went to a theological book and crammed my brains with sentences long enough to make the jaw of a Greek professor squeak for a week. It didn't amount to shucks. So I went and loaded up the old gun with rough-on-rats, ipecac, saltpeter, rock salt, dynamite and every other kind of explosive, and I pulled the trigger, and that Pharisee gang has been on the run ever since.

BILLY SUNDAY

[1285]
Euagelio (that we cal gospel) is a greke worde, and signyfyth good, mery, glad and joyfull tydings, that maketh a mannes hert glad, and maketh hym synge, daunce and leepe for joye.
WILLIAM TYNDALE

[1286]
My heart has always assured and reassured me that the Gospel of Christ must be a divine reality.
DANIEL WEBSTER

[1287]
God, not man, first communicated the Gospel of redemption.
WORLD CONGRESS ON EVANGELISM
Berlin, 1966

GOSSIP

[1288]
Avoid gossip, lest you come to be regarded as its originator.
CATO

[1289]
Do not give heed to all the things that men say, lest you hear your servant cursing you.
ECCLESIASTES 7:21 (RSV)

[1290]
Have you heard a word against your neighbor? Let it die within you, trusting that it will not burst you.
ECCLESIASTICUS 19:10

[1291]
Insinuations are the rhetoric of the devil.
JOHANN WOLFGANG VON GOETHE

[1292]
A real Christian is a person who can give his pet parrot to the town gossip.
BILLY GRAHAM

[1293]
Gossips are frogs; they drink and talk.
GEORGE HERBERT

[1294]
Never tell evil of a man if you do not know it for a certainty; and if you do know it for a certainty, then ask yourself: "Why should I tell it?"
JOHANN KASPAR LAVATER

[1295]
Believe nothing against another but upon good authority; nor report what may hurt another, unless it be a greater hurt to others to conceal it.
WILLIAM PENN

[1296]
Whoever gossips to you will gossip of you.
SPANISH PROVERB

[1297]
Never believe anything bad about anybody unless you positively know it to be true; never tell even that unless you feel that it is absolutely necessary—and that God is listening while you tell it.
HENRY VAN DYKE

[1298]
No one can have a gossiping tongue unless he has gossiping ears.

GOVERNMENT

[1299]
As the happiness of the people is the sole end of government, so the consent of the people is the only foundation of it.
JOHN ADAMS

[1300]
The foundation of our society and of our government rests so much on the teachings of the Bible that it would be difficult to support them if faith in these teachings should cease.

CALVIN COOLIDGE

[1301]
You can only govern men by serving them. The rule is without exception.

VICTOR COUSIN

[1302]
A good government remains the greatest of human blessings, and no nation has ever enjoyed it.

WILLIAM R. INGE

[1303]
The government will be upon his shoulder.

ISAIAH 9:6 (RSV)

[1304]
The basis of effective government is public confidence.

JOHN F. KENNEDY

[1305]
Every nation has the government it deserves.

JOSEPH LE MAISTRE

[1306]
No man is good enough to govern another man without that other's consent.

ABRAHAM LINCOLN

[1307]
I know not how long a republican form of government can flourish among a great people who have not the Bible.

WILLIAM H. SEWARD

[1308]
The people's government is made for the people, made by the people, and is answerable to the people.

DANIEL WEBSTER

[1309]
The firm basis of government is justice, not pity.

WOODROW WILSON

GRACE

[1310]
Grace freely justifies me and sets me free from slavery to sin.

BERNARD OF CLAIRVAUX

[1311]
Neither in heaven nor on earth is it possible just to settle down comfortably through grace and do nothing and care for nobody else. If I am saved by grace, then I am a worker through grace. If I am justified by grace, then through grace I am a worker for justice. If through grace I am placed within the truth, then through grace I am a servant of truth. If through grace I have been placed within peace, then through grace I am a servant of peace for all men.

CHRISTOPH BLUMHARDT

[1312]
Moody preached in a manner which led to the sort of effect produced by Luther. He exulted in the free grace of God. His joy was contagious. Men leaped out of darkness into light, and lived a Christian life afterward.

R. W. DALE

[1313]
A state of mind that sees God in everything is evidence of growth in grace and a thankful heart.

CHARLES G. FINNEY

[1314]
Grace is not sought nor bought nor wrought. It is a free gift of Almighty God to needy mankind.

BILLY GRAHAM

[1315]
The word "grace" is unquestionably the most significant single word in the Bible.

ILION T. JONES

[1316]
We may cast out the beam from the eye of the soul; we may "cleanse" it by all the actions of a virtuous life; we may direct it toward God by the processes of prayer and meditation; but all that is as nothing, unless God of his own free beneficence presents himself to the clarified vision and supplies the light wherewith he may be seen.

KENNETH E. KIRK

[1317]
Christ is no Moses, no exactor, no giver of laws, but a giver of grace, a Savior; he is infinite mercy and goodness, freely and bountifully giving to us.

MARTIN LUTHER

[1318]
Grace is God's unmerited, free spontaneous love for sinful man, revealed and made effective in Jesus Christ.

C. L. MITTON

[1319]
We cannot seek grace through gadgets.

J. B. PRIESTLY

[1320]
Grace is getting another chance even though you haven't earned it or deserved it. (You may not even want it!)

FRITZ RIDENOUR

[1321]
Christ, all the seasons of the year, is dropping sweetness; if I had vessels, I might fill them, but my old riven, holey and running-out dish, even when I am at the well, can bring little away. Nothing but glory will make tight and fast our leaking and rifty vessels.

SAMUEL RUTHERFORD

[1322]
There is nothing but God's grace. We walk upon it; we breathe it; we live and die by it; it makes the nails and axles of the universe.

ROBERT LOUIS STEVENSON

GRATITUDE

[1323]
Gratitude is not only the dominant note in Christian piety but equally the dominant motive of Christian action in the world. Such gratitude is for the grace that has been shown us by God. . . . A true Christian is a man who never for a moment forgets what God has done for him in Christ, and whose whole comportment and whole activity have their root in the sentiment of gratitude.

JOHN BAILLIE

[1324]
If gratitude is due from children to their earthly parent, how much more is the gratitude of the great family of men due to our Father in heaven?

HOSEA BALLOU

[1325]
Gratitude is not only the greatest of virtues, but the parent of all the others.

CICERO

[1326]
Gratitude is born in hearts that take time to count up past mercies.

CHARLES E. JEFFERSON

[1327]
Gratitude is the memory of the heart.

JEAN BAPTISTE MASSIEU

[1328]
How happy a person is depends upon the depth of his gratitude.

JOHN MILLER

[1329]
A favor is to a grateful man delightful always; to an ungrateful man only once.

SENECA

[1330]
O Lord, that lends me life,/ Lend me a heart replete with thankfulness!

SHAKESPEARE
King Henry the Sixth, Part II, I, i

[1331]
If you pick up a starving dog and make him prosperous, he will not bite you; that is the principal difference between a dog and a man.

MARK TWAIN

[1332]
Gratitude is the homage of the heart, rendered to God for his goodness.

NATHANIEL PARKER WILLIS

[1333]
The attitude of gratitude is both delicate and mysterious. It can be crushed by the uplifting of a skeptical eyebrow; yet its psychology is hidden in the divine love. Gratitude is a way of life, a temper of being, an index to spiritual health.*

GREATNESS

[1334]
The study of God's Word for the purpose of discovering God's will is the secret discipline which has formed the greatest characters.

JAMES W. ALEXANDER

[1335]
There is a great man who makes every man feel small. But the really great man is the man who makes every man feel great.

G. K. CHESTERTON

[1336]
The price of greatness is responsibility.

WINSTON S. CHURCHILL

[1337]
Great hopes make great men.

THOMAS FULLER

[1338]
Moses became the world's greatest jurist, not amid the luxuries of the palace of Egypt, but amid the solitude of the desert. In the desert he had time to meet and talk with God.

A. P. GOUTHEY

[1339]
No really great man ever thought himself so.

WILLIAM HAZLITT

[1340]
Nothing can make a man truly great but being truly good and partaking of God's holiness.

MATTHEW HENRY

[1341]
A retentive memory is a good thing, but the ability to forget is the true token of greatness.

ELBERT HUBBARD

[1342]
No man who wanted to be a great man ever was a great man.

JOHN HUNTER

[1343]
There is a greatness that can come to all of us, but it is a greatness that comes to us through prayer.

HAROLD LINDSELL

[1344]
He who is least among you all is the one who is great.

LUKE 9:48 (RSV)

[1345]
The final measure of greatness is whether you and I, by our individual lives, have increased the freedom of man, enhanced his dignity, and brought him nearer to the nobility of the divine image in which he was created.

HERBERT V. PROCHNOW

[1346]
Great minds are like eagles, and build their nest in some lofty solitude.

ARTHUR SCHOPENHAUER

[1347]
A solemn regard to spiritual and eternal things is an indispensable element of all true greatness.

DANIEL WEBSTER

GROWTH

[1348]
The strongest principle of growth lies in human choice.

GEORGE ELIOT

[1349]
When the divine owner takes possession of a property, he has a twofold objective: intense cultivation and abounding fruitfulness.

NORMAN P. GRUBB

[1350]
Keep the faith, baby; not the baby faith.

INTER-VARSITY GRAFFITO

[1351]
The earth produces of itself, first the blade, then the ear, then the full grain in the ear.

MARK 4:28 (RSV)

[1352]
Nature does not require that we be perfect; it requires only that we grow, and we can do this as well from a mistake as from a success.

ROLLO MAY

[1353]
The grace of God makes a man godly, and then proceeds to make him manly.

HENRIETTA MEARS

[1354]
Like newborn babes, long for the pure spiritual milk, that by it you may grow up to salvation.

1 PETER 2:2 (RSV)

[1355]
Jesus threw a dam across the desert canyon of my life and brought in living water. The arid cracks filled up, the desert blossomed, and now he controls the outflow.

CAROL RHODES

[1356]
God judges a man not by the point he has reached, but by the way he is facing; not by distance, but by direction.

JAMES S. STEWART

[1357]
Throw your sins into the middle of the sea and put up a sign, "No fishing."

CORRIE TEN BOOM

[1358]
Jesus Christ dredged me out of myself and has become the foundation of that new person I can see going up every day.

GUIDANCE

[1359]
It is one thing to climb above timber line to the summit and catch a view of the land of peace, but fail to find a trail leading to it, and so have to struggle through uncharted country, waylaid and beset by fugitives and deserters. It is quite another to move steadily down the posted highway to it, convoyed by the security troops of the King of heaven, unmolested by deserters who avoid the road like the plague.
AUGUSTINE OF HIPPO

[1360]
We need to learn to set our course by the stars and not by the lights of every passing ship.
OMAR BRADLEY

[1361]
Only if God is reinstated in the heart of the world will he furnish mankind and its leaders with ethical guidance through the dangers and pitfalls of the space age.
WERNHER VON BRAUN

[1362]
Since Jesus became my Supreme Programmer, he has kept the scanner and memory tapes moving rapidly and with a minimum of downtime.
DONALD R. BROWN

[1363]
Suppose one of the astronauts bound for the moon were to report, "We're off course," and the people at Mission Control replied in a tolerant and broadminded way, "Oh, it's all right. Many roads lead to the moon; just take the one you're on." There are many who say that about the way to heaven. Which road are you on today? Which direction are you traveling?
BILLY GRAHAM

[1364]
God not only orders our steps. He orders our stops.
GEORGE MÜLLER

[1365]
I praise God because he not only guides my directions but overrules my mistakes.
H. NORMAN PELL

[1366]
In everything you do, put God first, and he will direct you and crown your efforts with success.
PROVERBS 3:6
(The Living Bible)

[1367]
A man's mind plans his way, but the Lord directs his steps.
PROVERBS 16:9 (RSV)

[1368]
Men give advice; God gives guidance.
LEONARD RAVENHILL

[1369]
I came about like a well-handled ship. There stood at the wheel that . . . steersman whom we call God.
ROBERT LOUIS STEVENSON

GUILT

[1370]
Man falls according as God's providence ordains, but he falls by his own fault.
JOHN CALVIN

[1371]
Too many of our securities are guilt-edged.
MARIANNE CRISWELL

[1372]
A guilty conscience needs no accuser.
ENGLISH PROVERB

[1373]
Whoever keeps the whole law but fails in one point has become guilty of all of it.

JAMES 2:10 (RSV)

[1374]
When a psychotherapist speaks about guilt he almost always uses the word as short for "guilt-feeling," by which he means a psychological state or event. The theologian, on the other hand, in speaking of guilt refers not to a feeling but to an objective ethical or forensic relation between a man and God, or between one man and another. To *feel* guilty and to *be* guilty are not the same thing; the two do not even necessarily exist in direct proportion. When the two meanings are confused, needless conflict is generated.

MALCOLM A. JEEVES

[1375]
No creature that deserved redemption would need to be redeemed.

C. S. LEWIS

[1376]
Psychoanalysts relieve their patients from feeling guilty about things of which they are not guilty, and leave them with the sense of guilt about things of which they really are guilty.

GREGORY ZILBOORG

HABIT

[1377]
Thousands of Christians are swimming in a circle, repeating something they learned years ago.

FLORENCE ALLSHORN

[1378]
Habit is a shirt made of iron.

CZECH PROVERB

[1379]
We first make our habits, and then our habits make us.

JOHN DRYDEN

[1380]
Since habits become power, make them work with you and not against you.

E. STANLEY JONES

[1381]
Habit is a cable; we weave a thread of it every day, and at last we cannot break it.

HORACE MANN

[1382]
I never knew a man to overcome a bad habit gradually.

JOHN R. MOTT

[1383]
Train up a child in the way he should go, and when he is old he will not depart from it.

PROVERBS 22:6 (RSV)

[1384]
Habit is overcome by habit.

THOMAS À KEMPIS

HAPPINESS

[1385]
Happiness is living by inner purpose, not by outer pressures. Happiness is a happening-with-God.

DAVID AUGSBURGER

[1386]
If we would win gladness, we may well go to Jesus' springs.

WALTER RUSSELL BOWIE

[1387]
Make happiness the object of your pursuit, and it leads you on a wild-goose chase.

NATHANIEL HAWTHORNE

[1388]
The supreme happiness of life is the conviction that we are loved.

VICTOR HUGO

[1389]
God cannot give us happiness and peace apart from himself, because it is not there. There is no such thing.

C. S. LEWIS

[1390]
The moments of happiness we enjoy take us by surprise. It is not that we seize them, but that they seize us.

ASHLEY MONTAGU

[1391]
No one is born happy. Happiness is something that comes to you. It is brought about by inner productiveness and meaning found in a great life-task.

HATE

[1392]
There would be no place for hatred among wise men. For who but the foolish would hate good men? And there is no cause to hate bad men. Vice is a disease of the mind, just as feebleness shows ill health to the body.

BOETHIUS

[1393]
Hatred is blind as well as love.

THOMAS FULLER

[1394]
Short is the road that leads from fear to hate.

ITALIAN PROVERB

[1395]
Any one who hates his brother is a murderer.

1 JOHN 3:15 (RSV)

[1396]
These two sins, hatred and pride, deck and trim themselves out as the devil clothed himself in the Godhead. Hatred will be godlike; pride will be truth. These two are deadly sins: hatred is killing, pride is lying.

MARTIN LUTHER

[1397]
Our hatred of someone does not affect their peace of mind, but it certainly can ruin ours.

W. A. "DUB" NANCE

[1398]
It is better to eat soup with someone you love than steak with someone you hate.

PROVERBS 15:17
(The Living Bible)

[1399]
I will tell you what to hate. Hate hypocrisy, hate cant, hate intolerance, oppression, injustice; hate Pharisaism; hate them as Christ hated them, with a deep, living, godlike hatred.

F. W. ROBERTSON

[1400]
If we allow ourselves to hate, that is to insure our spiritual defeat and our likeness to what we hate.

GEORGE WILLIAM RUSSELL

[1401]
I shall never permit myself to stoop so low as to hate any man.

BOOKER T. WASHINGTON

HEALING

[1402]
He who has healing in his hands, be he physician, surgeon, psychiatrist, pastor or layman, may only thank God humbly that he is used in this ministry.

JOHN SUTHERLAND BONNELL

[1403]
The good Instructor, the Wisdom, the Word of the Father, who made man, cares for the whole nature of his creature. The all-sufficient Physician of humanity, the Savior, heals both our body and soul, which are the proper man.

CLEMENT OF ALEXANDRIA

[1404]
The temperature of the spiritual life of the church is the index of her power to heal.

EVELYN FROST

[1405]
With his stripes we are healed.

ISAIAH 53:5 (RSV)

[1406]
Stronger than all the evils in the soul is the Word, and the healing power that dwells in him.

ORIGEN

[1407]
I dressed his wounds; God healed him.

AMBROISE PARÉ
(father of modern surgery)

[1408]
He heals the brokenhearted, binding up their wounds.

PSALM 147:3
(The Living Bible)

[1409]
Even if you be healed by drugs (I grant you that point by courtesy), yet it behooves you to give testimony of the cure to God.

TATIAN

[1410]
The personality of the therapist is the most important human element in the therapeutic process.

THOMAS TYNDALL

HEALTH

[1411]
The trouble about always trying to preserve the health of the body is that it is so difficult to do without destroying the health of the mind.

G. K. CHESTERTON

[1412]
The secret of the physical well-being of the Christian is the vitality of the divine life welling up within by virtue of his incorporation in Christ.

EVELYN FROST

[1413]
He who has health is rich and does not know it.

ITALIAN PROVERB

[1414]
We should pray for a sane mind in a sound body.

JUVENAL

[1415]
What some call health, if purchased by perpetual anxiety about diet, isn't much better than tedious disease.

GEORGE DENNISON PRENTICE

[1416]
Look to your health; and if you have it, praise God, and value it next to a good conscience.

IZAAK WALTON

HEART

[1417]
Can you walk on water? You have done no better than a straw. Can you fly in the air? You have done no better than a bluebottle. Conquer your heart; then you may become somebody.

ANSARI OF HERAT

[1418]
To my God, a heart of flame; to my fellow men, a heart of love; to myself, a heart of steel.

AUGUSTINE OF HIPPO

[1419]
If it be true that the faith in Christ's blood justifieth me before God, and I confess it before all the bishops in England with my mouth, and believe it not with mine heart, then am I none the better.

JOHN FRITH

[1420]
There is but one question of the hour: how to bring the truth of God's Word into vital contact with the minds and hearts of all classes of people.

WILLIAM E. GLADSTONE

[1421]
At the heart of your need is the need of your heart.

DAVID MACLAGAN

[1422]
The heart has its reasons which reason does not know.

BLAISE PASCAL

[1423]
Men may tire themselves in a labyrinth of search and talk of God; but if we would know him indeed, it must be from the impressions we receive of him; and the softer our hearts are, the deeper and livelier those will be upon us.

WILLIAM PENN

[1424]
The capital of heaven is the heart in which Jesus Christ is enthroned as King.

SADHU SUNDAR SINGH

[1425]
Hardening of the heart ages more people than hardening of the arteries.

HEAVEN

[1426]
How many preachers, during these years, have dwelt on the joys of the heavenly rest with anything like the old ardent love and impatient longing, or have spoken of the world that now is as a place of sojourn and pilgrimage?

JOHN BAILLIE

[1427]
The best way to strengthen the faith of all our people in the heaven yonder is to bring down a little more heaven here.

JAMES BARR

[1428]
To believe in heaven is not to run away from life; it is to run toward it.

JOSEPH D. BLINCO

[1429]
All the way to heaven is heaven.

CATHERINE OF SIENA

[1430]
Every saint in heaven is as a flower in the garden of God, and every soul there is as a note in some concert of delightful music.

JONATHAN EDWARDS

[1431]
Heaven will be the perfection we have always longed for. All the things that made earth unlovely and tragic will be absent in heaven. There will be no night, no death, no disease, no sorrow, no tears, no ignorance, no disappointment, no war. It will be filled with health, vigor, virility, knowledge, happiness, worship, love, and perfection.

BILLY GRAHAM

[1432]
Serving God in heaven is work as free from care and toil and fatigue as is the wing-stroke of the jubilant lark when it soars into the sunlight of a fresh, clear day and, spontaneously and for self-relief, pours out its thrilling carol. Work up there is a matter of self-relief, as well as a matter of obedience to the ruling will of God. It is work according to one's tastes and delight and ability. If tastes vary there, if abilities vary there, then occupations will vary there.
DAVID GREGG

[1433]
You will get to heaven by accepting Christ as *Savior*, but by accepting Christ as *Lord* and Savior you will bring heaven down to yourself.
JORDAN C. KHAN

[1434]
A continual looking forward to the eternal world is not a form of escapism or wishful thinking, but one of the things a Christian is meant to do. It does not mean that we are to leave the present world as it is. If you read history, you will find that the Christians who did the most for the present world were just those who thought most of the next.
C. S. LEWIS

[1435]
A good many people will see little heaven hereafter if they do not begin to look for more of heaven now.
RICHARD MONTAGUE

[1436]
How far away is heaven? It is not so far as some imagine. It wasn't very far from Daniel. It was not so far off that Elijah's prayer, and those of others could not be heard there. Christ said when ye pray say, "Our Father, who art in heaven." Men full of the Spirit can look right into heaven.
DWIGHT L. MOODY

[1437]
Almost all systematic theologies devote infinitely more space to hell than to heaven, as, for instance, Shedd, who assigns two pages in his *Dogmatic Theology* to heaven, and eighty-seven pages to eternal punishment!
WILBUR M. SMITH

[1438]
Faith is the Christian's foundation, hope is his anchor, death is his harbor, Christ is his pilot, and heaven is his country.
JEREMY TAYLOR

[1439]
A little Swedish girl was walking with her father one night under the starry sky, intently meditating on the glories of heaven. At last, looking up to the sky, she said, "Father, I have been thinking that if the wrong side of heaven is so beautiful, what will the right side be?"

HELL

[1440]
The mission of Jesus cannot be defined without speaking of man being lost.
HENRI BLOCHER

[1441]
All hope abandon, ye who enter here.
DANTE'S *Inferno*
(inscription over the gate of hell)

[1442]
What is hell? . . . The suffering that comes from the consciousness that one is no longer able to love.

FYODOR DOSTOEVSKY
The Brothers Karamazov

[1443]
If there is no belief in hell the concept of judgment also becomes meaningless; and then all that is left of Christianity is a system of ethics.

GEOFFREY GORER

[1444]
Hell was not prepared for man. God never meant that man would ever go to hell. Hell was prepared for the devil and his angels, but man rebelled against God and followed the devil. . . . Hell is essentially and basically banishment from the presence of God for deliberately rejecting Jesus Christ as Lord and Savior.

BILLY GRAHAM

[1445]
Scripture holds out no hope of a second probation for those who have neglected or deliberately misused their present opportunities. Irretrievable loss awaits the deliberate rejecter of Christ at the Throne of Judgment.

T. C. HAMMOND

[1446]
There is nobody will go to hell for company.

GEORGE HERBERT

[1447]
Hell is paved with good intentions.

SAMUEL JOHNSON

[1448]
How thankful we should be that ever since our Father [Satan] entered hell . . . no square inch of infernal space and no moment of infernal time has been surrendered to either of those abominable forces [music and silence], but all has been occupied by Noise—Noise, the grand dynamism, the audible expression of all that is exultant, ruthless and virile.

C. S. LEWIS
Toadpipe, in *The Screwtape Letters*

[1449]
The one principle of hell is "I am my own."

GEORGE MACDONALD

[1450]
The fear of hell is not the fairest road to the feet of God, but, children of the Father, it is better than none at all.

The late Rev. ALISTAIR MacLEAN
of Daviot, Invernesshire, Scotland

[1451]
When we preach on hell, we might at least do it with tears in our eyes.

DWIGHT L. MOODY

[1452]
When you speak of heaven let your face light up. When you speak of hell—well, then your everyday face will do.

CHARLES H. SPURGEON

[1453]
Nothing burns in hell but self-will. . . . Hell is nothing but self-will, and if there were no self-will there would be no devil and no hell. When we say self-will, we mean: to will otherwise than as the One and Eternal Will of God wills.

THEOLOGIA GERMANICA

[1454]
If we had more hell in the pulpit, we'd
have less hell upon the streets and the
highways of our land, and in the homes
of our people.

GRADY B. WILSON

HELP

[1455]
God's help is nearer than the door.

GURNEY BENHAM

[1456]
A willing helper does not wait to be
called.

DANISH PROVERB

[1457]
He who sees a need and waits to be
asked for help is as unkind as if he had
refused it.

DANTE

[1458]
Mutual help is the law of nature.

FRENCH PROVERB

[1459]
I don't give tuppence for the man who
goes into the pulpit to tell me what my
duty is; but I give all I have to the man
who tells me from whence my help
cometh.

T. R. GLOVER

[1460]
The best help is not to bear the troubles of others for them, but to inspire
them with courage and energy to bear
their own burdens and to meet with the
difficulties of life bravely.

JOHN LUBBOCK

[1461]
Nisi Dominus frustra (Without the Lord,
everything fails).

MOTTO, EDINBURGH, SCOTLAND

[1462]
God is our refuge and strength, a very
present help in trouble.

PSALM 46:1 (RSV)

[1463]
Whom God will help nae man can hin-
der.

SCOTTISH PROVERB

[1464]
O Lord, help me to understand that
you ain't goin' to let nuthin' come my
way that You and me together can't
handle.

SOUTHERN PRAYER

HISTORY

[1465]
Golgotha was a historical event like the
murder of Julius Caesar; but we don't
meet God in the murder of Caesar.

EMIL BRUNNER

[1466]
What are all histories but God manifesting himself?

OLIVER CROMWELL

[1467]
Those who do not know history are
forever condemned to repeat it.

WILL DURANT

[1468]
History is a voice forever sounding
across the centuries the laws of right
and wrong.

JAMES ANTHONY FROUDE

[1469]
It is not the history of families, nor of
races and nations, nor of cultures that
holds within itself the final meaning of
history, but only the history of the salvation of persons in the Kingdom of
God.

THEODOR HAECKER

[1470]
A page of history is worth a volume of logic.
OLIVER WENDELL HOLMES

[1471]
We cannot escape history.
ABRAHAM LINCOLN

[1472]
The solution to history is that there is no solution.
REINHOLD NIEBUHR

[1473]
I predict that the twentieth century will spend a good deal of its time picking out of the wastebasket things that the nineteenth century threw into it.
ERNEST RENAN

[1474]
Hegel was right when he said that we learn from history that men never learn anything from history.
GEORGE BERNARD SHAW
Heartbreak House

[1475]
The history of the world is the judge of the world.
HERMANN ULLMANN

[1476]
There is one history, and that the most touching and most profound of all . . . the history of the human soul in its relations with its Maker; the history of its sin, and grief, and death, and of the way of its recovery to hope and life and to enduring joy.
ISAAC M. WISE

HOLINESS

[1477]
The beauty of holiness has done more, and will do more, to regenerate the world and bring in everlasting righteousness than all the other agencies put together.
THOMAS CHALMERS

[1478]
The destined end of man is not happiness, nor health, but holiness. God's one aim is the production of saints. He is not an eternal blessing-machine for men; he did not come to save men out of pity; he came to save men because he had created them to be holy.
OSWALD CHAMBERS

[1479]
He that sees the beauty of holiness, or true moral good, sees the greatest and most important thing in the world.
JONATHAN EDWARDS

[1480]
Put off your shoes from your feet, for the place on which you are standing is holy ground.
EXODUS 3:5 (RSV)

[1481]
There is no detour to holiness. Jesus came to the resurrection through the cross, not around it.
LEIGHTON FORD

[1482]
There is no true holiness without humility.
THOMAS FULLER

[1483]
In our era the road to holiness necessarily passes through the world of action.
DAG HAMMARSKJÖLD

[1484]
Holy, holy, holy is the Lord of Hosts;
the whole earth is filled with his glory.
ISAIAH 6:3
(The Living Bible)

[1485]
I have always been taught that God
seeks men, not men God; but it has
been only recently that I have begun to
know that the great longing for Spirit-
filled lives comes from the heart of
God; that it is the holy God who seeks
after men, who yearns and longs to fill
men. The secret of being filled with the
Spirit lies in letting God do for us what
he most desires to do, namely, to fill us.
L. L. LEGTERS

[1486]
It is a great deal better to live a holy life
than to talk about it.
DWIGHT L. MOODY

[1487]
The serene beauty of a holy life is the
most powerful influence in the world
next to the power of God.
BLAISE PASCAL

[1488]
Holiness is not a storage battery to be
used whenever and wherever, apart
from the ultimate source of its energy.
Holiness is a throbbing, pulsating connection with the divine Dynamo.
W. T. PURKISER

[1489]
The greatest miracle that God can do
today is to take an unholy man out of
an unholy world, and make that man
holy and put him back into that unholy
world and keep him holy in it.
LEONARD RAVENHILL

[1490]
Let the church be in earnest after
greater holiness in her own members,
and she will soon settle the question
whether her resources are competent
to change the face of the earth.
J. H. THORNWELL

[1491]
Holiness means something more than
the sweeping away of the old leaves of
sin: it means the life of Jesus developed
in us.
I. LILIAS TROTTER

HOLY SPIRIT

[1492]
He who does not know God the Holy
Spirit cannot know God at all.
THOMAS ARNOLD

[1493]
To the one who remembers the Spirit
there is always a way out, even in the
wilderness with the devil.
HERBERT F. BROKERING

[1494]
The presence of the Spirit endues men
with divine authority and power. . . .
The Holy Ghost does not come upon
methods, but upon men. He does not
anoint machinery, but men. He does
not work through organizations, but
through men. He does not dwell in
buildings, but in men.
SAMUEL CHADWICK

[1495]
Without the presence of the Spirit
there is no conviction, no regeneration, no sanctification, no cleansing, no
acceptable works. We can perform duties without him, but our service is dull
and mechanical. Life is in the quicken-
ing Spirit.
W. A. CRISWELL

[1496]
The Spirit-filled life is no mystery revealed to a select few, no goal difficult
of attainment. To trust and to obey is
the substance of the whole matter.
V. RAYMOND EDMAN

[1497]
Regardless of how sincere a soul-win-
ner may be, he cannot add one member
to the body of Christ. It would be like
putting waxed apples on a tree. The
Holy Spirit alone does the work.
ROY GUSTAFSON

[1498]
Blood is thicker than water, but Spirit
is thicker than blood.
REES HOWELLS

[1499]
I have never found anyone who prayed
so well as those who had never been
taught how. They who have no master
in man have one in the Holy Spirit.
PÈRE LA COMBE

[1500]
Those who have the gale of the Holy
Spirit go forward even in sleep.
BROTHER LAWRENCE

[1501]
God's sealing of believers is his gracious communication of the Holy
Ghost unto them, so as to enable them
unto all the duties of their holy calling.
The effects of this sealing are gracious
operations of the Spirit in and upon
believers; but the sealing itself is the
communication of the Spirit to them.
JOHN OWEN

[1502]
Every time we say, "I believe in the
Holy Spirit," we mean that we believe
that there is a living God able and willing to enter human personality and
change it.
J. B. PHILLIPS

[1503]
Any proposed psychological or sociological studies of the workings or operations of the Holy Spirit are meaningless and preposterous. Any attempt to
lift the curtain will achieve exactly
nothing. Yet this hidden One is the
power of God.
BERNARD RAMM

[1504]
In Canada I have watched the lumber-
jacks felling the mighty trees. The first
thing they do is seal the timber—brand
it with their peculiar mark as their private property. After this it is floated
downriver, and on the lakes it is gathered in booms ready for the sawmill.
Each log is immediately identified by
its seal. God chose you for himself and
purchased you through the blood of
his Son; on the very day you committed
your life to Jesus Christ, God sealed
you by giving you the gift of his Holy
Spirit. Every child of God bears the
same seal, is indwelt by the same Holy
Spirit.
TOM REES

[1505]
Before Christ sent the church into the
world, he sent the Spirit into the
church. The same order must be observed today.
JOHN R. W. STOTT

[1506]
To be sure, we cannot make the wind blow. But we do not need to do so, for it is already blowing. Wherever the Son of God goes, the winds of God are blowing, the streams of living water are flowing, and the sun of God is smiling. He is the bodily guarantee that the sun and streams and wind of God are round me. I do not need to seek them. I am already encircled by the rush of wind and water and the radiance of light when Jesus begins to speak.

HELMUT THIELICKE

[1507]
The idea of the Spirit held by the average church members is so vague as to be nearly nonexistent.

A. W. TOZER

[1508]
A young fellow came to our meeting in Plymouth, England, as he said, to pick a hole in the preacher's coat; and the Holy Spirit picked a hole in his heart.

GEORGE WHITEFIELD

HOME

[1509]
If anyone is really hungry he should eat at home.

1 CORINTHIANS 11:34
(The Living Bible)

[1510]
The music of the Gospel leads us home.

FREDERICK W. FABER

[1511]
What's the good of a home if you are never in it?

GEORGE AND WEEDON GROSSMITH

[1512]
They went each to his own house, but Jesus went to the Mount of Olives.

JOHN 7:53—8:1 (RSV)

[1513]
The Bible does not say very much about homes; it says a great deal about the things that make them. It speaks about life and love and joy and peace and rest. If we get a house and put these into it, we shall have secured a home.

JOHN HENRY JOWETT

[1514]
The foundation of the republic is the home.

BEN B. LINDSEY

[1515]
Home is where they understand you.

CHRISTIAN MORGENSTERN

HONESTY

[1516]
No man is really honest; none of us is above the influence of gain.

ARISTOPHANES

[1517]
Lock your door and keep your neighbor honest.

CHINESE PROVERB

[1518]
A man never surfeits of too much honesty.

ENGLISH PROVERB

[1519]
To appear an honest man, in one word you must be one.

FRENCH PROVERB

[1520]
Honesty is a fine jewel, but much out of fashion.

THOMAS FULLER

[1521]
No honest man ever repented of his
honesty.
GERMAN PROVERB

[1522]
Honesty is the first chapter of the book
of wisdom.
THOMAS JEFFERSON

[1523]
God regards pure hands, not full.
LATIN PROVERB

[1524]
Humility is pure honesty.
JACK MCALISTER

[1525]
An honest man's the noblest work of
God.
ALEXANDER POPE

[1526]
Let God inspire you, make you want to
begin to be your best self: not just to be
proved right, but to be willing to be
proved wrong when you are; to learn to
laugh when someone trips you up.
There is a great holy hilarity that we
haven't even touched in store for the
saints of God.
EUGENIA PRICE

[1527]
Honesty in public life is generally attributed to dumbness and is seldom re-
warded.
WILL ROGERS

[1528]
Let us walk honestly, as in the day.
ROMANS 13:13 (KJV)

[1529]
A thread will tie an honest man better
than a rope a rogue.
SCOTTISH PROVERB

[1530]
I hope I shall possess firmness and virtue enough to maintain what I consider
the most enviable of all titles, the character of an honest man.
GEORGE WASHINGTON

HONOR

[1531]
Honor is like a rocky island without a
landing place; once we leave it we can't
get back.
NICOLAS BOILEAU-DESPREAUX

[1532]
The louder he talked of his honor the
faster we counted our spoons.
RALPH WALDO EMERSON

[1533]
Honor your father and your mother.
EXODUS 20:12 (RSV)

[1534]
Those only deserve a monument who
do not need one.
WILLIAM HAZLITT

[1535]
If I honor myself, my honor is nothing.
JOHN 8:54 (KJV)

[1536]
When one has to seek the honor that
comes from God only, he will take the
withholding of the honor that comes
from men very quietly indeed.
GEORGE MACDONALD

[1537]
He who has lost honor can lose noth-
ing more.
PUBLILIUS SYRUS

HOPE

[1538]
Our hope lies not in the man we put on the moon, but in the Man we put on the cross.

DON BASHAM

[1539]
Other men see only a hopeless end, but the Christian rejoices in an endless hope.

GILBERT M. BEENKEN

[1540]
What oxygen is to the lungs, such is hope for the meaning of life.

EMIL BRUNNER

[1541]
The word *hope* I take for faith; and indeed hope is nothing else but the constancy of faith.

JOHN CALVIN

[1542]
We are afflicted in every way, but not crushed; perplexed, but not driven to despair; persecuted, but not forsaken; struck down, but not destroyed; always carrying in the body the death of Jesus, so that the life of Jesus may also be manifested in our bodies.

2 CORINTHIANS 4:8–10 (RSV)

[1543]
He brought light out of darkness, not out of a lesser light; he can bring your summer out of winter, though you have no spring; though in the ways of fortune, or understanding, or conscience, you have been benighted until now, wintered and frozen, clouded and eclipsed, damped and benumbed, smothered and stupefied till now, now God comes to you, not as in the dawning of the day, not as in the bud of the spring, but as the sun at noon.

JOHN DONNE

[1544]
Hope is one of the principal springs that keep mankind in motion.

ANDREW FULLER

[1545]
I know the world is filled with troubles and many injustices. But reality is as beautiful as it is ugly. I think it is just as important to sing about beautiful mornings as it is to talk about slums. I just couldn't write anything without hope in it.

OSCAR HAMMERSTEIN II

[1546]
The ground of our hope is Christ in the world, but the evidence of our hope is Christ in the heart.

MATTHEW HENRY

[1547]
The coffin of every hope is the cradle of a good experience.

FLORENCE NIGHTINGALE

[1548]
The very disillusionment of today is the raw material of the Christian hope.

JAMES S. STEWART

HUMANITY

[1549]
People may differ in tradition, language and religion, but they all have one common denominator: a desire to be treated like human beings.

STANLEY C. ALLYN

[1550]
Christianity is true humanity.

RALPH BRONKEMA

[1551]
Love, hope, fear, faith—these make humanity.

ROBERT BROWNING
"Paracelsus"

[1552]
Before one can become an evangelist, he must first be a human being.

EMIL BRUNNER

[1553]
There is but one law for all, namely, that law which governs all law, the law of our Creator, the law of humanity, justice, equity.

EDMUND BURKE

[1554]
Only as men believe in God can they believe in humanity.

CHARLES E. GARMAN

[1555]
It is easier to love humanity as a whole than to love one's neighbor.

ERIC HOFFER

[1556]
I love humanity; it's people I can't stand.

LINUS
(Charles M. Schulz)

[1557]
From Comte and the religion of humanity to Freud and Kinsey and Hitler is only a short and logical step.

ALBERT T. MOLLEGEN

[1558]
I am a man, and nothing human is foreign to me.

TERENCE

HUMILITY

[1559]
Pride changed angels into devils; humility makes men into angels.

AUGUSTINE OF HIPPO

[1560]
The true way to be humble is not to stoop until you are smaller than yourself, but to stand at your real height against some higher nature that will show you what the real smallness of your greatness is.

PHILLIPS BROOKS

[1561]
They are proud in humility, proud that they are not proud.

ROBERT BURTON

[1562]
Humility must always be the portion of any man who receives acclaim earned in the blood of his followers and the sacrifices of his friends.

DWIGHT D. EISENHOWER

[1563]
Too much humility is pride.

GERMAN PROVERB

[1564]
It is hard for a "superior" person to be used of the Lord.

RICHARD C. HALVERSON

[1565]
None are more humble than Spirit-filled Christians. Self must be crucified before the Holy Spirit will dwell within.

J. GILCHRIST LAWSON

[1566]
In the sight of God no man can look at himself except when he is down on his knees.

FRANÇOIS MAURIAC

[1567]
I used to think that God's gifts were on shelves one above the other and that the taller we grew in Christian character the more easily we could reach them. I now find that God's gifts are on shelves one beneath the other and that it is not a question of growing taller but of stooping lower.

F. B. MEYER

[1568]
What does the Lord require of you but to do justice, and to love kindness, and to walk humbly with your God?

MICAH 6:8 (RSV)

[1569]
One may be humble out of pride.

MICHEL DE MONTAIGNE

[1570]
Unless you humble yourself before [God] in the dust, and confess before him your iniquities and sins, the gate of heaven, which is open only for sinners saved by grace, must be shut against you forever.

DWIGHT L. MOODY

[1571]
Someone asked one of the ancient Fathers how he might obtain true humility, and he answered: "By keeping your eyes off other people's faults, and fixing them on your own."

ALPHONSE RODRIGUEZ

[1572]
Do not be haughty, but associate with the lowly; never be conceited.

ROMANS 12:16 (RSV)

[1573]
Humility is strong—not bold; quiet—not speechless; sure—not arrogant.

ESTELLE SMITH

[1574]
Oh, beware! Do not seek to be something! Let me be nothing, and Christ be all in all.

JOHN WESLEY
(in letter to Francis Asbury)

[1575]
In Christian service the branches that bear the most fruit hang the lowest.

HUMOR

[1576]
A case might be made for the potentially superior humor of the religious person who has settled once and for all what things are of ultimate value, sacred and untouchable. For then nothing else in the world need be taken seriously.

GORDON W. ALLPORT

[1577]
Humor is an affirmation of dignity, a declaration of man's superiority to all that befalls him.

ROMAIN GARY

[1578]
I have never understood why it should be considered derogatory to the Creator to suppose that he has a sense of humor.

WILLIAM R. INGE

[1579]
Humor is the harmony of the heart.

DOUGLAS JERROLD

[1580]
Think of what would happen to us . . . if there were no humorists; life would be one long Congressional Record.

THOMAS L. MASSON

[1581]
Insofar as the sense of humor is a recognition of incongruity, it is more profound than any philosophy which seeks to devour incongruity in reason. But the sense of humor remains healthy only when it deals with immediate issues and faces the obvious and surface irrationalities. It must move toward faith or sink into despair when the ultimate issues are raised. That is why there is laughter in the vestibule of the temple, the echo of laughter in the temple itself, but only faith and prayer, and no laughter, in the holy of holies.
REINHOLD NIEBUHR

[1582]
Everything is funny as long as it is happening to somebody else.
WILL ROGERS

[1583]
The secret source of humor itself is not joy but sorrow. There is no humor in heaven.
MARK TWAIN
Pudd'nhead Wilson's New Calendar

[1584]
Joy shatters pomposity and pride; it bubbles, is never heavy-handed, and is another name for the best kind of humor.
KENNETH L. WILSON

[1585]
A witty sinner is the worst of fools.

HYPOCRISY

[1586]
Don't stay away from church because there are so many hypocrites. There's always room for one more.
ARTHUR R. ADAMS

[1587]
If the world despises a hypocrite, what must they think of him in heaven?
JOSH BILLINGS

[1588]
Of all villainy there is none more base than that of the hypocrite, who, at the moment he is most false, takes care to appear most virtuous.
CICERO

[1589]
Better be a sinner than a hypocrite.
DANISH PROVERB

[1590]
No man, for any considerable period, can wear one face to himself and another to the multitude, without finally getting bewildered as to which may be the true.
NATHANIEL HAWTHORNE

[1591]
Hypocrites do the devil's drudgery in Christ's livery.
MATTHEW HENRY

[1592]
It is no fault of Christianity if a hypocrite falls into sin.
JEROME

[1593]
The joy of the godless is but for a moment.
JOB 20:5 (RSV)

[1594]
No man is a hypocrite in his pleasures.
SAMUEL JOHNSON

[1595]
Solemn prayers, rapturous devotions, are but repeated hypocrisies unless the heart and mind be conformable to them.
WILLIAM LAW

[1596]
A hypocrite is a person who—but who isn't?

DON MARQUIS

[1597]
When you pray, you must not be like the hypocrites.

MATTHEW 6:5 (RSV)

[1598]
Don't hunt through the church for a hypocrite. Go home and look in the glass.

BILLY SUNDAY

[1599]
The clergyman who affects worldliness in order to "relate" to those outside the church is only the latest in the parade of ecclesiastical hypocrites.*

IDENTIFICATION

[1600]
The cross stands for one thing only for us—a complete and entire and absolute identification with the Lord Jesus Christ. . . . But our Lord has told us how love to him is to manifest itself. "Lovest thou Me? Feed My sheep"—identify yourself with My interests in other people, not, identify Me with your interests in other people.

OSWALD CHAMBERS

[1601]
The true profession of a man is to find his way to himself.

HERMANN HESSE

[1602]
You can't run with dogs without getting fleas.

SAM JONES

[1603]
I do not of myself know what I am; I do not know, as St. Paul said, what I shall be. But, said the same St. Paul, "I press on, for Jesus Christ has made me his own." That is the self identified, the self located; "Jesus Christ has made me his own."

ALEXANDER MILLER

IDENTITY

[1604]
Man's problem rises from the fact that he has not only lost the way, but he has lost the address.

NICOLAS BERDYAEV

[1605]
Here is Christian identity: I know my past, where I came from. I came from God. I know what went wrong. I tried to play God instead of being satisfied to be a real man. I know my future. My destiny is Christ. And I know the present. I can face myself now—my problems, my hang-ups, my assets, my faults—because I have turned myself over to God.

LEIGHTON FORD

[1606]
Modern youth alternates between abysmal hang-ups and fanatical commitments. Psychologists call their malady an "identity crisis." Its chief symptom is the cry: "Who am I?" To them I say, "Have a confrontation with yourself. Then have a confrontation with Jesus Christ. Join the 'Jesus Generation' and find your true identity in him."

BILLY GRAHAM

[1607]
Too many Christians get lost in the wilderness between Easter and Pentecost.

C. PHILIP HINERMAN

[1608]
After I received him, Jesus restored my identity, filled my longing, erased my guilt and shame, and washed me from my sins.

JUSTINE KOVAR

[1609]
At a World War II army boxing tournament in France, between two bouts, they led round the ring a soldier from hospital who had lost his memory. The hope was that from the army corps of spectators with whom he had served, one man at least might recognize him and so assist his cure. None did. As the man was led down from the ring he threw out his arms and cried, "Will nobody tell me who I am?"

GEORGE F. MACLEOD

[1610]
The complete loss of one's identity is, with all propriety of theological definitions, hell. In diminished form it is insanity.

JOHN COURTNEY MURRAY

IDOLATRY

[1611]
Thou shalt not make unto thee any graven image, or any likeness of any thing that is in heaven above, or that is in the earth beneath, or that is in the water under the earth.

EXODUS 20:4 (KJV)

[1612]
Ephraim is joined to idols, let him alone.

HOSEA 4:17 (RSV)

[1613]
We easily fall into idolatry, for we are inclined to it by nature; and coming to us by inheritance, it seems pleasant.

MARTIN LUTHER

[1614]
An idol may be defined as any person or thing that has usurped in the heart the place of pre-eminence that belongs to the Lord.

ARTHUR WALLIS

IMMORTALITY

[1615]
I cannot conceive that [God] could make such a species as the human merely to live and die on this earth. If I did not believe in a future state, I should believe in no God.

JOHN ADAMS

[1616]
Immortality . . . is always a faith, never a demonstration.

GAIUS GLENN ATKINS

[1617]
Immortality is the glorious discovery of Christianity.

WILLIAM ELLERY CHANNING

[1618]
The blazing evidence of immortality is our dissatisfaction with any other solution.

RALPH WALDO EMERSON

[1619]
Millions long for immortality who do not know what to do with themselves on a rainy Sunday afternoon.

SUSAN ERTZ

[1620]
I believe in the immortality of the soul, not in the sense in which I accept the demonstrable truths of science, but as a supreme act of faith in the reasonableness of God's work. . . . The materialistic supposition that the life of the soul ends with the life of the body is perhaps the most colossal instance of baseless assumption known to the history of philosophy.

JOHN FISKE

[1621]
Man is immortal till his work is done.

THOMAS FULLER

[1622]
Any theory of the hereafter which modifies or weakens any doctrine plainly stated elsewhere in Scripture is to be held suspect.

T. C. HAMMOND

[1623]
Our Creator would never have made such lovely days, and have given us the deep hearts to enjoy them, above and beyond all thought, unless we were meant to be immortal.

NATHANIEL HAWTHORNE

[1624]
The belief of immortality is impressed upon all men, and all men act under an impression of it, however they may talk, and though, perhaps, they may be scarcely sensible of it.

SAMUEL JOHNSON

[1625]
Surely God would not have created such a being as man, with an ability to grasp the infinite, to exist only for a day. No, no, man was made for immortality.

ABRAHAM LINCOLN

[1626]
The universe is a stairway leading nowhere unless man is immortal.

EDGAR YOUNG MULLINS

[1627]
This carpenter of Galilee, who walked up and down the roads of Palestine two thousand years ago, lived and thought in terms of the immortal. His thoughts were the thoughts of one who was immortal. His talk was the talk of an immortal. He preached and healed like one immortal. He forgave like an immortal. He prayed like an immortal. He died like an immortal and he rose from the dead like an immortal, and he lives today as an immortal.

VICTOR B. NELSON

[1628]
Life is the childhood of immortality.

DANIEL A. POLING

[1629]
Almost every person I have ever talked to in my world travels has believed in life after death.

ELEANOR ROOSEVELT

[1630]
Let us live as people who are prepared to die, and die as people who are prepared to live.

JAMES S. STEWART

IMPOSSIBILITY

[1631]
Whoso loves believes the impossible.

ELIZABETH BARRETT BROWNING
"Aurora Leigh"

[1632]
Nothing is impossible when you put your trust in God.

EUGENE CLARK

[1633]
Impossible is a word which I never say.
COLLIN D'HARLEVILLE

[1634]
To a brave heart nothing is impossible.
FRENCH PROVERB

[1635]
To believe a business is impossible is the way to make it so.
THOMAS FULLER

[1636]
When God is about to do something great, he starts with a difficulty. When he is about to do something truly magnificent, he starts with an impossibility.
ARMIN GESSWEIN

[1637]
The Christian life is not just difficult for man; it is impossible. . . . That is why only this uniquely "impossible" faith—with a God who is, with an incarnation that is earthy and historical, with a salvation that is at cross-purposes with human nature, with a resurrection that blasts apart the finality of death—is able to provide an alternative to the sifting, settling dust of death and through a new birth open the way to new life.
OS GUINNESS

[1638]
Impossibilities recede as experience advances.
ARTHUR HELPS

[1639]
A wise man never attempts impossibilities.
PHILIP MASSINGER

[1640]
You never test the resources of God until you attempt the impossible.
F. B. MEYER

[1641]
To a willing mind nothing is impossible.
JOHN RAY

[1642]
To the timid and hesitating everything is impossible because it seems so.
WALTER SCOTT

[1643]
It is certain because it is impossible.
TERTULLIAN

INDEPENDENCE

[1644]
Let every tub stand upon its own bottom.
JOHN BUNYAN
The Pilgrim's Progress

[1645]
The man of independent mind,/ He looks and laughs at a' that.
ROBERT BURNS
"A Man's a Man for a' That"

[1646]
I never thrust my nose into other men's porridge.
MIGUEL DE CERVANTES

[1647]
Christianity promises to make men free; it never promises to make them independent.
WILLIAM R. INGE

[1648]
There must always be a struggle between a father and son, while one aims at power and the other at independence.
SAMUEL JOHNSON

[1649]
Independence? That's middle-class
blasphemy. We are all dependent on
one another, every soul of us on earth.
GEORGE BERNARD SHAW
Pygmalion

[1650]
Independence is good, but isolation is
too high a price to pay for it.
BENJAMIN R. TUCKER

[1651]
Men are still born alone, they still die
alone, and they still come to Jesus
Christ alone; but interdependence has
supplanted independence as the rule
of life.*

INDIFFERENCE

[1652]
By attempting to demonstrate the affi-
nity of the Christian faith to what members of the intelligentsia had already
accepted on other grounds, the
churches succeeded only in demon-
strating that they had so little of consequence to contribute that the person
outside the church could justifiably remain indifferent.
WINTHROP S. HUDSON

[1653]
Man cannot regard his fellow men with
complete indifference. Either he loves
them or else he regards them with hate
and hostility, or else finally the two
conflicting tendencies appear to cancel
each other, as in "Hamletism."
OSKAR PFISTER

[1654]
The worst sin toward our fellow creatures is not to hate them, but to be
indifferent to them.
GEORGE BERNARD SHAW

[1655]
The man who hates God is not far from
the Kingdom. It is the spiritually indifferent man who has placed himself almost beyond hope.*

INDIVIDUALITY

[1656]
Jesus Christ never met an unimportant
person. That is why God sent his Son
to die for us. If someone dies for you,
you must be important.
M. C. CLEVELAND

[1657]
Nature seems to have made everything
with a view to individuality.
JOHANN WOLFGANG VON GOETHE

[1658]
I am only one, but I am one. I can't do
everything, but I can do something.
And what I can do, that I ought to do.
And what I ought to do, by the grace of
God, I will do.
EDWARD EVERETT HALE

[1659]
There are a lot of different kinds of
nuts in the Lord's fruitcake.
WALTER HEARN

[1660]
Every man must do two things alone:
he must do his own believing, and his
own dying.
MARTIN LUTHER

[1661]
The only ultimate reason why man as
man has individual significance is that
Christ died for him.
GEORGE F. MACLEOD

[1662]
The modern world began with Christ's
discovery of the individual.
JOHN MACMURRAY

[1663]
Risk! Risk anything! Care no more for the opinions of others, for those voices. Do the hardest thing on earth for you. Act for yourself. Face the truth.

KATHERINE MANSFIELD

[1664]
The Christian church is not a trumpet corps but an orchestra. We are not all supposed to sound alike because each of us is a different-shaped instrument.

KEITH MILLER

[1665]
The individual is the end of the universe.

MIGUEL DE UNAMUNO

INSIGHT

[1666]
Good insight not only prevents a person from being deceived by his own rationalizations, but forces him to face objectively the weakness and strength of his personal equipment.

GORDON W. ALLPORT

[1667]
A moment's insight is sometimes worth a life's experience.

OLIVER WENDELL HOLMES

[1668]
Where man sees but withered leaves God sees sweet flowers growing.

ALBERT LAIGHTON

[1669]
To see new relationships of cause and effect, to gain new understanding of the meaning which behavior symptoms have had, to understand the patterning of one's behavior—such learnings constitute insight.

CARL R. ROGERS

[1670]
One of the first things for which we have to pray is a true insight into our condition.

OLIVE WYON

INSPIRATION

[1671]
Look well into yourself; there is a source which will always spring up if you will search there.

MARCUS ANTONINUS

[1672]
Genius is one per cent inspiration and ninety-nine per cent perspiration.

THOMAS A. EDISON

[1673]
Inspiration is an influence of the Holy Spirit on the minds of certain select men, which rendered them the organs of God for the infallible communication of his mind and will.

CHARLES HODGE

[1674]
In the pure, strong hours of the morning, when the soul of the day is at its best, lean upon the window sill of God and look into his face, and get the orders for the day. Then go out into the day with the sense of a Hand upon your shoulder and not a chip.

E. STANLEY JONES

[1675]
Inspiration is the name of that all-comprehensive operation of the Holy Spirit whereby he has bestowed on the church a complete and infallible Scripture.

ABRAHAM KUYPER

[1676]
Inspiration . . . is the determining influence exercised by the Holy Spirit on the writers of the Old and New Testaments in order that they might proclaim and set down in an exact and authentic way the message as received from God.

RENÉ PACHE

[1677]
All scripture is inspired by God and profitable for teaching, for reproof, for correction, and for training in righteousness.

2 TIMOTHY 3:16 (RSV)

[1678]
The Greek term [for "inspiration" in 2 Timothy 3:16] has nothing to say of inspiration. What it says of Scripture is, not that it is "breathed into by God" or is the product of the Divine "inbreathing" into its human authors, but that it is breathed out by God, "God-breathed," the product of the creative breath of God.

BENJAMIN B. WARFIELD

INSTINCT

[1679]
Instinct comes ready-made, and gives decisive—and usually successful—responses to stereotyped and ancestral situations; but it does not adapt the organism to change, it does not enable man to meet flexibly the fluid complexities of modern life.

WILL DURANT

[1680]
The operation of instinct is more sure and simple than that of reason.

EDWARD GIBBON

[1681]
Nothing shows a man's character more than what he laughs at.

JOHANN WOLFGANG VON GOETHE

[1682]
Beasts obey the prescript of their natures, and live up to the height of that instinct that Providence hath given them.

RICHARD POWER

INTEGRITY

[1683]
Always vote for a principle, though you vote alone, and you may cherish the sweet reflection that your vote is never lost.

JOHN QUINCY ADAMS

[1684]
My worth to God in public is what I am in private.

OSWALD CHAMBERS

[1685]
He that is good at making excuses is seldom good at anything else.

BENJAMIN FRANKLIN

[1686]
America was built not by politicians running for something, but by statesmen standing for something.

VANCE HAVNER

[1687]
Many men have too much will power. It's won't power they lack.

JOHN A. SHEDD

[1688]
A happily married man is one whose personality is essentially unchanged whether or not his wife is with him.

[1689]
Live so that the preacher can tell the truth at your funeral.

[1690]
People may doubt what you say, but they will always believe what you do.

INVOLVEMENT

[1691]
We do not have a personal Gospel and a social gospel. There is one Gospel, and one Gospel only, and that Gospel is the Gospel of God—this indivisible message from God has its individual application and its social application. It has the power to redeem the individual and also the power to redeem social order.

JESSE M. BADER

[1692]
Go for souls and go for the worst.

WILLIAM BOOTH

[1693]
Behold the turtle: he makes progress only when he sticks his neck out.

JAMES BRYANT CONANT

[1694]
The church as a whole must be concerned with both evangelism and social action. It is not a case of either-or; it is both-and. Anything less is only a partial Gospel, not the whole counsel of God.

ROBERT D. DE HAAN

[1695]
No man is an Iland, intire of it selfe; every man is a peece of the Continent, a part of the maine; if a Clod bee washed away by the Sea, Europe is the lesse, as well as if a Promontorie were, as well as if a Mannor of thy friends or of thine owne were; any mans death diminishes me, because I am involved in Mankinde; And therefore never send to know for whom the bell tolls; It tolls for thee.

JOHN DONNE

[1696]
Commitment to Christ must involve commitment to our neighbor and our world, for Christ's sake. Evangelism must sound this note today with the conviction of the classic evangelical tradition.

LEIGHTON FORD

[1697]
Be to the world a sign that while we as Christians do not have all the answers, we do know and care about the questions.

BILLY GRAHAM

[1698]
We are called to be thermostats instead of thermometers, affecting our environment, not reflecting it.

CHARLES R. HEMBREE

[1699]
We venture into the conflicts of our day —not in fear, but in faith that Christ and his Word will be vindicated as we pursue the light he gives us. We are sensitive to that which is around us, really concerned with our brother— not building up insulating walls so we don't really know what is happening, but responsive, involved, and obedient to the Head.

ROBERT BOYD MUNGER

[1700]
In every real encounter with life and with our fellow men we meet the living Spirit, the Creator of life. God is not to be found by leaving the world. He is not found by staying in the world. But those who in their daily living respond with their whole being to the "Thou" by whom they find themselves addressed are caught up into union with the true life of the world.

J. H. OLDHAM

[1701]
A man should be cause-oriented rather than ego-oriented.

FRED SMITH

[1702]
I should give a false impression of my own convictions if I did not [state] that there is no hope of establishing a more Christian social order except through the labor and sacrifice of those in whom the Spirit of Christ is active.

WILLIAM TEMPLE

[1703]
We are increasingly convinced that we must involve ourselves in the great social problems men are facing.

Wheaton Declaration of 1966

[1704]
If our Lord Jesus Christ was not Barabbas, stirring up rebellion against Rome, neither was he Simeon Stylites, living out his life atop a pillar.*

[1705]
The waste of life lies in the love we have not given, the powers we have not used, the selfish prudence which will risk nothing and which, shirking pain, misses happiness as well.

JESUS CHRIST

[1706]
All my theology is reduced to this narrow compass—Christ Jesus came into the world to save sinners.

ARCHIBALD ALEXANDER

[1707]
I find the name of Jesus Christ written on the top of every page of modern history.

GEORGE BANCROFT

[1708]
Jesus Christ [is] the condescension of divinity and the exaltation of humanity.

PHILLIPS BROOKS

[1709]
Jesus Christ is not the best human being, he is a being who cannot be accounted for by the human race at all. He is not man becoming God, but God Incarnate, God coming into human flesh, coming into it from outside. His life is the highest and the holiest entering in at the lowliest door.

OSWALD CHAMBERS

[1710]
Christ did not love humanity. He never said that he loved humanity. He loved men.

G. K. CHESTERTON

[1711]
No man can give at one and the same time the impression that he himself is clever and that Jesus Christ is mighty to save.

JAMES DENNEY

[1712]
Caesar hoped to reform men by changing institutions and laws; Christ wished to remake institutions, and lessen laws, by changing men.

WILL DURANT

[1713]
A man may go to heaven without health, without riches, without honors, without learning, without friends; but he can never go there without Christ.
JOHN DYER

[1714]
In him, as in no other, God lived; he lived, as no other ever did, in God. Since Jesus lived, God has been another and nearer Being to man.
A. M. FAIRBAIRN

[1715]
Jesus blew everything apart, and when I saw where the pieces landed I knew I was free.
GEORGE FOSTER

[1716]
To believe *on* Christ, I say: not merely to believe *in* him, or to believe something *about* him, but to believe *on* him; and this means to entrust your soul to him and to trust in him for wisdom and strength and salvation.
WASHINGTON GLADDEN

[1717]
Christ is greater than our faith in him.
JAMES HASTINGS

[1718]
Jesus clothes the Beatitudes with his own life.
CARL F. H. HENRY

[1719]
Jesus made a world of "differents" for me.
EVERETT N. HUNT, JR.

[1720]
If every person in the world had adequate food, housing, income; if all men were equal; if every possible social evil and injustice were done away with, men would still need one thing: Christ!
J. W. HYDE

[1721]
A man who was merely a man and said the sort of things Jesus said wouldn't be a great moral teacher. He'd either be a lunatic—on a level with a man who says he's a poached egg—or else he'd be the devil of hell. You must make your choice. Either this man was, and is, the Son of God, or else a madman or something worse.
C. S. LEWIS

[1722]
You cannot receive Christ in bits and pieces.
DAVID MARTYN LLOYD-JONES

[1723]
Many ran after Christ, not for the miracles, but for the loaves.
JOHN LUBBOCK

[1724]
No one is "getting along pretty well" without Jesus Christ. We are saved by a Person, and only by a Person, and only by one Person.
WILLIAM F. McDOWELL

[1725]
Jesus marks the point in history at which it becomes possible for man to adopt consciously as his own purpose the purpose which is already inherent in his own nature.
JOHN MACMURRAY

[1726]
Jesus Christ is the therapist for humanity.
ROLLO MAY

[1727]
Jesus Christ himself is the Way. If we have gone astray from the Way, it is because we have strayed from Jesus Christ. We return to the Way by returning to Jesus Christ. It is not just doctrine about him, or knowledge of him, or experience of the blessings he can give: it is his own living Presence which is the Way.

WESLEY W. NELSON

[1728]
I call the attention of you young people to Jesus, the greatest leader, the most proficient teacher, the most absolutely right person the world has ever known. I tell you that the only way this world can be saved is by Jesus.

WILLIAM LYON PHELPS

[1729]
The calm assumption of Jesus that he is not a sinner will take hold of the wrists of any thoughtful mind and twist them till it must come to its knees.

WILLIAM A. QUAYLE

[1730]
[Jesus Christ], being the holiest among the mighty, the mightiest among the holy, lifted with his pierced hand empires off their hinges, and the stream of centuries out of its channel, and still governs the ages.

JEAN PAUL RICHTER

[1731]
Jesus Christ came into my prison cell last night, and every stone flashed like a ruby.

SAMUEL RUTHERFORD

[1732]
I have a great need for Christ; I have a great Christ for my need.

CHARLES H. SPURGEON

[1733]
The demeanor, bearing and attitude of Jesus united . . . to arouse in others expectation and assurance of obtaining aid. . . . He ministered to people as he found them, touched life at every point, became the torchbearer of the bewildered. Small wonder that people had confidence in the one who had such a masterful spirit.

KARL RUF STOLZ

[1734]
There is reward for the obedient disciple, there are power and authority for the faithful disciple, there is glory of achievement for the zealous disciple; but there is the whisper of his love, the joy of his presence, and the shining of his face, for those who love Jesus for himself alone.

SUSAN B. STRACHAN

[1735]
Christ came not to talk about a beautiful light, but to be that light—not to speculate about virtue, but to be virtue.

H. G. TAYLOR

[1736]
I should be ashamed to acknowledge him as my Savior if I could comprehend him—he would be no greater than I. Such is my sense of sin, and consciousness of my inability to save myself, that I feel I need a superhuman Savior.

NOAH WEBSTER

[1737]
I am convinced that the need of the hour is not so much to discuss the Bread, as to break it and pass it out to the hungry multitude.

WILLIAM PARKER WHITE

[1738]
I have one passion only: It is He! It is He!

NICHOLAS VON ZINZENDORF

[1739]
Consider Jesus of Nazareth, the most generous-hearted person who ever lived. He never refused a request for help. Great multitudes followed him, and he healed them all. He went out of his way to cross racial and religious barriers. He compassed the whole world in his love.*

Jesus Christ, Attitude toward

[1740]
To treat Christ as the means to an end other than himself is to degrade salvation into a technique of social control.
DWIGHT P. BAKER

[1741]
If Jesus Christ were to come today people would not crucify him. They would ask him to dinner and hear what he had to say, and make fun of it.
THOMAS CARLYLE

[1742]
In all the history of Christianity, whenever there has been a new emphasis upon Jesus, there has been a fresh outburst of vitality and virility.
E. STANLEY JONES

[1743]
There are people today who, though they disdain the church, Christianity and religion, have limitless admiration for Jesus Christ, and are ready to listen to what he said and to what is said about him by persons they have learned to respect.
JOHN A. MACKAY

Jesus Christ, Birth of

[1744]
The shepherds did not go to Bethlehem seeking the birth of a great man, or a famous teacher, or a national hero. They were promised a Savior.
HANDEL H. BROWN

[1745]
It seemed so strange that on such slender thread as the feeble throb of an infant life the salvation of the world should hang—and no special care watch over its safety, no better shelter be provided it than a "stable," no other cradle than a manger! And it is still true. On what slender thread has the continued life of the church often seemed to hang! On what feeble throbbing that of every child of God—with no visible outward means to ward off danger, no home of comfort, no rest of ease.
ALFRED EDERSHEIM

[1746]
Theoretically a man can believe in the resurrection . . . without believing in the virgin birth, yet such a halfway conviction is not likely to endure. The virgin birth is an integral part of the New Testament witness about Christ, and that witness is strongest when it is taken as it stands.
J. GRESHAM MACHEN

[1747]
Jesus was born twice. The birth at Bethlehem was a birth into a life of weakness. The second time he was born from the grave—"the first-born from the dead"—into the glory of heaven and the throne of God.
ANDREW MURRAY

[1748]
The whole question of the virgin birth of Jesus need not afflict the average man. If Jesus is unique, unlike any other person, it is not illogical to believe that his birth was unique.
WILLIAM LYON PHELPS

[1749]
Christ is the great central fact in the world's history. To him everything looks forward or backward. All the lines of history converge upon him. All the great purposes of God culminate in him. The greatest and most momentous fact which the history of the world records is the fact of his birth.

CHARLES H. SPURGEON

Jesus Christ, Blood of

[1750]
In our scientific age there are thousands living who owe their lives to blood transfusions. By analogy, it can be reverently said that, in a mystical sense, the Son of God is the great universal Donor, giving new life to the sinner who trusts his shed blood for cleansing.

L. NELSON BELL

[1751]
In Christ Jesus you who once were far off have been brought near in the blood of Christ.

EPHESIANS 2:13 (RSV)

[1752]
A blood-bought redemption has always been God's firm plan. We cannot explain why this was in God's mind. We can only point to the record that it is so. He never changed the pattern.

PAUL P. FRYHLING

[1753]
I'm going to heaven and I believe I'm going by the blood of Christ. That's not popular preaching, but I'll tell you it's all the way through the Bible and I may be the last fellow on earth who preaches it, but I'm going to preach it because it's the only way we're going to get there.

BILLY GRAHAM

[1754]
Without the shedding of blood there is no forgiveness of sins.

HEBREWS 9:22 (RSV)

[1755]
The holy walk, the devoted life of our Lord Jesus Christ could not avail to put away sin. It was life poured out in death that saved. Apart from his death, his life could only bring out in bold relief our exceeding sinfulness. But his blood shed for us was life given up, poured out in death that we might live eternally.

H. A. IRONSIDE

[1756]
The work of the Lord Jesus . . . is represented by "the blood" shed for our justification through "the remission of sins." The blood deals with what we have done, whereas the cross deals with what we are. The blood disposes of our sins, while the cross strikes at the root of our capacity for sin.

WATCHMAN NEE

[1757]
The blood is the poured-out life of the Son of God, given as the price, the atonement, the substitute, for the forfeited life of the believer in Jesus Christ. Any sinner who receives Christ as God's gift is cleansed from all sin by his blood.

MARCUS RAINSFORD

Jesus Christ, Deity of

[1758]
As all the sweetness that is in the flowers of the field and in the garden is brought by the bees into the hive, and is there embodied in one hive; so all the attributes of God and the sweetness of them are hived in Christ, in whom all the fulness of the Godhead dwells bodily.

WILLIAM BRIDGE

[1759]
Jesus Christ alone stands at the absolute center of humanity, the one completed harmonious man. He is the absolute and perfect truth, the highest that humanity can reach; at once its perfect image and supreme Lord.

CHARLES W. FRENCH

[1760]
The most profound tendencies of Luther's thought [show that] in the human words and works of Jesus, God is revealed. . . . He had from the beginning thought of the two natures of Christ as so united that the man Jesus was, in all his words and works, the expression and organ of his divine nature. He knew no God except the One revealed in the man Jesus.

REINHOLD SEEBERG

[1761]
[Jesus] does not have to rely on the authority of the past or on other teachers. It is in himself. He acts with the manifest authority of God; he is the creative Word of God. In him we are to see what is the purpose of God in making the world and in making us.

WILLIAM TEMPLE

[1762]
They should have known that [Christ] was God. His patience should have proved that to them.

TERTULLIAN

Jesus Christ, Description of

[1763]
When I nominated Jesus as my supreme ecologist, years of inner pollution became instantly biodegradable.

DONALD R. BROWN

[1764]
I was going to waste until Jesus recycled me.

RICHELLE CROSS

[1765]
Jesus is the rosetta stone in the language of love.

NORA JANE ISON

[1766]
My life's horizontal started focusing when Jesus Christ introduced me to vertical fine-tuning.

NANCY WHITE KELLY

[1767]
I was a sour note on Adam's reed when the Master Musician reorchestrated my life and gave the angels something to sing about.

NANCY THOMAS

Jesus Christ, Example of

[1768]
Jesus alone is able to offer himself as the sufficient illustration of his own doctrine.

HERBERT HENSLEY HENSON

[1769]
The Lord Jesus Christ is the perfect example for all his followers, for he said, "I am among you as one who serves" (Luke 22:27).

PHILIP E. HOWARD, JR.

[1770]
Anyone who says he is a Christian should live as Christ did.

1 JOHN 2:6
(*The Living Bible*)

[1771]
Jesus is the true prototype of the human race.

CHRISTOPH ERNST LUTHARDT

Jesus Christ, Indwelling of

[1772]
Jesus Christ bought the controlling interest in my family business of Self & Co. He has brought stability to the firm. He has a gift for dealing with personnel problems and takes an optimistic view of future projects.

ALEX BEALE

[1773]
Christ always lives where there is room for him. If there is room in your heart for Christ, he lives there; if there is room in a law office for Christ, he lives there; if there is room on a locomotive engine, he will be there; if there is room in a baggage car, he will be there.

SAM JONES

[1774]
We get no deeper into Christ than we allow him to get into us.

JOHN HENRY JOWETT

Jesus Christ, Lordship of

[1775]
Jesus Christ will be Lord of all or he will not be Lord at all.

AUGUSTINE OF HIPPO

[1776]
I came to Christ as a country boy. I did not understand all about the plan of salvation. One does not have to understand it; one has only to stand on it. I do not understand all about electricity, but I do not intend to sit around in the dark until I do! One thing I did understand even as a lad: I understood that I was under new management. I belonged to Christ and he was Lord.

VANCE HAVNER

[1777]
The core of the Christian revelation is that Jesus Christ is the sole legitimate Lord of all human lives.

HENDRIK KRAEMER

[1778]
Christ attributes all he does and says to the Father, and this makes God's name no longer terrible to us, but comforting.

MARTIN LUTHER

[1779]
You cannot have Christian principles without Christ.

DOROTHY L. SAYERS

Jesus Christ, Love of

[1780]
The people who love Christ are set apart, like the soft, glorious Pleiades that keep together in the sky.

STORM JAMESON

[1781]
When men are animated by the love of Christ they feel united, and the needs, sufferings and joys of others are felt as their own.

POPE JOHN XXIII

[1782]
Do you love the Son? Is he the captain of ambition and desire? Are you receiving daily into your spirit those marvelous resources and powers which are available from Christ? Are you living an everlasting life? Are you happy? Are you calm? When you can say Yes to these questions you have come to the point where your partnership with Christ begins.

The late Rev. ALISTAIR MACLEAN
of Daviot, Invernesshire, Scotland

[1783]
A man who loves his wife will love her letters and her photographs because they speak to him of her. So if we love the Lord Jesus we shall love the Bible because it speaks to us of him.
JOHN R. W. SCOTT

[1784]
God and I have this in common—we both love his Son, Jesus Christ.
LANCE ZAVITZ

Jesus Christ, Relationship to

[1785]
The big end of the branch is always toward the vine. The fruit comes on the little end. When we daily direct the big end of our lives toward Christ and his Word, an amazing thing takes place. The fruit comes on the little end. It will come in a way that will let us know that it was because of him and in spite of us.
LANE ADAMS

[1786]
To be a Christian means to have a vital, personal relationship with Jesus Christ, and until that is established all other concerns are secondary.
L. NELSON BELL

[1787]
What we need is not a concession to modern man, but a concentration on Jesus Christ.
GERHARD BERGMANN

[1788]
Jesus Christ is no crutch; he is the ground to walk on.
LEIGHTON FORD

[1789]
Christ came not to be ministered to, but to minister; and our first duty, therefore, is to be ministered to by him. First faith, then works.
P. T. FORSYTH

[1790]
God will answer all our questions in one way and one way only, namely, by showing us more of his Son.
WATCHMAN NEE

[1791]
Without Christ I was like a fish out of water. With Christ I am in the ocean of love.
SADHU SUNDAR SINGH

[1792]
You are redeemed from the penalty of your sin, and you are on your way to heaven, in order that Jesus Christ might come in the power of his resurrection to occupy your redeemed humanity upon earth today, and that you might present your body a living sacrifice, totally, wholly available to him. It is your reasonable service, with no margin or latitude for self-pleasing. When you have reached that place, you don't have to pray for blessing any more; it is inevitable.
IAN THOMAS

[1793]
Soul winners are not soul winners because of what they know, but because of Whom they know, and how well they know him, and how much they long for others to know him.
DAWSON TROTMAN

Jesus Christ, as Savior

[1794]
The question remains, "How can God be just—that is, true to himself in nature and true to himself in holiness, and yet justify the sinner?" The only solution was for an innocent party to volunteer to die physically and spiritually as a substitution before God. There was only one possibility. God's own Son was the only personality in the universe who had the capacity to bear in his own body the sins of the world.

BILLY GRAHAM

[1795]
At the supreme moment of his dying Jesus so identified himself with men and the depths of their predicament and agony that no man can now sink so low that God has not gone lower.

OS GUINNESS

[1796]
Jesus did not hang on the cross on his own account, but as our Representative. It was our death. . . . By his death he paid the wages of sin for us. . . . There is no longer any cause for anxiety except in the case of those who refuse to acknowledge their sinfulness, and turn their backs on the Man of Sorrows on the cross. *We* are delivered. . . . Whatever confusion and desolation may yet come upon our world, its future is secure.

F. W. KRUMMACHER

[1797]
Peace comes only when a man recognizes that all his striving to be right with God, all his feverish endeavor to keep the law before he can be saved, is unnecessary, and that the Lord Jesus has wiped out the handwriting that was against him by dying instead of him on the cross.

J. GRESHAM MACHEN

[1798]
I think I may have to go through the agony of hearing all my sins recited in the presence of God. But I believe it will be like this—Jesus will come over and lay his hand across my shoulders and say to God, "Yes, all these things are true, but I'm here to cover up for Peter. He is sorry for all his sins, and by a transaction made between us, I am now solely responsible for them."

PETER MARSHALL

[1799]
When I was saved, I accepted death as my only deliverance. Christ died in my place. I was indeed a dead man but for Christ. When I accepted Christ's death for my sin, I could not avoid accepting my own death to sin. I am committed to the cross. My only logical standing is one of death. I have been "born crucified."

L. E. MAXWELL

[1800]
I stand before my neighbors on my character; but in heaven I have no standing myself at all. I stand there in the character of my Savior.

PAUL RADER

[1801]
The death of Christ differs from the death of prophets, patriots and martyrs in many respects. It was foretold in prophecy; it was for the propitiation of sin; it was accompanied by manifestation; it was followed by supernatural victory over death and resurrection. But the real point of difference is in the Person who died. In him dwelt all the fulness of the Godhead bodily. The Word was made flesh and crucified for us.

SAMUEL M. ZWEMER

Jesus Christ, as Son of God

[1802]
Who can deny that Jesus of Nazareth, the incarnate Son of the Most High God, is the eternal glory of the Jewish race?

BENJAMIN DISRAELI

[1803]
We can form no idea of the natural distance between God and man, but the infinite vacuum is filled up by the Messiah.

CHRISTMAS EVANS

[1804]
None but the God we see in Jesus Christ will meet men's case.

ARTHUR JOHN GOSSIP

[1805]
Others had applied the name "Father" to God, but the point is that when Jesus called God "Father" he knew him as the Father.

BRUCE M. METZGER

[1806]
After six years given to the impartial investigation of Christianity as to its truth or falsity, I have come to the deliberate conclusion that Jesus Christ is the Messiah of the Jews, the Savior of the world, and my personal Savior.

LEW WALLACE

[1807]
I believe Jesus Christ to be the Son of God. The miracles which he wrought establish in my mind, his personal authority, and render it proper for me to believe whatever he asserts. I believe, therefore, all his declarations, as well when he declares himself to be the Son of God, as when he declares any other proposition. And I believe there is no other way of salvation than through the merits of his atonement.

DANIEL WEBSTER

JOY

[1808]
Those who bring sunshine to the lives of others cannot keep it from themselves.

JAMES M. BARRIE

[1809]
The joy that Jesus gives is the result of our disposition being at one with his own disposition.

OSWALD CHAMBERS

[1810]
When I think of God, my heart is so full of joy that the notes leap and dance as they leave my pen; and since God has given me a cheerful heart, I serve him with a cheerful spirit.

FRANZ JOSEPH HAYDN

[1811]
Claudel, the French poet, said after listening to Beethoven's Fifth Symphony that he knew now that at the heart of the universe there is joy.

GERALD KENNEDY

[1812]
Joy is a necessity, not a luxury.

HAROLD F. LEESTMA

[1813]
Joy is the serious business of heaven.

C. S. LEWIS

[1814]
Joy seems to be distilled from a strange mixture of challenge, risk and hope.

KEITH MILLER

[1815]
Jesus Christ can put joy into the joyless work of the twentieth century.

BERNARD RAMM

[1816]
The surest mark of a Christian is not faith, or even love, but joy.

SAMUEL M. SHOEMAKER

[1817]
Joy is the standard that flies on the bat-
tlements of the heart when the King is
in residence.

R. LEONARD SMALL

[1818]
To miss the joy is to miss all.

ROBERT LOUIS STEVENSON

[1819]
If there is joy in the world, surely the
man of pure heart possesses it.

THOMAS À KEMPIS

[1820]
Joy is not gush; joy is not jolliness. Joy
is perfect acquiescence in God's will
because the soul delights itself in God
himself.

H. W. WEBB-PEPLOE

[1821]
Joy is not happiness so much as gladness; it is the ecstasy of eternity in a
soul that has made peace with God and
is ready to do his will.*

JUDGMENT

[1822]
The coming again of Christ will be a
vindication of the moral order of the
universe and a revelation of God's sovereign purpose in history.

WILLIAM FITCH

[1823]
I believe the troubles that have come
upon us are in part a judgment of God
on us for our sins; and that unless we
repent and turn to God we are finished
as a free democratic society.

BILLY GRAHAM

[1824]
He who has spoken in love will soon be
obliged to speak in judgment.

KAY GUDNASON

[1825]
There is no fear of judgment for the
man who judges himself according to
the Word of God.

HOWARD G. HENDRICKS

[1826]
The promises of sin are fair but the
payoff is cruel.

ALBERT NIELSEN

[1827]
Your riches won't help you on Judgment Day; only righteousness counts
then.

PROVERBS 11:4
(The Living Bible)

[1828]
A man's judgment of another depends
more on the one judging and on his
passions than on the one being judged
and his conduct.

PAUL TOURNIER

JUSTICE

[1829]
Let justice roll down like waters, and
righteousness like an everflowing
stream.

AMOS 5:24 (RSV)

[1830]
The imperfection of justice in this life
is the strongest proof that in the next
world justice and vengeance will be
fulfilled to the utmost.

DAVID AUGSBURGER

[1831]
Justice travels with a leaden heel but
strikes with an iron hand.

JEREMIAH S. BLACK

[1832]
Justice is the great standing policy of
civil society.

EDMUND BURKE

[1833]
The fundamentals of justice are that no one shall suffer wrong, and that the public good be served.

CICERO

[1834]
Justice is simply the condition of free men living harmoniously in society.

EVERETT MCKINLEY DIRKSEN

[1835]
History shows that Christ on the cross has been more potent than anything else in arousing a compassion for suffering and indignation at injustice.

F. J. FOAKES-JACKSON

[1836]
We may think we want justice. What we want is mercy. We need it.

B. C. FORBES

[1837]
Justice is the sum of all moral duty.

WILLIAM GODWIN

[1838]
Indeed, I tremble for my country when I reflect that God is just.

THOMAS JEFFERSON

[1839]
Delay of justice is injustice.

WALTER SAVAGE LANDOR

[1840]
[God] has told you what he wants, and this is all it is: to be fair and just and merciful, and to walk humbly with your God.

MICAH 6:8
(The Living Bible)

[1841]
Where justice reigns, 'tis freedom to obey.

JAMES MONTGOMERY

[1842]
The Christian demand for justice does not come from Karl Marx. It comes from Jesus Christ and the Hebrew prophets.

G. BROMLEY OXNAM

[1843]
The message of the Gospel is that in some true sense Christ died, not for general justice, but for me.

WILLISTON WALKER

KINDNESS

[1844]
It is difficult to tell how much men's minds are conciliated by a kind manner and gentle speech.

CICERO

[1845]
Kindness is like a garden of blessing, and love endures forever.

ECCLESIASTICUS 40:17
(Goodspeed)

[1846]
Kindness has converted more sinners than zeal, eloquence or learning.

FREDERICK W. FABER

[1847]
I shall pass through this world but once. If, therefore, there be any kindness I can show, or any good thing I can do, let me do it now; let me not defer it or neglect it, for I shall not pass this way again.

ÉTIENNE DE GRELLET (attr.)

[1848]
Wise sayings often fall on barren ground; but a kind word is never thrown away.

ARTHUR HELPS

[1849]
One kind word can warm three winter
months.

JAPANESE PROVERB

[1850]
Kindness is the rule for everything she
says.

PROVERBS 31:26
(*The Living Bible*)

[1851]
It is a kindness to refuse gently what
you intend to deny.

PUBLILIUS SYRUS

[1852]
Be kind. Remember everyone you
meet is fighting a hard battle.

T. H. THOMPSON

[1853]
Kind words don't wear out the tongue.

KNOWLEDGE

[1854]
Our knowledge, compared with Yours,
is ignorance.

AUGUSTINE OF HIPPO

[1855]
A religion that is jealous of the variety
of learning, discourse, opinions, and
sects, as misdoubting it may shake the
foundations, or that cherisheth devotion upon simplicity and ignorance, as
ascribing ordinary effects to the immediate working of God, is adverse to
knowledge.

FRANCIS BACON

[1856]
There is knowledge and knowledge:
knowledge that resteth in the bare
speculation of things, and knowledge
that is accompanied with the grace of
faith and love, which puts a man upon
doing even the will of God from the
heart.

JOHN BUNYAN

[1857]
Grace is given of God, but knowledge
is bought in the market.

ARTHUR HUGH CLOUGH

[1858]
To be conscious that you are ignorant
is a great step to knowledge.

BENJAMIN DISRAELI

[1859]
Knowledge we ask not—knowledge
Thou hast lent,/ But Lord, the will—
there lies our bitter need.

JOHN DRINKWATER
"A Prayer"

[1860]
Where is the wisdom we have lost in
knowledge?/ Where is the knowledge
we have lost in information?

T. S. ELIOT
The Rock

[1861]
It is not the tree of knowledge that destroys—it is disobedience that proves
destructive.

Epistle to Diognetus

[1862]
Knowledge is a process of piling up
facts; wisdom lies in their simplifica-
tion.

MARTIN H. FISCHER

[1863]
He that boasts of his own knowledge
proclaims his own ignorance.

GERMAN PROVERB

[1864]
Knowledge is folly except grace guide
it.
GEORGE HERBERT

[1865]
It isn't how much you know; it's what
you do with what you do know.
JOHN HUNTER

[1866]
Only a great Christian can be a great
Biblical scholar.
KENNETH S. LATOURETTE

[1867]
A child in our Sunday Schools knows
more about God than all you can find
in all the analects of Confucius.
CHARLES OGILVIE

[1868]
Things human must be known to be
loved; things divine must be loved to
be known.
BLAISE PASCAL

[1869]
The fear of the Lord is the beginning of
knowledge.
PROVERBS 1:7 (RSV)

[1870]
A wise man is mightier than a strong
man, and a man of knowledge than he
who has strength.
PROVERBS 24:5 (RSV)

[1871]
We know lots of things we didn't use to
know but we don't know any way to
prevent 'em happening.
WILL ROGERS

[1872]
Knowledge is strong, but love is sweet.
CHRISTINA GEORGINA ROSSETTI

[1873]
There is nothing so practical as a cor-
rect theory.
FRED SMITH

[1874]
To know God is at once the easiest and
the most difficult thing in the world. It
is easy because the knowledge is not
won by hard mental toil, but is something freely given. As sunlight falls free
on the open field, so the knowledge of
the holy God is a free gift to men who
are open to receive it. But this knowledge is difficult because there are conditions to be met and the obstinate nature of fallen man does not take kindly
to them.
A. W. TOZER

LAUGHTER

[1875]
Man is distinguished from all other
creatures by the faculty of laughter.
JOSEPH ADDISON

[1876]
Keep company with the more cheerful
sort of the godly; there is no mirth like
the mirth of believers.
RICHARD BAXTER

[1877]
Millionaires seldom laugh.
ANDREW CARNEGIE

[1878]
Men don't go to heaven laughing.
DUTCH PROVERB

[1879]
For as the crackling of thorns under a
pot, so is the laughter of the fools; this
also is vanity.
ECCLESIASTES 7:6 (RSV)

[1880]
No man ever distinguished himself
who could not bear to be laughed at.
MARIA EDGEWORTH

[1881]
One shows his character by what he laughs at.
GERMAN PROVERB

[1882]
If I did not laugh, I should die.
ABRAHAM LINCOLN

[1883]
Everyone likes a man who can enjoy a laugh at his own expense.
JOHN LUBBOCK

[1884]
Laughter brightens the eye, increases the perspiration, expands the chest, forces the poisoned air from the least-used cells, and tends to restore that exquisite poise or balance which we call health.
O. S. MARDEN

[1885]
God is the creator of laughter that is good.
PHILO

[1886]
No one is sadder than the man who laughs too much.
JEAN PAUL RICHTER

[1887]
One who is always laughing is a fool, and one who never laughs a knave.
SPANISH PROVERB

[1888]
The greatest saints are the merriest-hearted people.
MARY WEBB

LAW

[1889]
Knowledge of grace presupposes the law. Without the law there is no experience of the grace of God. Without the Sermon on the Mount there would be no Epistle to the Romans.
EMIL BRUNNER

[1890]
Moral law is more than a test, it is for man's own good. Every law that God has given has been for man's benefit. If man breaks it, he is not only rebelling against God, he is hurting himself. . . . The law is a mirror that shows us that we are lawbreakers and reflects our need for Christ.
BILLY GRAHAM

[1891]
Statutory law is based upon common law; common law is based upon moral law; and moral law is based upon divine law.
JEWISH CHAPLAIN, World War II

[1892]
Moses gave us only the Law with its rigid demands and merciless justice, while Jesus Christ brought us loving forgiveness as well.
JOHN 1:17
(The Living Bible)

[1893]
Man's inability to keep the law of God inevitably brings him under the curse of God, i.e., God's judgment upon sin. There is, therefore, no way for man to be saved by the law, for only through perfect obedience could that occur. It is through faith, and faith alone, that man is justified before God and attains unto life. The believer is redeemed from the curse of the law since Christ, in his crucifixion, became a curse for us.

HAROLD LINDSELL

[1894]
The little word "law" you must not understand in its human or everyday sense as applying to things you do or do not do. By human standards it is enough just to observe the law even though your heart may not be in it. Paul says that the law is spiritual. Since it is spiritual, no man keeps it, unless everything he does comes from the bottom of his heart. But nobody has a heart like that. Only the Holy Spirit can give a man such a heart. Thus it comes about that faith alone justifies a man and fulfils the law, for faith brings the Holy Spirit through the merits of Christ.

MARTIN LUTHER

[1895]
A low view of law leads to legalism in religion; a high view makes man a seeker after grace.

J. GRESHAM MACHEN

[1896]
The laws are good when used as God intended.

1 TIMOTHY 1:8
(The Living Bible)

[1897]
Before I can preach love and grace, I must preach sin, law and judgment.

JOHN WESLEY

[1898]
The role which law fulfils in relation to the Gospel has been traditionally described in a scheme of three uses: (1) It serves to preserve the order of creation where there is no saving faith. (2) By reason of fallen man's impotence to fulfil it, it drives man to realize the need for grace, and summons him to Christ the only Savior. (3) For believers it is a standard of obedience to God, by the guidance of which the fruits of the Spirit may be brought forth.

W. A. WHITEHOUSE

LEADERSHIP

[1899]
If the bugle gives an indistinct sound, who will get ready for battle?

1 CORINTHIANS 14:8 (RSV)

[1900]
An institution is the lengthened shadow of one man.

RALPH WALDO EMERSON

[1901]
Leadership is achieved by ability, alertness, experience; by willingness to accept responsibility; by a knack for getting along with people; by an open mind and a head that stays clear under stress.

E. F. GIRARD

[1902]
A good leader takes a little more than his share of blame; a little less than his share of credit.

ARNOLD H. GLASSGOW

[1903]
If the blind lead the blind, both shall
fall into the ditch.

MATTHEW 15:14 (KJV)

[1904]
I would rather set ten men to work than
do the work of ten men.

DWIGHT L. MOODY

[1905]
Whether Christianity can be adequate
to the moral leadership of our civilization today and tomorrow depends on
whether it can recapture that "first fine,
careless rapture" of its earliest days.

KIRBY PAGE

[1906]
O for a living man to lead!/ That will
not babble when we bleed;/ . . . And
one that in a nation's night/ Hath solitary certitude of light.

STEPHEN PHILLIPS
"A Man"

[1907]
If human progress had been merely a
matter of leadership we should be in
Utopia today.

THOMAS B. REED

[1908]
For every man who has the ability to
lead there are a thousand waiting to be
led.

ROY L. SMITH

[1909]
Reason and calm judgment are the
qualities of a leader.

TACITUS

[1910]
The would-be leader of men who
affirms and proclaims that he pays no
heed to the things of the Spirit is not
worthy to lead them.

MIGUEL DE UNAMUNO

[1911]
If you wish to be a leader you will be
frustrated, for very few people wish to
be led. If you aim to be a servant you
will never be frustrated.

FRANK F. WARREN

[1912]
Good management is showing average
people how to do the work of superior
people.

LIBERTY

[1913]
Liberty is not a means to a higher political end. It is itself the highest political
end.

LORD ACTON

[1914]
Among a people generally corrupt, liberty cannot long exist.

EDMUND BURKE

[1915]
O Liberty, what things are done in thy
name!

THOMAS CARLYLE

[1916]
Where the Spirit of the Lord is, there is
liberty.

2 CORINTHIANS 3:17 (RSV)

[1917]
The condition upon which God hath
given liberty to man is eternal vigi-
lance.

JOHN PHILPOT CURRAN

[1918]
When liberty becomes license, dicta-
torship is near.

WILL DURANT

[1919]
Christ has made us free. Now make sure that you stay free and don't get all tied up again in the chains of slavery.
GALATIANS 5:1
(*The Living Bible*)

[1920]
Liberty is the power that we have over ourselves.
HUGO GROTIUS

[1921]
The spirit of liberty is the spirit of him who, near two thousand years ago, taught mankind that lesson it has never learned, but has never quite forgotten: that there is a kingdom where the least shall be heard and considered side by side with the greatest.
LEARNED HAND

[1922]
The love of liberty is the love of others; the love of power is the love of ourselves.
WILLIAM HAZLITT

[1923]
Is life so dear, or peace so sweet, as to be purchased at the price of chains and slavery? Forbid it, Almighty God! I know not what course others may take, but as for me, give me liberty, or give me death!
PATRICK HENRY

[1924]
The God who gave us life gave us liberty at the same time.
THOMAS JEFFERSON

[1925]
The world has never had a good definition of the word liberty.
ABRAHAM LINCOLN

[1926]
The liberties we talk about defending today were established by men who took their conception of man from the great religious tradition of Western civilization, and the liberties we inherit can almost certainly not survive the abandonment of that tradition.
WALTER LIPPMANN

[1927]
Liberty without obedience is confusion, and obedience without liberty is slavery.
WILLIAM PENN

[1928]
To obey God is perfect liberty.
SENECA

[1929]
God grants liberty only to those who love it.
DANIEL WEBSTER

[1930]
Liberty is the only thing you cannot have unless you are willing to give it to others.
WILLIAM ALLEN WHITE

[1931]
The history of liberty is a history of resistance.
WOODROW WILSON

LIFE

[1932]
Life is a long lesson in humility.
JAMES M. BARRIE
The Little Minister

[1933]
All real life is meeting.
MARTIN BUBER

[1934]
The quality of life is more important than life itself.

ALEXIS CARREL

[1935]
One person who has mastered life is better than a thousand persons who have mastered only the contents of books, but no one can get anything out of life without God.

MEISTER ECKHART

[1936]
I have measured out my life with coffee spoons.

T. S. ELIOT
"The Love Song
of J. Alfred Prufrock"

[1937]
Being a Christian is a way of life, not a method or a technique, but a life-style all its own.

FEMI ILESANMI

[1938]
The glory of God is man fully alive.

IRENAEUS

[1939]
What is your life? For you are a mist that appears for a little time and then vanishes.

JAMES 4:14 (RSV)

[1940]
Life can only be understood backward; it must be lived forward.

SØREN KIERKEGAARD

[1941]
Live your own life, and you will die your own death.

LATIN PROVERB

[1942]
A man's life does not consist in the abundance of his possessions.

LUKE 12:15 (RSV)

[1943]
If he [God] has work for me to do I cannot die.

HENRY MARTYN

[1944]
Life's a voyage that's homeward bound.

HERMAN MELVILLE (attr.)

[1945]
Fear not that your life shall come to an end, but rather that it shall never have a beginning.

JOHN HENRY NEWMAN

[1946]
Thus has the Lord been teaching me to live upon himself: not upon anything received from him but upon the Life itself.

ISAAC PENNINGTON

[1947]
Religion can offer a man a burial service, but Christ offers every man new, abundant and everlasting life.

WILMA REED

[1948]
It matters not how long you live, but how well.

PUBLILIUS SYRUS

[1949]
God hath given to man a short time here upon earth, and yet upon this short time eternity depends.

JEREMY TAYLOR

LIGHT

[1950]
I send you to open their eyes, that they may turn from darkness to light and from the power of Satan to God.

ACTS 26:17–18 (RSV)

[1951]
The light that shines from the Crucified is a light . . . which both illumi-
nates the obscurity of being and overcomes the darkness of nonbeing.
NICOLAS BERDYAEV

[1952]
To the church, Pentecost brought
light, power, joy. There came to each
illumination of mind, assurance of
heart, intensity of love, fulness of
power, exuberance of joy. No one
needed to ask if they had received the
Holy Ghost. Fire is self-evident. So is
power!
SAMUEL CHADWICK

[1953]
This is the judgment, that the light has
come into the world, and men loved
darkness rather than light, because
their deeds were evil.
JOHN 3:19 (RSV)

[1954]
Be of good comfort, Master Ridley,
and play the man. We shall this day
light such a candle by God's grace in
England, as I trust shall never be put
out.
HUGH LATIMER
(at the stake)

[1955]
You are the light of the world, but the
switch must be turned on.
AUSTIN ALEXANDER LEWIS

[1956]
In darkness there is no choice. It is
light that enables us to see the differences between things; and it is Christ
who gives us light.
C. T. WHITMELL

[1957]
When Jesus healed the man blind from
birth, he let him grope his way, still
blind, to wash in the pool—and *then* the
light broke. We don't need to know
what we're groping toward—or why. It
is enough that we have Christ's direction. The light will break in God's own
time.

LOGIC

[1958]
The healthy understanding, we should
say, is not the logical or argumentative,
but the intuitive.
THOMAS CARLYLE

[1959]
"Contrariwise," continued Tweed-
ledee, "if it was so, it might be; and if
it were so, it would be: but as it isn't, it
ain't. That's logic."
LEWIS CARROLL
Through the Looking-Glass

[1960]
We must beware of needless innova-
tions, especially when guided by logic.
WINSTON S. CHURCHILL

[1961]
Logical reason enables a man to adapt
himself to circumstances, instead of
seeking blindly to satisfy his impulses.
LINDSAY DEWAR

[1962]
Men are apt to mistake the strength of
their feeling for the strength of their
argument. The heated mind resents
the chill touch and relentless scrutiny
of logic.
WILLIAM E. GLADSTONE

LONELINESS

[1963]
Columbus discovered no isle or key so lonely as himself.
RALPH WALDO EMERSON

[1964]
The essential loneliness is an escape from an inescapable God.
WALTER FARRELL

[1965]
The deepest need of man is the need to overcome his separateness, to leave the prison of his aloneness.
ERICH FROMM

[1966]
Then all the disciples forsook him and fled.
MATTHEW 26:56 (RSV)

[1967]
Loneliness is the first thing which God's eye nam'd not good.
JOHN MILTON

[1968]
Loneliness is only an opportunity to cut adrift and find yourself.
ANNA MONROE

[1969]
Shakespeare, Leonardo da Vinci, Benjamin Franklin, and Lincoln . . . were not afraid of being lonely because they knew that was when the creative mood in them would work.
CARL SANDBURG

[1970]
My heart is a lonely hunter that hunts on a lonely hill.
WILLIAM SHARP

[1971]
The soul hardly ever realizes it, but whether he is a believer or not, his loneliness is really a homesickness for God.
HUBERT VAN ZELLER

[1972]
Loneliness, far from being a rare and curious phenomenon peculiar to myself and to a few other solitary men, is the central and inevitable fact of human existence.
THOMAS WOLFE

[1973]
People are lonely because they build walls instead of bridges.

LORD'S SUPPER

[1974]
The cup of blessing which we bless, is it not a participation in the blood of Christ? The bread which we break, is it not a participation in the body of Christ?
1 CORINTHIANS 10:16 (RSV)

[1975]
When we come to Christ's table to commune, we come with a prayer that we may be filled with the fulness of his life, may grow into his likeness, and may evermore dwell in him and he in us.
HOWARD W. ELLIS

[1976]
The Lord's Supper testifies to us that we have complete forgiveness of all our sins through the one sacrifice of Jesus Christ which he himself has accomplished on the cross once for all.
THE HEIDELBERG CATECHISM

[1977]

In the holy sacrament of the altar there are three things we must observe: the sign, which should be outward, visible, and in a bodily shape; the thing signified, which is inward, spiritual, and in the mind of man; and faith, which makes use of both. . . . There is no closer, deeper or more indivisible union than that which takes place between the food and the body which the food nourishes. Christ is so united to us in the sacrament [of the Lord's Supper] that he acts as if he were ourselves. Our sins assail him; his righteousness defends us.

MARTIN LUTHER

[1978]

When we come to the holy communion acknowledging who God is and who we are, we are fed with God's holy food. We are nourished, healed, restored and enlivened. We can go from God's table strengthened to live a new style of life. How? By taking Jesus Christ at his word and then going out in his strength and in his love.

MOULTRIE H. McINTOSH

[1979]

To speak of the social significance of holy communion is no longer novel. The great community problem of our modern world is how to share bread.

GEORGE F. MACLEOD

[1980]

I believe that Christ is truly in the Supper, nay, I do not believe it is the Lord's Supper unless Christ is there. . . . To eat the body of Christ spiritually is . . . to trust in spirit and heart upon the mercy and goodness of God through Christ, that is, to be sure with unshaken faith that God is going to give us pardon for our sins and the joy of everlasting blessedness on account of his Son, who was made wholly ours, was offered for us, and reconciled the divine righteousness to us.

ULRICH ZWINGLI

LOVE

[1981]

I feel that God would sooner we did wrong in loving than never love for fear we should do wrong.

FATHER ANDREW

[1982]

They [the Christians] know one another by secret marks and signs, and they love one another almost before they know one another.

STATIUS CAECILIUS

[1983]

You can give without loving, but you cannot love without giving.

AMY CARMICHAEL

[1984]

When iron is rubbed against a magnet it becomes magnetic. Just so, love is caught, not taught. One heart burning with love sets another on fire. The church was built on love; it proves what love can do.

FRANK C. LAUBACH

[1985]
We can do little things for God: I turn the cake that is frying on the pan, for love of him; and that done, if there is nothing else to call me, I prostrate myself in worship before him who has given me grace to work; afterward I rise happier than a king.
BROTHER LAWRENCE

[1986]
He who loves not, lives not.
RAMÓN LULL

[1987]
Love makes everything lovely; hate concentrates itself on the one thing hated.
GEORGE MACDONALD

[1988]
Blessed is the season that engages the whole world in a conspiracy of love.
HAMILTON WRIGHT MABIE

[1989]
Let me never fancy that I have zeal until my heart overflows with love to every human being.
HENRY MARTYN

[1990]
Love is the key to the entire therapeutic program of the modern psychiatric hospital.
KARL A. MENNINGER

[1991]
Love seeks one thing only: the good of the one loved. It leaves all the other secondary effects to take care of themselves. Love, therefore, is its own reward.
THOMAS MERTON

[1992]
Joy is love exalted; peace is love in repose; long-suffering is love enduring; gentleness is love in society; goodness is love in action; faith is love on the battlefield; meekness is love in school; and temperance is love in training.
DWIGHT L. MOODY

[1993]
There is no surprise more wonderful than the surprise of being loved; it is God's finger on man's shoulder.
CHARLES MORGAN

[1994]
The love that we need is God himself coming into our hearts. When the soul is perfected in love, it has such a sense of that love that it can rest in it for eternity, and though it has as much as it can contain for the time being, it can always receive more.
ANDREW MURRAY

[1995]
Love must be learned and learned again and again; there is no end to it. Hate needs no instruction, but waits only to be provoked.
KATHERINE ANNE PORTER

[1996]
When the satisfaction or security of another person becomes as important to one as one's own, then a state of love exists.
HARRY STACK SULLIVAN

[1997]
Our Lord does not care so much for the importance of our works as for the love with which they are done.
TERESA OF AVILA

[1998]
Tell me how much you know of the sufferings of your fellow men and I will tell you how much you have loved them.

HELMUT THIELICKE

[1999]
You want to compete with his affection before you have understood it; that is your mistake. . . . Come, then! Show a little more deference to our Lord and allow him to go first. Let him love you a great deal before you have succeeded in loving him even a little as you would wish to love him. That is all that our Lord asks of you.

HENRI DE TOURVILLE

[2000]
To believe in God is to love him.

MIGUEL DE UNAMUNO

[2001]
It is always springtime in the heart that loves God.

JEAN-MARIE VIANNEY

[2002]
There is a land of the living and a land of the dead and the bridge is love, the only survival, the only meaning.

THORNTON WILDER

[2003]
Love is not only something you feel. It's something you do.

DAVID WILKERSON

[2004]
What's so remarkable about love at first sight? It's when people have been looking at each other for years that it becomes remarkable.

MAN

[2005]
Man is a good thing spoiled.

AUGUSTINE OF HIPPO

[2006]
European man strode into history full of confidence in himself and his creative powers. Today he leaves it to pass into an unknown epoch, discouraged, his faith in shreds.

NICOLAS BERDYAEV

[2007]
The church is looking for better methods; God is looking for better men.

E. M. BOUNDS

[2008]
The worker is far more important to our Lord than the work.

LETTIE COWMAN

[2009]
We have learned to fly through the air like birds and to swim through the sea like fish. When will we learn to walk the earth like men?

R. W. HUGH JONES

[2010]
It is becoming more and more obvious that it is not starvation, not microbes, not cancer, but man himself who is mankind's greatest danger.

CARL GUSTAV JUNG

[2011]
The most important thing to come out of the mine is the miner.

FRÉDÉRIC LE PLAY

[2012]
Man finds himself today, perhaps largely as a result of his technological triumphs, engulfed in difficulties with his fellow men which threaten to despoil him of his enjoyment of the choicest fruits that science has placed within his reach.

GEORGE A. LUNDBERG

[2013]
Mr. Average North American is typed as the installment buyer who is busy buying things he doesn't want, with money he doesn't have, to impress people he doesn't like.

O. DONALD OLSEN

[2014]
What a chimera, then, is man! What a novelty! What a monster, what a chaos, what a contradiction, what a prodigy! Judge of all things, feeble worm of the earth, depository of truth, a sink of uncertainty and error, the glory and the shame of the universe.

BLAISE PASCAL

[2015]
Abdallah the Saracen, having been asked what could be seen on the earthly stage that was most to be wondered at, answered that nothing could be seen more wonderful than man.

PICO DELLA MIRANDOLA

[2016]
We live less than the time it takes to blink an eye, if we measure our lives against eternity. . . . I learned a long time ago that a blink of an eye in itself is nothing. But the eye that blinks, *that* is something. A span of life is nothing. But the man who lives that span, *he* is something. He can fill that tiny span with meaning, so its quality is immeasurable though its quantity may be insignificant.

CHAIM POTOK
The Chosen

[2017]
What is man that thou art mindful of him?

PSALM 8:4 (RSV)

[2018]
Made in God's image, man was made to be great, he was made to be beautiful and he was made to be creative in life and art. But his rebellion has led him into making himself into nothing but a machine.

FRANCIS A. SCHAEFFER

[2019]
Man is like nothing so much as a lump of muddy earth plunged into a very clear, pure brook.

ULRICH ZWINGLI

MARRIAGE

[2020]
Marryin' a man ain't like setting alongside him nights and hearing him talk pretty; that's the fust prayer. There's lots and lots o' meetin' after that.

ROSE TERRY COOKE

[2021]
Never get married until you have kissed the Blarney Stone. Praising a woman before marriage is a matter of inclination. But praising one after you marry her is a matter of necessity. Matrimony is no place for candor. It is a field for diplomacy.
DOROTHY DIX

[2022]
Choose a wife rather by your ear than your eye.
THOMAS FULLER

[2023]
In marriage, being the right person is as important as finding the right person.
WILBERT DONALD GOUGH

[2024]
The best advice I can give to unmarried girls is to marry someone you don't mind adjusting to. God tailors the wife to fit the husband, not the husband to fit the wife.
RUTH BELL GRAHAM

[2025]
A happy marriage is the union of two good forgivers.
ROBERT QUILLEN

[2026]
One of the great similarities between Christianity and marriage is that, for Christians, they both get better as we get older.
JEAN A. REES

[2027]
The heart of marriage is its communication system. It can be said that the success and happiness of any married pair is measurable in terms of the deepening dialogue which characterizes their union.
DWIGHT SMALL

[2028]
One never realizes how the human voice can change until a woman stops scolding her husband to answer the phone.

MARTYRDOM

[2029]
Were the happiness of the next world as closely apprehended as the felicities of this, it were a martyrdom to live.
THOMAS BROWNE

[2030]
All have not the gift of martyrdom.
JOHN DRYDEN

[2031]
It is not suffering but the cause which makes a martyr.
ENGLISH PROVERB

[2032]
It is the truth of the doctrine that makes the martyr.
GUSTAVE FLAUBERT

[2033]
Perhaps there is no happiness in life so perfect as the martyr's.
O. HENRY

[2034]
When a Christian is martyred, tremendous things begin to happen.
IAN RENNIE

[2035]
The blood of the martyrs is seed.
TERTULLIAN

[2036]
Love makes the whole difference between an execution and a martyrdom.
EVELYN UNDERHILL

MATERIALISM

[2037]
No government can inoculate its people against the fatal materialism that plagues our age. Happily our people, though blessed with more material goods than any people in history, have always reserved their first allegiance to the kingdom of spirit, which is the true source of that freedom we value above all material things.

DWIGHT D. EISENHOWER

[2038]
Lives based on *having* are less free than lives based either on doing or on being.

WILLIAM JAMES

[2039]
A purely materialistic philosophy is to me the height of unintelligence.

ROBERT A. MILLIKAN

MATURITY

[2040]
So far in the history of the world there have never been enough mature people in the right places.

GEORGE B. CHISHOLM (attr.)

[2041]
When I was a child I spoke and thought and reasoned as a child does. But when I became a man my thoughts grew far beyond those of my childhood, and now I have put away the childish things.

1 CORINTHIANS 13:11
(*The Living Bible*)

[2042]
It is a great pity that men and women forget that they have been children. Parents are apt to be foreigners to their sons and daughters. Maturity is the gate of Paradise which shuts behind us; and our memories are gradually weaned from the glories in which our nativity was cradled.

GEORGE WILLIAM CURTIS

[2043]
His gifts were that some should be apostles, some prophets, some evangelists, some pastors and teachers . . . until we all attain to the unity of the faith and of the knowledge of the Son of God, to mature manhood . . . so that we may no longer be children . . . carried about with every wind of doctrine.

EPHESIANS 4:11–14 (RSV)

[2044]
To know Jesus personally is authentic maturity.

RICHARD C. HALVERSON

[2045]
Please be patient. God isn't finished with me yet.

INTER-VARSITY GRAFFITO

[2046]
Men return again and again to the few who have mastered the spiritual secret, whose life has been hid with Christ in God. These are of the old-time religion, hung to the nails of the cross.

ROBERT MURRAY MCCHEYNE

[2047]
The characteristic of the mature person is that he affirms life.

HARRY A. OVERSTREET

[2048]
Mature people are made not out of good times but out of bad times.

HYMAN JUDAH SCHACHTEL

[2049]
It takes a long time to bring excellence
to maturity.

PUBLILIUS SYRUS

[2050]
Maturity is the art of living in peace
with that which we cannot change.

MEANING

[2051]
Our life has no meaning in itself; it has
meaning only in relation to God.

CHRISTOPH BLUMHARDT

[2052]
This world's no blot for us,/ Nor blank;
it means intensely, and means good;/
To find its meaning is my meat and
drink.

ROBERT BROWNING
"Fra Lippo Lippi"

[2053]
Only as man brings his life into harmony with God does that life have balance and meaning. Then man finds
that he is not simply a mass of dancing
dirt, coming from nowhere and going
nowhere.

HENRY J. SCHMIDT

[2054]
Having sought for so long the real
meaning and key to life, and having
found it in Christ, I couldn't keep quiet
about this discovery. Everybody had to
know!

GEOFFREY SHAW

MEDITATION

[2055]
He who hath not much meditated upon
God . . . may possibly make a thriving
earthworm, but will most indubitably
make a sorry patriot and a sorry statesman.

GEORGE BERKELEY

[2056]
I thank God for my happy dreams, as I
do for my good rest; for there is a satisfaction in them unto reasonable
desires, and such as can be content
with a fit of happiness; and surely it is
not a melancholy conceit to think we
are all asleep in this world, and that the
conceits of this life are as mere dreams
to those of the next. [I never go to
sleep] without my prayers, and a half
adieu unto the world, and take my fare-
well in a colloquy with God.

THOMAS BROWNE

[2057]
I neglect God and his angels for the
noise of a fly, for the rattling of a coach,
for the whining of a door.

JOHN DONNE

[2058]
Every man has a train of thought on
which he rides when he is alone. The
dignity and nobility of his life, as well as
his happiness, depend upon the direction in which that train is going, the
baggage it carries, and the scenery
through which it travels.

JOSEPH FORT NEWTON

[2059]
His delight is in the law of the Lord,
and on his law he meditates day and
night.

PSALM 1:2 (RSV)

154 MERCY

MEEKNESS

[2060]
Meekness is not weakness.
WILLIAM GURNEY BENHAM

[2061]
Meekness takes injuries like pills, not chewing, but swallowing them down.
THOMAS BROWNE

[2062]
Learn the blessedness of the unoffended in the face of the unexplainable.
AMY CARMICHAEL

[2063]
Meekness in itself is nought else but a true knowing and feeling of man's self as he is.
The Cloud of Unknowing

[2064]
The meek, the terrible meek, the fierce agonizing meek, are about to enter into their inheritance.
CHARLES RANN KENNEDY
The Terrible Meek

[2065]
I am gentle and lowly in heart.
MATTHEW 11:29 (RSV)

[2066]
The meek shall possess the land, and delight themselves in abundant prosperity.
PSALM 37:11 (RSV)

[2067]
The meek are not simply the jaunty, as some would derive from the French translation of the Beatitude: "Heureux les débonnaires; car ils hériteront de la terre." Nor are they those who possess a vague "faith in the friendliness of the universe" (Ligon). First and foremost, the blessed meek are those who have given their lives over to the Savior that he might live in them.*

MERCY

[2068]
Thomas Hooker, the courageous English preacher who brought his flock to the new world and became one of the founders of Connecticut, lay dying in his Hartford home in 1647. Gathered at his bedside were his friends, who sought to comfort him. "Mr. Hooker," they said to him, "you are now going to receive your reward." But the old Puritan turned and retorted, "I go to receive mercy."
ROLAND H. BAINTON

[2069]
Among the attributes of God, although they are all equal, mercy shines with even more brilliancy than justice.
MIGUEL DE CERVANTES

[2070]
Mercy is as beautiful in a time of trouble as rain clouds in a time of drought.
ECCLESIASTICUS 35:20
(Goodspeed)

[2071]
You have reason to open your mouth in God's praises, both here and to all eternity, for his rich and sovereign mercy to you.
JONATHAN EDWARDS

[2072]
Ultimately this is what you go before God for: you've had bad luck and good luck and all you really want in the end is mercy.
ROBERT FROST

[2073]
There will be no mercy to those who have shown no mercy.
JAMES 2:13
(The Living Bible)

[2074]
Mercy does not always express itself by withholding punishment.

ERNEST M. LIGON

[2075]
Blessed are the merciful, for they shall obtain mercy.

MATTHEW 5:7 (RSV)

[2076]
The good news of the Gospel is that there is a resource of divine mercy which is able to overcome a contradiction within our own souls, which we cannot overcome ourselves.

REINHOLD NIEBUHR

[2077]
Mercy's indeed the attribute of heaven.

THOMAS OTWAY

[2078]
If we refuse mercy here, we shall have justice in eternity.

JEREMY TAYLOR

[2079]
A God all mercy is a God unjust.

EDWARD YOUNG

[2080]
Mercy is unmerited favor from God himself to an erring people who can do nothing to earn it except to hold out their hands.*

MIND

[2081]
I had rather believe all the fables in the Legend and the Talmud and the Alcoran than that this universal frame is without a mind.

FRANCIS BACON

[2082]
Rule your mind or it will rule you.

HORACE

[2083]
Mind no longer appears as an accidental intruder into the realm of matter. The universe begins to look more like a great thought than a great machine.

JAMES JEANS

[2084]
The sins of the mind are the last habitation of the devil.

JAROL JOHNSON

[2085]
You shall love the Lord your God . . . with all your mind.

LUKE 10:27 (RSV)

[2086]
Sometimes an open mind is one that is too porous to hold a conviction.

W. NORMAN MACFARLANE

[2087]
The modern intelligent mind, which has had its horizons widened in dozens of different ways, has got to be shocked afresh by the audacious central fact that as a sober matter of history, God became one of us.

J. B. PHILLIPS

[2088]
It does not take a great mind to be a Christian, but it takes all the mind a man has.

RICHARD C. RAINES

[2089]
Physical theory in its present stage strongly suggests the indestructibility of Mind in Time.

ERWIN SCHRÖDINGER

MIRACLES

[2090]
Miracles are not contrary to nature, but only contrary to what we know about nature.

AUGUSTINE OF HIPPO

[2091]
Every believer is God's miracle.

PHILIP JAMES BAILEY

[2092]
We must first make up our minds about Christ before coming to conclusions about the miracles attributed to him.

F. F. BRUCE

[2093]
A ministry that is college-trained but not Spirit-filled works no miracles.

SAMUEL CHADWICK

[2094]
The divine art of miracle is not an art of suspending the pattern to which events conform, but of feeding new events into that pattern.

C. S. LEWIS

[2095]
Jesus was himself the one convincing and permanent miracle.

IAN MACLAREN

[2096]
There are laws of the universe that are still waiting to be discovered by painful research. . . . I venture to suggest that if we are truly to understand the miracles of healing in the New Testament we shall have to discover the secret already at least partially revealed to those who make prayer the chief factor in their healing ministries.

E. R. MICKLEM

[2097]
We do not hug our miracles close. We put them hastily away, preferring the commonplace to live with.

FULTON OURSLER

[2098]
A miracle in the Biblical sense is an event which happens in a manner contrary to the regularly observed processes of nature. . . . It may happen according to higher laws as yet but dimly discerned by scientists, and therefore must not be thought of as an irrational irruption of divine power into the orderly realm of nature.

ALAN RICHARDSON

[2099]
God raises the level of the impossible.

CORRIE TEN BOOM

[2100]
Miracles do not appear on the page of Scripture vagrantly, here, there and elsewhere indifferently, without assignable reason. They belong to revelation periods, and appear only when God is speaking to his people through accredited messengers, declaring his gracious purposes.

BENJAMIN B. WARFIELD

MISSION

[2101]
If [people] ask, "Why did he not appear by means of other parts of creation, and use some nobler instrument, as the sun or moon or stars or fire or air, instead of man merely?" let them know that the Lord came not to make a display, but to heal and teach those who were suffering.

ATHANASIUS

[2102]
If the redemption of man awaits his faith in Christ and his Kingdom, then to summon men to that faith (the missionary task of the church) is no fussy meddling: it is the pivotal activity of history. Indeed, it is possible to say that it is the only hope of mankind.

JOHN BRIGHT

[2103]
A church exists by mission as fire exists by burning.

EMIL BRUNNER

[2104]
The posture of Christianity toward the religions of the world is not one of condemnation. It is rather one of illumination and the offering of the Good News.

GARY W. DEMAREST

[2105]
The Bible is a missionary book. Jesus Christ is the Father's missionary to a lost world.

HAROLD LINDSELL

[2106]
God had an only Son, and he was a missionary and a physician.

DAVID LIVINGSTONE

[2107]
The whole church must become a mobile missionary force, ready for a wilderness life. It is a time for us all to be thinking of campaign tents rather than of cathedrals.

JOHN A. MACKAY

[2108]
The Spirit of Christ is the spirit of missions, and the nearer we get to him the more intensely missionary we must become.

HENRY MARTYN

[2109]
As we look back over history and consider the enormous difficulties to be overcome, the unwillingness of many great Western churches to take part in missionary work at all, the miserable niggardliness with which the work of missions has always been supported, the lack of distinction in some of those who have undertaken this service, it seems a sheer miracle that there are any Christians at all in the lands of the younger churches. And yet there they are.

STEPHEN NEILL

[2110]
Do we still want missionaries? Yes, but we want missionaries who are "God-intoxicated" men.

BISHOP ODUTOLA OF NIGERIA

[2111]
You are either a missionary or a mission field: one of the two.

OLAF SKINSNES

[2112]
Those who deblaterate against missions have only one thing to do: to come and see them on the spot.

ROBERT LOUIS STEVENSON

[2113]
There is no argument for missions. The total action of God in history, the whole revelation of God in Christ—this is the argument.

JAMES S. STEWART

[2114]
I am frequently told of doors closing to the Gospel. It is my job to negotiate with diplomatic embassies on behalf of evangelical societies and individuals. I could count on my fingers the number of closed doors, but there are countless open ones.

CLYDE W. TAYLOR

[2115]
I look upon foreign missionaries as the scaffolding around a rising building. The sooner it can be dispensed with, the better; or rather, the sooner it can be transferred to other places, to serve the same temporary use, the better.
                              J. HUDSON TAYLOR

[2116]
That land is henceforth my country which most needs the Gospel.
                      NICHOLAS VON ZINZENDORF

[2117]
Every life without Christ is a mission field; every life with Christ is a missionary.

MISTAKES

[2118]
There is nothing final about a mistake except its being taken as final.
                            PHYLLIS BOTTOME
                                Strange Fruit

[2119]
Reas'ning at every step he treads,/ Man yet mistakes his way.
                          WILLIAM COWPER
                                "The Doves"

[2120]
I beseech you, in the bowels of Christ, think it possible you may be mistaken.
                          OLIVER CROMWELL
            (in letter to General Assembly of the
                          Church of Scotland)

[2121]
Mistakes are often the best teachers.
                      JAMES ANTHONY FROUDE

[2122]
The man who makes no mistakes does not usually make anything.
                      WILLIAM CONNOR MAGEE

[2123]
He is always right who suspects that he makes mistakes.
                            SPANISH PROVERB

MONEY

[2124]
The only money of God is God.
                      RALPH WALDO EMERSON

[2125]
Money never made a man happy yet, nor will it. There is nothing in its nature to produce happiness. The more a man has, the more he wants. That was a true proverb of the wise man, rely upon it: "Better is little with the fear of the Lord, than great treasure, and trouble therewith."
                        BENJAMIN FRANKLIN

[2126]
Come . . . without money and without price. Why do you spend your money for that which is not bread?
                        ISAIAH 55:1–2 (RSV)

[2127]
Resolve not to be poor: whatever you have, spend less.
                          SAMUEL JOHNSON

[2128]
The real measure of our wealth is how much we'd be worth if we lost all our money.
                        JOHN HENRY JOWETT

[2129]
The moral problem of our age is concerned with the love of money, with the habitual appeal to the money motive in nine-tenths of the activities of life.
                              J. M. KEYNES

[2130]
The man who loves money is the man who has never grown up.
ROBERT LYND

[2131]
Trust in your money and down you go! Trust in God and flourish as a tree.
PROVERBS 11:28
(The Living Bible)

[2132]
No man is really consecrated until his money is dedicated.
ROY L. SMITH

[2133]
Nothing that is God's is obtainable by money.
TERTULLIAN

[2134]
Make all you can, save all you can, give all you can.
JOHN WESLEY

[2135]
Money buys everything except love, personality, freedom, immortality.

MORALITY

[2136]
Not guided missiles but guided morals constitute our great need today.
GEORGE L. FORD

[2137]
To deny the freedom of the will is to make morality impossible.
JAMES ANTHONY FROUDE

[2138]
All moral obligation resolves itself into the obligation of conformity to the will of God.
CHARLES HODGE

[2139]
Nothing is settled until it is settled right.
ABRAHAM LINCOLN

[2140]
To give a man full knowledge of true morality, I would send him to no other book than the New Testament.
JOHN LOCKE

[2141]
The doctors treat venereal disease as a medical problem. Lately they have been calling it a social problem. I say it is a moral problem.
ALVIE L. McKNIGHT

[2142]
The health of a community is an almost unfailing index of its morals.
JAMES MARTINEAU

[2143]
The social revolution will be moral, or it will not be.
CHARLES PÉGUY

[2144]
Right is right, even if everyone is against it; and wrong is wrong, even if everyone is for it.
WILLIAM PENN

[2145]
The Puritan Christian held, incredible as it may seem, that morals are more important than athletics, business or art; that the good life must be founded on virtue.
RALPH BARTON PERRY

[2146]
Where there is no free agency, there can be no morality.
WILLIAM PRESCOTT

[2147]
Aim above morality. Be not simply good; be good for something.
HENRY DAVID THOREAU

[2148]
In morality we are as sure as in mathematics.

BENJAMIN WHICHCOTE

[2149]
Morality does not make a Christian, yet no man can be a Christian without it.

DANIEL WILSON

MOTHERHOOD

[2150]
It was because my salvation was at stake that [my mother] loved Ambrose greatly, and he loved her because of her fervent life of devotion, which took the form of good works and frequent churchgoing. Sometimes when he saw me he would break out in praise of her and congratulate me on having such a mother—not knowing what a son she had!

AUGUSTINE OF HIPPO

[2151]
This is the promise: that if you honor your father and mother, yours will be a long life, full of blessing.

EPHESIANS 6:2
(The Living Bible)

[2152]
No man is poor who has had a godly mother.

ABRAHAM LINCOLN

[2153]
Even he that died for us upon the cross, in the last hour, in the unutterable agony of death, was mindful of his mother, as if to teach us that this holy love should be our last worldly thought—the last point of earth from which the soul should take its flight for heaven.

HENRY WADSWORTH LONGFELLOW

[2154]
Her children rise up and call her blessed.

PROVERBS 31:28 (RSV)

[2155]
God pays a good mother. Mothers, get your names on God's payroll.

BILLY SUNDAY

[2156]
Mother is the name for God in the lips and hearts of little children.

WILLIAM MAKEPEACE THACKERAY
Vanity Fair

MOTIVATION

[2157]
In the course of development relatively stable units of personality gradually emerge. Such units are always the product of the two central and vital functions of mental life: motivation and organization. Motivation refers to the "go" of mental life, organization to its patterning. . . . Organized motive . . . is a system of readiness, a mainspring of conduct, preparing the person for adaptive behavior whenever the appropriate stimulus or associations are presented.

GORDON W. ALLPORT

[2158]
We do not evangelize because we expect results. We evangelize because we are sent men.

JOSEPH D. BLINCO

[2159]
If no action is to be deemed virtuous for which malice can imagine a sinister motive, then there was never a virtuous action; no, not even in the life of our Savior himself. But he has taught us to judge the tree by its fruit, and to leave motives to him who can alone see into them.

THOMAS JEFFERSON

[2160]
The morality of an action depends on the motive from which we act.

SAMUEL JOHNSON

[2161]
It was God's love that motivated him to do something for the lostness of the world.

HOWARD O. JONES

[2162]
We must judge a man's motives from his overt acts.

LORD KENYON

[2163]
I go at what I have to do as if there were nothing else in the world for me to do.

CHARLES KINGSLEY

[2164]
Man sees your actions, but God your motives.

THOMAS À KEMPIS

[2165]
If a man does not keep pace with his companions, perhaps it is because he hears a different drummer.

HENRY DAVID THOREAU

[2166]
God give me a deep humility, a well-guided zeal, a burning love and a single eye, and then let men or devils do their worst.

GEORGE WHITEFIELD

MUSIC

[2167]
[Good music is] that which penetrates the ear with facility and quits the memory with difficulty.

THOMAS BEECHAM

[2168]
Music is a part of us, and either ennobles or degrades our behavior.

BOETHIUS

[2169]
Music strikes in me a profound contemplation of the First Composer.

THOMAS BROWNE

[2170]
The best days of the church have always been its singing days.

THEODORE L. CUYLER

[2171]
A nation creates music—the composer only arranges it.

MIKHAIL GLINKA

[2172]
Why should the devil have all the good tunes?

ROWLAND HILL

[2173]
Music is love in search of a word.

SIDNEY LANIER

[2174]
Music is the universal language of mankind.

HENRY WADSWORTH LONGFELLOW

[2175]
Next to theology I give to music the highest place and honor. Music is the art of the prophets, the only art that can calm the agitations of the soul; it is one of the most magnificent and delightful presents God has given us.

MARTIN LUTHER

[2176]
We must observe what are the natural rhythms of a well-regulated and manly life, and when we have discovered these we must compel the foot and the music to suit themselves to the sense of such a life, and not the sense to suit itself to the foot and the music.

PLATO

[2177]
[Sing] not lolling at ease or in the indecent posture of sitting, drawling out one word after another, but all standing before God, and praising him lustily, and with good courage.

JOHN WESLEY

NATURE

[2178]
All art, all education, can be merely a supplement to nature.

ARISTOTLE

[2179]
Nature is not governed except by obeying her.

FRANCIS BACON

[2180]
I love to think of nature as an unlimited broadcasting station through which God speaks to us every hour, if we will only tune in.

GEORGE WASHINGTON CARVER

[2181]
Nature is but a name for an effect whose cause is God.

WILLIAM COWPER

[2182]
Nature is the art of God.

DANTE

[2183]
Nature never breaks her own laws.

LEONARDO DA VINCI

[2184]
Nature is a volume of which God is the author.

WALTER HARVEY

[2185]
Man cannot control nature; he can gain his commodity by cooperating with her and in no other way.

EDWARD HYAMS

[2186]
I hold that we have a very imperfect knowledge of the works of nature till we view them as the works of God.

JAMES McCOSH

[2187]
Let us permit nature to have her way: she understands her business better than we do.

MICHEL DE MONTAIGNE

[2188]
Nature has some perfections, to show that she is the image of God; and some defects, to show that she is only his image.

BLAISE PASCAL

[2189]
One touch of nature makes the whole world kin.

SHAKESPEARE
Troilus and Cressida, III, iii

[2190]
There are no impasses in nature.

TONI WOLFF

NEEDS

[2191]
He who buys what he doesn't need sells what he does need.

MATEO ALEMÁN

[2192]
It is not book-learning young men need, nor instruction about this and that, but a stiffening of the vertebrae which will cause them to be loyal to a trust, to act promptly, concentrate their energies, do a thing—carry a message to Garcia.

ELBERT HUBBARD

[2193]
The world needs fewer man-made goods and more God-made men and women.

SARAH ANNE JEPSON

[2194]
One thing is needful. Mary has chosen the good portion.

LUKE 10:42 (RSV)

[2195]
A great interpreter of life ought not himself to need interpretation.

JOHN MORLEY

NEIGHBOR

[2196]
You shall not bear false witness against your neighbor.

EXODUS 20:16 (RSV)

[2197]
We never love our neighbor so truly as when our love for him is prompted by the love of God.

FRANÇOIS DE LA MOTHE FÉNELON

[2198]
We can live without our friends but not without our neighbors.

THOMAS FULLER

[2199]
A good neighbor doubles the value of a house.

GERMAN PROVERB

[2200]
He who prays for his neighbor will be heard for himself.

HEBREW PROVERB

[2201]
All is well with him who is beloved of his neighbors.

GEORGE HERBERT

[2202]
You shall not take vengeance or bear any grudge against the sons of your own people, but you shall love your neighbor as yourself.

LEVITICUS 19:18 (RSV)

[2203]
Who gives himself with his alms feeds three—/ Himself, his hungering neighbor, and me.

JAMES RUSSELL LOWELL
"The Vision of Sir Launfal"

[2204]
The love of our neighbor is the only door out of the dungeon of self.

GEORGE MACDONALD

[2205]
Though we do not have our Lord with us in bodily presence, we have our neighbor, who, for the ends of love and loving service, is as good as our Lord himself.

TERESA OF AVILA

[2206]
Man becomes a holy thing, a neighbor, only if we realize that he is the property of God and that Jesus Christ died for him.

HELMUT THIELICKE

[2207]
Faith without ethical consequences is a lie. God does not need our sacrifices but he has, nevertheless, appointed a representative to receive them, namely our neighbor. The neighbor always represents the invisible Christ.

J. S. WHALF

[2208]
If you want your neighbor to know what Christ will do for him, let the neighbor see what Christ has done for you.

NEW TESTAMENT

[2209]
I do not dare to read the New Testament for fear of its awakening a storm of anxiety and self-reproach and doubt and dread of having taken the wrong path, of having been traitor to the plain and simple God.

GAMALIEL BRADFORD

[2210]
The theological principles underlying God's dealings with Israel are also the same as those underlying his dealings with Christians and the Christian church. The Old Testament and the New Testament belong together, the one as preparation, the other as fulfillment.

GEOFFREY W. BROMILEY

[2211]
The New Testament Scriptures speak of the Holy Spirit as a Person, and never merely as an influence. They always speak of him, and never of it.

SAMUEL CHADWICK

[2212]
The difference between the Old and the New Testaments is the difference between a man who said, "There is nothing new under the sun," and a God who says, "Behold, I make all things new."

RONALD A. KNOX

[2213]
The New Testament is a love letter to you from God.

GREGORIO TINGSON

[2214]
All four Gospels agree in giving us a picture of a very definite personality. One is obliged to say, "Here was a man. This could not have been invented."

H. G. WELLS

[2215]
If you really want some mail, read a letter from Paul.

NURTURE

[2216]
Train up a child in the way he should go and walk there yourself once in a while.

JOSH BILLINGS

[2217]
To discipline a child is not to punish him for stepping out of line, but to teach that child the way he ought to go. Discipline therefore includes everything that you do in order to help children learn.

HENRY R. BRANDT

[2218]
Do not provoke your children to anger, but bring them up in the discipline and instruction of the Lord.

EPHESIANS 6:4 (RSV)

[2219]
A child who is allowed to be disrespectful to his parents will not have true respect for anyone.

BILLY GRAHAM

[2220]
For the Lord disciplines him whom he loves, and chastises every son whom he receives.

HEBREWS 12:6 (RSV)

[2221]
A child who has been taught to respect the laws of God will have little difficulty respecting the laws of men.

J. EDGAR HOOVER

[2222]
Culture shapes, but self-awareness reshapes, and the resources of God are ever available for the reconstruction.

JAMES L. JOHNSON

[2223]
That best academy, a mother's knee.

JAMES RUSSELL LOWELL
"The Cathedral"

[2224]
I get my meat from Christ with nurture.

SAMUEL RUTHERFORD

[2225]
The greatest preferment we can give a child is learning and nurture, to train him to live.

THOMAS TUSSER

[2226]
Training is everything. The peach was once a bitter almond; cauliflower is nothing but cabbage with a college education.

MARK TWAIN

OBEDIENCE

[2227]
I mean to live my life an obedient man, but obedient to God, subservient to the wisdom of my ancestors; never to the authority of political truths arrived at yesterday at the voting booth.

WILLIAM F. BUCKLEY, JR.

[2228]
Throughout the Bible . . . when God asked a man to do something, methods, means, materials and specific directions were always provided. The man had one thing to do: obey.

ELISABETH ELLIOT

[2229]
Enthusiasm is easier than obedience.

MICHAEL GRIFFITH

[2230]
An office-bearer who wants something other than to obey his King is unfit to bear his office.

ABRAHAM KUYPER

[2231]
God delivers us from sin; we have to deliver ourselves from individuality, that is, to present our natural life to God and sacrifice it until it is transformed into a spiritual life by obedience.

D. W. LAMBERT

[2232]
Spiritual maturity comes not by erudition, but by compliance with the known will of God.

LEONARD RAVENHILL

[2233]
Faith and obedience are bound up in the same bundle. He that obeys God, trusts God; and he that trusts God, obeys God.

CHARLES H. SPURGEON

[2234]
Wherever God has placed a period, don't try to change it to a question mark.

OMNIPOTENCE

[2235]
According to the avowal of the whole human race, God is the Cause and Principle of things.

ARISTOTLE

[2236]
There is nothing which God cannot accomplish.

CICERO

[2237]
The right of God's sovereignty is derived from his omnipotence.

THOMAS HOBBES

[2238]
[God's] omnipotence means power to do all that is intrinsically possible, not to do the intrinsically impossible. You may attribute miracles to him, but not nonsense.

C. S. LEWIS

[2239]
If Providence is omnipotent, Providence intends whatever happens, and the fact of its happening proves that Providence intended it.

JOHN STUART MILL

[2240]
Where man's method fails and can reach no higher, there God's method begins.

JAN RUYSBROECK

[2241]
God, the great Creator of all things, doth uphold, direct, dispose, and govern all creatures, actions, and things from the greatest even to the least, by his most wise and holy providence, according to his infallible foreknowledge, and the free and immutable counsel of his own will, to the praise of the glory of his wisdom, power, justice, goodness, and mercy.

WESTMINSTER CONFESSION OF FAITH

OMNIPRESENCE

[2242]
Most Christians do not believe in the omnipresence of God; they only believe in his ubiquity.

LYMAN ABBOTT

[2243]
I know that nothing can exist without you; does that mean that whatever exists contains you? . . . Do the heavens and the earth contain you, since you fill them? Or do you cram them to overflowing? And if you do overflow the universe, into what do you overflow? . . . And then, when you fill all things, do you fill it with your whole Being?

AUGUSTINE OF HIPPO

[2244]
The almighty and ever-present power of God whereby he still upholds, as it were by his own hand, heaven and earth together with all creatures, and rules in such a way that . . . everything . . . comes to us not by chance but by his fatherly hand.

THE HEIDELBERG CATECHISM

[2245]
It is proper to the divine nature to be infinite, omnipotent, omnipresent.

WILLIAM WILLET

OMNISCIENCE

[2246]
We cannot too often think there is a never-sleeping eye which reads the heart and registers our thoughts.

FRANCIS BACON

[2247]
By comparison with God's perfect understanding, we are like a man inside a barrel looking through a bunghole.

R. R. BROWN

[2248]
I cannot believe that God plays dice with the world.

ALBERT EINSTEIN

[2249]
Divine wisdom knows infinitely more propositions [than human wisdom] because it knows them all.

GALILEO

[2250]
What can escape the eye of God all seeing, or deceive his heart omniscient?

JOHN MILTON

[2251]
We are always punched in on God's timecard.

RICHARD RIIS

OPINION

[2252]
How long are you going to waver between two opinions? . . . If the Lord is God, follow him! But if Baal is God, then follow him!

1 KINGS 18:21
(The Living Bible)

[2253]
It is natural for a wise man to change his opinion.

LATIN PROVERB

[2254]
Opinion in good men is but knowledge in the making.

JOHN MILTON

[2255]
It seems to me that the nursing mother of most false opinions, both public and private, is the too high opinion which man has of himself.

MICHEL DE MONTAIGNE

[2256]
Public opinion does not decide whether things are good or bad.

TACITUS

OPPORTUNITY

[2257]
A wise man will make more opportunities than he finds.

FRANCIS BACON

[2258]
When one door is shut, another opens.

MIGUEL DE CERVANTES

[2259]
Small opportunities are often the beginning of great enterprises.

DEMOSTHENES

[2260]
Watch your opportunity.

ECCLESIASTICUS 4:20
(Goodspeed)

[2261]
God is not saying to us, "Come, boys, each of you do your thing and try to get along." He is saying, "It is time to do my thing. Take these keys—a Gospel that is true, a love that has flesh on it, and the power that belongs to me alone —and open the door to the world."

LEIGHTON FORD

[2262]
As we have opportunity, let us do good
to all men.
                    GALATIANS 6:10 (RSV)

[2263]
Don't ever say we have no opportunity
to reach people. It is not that the
chances are missing, but we are missing the chances.
                          CHARLES GUILLOT

[2264]
Faith is the hinge that opens the door
to opportunity.
                          JOHN HUNTER

[2265]
Seek the first possible opportunity to
act on every good resolution you make.
                          WILLIAM JAMES

[2266]
Hell is paved with good intentions and
roofed with lost opportunities.
                      PORTUGUESE PROVERB

[2267]
God often gives in one brief moment
that which he has for a long time de-
nied.
                      THOMAS À KEMPIS
                  The Imitation of Christ

PAIN

[2268]
Certain pains are bad in an absolute
manner, others are bad only insofar as
they deprive us of some good.
                          ARISTOTLE

[2269]
Prayer and pains through faith in Jesus
Christ can do anything.
                          JOHN ELIOT

[2270]
The least pain in our little finger gives
us more concern and uneasiness than
the destruction of millions of our fellow beings.
                      WILLIAM HAZLITT

[2271]
When pain is to be borne, a little courage helps more than much knowledge,
a little human sympathy more than
much courage, and the least tincture of
the love of God more than all.
                          C. S. LEWIS

[2272]
To get the whole world out of bed/
And washed, and dressed, and
warmed, and fed,/ To work, and back
to bed again,/ Believe me, Saul, costs
worlds of pain.
                      JOHN MASEFIELD
                  The Everlasting Mercy

[2273]
And God shall wipe away all tears from
their eyes; and there shall be no more
death, neither sorrow, nor crying, neither shall there be any more pain.
                      REVELATION 21:4 (KJV)

[2274]
To a person with a toothache, even if
the world is tottering, there is nothing
more important than a visit to a dentist.
                  GEORGE BERNARD SHAW

[2275]
The pain of the mind is worse than the
pain of the body.
                      PUBLILIUS SYRUS

PASSION

[2276]
A man without passion is only a latent force, only a possibility, like a stone waiting for the blow from the iron to give forth sparks.

HENRI FRÉDÉRIC AMIEL

[2277]
Do not kindle the coals of a sinner, or you may be burned with the flame of his fire.

ECCLESIASTICUS 8:10
(Goodspeed)

[2278]
Pure prayer directed to heaven subdues passion, for it is a citadel inaccessible to the enemy.

DESIDERIUS ERASMUS

[2279]
Proof that the Lord who will come is that same Jesus who went into heaven will lie in the scars of the cross. The marks of his passion will never be effaced from his body.

MARCUS L. LOANE

[2280]
The natural man has only two primal passions, to get and to beget.

WILLIAM OSLER

[2281]
The passions are innate in man, and have not entered him from without; and if strict discipline did not come to his assistance, man would probably be no tamer than the wildest of the beasts.

PLUTARCH

[2282]
We should employ our passions in the service of life, not spend life in the service of our passions.

RICHARD STEELE

[2283]
The happiness of a man in this life does not consist in the absence but in the mastery of his passions.

ALFRED TENNYSON

PATIENCE

[2284]
We are called to be the Lord's diehards, to whom can be committed any kind of trial of endurance, and who can be counted upon to stand firm whatever happens. Surely fortitude is the sovereign virtue of life; not patience, though we need it too, but fortitude. O God, give me fortitude.

AMY CARMICHAEL

[2285]
When the darkness of dismay comes, endure until it is over, because out of it will come that following of Jesus which is an unspeakable joy.

OSWALD CHAMBERS

[2286]
We must wait for God, long, meekly, in the wind and wet, in the thunder and lightning, in the cold and the dark. Wait, and he will come. He never comes to those who do not wait.

FREDERICK W. FABER

[2287]
Patience is a bitter plant but it bears sweet fruit.

GERMAN PROVERB

[2288]
God takes a text, and preaches patience.

GEORGE HERBERT

[2289]
We count them happy which endure. Ye have heard of the patience of Job.

JAMES 5:11 (KJV)

[2290]
Patience and diligence, like faith, remove mountains.

WILLIAM PENN

PEACE

[2291]
In war: resolution. In defeat: defiance. In victory: magnanimity. In peace: goodwill.

WINSTON S. CHURCHILL

[2292]
If we will have peace without a worm in it, lay we the foundations of justice and righteousness.

OLIVER CROMWELL

[2293]
God takes life's broken pieces and gives us unbroken peace.

WILBERT DONALD GOUGH

[2294]
The storm was raging. The sea was beating against the rocks in huge, dashing waves. The lightning was flashing, the thunder was roaring, the wind was blowing; but the little bird was sound asleep in the crevice of the rock, its head tucked serenely under its wing. That is peace: to be able to sleep in the storm! In Christ we are relaxed and at peace in the midst of the confusions, bewilderments and perplexities of this life. The storm rages, but our hearts are at rest. We have found peace—at last!

BILLY GRAHAM

[2295]
Peace is such a precious jewel that I would give anything for it but truth.

MATTHEW HENRY

[2296]
We [do not] eschew concord and peace, but to have peace with man we will not be at war with God.

JOHN JEWEL

[2297]
If man does find the solution for world peace it will be the most revolutionary reversal of his record we have ever known.

GEORGE C. MARSHALL

[2298]
A great many people are trying to make peace, but that has already been done. God has not left it for us to do; all we have to do is to enter into it.

DWIGHT L. MOODY

[2299]
Peace *with* God brings the peace *of* God. It is a peace that settles our nerves, fills our mind, floods our spirit, and in the midst of the uproar around us, gives us the assurance that everything is all right.

BOB MUMFORD

[2300]
There will be no peace so long as God remains unseated at the conference tables.

WILLIAM M. PECK

PERFECTION

[2301]
Perfection does not consist in macerating or killing the body, but in killing our perverse self-will.

CATHERINE OF SIENA

[2302]
I know of no one man perfect in all things at once but still human . . . except him alone who for us clothed himself with humanity.

CLEMENT OF ALEXANDRIA

[2303]
He said to me, "My grace is sufficient for you, for my power is made perfect in weakness."

2 CORINTHIANS 12:9 (RSV)

[2304]
True perfection consists . . . in having but one fear, the loss of God's friendship.

GREGORY OF NYSSA

[2305]
He who is faultless is lifeless.

JOHN HEYWOOD

[2306]
You, therefore, must be perfect, as your heavenly Father is perfect.

MATTHEW 5:48 (RSV)

[2307]
Trifles make perfection and perfection is no trifle.

MICHELANGELO

[2308]
Perfection is being, not doing; it is not to effect an act but to achieve a character.

FULTON J. SHEEN

[2309]
If you check out the life of Jesus you will discover what made him perfect. He did not attain a state of perfection by carrying around in his pocket a list of rules and regulations, or by seeking to conform to the cultural mores of his time. He was perfect because he never made a move without his Father.

TOM SKINNER

[2310]
What is Christian perfection? Loving God with all our heart, mind, soul and strength.

JOHN WESLEY

[2311]
The divine nature is perfection; and to be nearest to the divine nature is to be nearest to perfection.

XENOPHON

PERSECUTION

[2312]
A man who is possessed by fear often begins to persecute.

NICOLAS BERDYAEV

[2313]
Religious persecution may shield itself under the guise of a mistaken and over-zealous piety.

EDMUND BURKE

[2314]
Far be it from us to approve as right those inhuman methods whereby many up to now have sought to force such people to accept our faith, denying them food, warmth and life's commonest amenities, and persecuting them with fire and sword.

JOHN CALVIN

[2315]
Opposition may become sweet to a man when he has christened it persecution.

GEORGE ELIOT

[2316]
The way of this world is to praise dead saints and persecute living ones.

NATHANIEL HOWE

[2317]
Wherever you see persecution, there is more than a probability that truth is on the persecuted side.

HUGH LATIMER

[2318]
When you are reviled and persecuted
and lied about because you are my followers—wonderful! Be happy about it!
Be very glad! For a tremendous reward
awaits you up in heaven.
                    MATTHEW 5:11–12
                    (The Living Bible)

[2319]
Whoever is right, the persecutor must
be wrong.
                    WILLIAM PENN

[2320]
Bless those who persecute you; bless
and do not curse them.
                    ROMANS 12:14 (RSV)

[2321]
Peple which hung idiotic old wimin for
witches, burnt holes in Quakers'
tongues, and consined their feller crit-
ters to the tredmill and pillery on the
slitest provocashun may hav bin very
nice folks in their way, but I must confess I don't admire their stile.
                    ARTEMUS WARD

[2322]
Persecution is not wrong because it is
cruel; it is cruel because it is wrong.
                    RICHARD WHATELY

PERSEVERANCE

[2323]
Genius, that power which dazzles mortal eyes,/ Is oft but perseverance in dis-
guise.
                    HENRY W. AUSTIN
                    "Perseverance Conquers All"

[2324]
Consider the postage stamp, my son.
Its usefulness consists in sticking to
one thing till it gets there.
                    JOSH BILLINGS

[2325]
Never give in! Never give in! Never,
never, never. Never—in anything great
or small, large or petty—never give in
except to convictions of honor and
good sense.
                    WINSTON S. CHURCHILL

[2326]
Even the woodpecker owes his success
to the fact that he uses his head and
keeps pecking away until he finishes
the job he starts.
                    COLEMAN COX

[2327]
Great works are performed not by
strength but by perseverance.
                    SAMUEL JOHNSON

[2328]
It takes time and perseverance to do
big things.
                    JAWAHARLAL NEHRU

[2329]
The will to persevere is often the difference between failure and success.
                    DAVID SARNOFF

[2330]
Today's mighty oak is just yesterday's
little nut that held its ground.

[2331]
When the going gets tough, the tough
get going.

PERSONALITY

[2332]
God himself I may declare to be the
supreme expression of personality.
                    GORDON W. ALLPORT

[2333]
Human personality and individuality
written and signed by God on each human countenance . . . is something altogether sacred, something for the
resurrection, for eternal life.
LEON BLOY

[2334]
The essential meaning of personality is
selfhood, self-consciousness, self-control, and the power to know.
B. P. BOWNE

[2335]
Personality is the integration of all the
traits which might determine the role
and status of the person in society.
E. W. BURGESS

[2336]
Only when the Spirit of God takes
possession of the "old" man to transform him is the man made whole again.
It is only when this threshold is crossed
that personality takes on full meaning
and significance.
EMILE CAILLIET

[2337]
Our possibilities . . . are limited much
more by our personality traits than by
our intellect.
HENRY GREBER

[2338]
What our eyes see as they look out on
the world is closely related to the kind
of person we are.
HALFORD E. LUCCOCK

[2339]
The secret of the universe, as by slow
degrees it reveals itself to us, turns out
to be personality.
JOHN COWPER POWYS

[2340]
Personality is the sum-total of all the
biological innate dispositions, impulses, tendencies, appetites and in-
stincts of the individual, and the acquired dispositions and tendencies—
acquired by experience.
MORTON PRINCE

[2341]
The world is a looking glass and gives
back to every man the reflection of his
own face.
WILLIAM MAKEPEACE THACKERAY

[2342]
Either heaven or hell will have continuous background music piped in. Which
one you think it is tells a lot about your
personality.
BILL VAUGHAN

[2343]
Personality is the entire organization of
a human being at any stage of his development.
H. C. WARREN AND L. CARMICHAEL

[2344]
Personality is individuality which has
become objective to itself.
W. WINDELBAND

PIETY

[2345]
Piety is a silver chain uniting heaven
and earth, temporal and spiritual, God
and man together.
NICOLAS CAUSSIN

[2346]
Piety is the foundation of all virtues.
CICERO

[2347]
All is vanity which is not honest, and
there is no solid wisdom but in true
piety.

JOHN EVELYN

[2348]
How easy is pen-and-paper piety! I will
not say it costs nothing; but it is far
cheaper to work one's head than one's
heart to goodness. I can write a hundred meditations sooner than subdue
the least sin in my soul.

THOMAS FULLER

[2349]
Genuine piety is the spring of peace of
mind.

JEAN DE LA BRUYÈRE

[2350]
Piety requires us to renounce no ways
of life where we can act reasonably and
offer what we do to the glory of God.

WILLIAM LAW

[2351]
A pious mind prizes honor above
worldly goods.

REMBRANDT VAN RIJN

[2352]
Piety, stretched beyond a certain point,
is the parent of impiety.

SYDNEY SMITH

[2353]
Some persons think they have to look
like a hedgehog to be pious.

BILLY SUNDAY

[2354]
Let them learn first to show piety at
home.

1 TIMOTHY 5:4 (KJV)

[2355]
He who is pious does not contend but
teaches in love.

ULRICH ZWINGLI

POLITICS

[2356]
You have no commission to preach
politics.

BISHOPS JAMES O. ANDREW,
ROBERT PAINE, AND
GEORGE F. PIERCE
(to Methodist Episcopal Church,
South, clergy, 1865)

[2357]
What has the emperor to do with the
church?

DONATUS THE GREAT

[2358]
Politics makes strange postmasters.

KIN HUBBARD

[2359]
We know that separation of state and
church is a source of strength, but the
conscience of our nation does not call
for separation between men of state
and faith in the Supreme Being. The
men who have guided the destiny of
the United States have found the
strength for their tasks by going to
their knees. This private unity of public
men and their God is an enduring
source of . . . reassurance for the people of America.

LYNDON B. JOHNSON

[2360]
Christian political action does not
mean waiting for the orders of the
bishop or campaigning under the banner of the church; rather, it means
bringing to politics a sense of Christian
responsibility.

FRANZISKUS KOENIG

POLLUTION

[2361]
If you want to clear the stream, get the hog out of the spring.
AMERICAN PROVERB

[2362]
The central problem of our age has become the contamination of man's total environment.
RACHEL CARSON

[2363]
The path of civilization is paved with tin cans.
ELBERT HUBBARD

[2364]
Only if we determine not to desecrate it will we be enabled to complete our God-given task—which is to control the earth and provide a suitable habitation for all men. The choice is ours.
E. JAMES KENNEDY

[2365]
You shall not thus pollute the land in which you live.
NUMBERS 35:33 (RSV)

[2366]
To waste, to destroy, our natural resources, to skin and exhaust the land instead of using it so as to increase its usefulness, will result in undermining in the days of our children the very prosperity which we ought by right to hand down to them amplified and developed.
THEODORE ROOSEVELT

[2367]
In two generations this nation [America] will self-destruct.
FRED SMITH

POWER

[2368]
Power in the Christian life depends upon our connection with the source of power.
L. NELSON BELL

[2369]
The real function of power and the order it creates is the liberation of men and women to think and be and make the most of themselves.
ADOLF A. BERLE

[2370]
Dominion is impossible without authority, and authority is useless without power.
SAMUEL CHADWICK

[2371]
A witness is not one who is entranced by Jesus, by the revelation he gives or by what he has done. A witness is one who has received the energy Jesus himself had, and has become a witness that pleases him, wherever he may be placed, whatever he may be doing, and whether he is known or unknown.
OSWALD CHAMBERS

[2372]
The center of power is not to be found in summit meetings or in peace conferences. It is not in Peking or Washington or the United Nations, but rather where a child of God prays in the power of the Spirit for God's will to be done in his life, in his home, and in the world about him.
RUTH BELL GRAHAM

[2373]
God does not invest a man with power for any other work than that of the Kingdom.
J. STUART HOLDEN

[2374]
No man can do the work of God until he have the Holy Spirit and is endued with power. It is impossible to preach the Gospel save in the power of the Spirit.

G. CAMPBELL MORGAN

[2375]
The same power that brought Christ back from the dead is operative within those who are Christ's. The resurrection is an ongoing thing.

LEON MORRIS

[2376]
If we would answer the question, "Where is the Church?" we must ask, "Where is the Holy Spirit recognizably present with power?"

LESSLIE NEWBIGIN

[2377]
There is a pride of power in which the human ego assumes its self-sufficiency and self-mastery and imagines itself secure against all vicissitudes.

REINHOLD NIEBUHR

[2378]
Goals have little to do with creating the power to get from here to there.

STEPHEN C. ROSE

[2379]
It would take a theologian with a fine-toothed comb to find the Holy Spirit recognizably present with power in much of our ecclesiastical routine.

SAMUEL M. SHOEMAKER

[2380]
Power over other people, power over nature, power over supernatural forces, and power over himself—such is the four-sided goal of natural man.*

PRAISE

[2381]
One thing scientists have discovered is that often-praised children become more intelligent than often-blamed ones. There's a creative element in praise.

THOMAS DREIER

[2382]
Praise makes good men better and bad men worse.

THOMAS FULLER

[2383]
Praise is like a plow set to go deep into the soil of believers' hearts. It lets the glory of God into the details of daily living.

C. M. HANSON

[2384]
They loved the praise of men more than the praise of God.

JOHN 12:43
(The Living Bible)

[2385]
All censure of a man's self is oblique praise.

SAMUEL JOHNSON

[2386]
The continual offering of praise requires stamina; we ought to praise God even when we do not feel like it. Praising him takes away the blues and restores us to normal.

HAROLD LINDSELL

[2387]
The trouble with most of us is that we would rather be ruined by praise than saved by criticism.

NORMAN VINCENT PEALE

[2388]
Let another praise you, and not your own mouth.

PROVERBS 27:2 (RSV)

[2389]
I will praise him as long as I live, yes,
even with my dying breath.
PSALM 146:2
(The Living Bible)

[2390]
Let everything that breathes praise the
Lord!
PSALM 150:6 (RSV)

[2391]
Praise from a wife is praise indeed.
ERNEST R. PUNSHON

[2392]
Try praising your wife even if it does
frighten her at first.
BILLY SUNDAY

PRAYER

[2393]
Between the humble and contrite heart
and the majesty of heaven there are no
barriers; the only password is prayer.
HOSEA BALLOU

[2394]
If you are swept off your feet, it's time
to get on your knees.
FRED BECK

[2395]
No heart thrives without much secret
converse with God, and nothing will
make amends for the want of it.
JOHN BERRIDGE

[2396]
Prayer is a shield to the soul, a sacrifice
to God, and a scourge to Satan.
JOHN BUNYAN

[2397]
Prayer does not enable us to do a
greater work for God. Prayer is a
greater work for God.
THOMAS CHALMERS

[2398]
Most of us have much trouble praying
when we are in little trouble, but we
have little trouble praying when we are
in much trouble.
RICHARD P. COOK

[2399]
The man who kneels to God can stand
up to anything.
LOUIS H. EVANS, JR.

[2400]
Prayer is for the religious life what
original research is for science—by it
we get direct contact with reality. . . .
We pray because we were made for
prayer, and God draws us out by
breathing himself in.
P. T. FORSYTH

[2401]
To pray is nothing more involved than
to lie in the sunshine of God's grace.
OLE HALLESBY

[2402]
Prayer is the breath of the new-born
soul, and there can be no Christian life
without it.
ROWLAND HILL

[2403]
He who has learned how to pray has
learned the greatest secret of a holy
and a happy life.
WILLIAM LAW

[2404]
What a man is on his knees before God,
that he is—and nothing more.
ROBERT MURRAY McCHEYNE

[2405]
The Christian on his knees sees more
than the philosopher on tiptoe.
DWIGHT L. MOODY

[2406]
The Lord hates the gifts of the wicked, but delights in the prayers of his people.

PROVERBS 15:8
(*The Living Bible*)

[2407]
The self-sufficient do not pray, the self-satisfied will not pray, the self-righteous cannot pray. No man is greater than his prayer life.

LEONARD RAVENHILL

[2408]
Prayer enlarges the heart until it is capable of containing God's gift of himself.

MOTHER TERESA OF CALCUTTA

[2409]
I don't know of a single foreign product that enters this country untaxed except the answer to prayer.

MARK TWAIN

[2410]
If your troubles are deep-seated or long-standing, try kneeling.

[2411]
Seven days without prayer make one weak.

[2412]
When the outlook is bad, try the uplook.

Prayer and Action

[2413]
Prayer is the most powerful form of energy that one can generate.

ALEXIS CARREL

[2414]
If God is going to do it, it has to be by prayer.

ARMIN GESSWEIN

[2415]
Prayer is the principal work of a minister, and it is by this he must carry on the rest.

THOMAS HOOKER

[2416]
In prayer we see the issues; by prayer we are moved to act.

ROY NEEHALL

[2417]
He who prays as he ought will endeavor to live as he prays.

JOHN OWEN

Prayer, Answer to

[2418]
I am not so sure that I believe in "the power of prayer," but I do believe in the power of the Lord who answers prayer.

DONALD GREY BARNHOUSE

[2419]
God answers sharp and sudden on some prayers,/ And thrusts the thing we have prayed for in our face.

ELIZABETH BARRETT BROWNING
"Aurora Leigh"

[2420]
God always answers us in the deeps, never in the shallows of our soul.

AMY CARMICHAEL

[2421]
I believe that we get an answer to our prayers when we are willing to obey what is implicit in that answer. I believe that we get a vision of God when we are willing to accept what that vision does to us.

ELSIE CHAMBERLAIN

[2422]
Keep praying, but be thankful that God's answers are wiser than your prayers!

WILLIAM CULBERTSON

[2423]
We do not receive things by prayer. We
receive them by Jesus.

ARMIN GESSWEIN

[2424]
The privilege of prayer, to me, is one of
the most cherished possessions, because faith and experience alike con-
vince me that God himself sees and answers, and his answers I never venture
to criticize. It is only my part to ask.

WILFRED T. GRENFELL

[2425]
Some prayers have a longer voyage
than others, but they return with the
richer lading at last, so that the praying
soul is a gainer by waiting for an answer.

WILLIAM GURNALL

[2426]
Prayer is the slender nerve that moves
the muscle of Omnipotence.

J. EDWIN HARTILL

[2427]
When we are praying, the thought will
often cross our minds that (if only we
knew it) the event is already decided
one way or the other. I believe this to
be no good reason for ceasing our
prayers. The event certainly has been
decided—in a sense it was decided
"before all worlds." But one of the
things that really cause it to happen
may be this very prayer that we are now
offering.

C. S. LEWIS

[2428]
Prayer is a powerful thing, for God has
bound and tied himself thereto. None
can believe how powerful prayer is, and
what it is able to effect, but those who
have learned it by experience.

MARTIN LUTHER

[2429]
If you will pray in union to Jesus, having childlike confidence toward God,
having the spirit of adoption, crying
Abba within you, seeking the glory of
God more than all personal benefits, I
believe that in all such cases you will
get the very thing you ask, at the very
time you ask it. Before you call, God
will answer; and while you are speaking, he will hear. God will either give
you what you ask, or something far better.

ROBERT MURRAY MCCHEYNE

[2430]
Prayer is not an argument with God to
persuade him to move things our way,
but an exercise by which we are enabled by his Spirit to move ourselves
his way.

LEONARD RAVENHILL

Prayer, as Communication

[2431]
When the Spirit prays through us, he
trims our praying down to the will of
God. . . . The Holy Spirit is both
teacher and lesson. We pray, not by the
truth he reveals to us, but we pray by
the actual presence of the Holy Spirit.
He kindles the desire in hearts by his
own flame.

E. M. BOUNDS

[2432]
Prayer is simply intelligent, purposeful, devoted contact with God. Where
that contact is established and sustained, prayer will work infallibly according to its own inherent laws.

CHARLES H. BRENT

[2433]
Prayer is and remains always a native
and deep impulse of the soul of man.

THOMAS CARLYLE

[2434]
Since the lines have been cleared between the Lord and me, the telephone has never stopped ringing.
BERNARD L. CLARK

[2435]
Prayer is conversation with God.
CLEMENT OF ALEXANDRIA

[2436]
And Satan trembles when he sees / The weakest saint upon his knees.
WILLIAM COWPER

[2437]
We can prove the reality of prayer only by praying.
SHERWOOD EDDY

[2438]
Tell God all that is in your heart, as one unloads one's heart to a dear friend. People who have no secrets from each other never want subjects of conversation; they do not weigh their words, because there is nothing to be kept back. Neither do they seek for something to say; they talk out of the abundance of their hearts, just what they think. Blessed are they who attain to such familiar, unreserved intercourse with God.
FRANÇOIS DE LA MOTHE FÉNELON

[2439]
Prayer is the highest use to which speech can be put.
P. T. FORSYTH

[2440]
A good prayer, though often used, is still fresh and fair in the eyes and ears of heaven.
THOMAS FULLER

[2441]
He who has learned to pray has learned the greatest secret of a holy and happy life.
WILLIAM LAW

[2442]
To be with God, there is no need to be continually in church. We may make an oratory of our heart wherein to retire from time to time to converse with him in meekness, humility and love. There is not in the world a kind of life more sweet and delightful than that of a continual conversation with God.
BROTHER LAWRENCE

[2443]
If your knees are knocking, kneel on them.
LONDON AIR RAID GRAFFITO,
World War II

[2444]
No one can say his prayers are poor prayers when he is using the language of love.
JOHN MAILLARD

[2445]
The first thing I do, after having asked in a few words the Lord's blessing upon his precious Word, is to begin to meditate on the Word of God, searching as it were into every verse to get blessing out of it . . . for the sake of obtaining food for my soul. The result I have found to be almost invariably this, that after a very few minutes my soul has been led to confession, or to thanksgiving, or to intercession, or to supplication; so that, though I did not, as it were, give myself to prayer but to meditation, it had turned almost immediately more or less into prayer.
GEORGE MÜLLER

[2446]
Where God is concerned the only language open to us is prayer.
J. H. OLDHAM

[2447]
In a single day I have prayed as many
as a hundred times, and in the night
almost as often.
                    PATRICK OF IRELAND

[2448]
If we are willing to take hours on end
to learn to play a piano, or operate a
computer, or fly an airplane, it is sheer
nonsense for us to imagine that we can
learn the high art of getting guidance
through communion with the Lord
without being willing to set aside time
for it. It is no accident that the Bible
speaks of prayer as a form of waiting on
God.
                    PAUL S. REES

[2449]
A hurried glance at Christ snatched
after lying abed too late will never
effect a radical transformation of character.
                    J. OSWALD SANDERS

[2450]
We are always in the presence of God,
yet it seems to me that those who pray
are in his presence in a very different
sense.
                    TERESA OF AVILA

[2451]
Pray constantly.
        1 THESSALONIANS 5:17 (RSV)

[2452]
Hezekiah took his morning mail, with
its bad news, and forwarded it to God.
                    WILLIAM VANDER HOVEN
                    (on 2 Kings 19:14)

Prayer, Corporate

[2453]
The spectacle of a nation praying is
more awe-inspiring than the explosion
of an atomic bomb. Prayer is man's
greatest means of tapping the infinite
resources of God.
                    J. EDGAR HOOVER

[2454]
The very act of prayer honors God and
gives glory to God, for it confesses that
God is what he is.
                    CHARLES KINGSLEY

[2455]
Again I tell you this: if two of you agree
on earth about any request you have to
make, that request will be granted by
my heavenly Father. For where two or
three have met together in my name, I
am there among them.
                    MATTHEW 18:19–20 (NEB)

[2456]
If we ever forget our basic charter—
"My house is a house of prayer"—we
might as well shut the church doors
forever. For if we lose that emphasis,
all the rest—the dynamic of our corporate witness, the impact on society, the
outreach existentially into the lives of
men—will soon rot and wither and die.
                    JAMES S. STEWART

Prayer, Intercessory

[2457]
Talking to men for God is a great
thing, but talking to God for men is
greater still.
                    E. M. BOUNDS

[2458]
In the morning I spent, I believe, an hour in prayer, with great intenseness and freedom, and with the most soft and tender affection toward mankind. I longed that those who, I have reason to think, owe me ill will, might be eternally happy. It seemed refreshing to think of meeting them in heaven, how much soever they had injured me on earth. I had no disposition to insist upon any confession from them in order to effect reconciliation between us, and the exercise of love and kindness to them on my part.

DAVID BRAINERD

[2459]
We know that God's nature is unchangeable; are we sure that his will is equally so? Is the wish, the submitted wish of a human heart, able to alter the counsel of the Almighty? Can the humble request of believing lips restrain, accelerate, change the settled order of events? Can prayer make things that are not to be as though they were? Yes, a thousand times yes! Intercession is the mother tongue of the whole family of Christ.

DORA GREENWELL

[2460]
There are three things to be seen in an intercessor which are not necessarily found in ordinary prayer: identification, agony, and authority.... Intercession so identifies the intercessor with the sufferer that it gives him a prevailing place with God.

NORMAN P. GRUBB

[2461]
One only asks God to do through another what he is willing for the Lord to do through him. That is the law of intercession on every level of life. Only so far as we have been tested and proved willing to do a thing ourselves can we intercede for others. Christ is an Intercessor, because he took the place of each one prayed for. We are never called to intercede for sin—that has been done once and for all; but we are often called to intercede for sinners and their needs, and the Holy Spirit can never "bind the strong man" through us on a higher level than that in which he has first had victory in us.

REES HOWELLS

[2462]
There is nothing that makes us love a man so much as praying for him.

WILLIAM LAW

[2463]
If I could hear Christ praying for me in the next room, I would not fear a million enemies. Yet distance makes no difference. He *is* praying for me.

ROBERT MURRAY MCCHEYNE

[2464]
The prayer that we find hardest to comprehend, namely, the intercessory, Jesus took most easily and naturally for granted.

FRANCIS J. MCCONNELL

[2465]
We do not know what and how we ought to pray, but the Spirit himself intercedes on our behalf with sighs too deep for words.

ROMANS 8:26
(Berkeley)

[2466]
[Christ] is the one who died for us and came back to life again for us and is sitting at the place of highest honor next to God, pleading for us there in heaven.

ROMANS 8:34
(The Living Bible)

[2467]
To intercede means literally "to pass between." . . . How the intercession of Christ is conducted, it does not become us either anxiously to inquire, or dogmatically to affirm. . . . Among the innumerable multitude of the chosen of God, not one shall be omitted. Nor is it for all in the mass that the Savior makes intercession. He prays for each by himself. With infinite compassion and skill is every special case of each individual presented by this divine Advocate to his Father.

WILLIAM SYMINGTON

[2468]
Prayer is not conquering God's reluctance but laying hold of God's willingness.

Prayer, Petitionary

[2469]
As a physician I have seen men, after all other therapy had failed, lifted out of disease and melancholy by the serene effort of prayer.

ALEXIS CARREL

[2470]
Talk to him in prayer of all your wants, your troubles, even of the weariness you feel in serving him. You cannot speak too freely, too trustfully, to him.

FRANÇOIS DE LA MOTHE FÉNELON

[2471]
I like ejaculatory prayer; it reaches heaven before the devil can get a shot at it.

ROWLAND HILL

[2472]
The prayer of a righteous man has great power in its effects.

JAMES 5:16 (RSV)

[2473]
Many a fellow is praying for rain with his tub the wrong side up.

SAM JONES

[2474]
You need not cry very loud: he is nearer to us than we think.

BROTHER LAWRENCE

[2475]
I have been driven many times to my knees by the overwhelming conviction that I had nowhere else to go.

ABRAHAM LINCOLN

[2476]
Spread out your petition before God, and then say, "Thy will, not mine, be done." The sweetest lesson I have learned in God's school is to let the Lord choose for me.

DWIGHT L. MOODY

[2477]
If I had cherished iniquity in my heart, the Lord would not have listened.

PSALM 66:18 (RSV)

[2478]
Much of our praying is just asking God to bless some folks that are ill, and to keep us plugging along. But prayer is not merely prattle: it is warfare.

ALAN REDPATH

[2479]
Whether we like it or not, asking is the rule of the Kingdom.

CHARLES H. SPURGEON

[2480]
Prayer is not overcoming God's reluctance: it is laying hold of his highest willingness.

RICHARD CHENEVIX TRENCH

PREACHERS, PREACHING

[2481]
Actors speak of things imaginary as if they were real, while you preachers too often speak of things real as if they were imaginary.

THOMAS BETTERTON

[2482]
A good sermon should be as exciting as a baseball game.

ANDREW W. BLACKWOOD

[2483]
Preach faith till you have it; and then, because you have it, preach faith.

PETER BOHLER
(to John Wesley)

[2484]
The life-giving preacher is a man of God, whose heart is ever athirst for God, whose soul is following hard after God, whose eye is single to God, and in whom by the power of God's Spirit the flesh and the world have been crucified; his ministry is like the generous flood of a life-giving river. Life-giving preaching costs the preacher much—death to self, crucifixion to the world, the travail of his own soul. Only crucified preaching can give life. Crucified preaching can come only from a crucified man.

E. M. BOUNDS

[2485]
Preaching is truth given through personality.

PHILLIPS BROOKS

[2486]
He preaches well who lives well. That's all the divinity I know.

MIGUEL DE CERVANTES

[2487]
Don't preach any more. Let's have a moratorium on preaching. There has been too much preaching. Let's just take an outline and go into the pulpit and tell the story of Jesus and how he died for our sins and how he took them away, and sets us free. That's what we need to hear.

J. WILBUR CHAPMAN

[2488]
To love to preach is one thing—to love those to whom we preach, quite another.

RICHARD CECIL

[2489]
The Christian messenger cannot think too highly of his Prince, or too humbly of himself.

CHARLES C. COLTON

[2490]
It pleased God through the folly of what we preach to save those who believe.

1 CORINTHIANS 1:21 (RSV)

[2491]
If it is possible to train elephants to dance, lions to play, and leopards to hunt, it should be possible to teach preachers to preach.

DESIDERIUS ERASMUS

[2492]
When power goes out of the message it is because the Word has become not flesh, but words.

LEIGHTON FORD

[2493]
A preacher whose chief power is not in studious prayer is, to that extent, a man who does not know his business. Prayer is the minister's business. He cannot be a sound preacher unless he is a priest.

P. T. FORSYTH

[2494]
Wherever the Gospel is preached, no matter how crudely, there are bound to be results.

BILLY GRAHAM

[2495]
No preaching can be evangelistic which does not stress the utter, essential need that man, however cultured and civilized, has for God.

BRYAN GREEN

[2496]
A strong and faithful pulpit is no mean safeguard of a nation's life.

JOHN HALL

[2497]
It is not the business of the preacher to fill the house. It is his business to fill the pulpit.

VANCE HAVNER

[2498]
We are sent to preach not sociology but salvation; not economics but evangelism; not reform but redemption; not culture but conversion; not progress but pardon; not the new social order but the new birth; not a new organization but a new creation; not democracy but the Gospel; not civilization but Christ. We are ambassadors, not diplomats.

HUGH THOMSON KERR

[2499]
When I hear a man preach I like to see him act as if he were fighting bees.

ABRAHAM LINCOLN

[2500]
If the church does not fulfil its destiny the Gospel will not be preached. Even the angels cannot preach the Gospel. This is reserved for the church of Jesus Christ alone.

HAROLD LINDSELL

[2501]
It is not our comment on the Word that saves, but the Word itself.

ROBERT MURRAY MCCHEYNE

[2502]
Preaching is a manifestation of the incarnate Word, from the written Word, by the spoken word.

BERNARD MANNING

[2503]
The best way to revive a church is to build a fire in the pulpit.

DWIGHT L. MOODY

[2504]
My grand point in preaching is to break the hard heart and to heal the broken one.

JOHN NEWTON

[2505]
I think that some of our voices in the pulpit today tend to speak too much about religion in the abstract, rather than in the personal, simple terms which I heard in my earlier years. More preaching from the Bible, rather than just about the Bible, is what America needs.

RICHARD NIXON

[2506]
Preaching is not the art of making a sermon and delivering it. Preaching is the art of making a preacher and delivering that.

WILLIAM A. QUAYLE

[2507]
If the houses of worship in the big town are not drawing the customers as they should, it is not because religion is at a low ebb; it is because the preachers are too dull. Our greatest need in the New York pulpit is a few preachers who will haul off and slap the ears off evil in words that the lads around Lindy's will savvy, in the remote event they read them.

DAMON RUNYON

[2508]
Preaching is thirty minutes in which to raise the dead.

JOHN RUSKIN

[2509]
I have known what it is to use up all my ammunition, and then I have, as it were, rammed myself into the great Gospel gun, and I have fired myself at my hearers; all my experience of God's goodness, all my consciousness of sin, and all my sense of the power of the Gospel. And there are some people upon whom that kind of preaching tells when nothing else does, for they see that then you are communicating to them not only the Gospel, but yourself also.

CHARLES H. SPURGEON

[2510]
Preach nothing down but the devil, nothing up but the Christ.

CHARLES H. SPURGEON

[2511]
In Washington they preach to Daniel Webster, the statesman, but this [country preacher] has been telling Daniel Webster, the sinner, of Jesus, and it has been helping him.

DANIEL WEBSTER

[2512]
Give me one hundred preachers who fear nothing but sin and desire nothing but God, and I care not a straw whether they be clergymen or laymen, such alone will shake the gates of hell and set up the Kingdom of God upon earth.

JOHN WESLEY

[2513]
The Christian world is in a dead sleep. Nothing but a loud voice can awaken them out of it.

GEORGE WHITEFIELD

PREDESTINATION

[2514]
I would ask, "Who made me? Not my God, who is not only good but Goodness itself. For if he did, how is it I will to do evil and bypass the good, and so earn punishment for myself? Who gave me this will? Who planted this seed of bitterness in me when all I am is what God made me, and he is Sweetness itself? If the devil is to blame, where did the devil come from? . . . Didn't the Creator, who is all good, make his angels all good?"

AUGUSTINE OF HIPPO

[2515]
God has an exasperating habit of laying his hands on the wrong man.

JOSEPH D. BLINCO

[2516]
From the very beginning God decided that those who came to him—and all along he knew who would—should become like his Son, so that his Son would be the First, with many brothers.

ROMANS 8:29
(*The Living Bible*)

[2517]
God is preparing his heroes; and when the opportunity comes, he can fit them into their places in a moment, and the world will wonder where they came from.

A. B. SIMPSON

[2518]
Lord, save all the elect, and then elect some more.

CHARLES H. SPURGEON

[2519]
All those whom God hath predestinated unto life . . . he is pleased, in his appointed and accepted time, effectually to call by his Word and Spirit.

WESTMINSTER CONFESSION OF FAITH

[2520]
God predestines every man to be saved. The devil predestines every man to be damned. Man has the casting vote.

PREJUDICE

[2521]
Prejudice, put theologically, is one of man's several neurotic and perverted expressions of his will to be God.

KYLE HASELDEN

[2522]
Prejudice is the child of ignorance.

WILLIAM HAZLITT

[2523]
Beware lest we mistake our prejudices for our convictions.

H. A. IRONSIDE

[2524]
A great many people think they are thinking when they are merely rearranging their prejudices.

WILLIAM JAMES

[2525]
Remember, when the judgment is weak, the prejudice is strong.

KANE O'HARA

[2526]
Very few people take the trouble to use their brains as long as their prejudices are in working condition.

ROY L. SMITH

[2527]
No person is strong enough to carry a cross and a prejudice at the same time.

WILLIAM A. WARD

[2528]
Passion and prejudice govern the world, only under the name of reason.

JOHN WESLEY

[2529]
Prejudices are often carefully taught, and once established they are strengthened by superstitions, old wives' tales and downright lies.

PRIDE

[2530]
Pride is detested in the sight of the Lord and of men, and injustice is wrong in the sight of both.

ECCLESIASTICUS 10:7
(Goodspeed)

[2531]
An ass may bray a good while before he shakes the stars down.

GEORGE ELIOT

[2532]
You can have no greater sign of a confirmed pride than when you think you are humble enough.

WILLIAM LAW

[2533]
A proud man is always looking down
on things and people; and, of course,
as long as you're looking down, you
can't see something that's above you.
C. S. LEWIS

[2534]
God sends no one away empty except
those who are full of themselves.
DWIGHT L. MOODY

[2535]
Before we become too arrogant with
the most deadly of the seven deadly
sins, the sin of pride, let us remember
that the two great wars of this century,
wars which cost twenty million dead,
were fought between Christian nations
praying to the same God.
RICHARD NIXON

[2536]
"For if a man thinketh himself to be
something, when he is nothing, he de-
ceiveth himself"—and nobody else.
JOSEPH PARKER

[2537]
An inferiority complex would be a
blessing, if only the right people had it.
ALAN REED

[2538]
The earth is strewn with the exploded
bladders of the puffed up.
CARL SANDBURG

[2539]
Be not proud of race, face, place, or
grace.
CHARLES H. SPURGEON

PROBLEMS

[2540]
To solve a problem it is necessary to
think. It is necessary to think even to
decide what facts to collect.
ROBERT MAYNARD HUTCHINS

[2541]
Problems are only opportunities in
work clothes.
HENRY J. KAISER

[2542]
A problem well stated is a problem half
solved.
CHARLES F. KETTERING

[2543]
Learn to eat problems for breakfast.
ALFRED ARMAND MONTAPERT

[2544]
I believe that problems can be dissolved by grace, like a mist that is dis-
sipated by the sunshine. One sees the
Christian Gospel of salvation quite
concretely at work in the gradual disso-
lution of tangled problems, without
any of them being solved in the usual
sense of the word.
PAUL TOURNIER

[2545]
If a care is too small to be turned into
a prayer, it is too small to be made into
a burden.

[2546]
Obstacles are those terrifying things
we see when we take our eyes off our
goals.

PROCLAMATION

[2547]
Without continued proclamation of the
Good News in Christ the church would
never have got off the ground. In a
generation it would have become ex-
tinct.
OSWALD C. J. HOFFMANN

[2548]
The word of man does not become the
Word of God by being loudly proclaimed. No amount of noise and lather
can substitute for the note of authority.
God does not promise to bless the
proclamation of our own clever ideas;
but he does promise, "My word . . .
shall not return unto me void" (Isaiah
55:11).
CHARLES W. KOLLER

[2549]
Proclaim liberty throughout the land to
all its inhabitants.
LEVITICUS 25:10 (RSV)

[2550]
Traditional Christianity begins with a
triumphant indicative.
J. GRESHAM MACHEN

[2551]
The proclamation and promulgation of
the Christian faith must arise out of the
continued rehearsal of the events recorded in the Bible.
DONALD G. MILLER

[2552]
The world does not require so much to
be informed as to be reminded.
HANNAH MORE

[2553]
The heavens are telling the glory of
God; and the firmament proclaims his
handiwork.
PSALM 19:1 (RSV)

PROCRASTINATION

[2554]
I could give no reply except a lazy and
drowsy, "Yes, Lord, yes, I'll get to it
right away; just don't bother me for a
little while." But "right away" didn't
happen right away; and "a little while"
turned out to be a very long while.
AUGUSTINE OF HIPPO

[2555]
Do not put off turning to the Lord, and
do not postpone it from day to day.
ECCLESIASTICUS 5:9
(Goodspeed)

[2556]
Procrastination brings loss, delay, dan-
ger.
DESIDERIUS ERASMUS

[2557]
The procrastinating man is forever
struggling with ruin.
HESIOD

[2558]
Procrastination is the thief of time.
EDWARD YOUNG

PROMISES

[2559]
The promises of God are just as good
as ready money any day.
BILLY BRAY

[2560]
All the promises of God find their Yes
in [Jesus]. That is why we utter the
Amen through him, to the glory of
God.
2 CORINTHIANS 1:20 (RSV)

[2561]
Promises may get friends, but it is performance that must nurse and keep
them.

OWEN FELTHAM

[2562]
Not only does the Old Testament tell
us to expect the Second Coming of
Christ, not only is the New Testament
filled with the promise of it, but if we
would study the historic documents of
our major denominations, we would
find that our founders all believed and
accepted it. The most thrilling, glorious truth in all the world is the Second
Coming of Jesus Christ. It is the sure
promise of the future.

BILLY GRAHAM

[2563]
Certainly there are promises in the Old
Testament which relate to material
things. But if God was faithful and merciful to Israel, whom he chose not because of their righteousness but only
because of his love for them, how much
more reason today to rest on the faithfulness of him who gave his beloved
Son for us! In that faithfulness is assured our right to God's promises.

PHILIP E. HOWARD, JR.

[2564]
Jesus promised his disciples three
things: that they would be completely
fearless, absurdly happy, and in constant trouble.

F. R. MALTBY

[2565]
God's promises are like the stars; the
darker the night the brighter they
shine.

DAVID NICHOLAS

[2566]
Remember that Jesus Christ came to
show that God is true to his promises
and to help the Jews. And remember
that he came also that the Gentiles
might be saved and give glory to God
for his mercies to them.

ROMANS 15:8–9
(*The Living Bible*)

[2567]
Swim through your temptations and
troubles. Run to the promises; they be
our Lord's branches hanging over the
water so that his half-drowned children
may take a grip of them. Let go that
grip and you sink to the bottom.

SAMUEL RUTHERFORD

PROOFS

[2568]
[Jesus] presented himself alive after his
passion by many proofs.

ACTS 1:3 (RSV)

[2569]
All the proof of a pudding is in the
eating.

WILLIAM CAMDEN

[2570]
No one ever proved the beauty of Beethoven's Fifth Symphony by holding it
over a bunsen burner.

ELAM DAVIS

[2571]
That which proves too much proves
nothing.

THOMAS FULLER

[2572]
A Christianity which does not prove its
worth in practice degenerates into dry
scholasticism and idle talk.

ABRAHAM KUYPER

[2573]
Confidence in the goodness of another
is good proof of one's own goodness.
MICHEL DE MONTAIGNE

[2574]
Test everything; hold fast what is good.
1 THESSALONIANS 5:21 (RSV)

[2575]
Some circumstantial evidence is very
strong, as when you find a trout in the
milk.
HENRY DAVID THOREAU

[2576]
The ultimate verification of our religion consists of the changed lives to
which it can point and for which it is
responsible.
ELTON TRUEBLOOD

PROPHET, PROPHECY

[2577]
Fulfillment of prophecies was only one
important element in the validation of
a "true" prophet. More important still
was the moral and religious content of
a prophet's message.
WILLIAM FOXWELL ALBRIGHT

[2578]
The prophet and the martyr do not see
the hooting throng. Their eyes are
fixed on the eternities.
BENJAMIN N. CARDOZO

[2579]
The task of prophecy has been to "dis-
cern the signs of the times," to see
what God is bringing to pass as the history of peoples and societies unfolds,
to point to the judgment he brings
upon all institutions.
JOHN B. COBURN

[2580]
Our knowledge is imperfect and our
prophecy is imperfect; but when the
perfect comes, the imperfect will pass
away.
1 CORINTHIANS 13:9–10 (RSV)

[2581]
There is only one real inevitability: It is
necessary that the Scripture be
fulfilled.
CARL F. H. HENRY

[2582]
I will pour out my spirit on all flesh;
your sons and your daughters shall
prophesy.
JOEL 2:28 (RSV)

[2583]
The Hebrew prophets were . . .
primarily exhorters, interpreters of the
will of God . . . men impelled by their
vision of God as a God of justice, holiness, love and the one and only God in
a polytheistic world.
RAPHAEL H. LEVINE

[2584]
A prophet is honored everywhere ex-
cept in his own hometown and among
his relatives and by his own family.
MARK 6:4
(The Living Bible)

[2585]
Beware of false prophets, who come to
you in sheep's clothing but inwardly
are ravenous wolves.
MATTHEW 7:15 (RSV)

[2586]
No prophecy recorded in Scripture was
ever thought up by the prophet himself. It was the Holy Spirit within these
godly men who gave them true messages from God.
2 PETER 1:20–21
(The Living Bible)

[2587]
Do not despise prophesying.
1 Thessalonians 5:20 (rsv)

PROVIDENCE

[2588]
Behind a frowning Providence / He
hides a smiling face.
William Cowper
"Light Shining Out of Darkness"

[2589]
What God sends is better than what
men ask for.
Croatian Proverb

[2590]
God's ways are behind the scenes, but
he moves all the scenes which he is behind.
John Nelson Darby

[2591]
The longer I live, the more faith I have
in Providence, and the less faith in my
interpretation of Providence.
Jeremiah Day

[2592]
Providence is the care God takes of all
existing things.
John of Damascus

[2593]
By going a few minutes sooner or later,
by stopping to speak with a friend on
the corner, by meeting this man or
that, or by turning down this street instead of the other, we may let slip some
impending evil, by which the whole
current of our lives would have been
changed. There is no possible solution
in the dark enigma, but the one word
"Providence."
Henry Wadsworth Longfellow

[2594]
Providence gives us chance—and man
must mold it to his own designs.
Johann Friedrich von Schiller

[2595]
There's a special providence in the fall
of a sparrow.
Shakespeare
Hamlet, V, ii

[2596]
God tempers the wind to the shorn
lamb.
Laurence Sterne

[2597]
God needs no props for his stars and
planets. He hangs them on nothing.
So, in the working of God's providence, the unseen is prop enough for
the seen.
Augustus Hopkins Strong

[2598]
God builds the nest of the blind bird.
Turkish Proverb

[2599]
Providence has at all times been my
only dependence, for all other resources seem to have failed us.
George Washington

PSYCHIATRY, PSYCHOLOGY

[2600]
Love—incomparably the greatest psy-
chotherapeutic agent—is something
that professional psychiatry cannot of
itself create, focus, or release.
Gordon W. Allport

[2601]
A sound philosophy or a sincere religious belief does not obviate the need for psychiatric assistance with emotional disorders.
FRANCIS J. BRACELAND

[2602]
Psychoanalysis is confession without absolution.
G. K. CHESTERTON

[2603]
The terminology of psychiatry is simply a roundabout and veiled corroboration of Christian doctrine.
JOHN E. LARGE

[2604]
Psychology alone is never enough for man's great adventure—life. It is a key to the temple, not the temple itself.
JOSHUA LOTH LIEBMAN

[2605]
The business of psychology is to tell us what actually goes on in the mind. It cannot possibly tell us whether the beliefs are true or false.
HASTINGS RASHDALL

[2606]
Prayer has an important place in psychiatric treatment.
EDWARD S. STRECKER

[2607]
One out of every four Americans is mentally ill. If three of your friends are okay, you're in trouble!

PURPOSE

[2608]
In Christ may be seen that for which the whole universe has come into existence.
EDWYN BEVAN

[2609]
We are not taken up into conscious agreement with God's purpose; we are taken up into God's purpose without any consciousness at all.
OSWALD CHAMBERS

[2610]
Our lives will be complete only when we express the full intent of the Master.
CHARLES R. HEMBREE

[2611]
[We must sail through the sea of life] beeing full fraught with humility, bound for the land of promise, hauing our sayles of heauenlie hope fylled with the winde of God's Spirite, being dyrected by the roother [rudder] of wisedome, with the anchor of faith, and the mainemast of an vpright conscience and smothe conuersation in Christ Iesu.
RICHARD MADDOXE

[2612]
Man, made in the image of God, has a purpose—to be in relationship to God, who is there. Man forgets his purpose and thus he forgets who he is and what life means.
FRANCIS A. SCHAEFFER

[2613]
More men fail through lack of purpose than through lack of talent.
BILLY SUNDAY

[2614]
The first consideration a wise man fixes upon is the great end of his creation: what it is and wherein it consists. The next is of the most proper means to that end.

JAMES BARR WALKER

[2615]
When you're up to your waist in alligators, it's difficult to remember that your main objective was to drain the swamp.

QUIETNESS

[2616]
I discover an arrant laziness in my soul. For when I am to read a chapter in the Bible, before I begin I look where it endeth. And if it endeth not on the same side, I cannot keep my hands from turning over the leaf, to measure the length thereof on the other side; if it swells to many verses, I begin to grudge. Surely my heart is not rightly affected. Were I truly hungry after heavenly food, I would not complain of meat. Scourge, Lord, this laziness of my soul; make the reading of thy Word not a penance but a pleasure unto me; so I may esteem that chapter in Thy Word the best which is the longest.

THOMAS FULLER

[2617]
As the morning is to you the beginning of a new life; as God has then given you a new enjoyment of yourself and a fresh entrance into the world, it is highly proper that your first devotions should be a praise and thanksgiving to God, as for a new creation; and that you should offer and devote body and soul, all that you are, and all that you have, to his service and glory.

WILLIAM LAW

[2618]
A habit of devout fellowship with God is the spring of all our life, and the strength of it. Such prayer, meditation and converse with God restores and renews the temper of our minds; so that by this contact with the world unseen we receive continual accesses of strength.

HENRY E. MANNING

[2619]
The more I pray, the more I feel my need of the Word. The more I read God's Word, the more I have to pray, and the more power I have in prayer.

ANDREW MURRAY

[2620]
I grew up in the generation of the giants—John R. Mott and his disciples —among whom it was taken for granted that if you were going to live the Christian life at all, you would give at least one hour daily, before the first meal of the day, to seeking God through his Word and to listening to his voice.

STEPHEN NEILL

[2621]
All the troubles of life come upon us because we refuse to sit quietly for a while each day in our rooms.

BLAISE PASCAL

[2622]
If you can beat the devil in the matter of regular daily prayer, you can beat him anywhere. If he can beat you there, he can possibly beat you anywhere.

PAUL RADER

[2623]
Don't pray when you feel like it. Have an appointment with the Lord and keep it. A man is powerful on his knees.

CORRIE TEN BOOM

[2624]
Every bearer of the Good News must
tarry first, in order to have time to
blend his will with the Master's and to
discover his purposes.

MARY S. WOOD

[2625]
A man said to his body, "Today I will
go with you three times to eat, but you
will come with me three times to pray."

RACE

[2626]
God that made the world and all things
therein . . . hath made of one blood all
nations of men for to dwell on the face
of the earth.

ACTS 17:24,26 (KJV)

[2627]
Whatever the color of a man's skin, we
are all mankind. So every denial of
freedom, of equal opportunity for a
livelihood, or for an education, diminishes me.

EVERETT MCKINLEY DIRKSEN

[2628]
The essential corruption of racial segregation is not that it is supported by
lies but that people believe the lies.

HARRY GOLDEN

[2629]
God will judge any society, people or
nation that does not repent of its sins,
and one of the sins we need to repent
of is racism. Skin color does not matter
to God, for he is looking upon the
heart. . . . When men are standing at
the foot of the cross there are no racial
barriers.

BILLY GRAHAM

[2630]
The plague of racial injustice is not
contained within geographical limits. It
is not a regional issue. It is a national
issue and a national disgrace.

PAUL J. HALLINAN

[2631]
Even though human beings differ from
one another by virtue of their ethnic
peculiarities, they all possess certain
common elements and are inclined by
nature to meet each other in the world
of spiritual values.

POPE JOHN XXIII

[2632]
Until justice is blind to color, until education is unaware of race, until opportunity is unconcerned with the color of
men's skins, emancipation will be a
proclamation but not a fact.

LYNDON B. JOHNSON

[2633]
I want to be the white man's brother,
not his brother-in-law.

MARTIN LUTHER KING, JR.

[2634]
The Constitution of the United States
does not, I think, permit any authority
to know the race of those entitled to be
protected in the enjoyment of . . . civil
rights, common to all citizens.

JOHN MARSHALL

[2635]
The chief sin of segregation is the dis-
tortion of human personality. It dam-
ages the soul of both the segregator
and the segregated.

BENJAMIN E. MAYS

[2636]
After all there is but one race—
humanity.

GEORGE MOORE

[2637]
The sin of racial pride still represents
the most basic challenge to the American conscience.
                ARTHUR M. SCHLESINGER, JR.

[2638]
The new evangelical finds it incredible
that anyone—Christian or non-Christian—should judge himself to be superior to another person on the basis
of racial origin.*

[2643]
Though it is easy to crown an ass with
laurel leaves, yet his ears will always
spoil the effect.

[2644]
What a real spiritual awakening does is
to take Jesus Christ out of the realm of
"religion" and into the world of reality.
It makes people look at themselves
honestly, stripped of their usual pro-
tective coloring.*

REALITY

[2639]
Fragrance is like light. It cannot be hidden. It is like love: intangible, invisible,
but always at once recognized. Though
it is neither to be touched, nor heard,
nor seen, we know that it is there. And
its opposite is just as impossible to
hide. This brings us to a solemn truth:
it is what we *are* that tells.
                AMY CARMICHAEL

[2640]
Make the application of Christianity to
present-day life a reality, and none will
support it with more zeal than the
workers.
                KEIR HARDIE

[2641]
If we spend sixteen hours a day dealing
with tangible things and only five minutes a day dealing with God, is it any
wonder that tangible things are two
hundred times more real to us than
God?
                WILLIAM R. INGE

[2642]
Christ moves among the pots and pans.
                TERESA OF AVILA

REASON

[2645]
Reason is a light that God has kindled
in the soul.
                ARISTOTLE

[2646]
The Almighty does nothing without
reason, though the frail mind of man
cannot explain the reason.
                AUGUSTINE OF HIPPO

[2647]
Reason is the life of the law; nay, the
Common Law itself is nothing else but
reason.
                EDWARD COKE

[2648]
I do not feel obliged to believe that the
same God who has endowed us with
sense, reason and intellect has intended us to forego their use.
                GALILEO

[2649]
Reason inspired by love of truth is the
only eye with which man can see the
spiritual heavens above us.
                CHARLES E. GARMAN

[2650]
Christian theology involves a revelational philosophy. The appeal to revealed truth involves not the rejection of the authority of reason, but an appeal from a limited and unenlightened reason to a reason fully informed. . . . Reason should be viewed not as a source of knowledge and contrasted with revelation, but as a means of comprehending revelation.

CARL F. H. HENRY

[2651]
Come now, let us reason together, says the Lord; though your sins are like scarlet, they shall be as white as snow; though they are red like crimson, they shall become like wool.

ISAIAH 1:18 (RSV)

[2652]
Error of opinion may be tolerated where reason is left free to combat it.

THOMAS JEFFERSON

[2653]
[Reason is] a free activity of the mind, reaching conclusions under no compulsion save that of evidence.

C. E. M. JOAD

REBELLION

[2654]
The task of life is not to be engaged in perpetual rebellion, but to find and serve our true Master.

E. L. ALLEN

[2655]
The rebellion that seethes in youth today has no foundation. They rebel against they know not what. They are searching for something, but what the something is they cannot say. We are the hope of the world, but we have no hope.

A Girl College Student
(aged 21)

[2656]
All the way through the Bible man is rebellious. Adam and Eve rebelled in the Garden of Eden against God. Cain rebelled against the teachings of God. The Tower of Babel was nothing but a rebellion. Lot rebelled against Abraham. Esau rebelled against Jacob. Absalom rebelled against David. And every one of us today is a rebel. Earth is a planet in rebellion against God.

BILLY GRAHAM

[2657]
What greater rebellion, impiety, or insult to God can there be, than not to believe his promises?

MARTIN LUTHER

[2658]
The religious dimension of sin is man's rebellion against God. The moral and social dimension of sin is injustice.

REINHOLD NIEBUHR

[2659]
Jesus Christ is the only platform from which a true radical, revolutionary program can be launched. . . . If you want to radicalize the world, if you want to radicalize your church, if you want to see things changed, you must begin with a change in yourself. Come to Christ and let him live his life through you.

TOM SKINNER

REBIRTH

[2660]
When Christ said, "Ye must be born again," the literal-minded Nicodemus was puzzled and asked, "Can a man enter a second time into his mother's womb and be born?" A statement intended to be prescriptive and incitive was mistaken for something informative and designative.

GORDON W. ALLPORT

[2661]
There could be no growth if there were not something planted. . . . Until the new man is born, or begotten, the soul abideth in death, and therefore cannot grow.

HORACE BUSHNELL

[2662]
Truly, truly, I say to you, unless one is born anew, he cannot see the kingdom of God.

JOHN 3:3 (RSV)

[2663]
Clang! Clang! went every bell in heaven, for Richard Knill was born again.

RICHARD KNILL

[2664]
By [God's] great mercy we have been born anew to a living hope through the resurrection of Jesus Christ from the dead, and to an inheritance which is imperishable, undefiled, and unfading, kept in heaven for you.

1 PETER 1:3–4 (RSV)

[2665]
As you have made a pretty considerable progress in the mysteries of electricity, I would now honestly recommend to your diligent unprejudiced pursuit and study the mysteries of the new birth.

GEORGE WHITEFIELD
(in letter to Benjamin Franklin)

[2666]
To be highborn is nice, but to be newborn is necessary!

REDEMPTION

[2667]
Redemption means that Jesus Christ can put into any man the heredity disposition that was in himself.

OSWALD CHAMBERS

[2668]
I know that my Redeemer lives, and at last he will stand upon the earth.

JOB 19:25 (RSV)

[2669]
Redemption [is] the liberation of man through Christ and the Holy Spirit from forces and thralldoms that hold him bound, individually and collectively.

JOHN A. MACKAY

[2670]
Redemption does not only look back to Calvary. It looks forward to the freedom in which the redeemed stand. Precisely because they have been redeemed at such a cost, believers must be God's men.

LEON MORRIS

[2671]
The experience of redemption which Christians now possess is but the firstfruits of that full redemption whose scope will embrace all history and nature. In Christ full redemption has already entered into the world but awaits its final consummation.

F. J. TAYLOR

RELATIONSHIPS

[2672]
If a man be gracious and courteous to strangers, it shows he is a citizen of the world, and that his heart is no island cut off from other lands, but a continent that joins them.

FRANCIS BACON

[2673]
Each of us has a capacity for God and an ability to relate to him in a personal way. When we do, he brings to us pardon for the past, peace for the present, and a promise for the future.

RALPH S. BELL

[2674]
Before any congregation can hope to excel in soul-winning, the officers and members must first be at peace with each other.

ANDREW W. BLACKWOOD

[2675]
God does not make the other person as I would have made him. He did not give him to me as a brother for me to dominate and control, but in order that I might find above him the Creator.

DIETRICH BONHOEFFER

[2676]
Do not fight with a hot-tempered man, and do not travel across the desert with him.

ECCLESIASTICUS 8:16
(Goodspeed)

[2677]
Do not neglect to show hospitality to strangers, for thereby some have entertained angels unawares.

HEBREWS 13:2 (RSV)

[2678]
In our relationship with ourselves, we should accept the unchangeable and change the unacceptable.

BERNARD O'BRIEN

[2679]
Repay no one evil for evil.

ROMANS 12:17 (RSV)

[2680]
We cannot exist without mutual help. All therefore that need aid have a right to ask it from their fellow men; and no one who has the power of granting can refuse it without guilt.

WALTER SCOTT

[2681]
It is better to be alone than in bad company.

GEORGE WASHINGTON

RELEVANCE

[2682]
Mustn't the churches adapt Christianity to suit the ideas of our time? No, they must not. Our ideas are killing us spiritually. When your child swallows poison, you don't sit around thinking of ways to adapt his constitution to a poisonous diet. You give him an emetic.

JOY DAVIDMAN

[2683]
In the world we live in, nothing can be
finally irrelevant. [Therefore] it is impossible to argue about religious faith
on the basis of relevance. We must, instead, insist upon the irrelevance of
relevance and argue upon the basis of
truth and truth claims.

KENNETH HAMILTON

[2684]
You can only find God in the now. Our
God is a God that moves. Only in the
contemporaneous does God converse
with men. His very name is "Now": "I
am that I am," and, "I will be that I will
be." God is still sovereign. He is at the
hub, while the church gnaws its fingers
in mystification that the vast majority in
East and West pass us by as irrelevant.
All through the Bible the contemporary situation is the arena in which you
meet God.

GEORGE F. MacLEOD

[2685]
The church that is married to the spirit
of the age will find itself a widow in the
next generation.

JOSEPH R. SIZOO

[2686]
Trying to be a "relevant social activist"
Christian without a personal relationship to Christ is like having the hiccups;
it doesn't leave much time for anything
else, and it can prove fatal.*

[2687]
Here is the tragic paradox of religion:
If we should seriously undertake to
turn as pilgrims toward that far-off land
which is our home . . . we only display
the catastrophe of human impotence in
the things of God. . . . What is our
undertaking of a visible relationship,
our scaling of the summit of human
possibility, but our completest separation from the true invisible relationship? Seen from God's standpoint, religion is precisely that which we had
better leave undone. . . . Religion is not
at all to be "in tune with the infinite" or
to be at "peace with oneself.". . . Religion is an abyss; it is terror. . . . Death
is the meaning of religion.

KARL BARTH

[2688]
Man is by his constitution a religious
animal.

EDMUND BURKE

[2689]
Very religious people always shock
slightly religious people by their blas-
phemous attitude toward religion, and
it was precisely for blasphemy that
Jesus was crucified.

R. G. COLLINGWOOD

[2690]
Science without religion is lame, religion without science is blind.

ALBERT EINSTEIN

[2691]
Religion is the best armor in the world
but the worst cloak.

THOMAS FULLER

[2692]
Religion is man's quest for God; the Gospel is the Savior God seeking lost men. Religion originates on earth; the Gospel originated in heaven. Religion is man-made; the Gospel is the gift of God. Religion is the story of what a sinful man tries to do for a holy God; the Gospel is the story of what a holy God has done for sinful men. Religion is good views; the Gospel is good news.

ROY GUSTAFSON

[2693]
Religion is a stalking horse to shoot other fowl.

GEORGE HERBERT

[2694]
Religion that is pure and undefiled before God and the Father is this: to visit orphans and widows in their affliction, and to keep oneself unstained from the world.

JAMES 1:27 (RSV)

[2695]
Religion is a monumental chapter in the history of human egotism.

WILLIAM JAMES

[2696]
Religion's in the heart, not in the knee.

DOUGLAS WILLIAM JERROLD

[2697]
What I want is not to possess a religion, but to have a religion that shall possess me.

CHARLES KINGSLEY

[2698]
Religious contention is the devil's harvest.

JEAN DE LA FONTAINE

[2699]
Things are coming to a pretty pass when religion is allowed to invade private life.

WILLIAM LAMB

[2700]
The heart of religion lies in its personal pronouns.

MARTIN LUTHER

[2701]
I find no quality so easy to counterfeit as religious devotion.

MICHEL DE MONTAIGNE

[2702]
There is no disagreement greater than one which proceeds from religion.

MONTANUS

[2703]
The religion of some people is constrained, like the cold bath when used, not for pleasure, but from necessity for health, into which one goes with reluctance and is glad when able to get out. But religion to the true believer is like water to a fish; it is his element; he lives in it and could not live out of it.

JOHN NEWTON

[2704]
Men never do evil so completely and cheerfully as when they do it from religious conviction.

BLAISE PASCAL

[2705]
That religion cannot be right that a man is the worse for having.

WILLIAM PENN

[2706]
I do not know how philosophers may ultimately define religion; but from Micah to James it has been defined as service to one's fellow men rendered by following the great rule of justice and mercy, of wisdom and righteousness.

THEODORE ROOSEVELT

[2707]
Religion which is merely ritual and ceremonial can never satisfy. Neither can we be satisfied by a religion which is merely humanitarian or serviceable to mankind. Man's craving is for the spiritual.
SAMUEL M. SHOEMAKER

[2708]
No man's religion ever survives his morals.
ROBERT SOUTH

[2709]
I would not give much for your religion unless it can be seen. Lamps do not talk, but they do shine.
CHARLES H. SPURGEON

[2710]
We have just enough religion to make us hate, but not enough to make us love one another.
JONATHAN SWIFT

[2711]
Some people have just enough religion to make them uncomfortable.
JOHN WESLEY

RENEWAL

[2712]
Since we believe that Christ died for all of us, we should also believe that we have died to the old life we used to live. He died for all so that all who live—having received eternal life from him—might live no longer for themselves, to please themselves, but to spend their lives pleasing Christ who died and rose again for them.
2 CORINTHIANS 5:14–15
(The Living Bible)

[2713]
That sense of newness is simply delicious. It makes new the Bible and friends, and all mankind and love and spiritual things and Sunday and church and God himself.
TEMPLE GAIRDNER

[2714]
God cared so much about man's renewal that he sent his Son into the world to accomplish this purpose.
W. CURRY MAVIS

[2715]
April prepares her green traffic light and the world thinks go.
CHRISTOPHER MORLEY

[2716]
We are not called upon to renew our minds in order that we may be transfigured; we are only to yield ourselves unto God, and he does all the rest.
WILLIAM L. PETTINGILL

[2717]
For, lo, the winter is past, the rain is over and gone; the flowers appear on the earth; the time of the singing of birds is come, and the voice of the turtle is heard in our land.
THE SONG OF SOLOMON 2:11–12 (KJV)

REPENTANCE

[2718]
The Lord's mercy may be found between bridge and stream.
AUGUSTINE OF HIPPO

[2719]
Repentance is despair of self, despairing of self-help in removing the guilt that we have brought upon us. Repentance means a radical turning away from self-reliance to trust in God alone. To repent means to recognize self-trust to be the heart of sin.

EMIL BRUNNER

[2720]
Betwixt the stirrup and the ground /
Mercy I asked, mercy I found.

WILLIAM CAMDEN

[2721]
The question is not, shall I repent? For that is beyond a doubt. But the question is, shall I repent now, when it may save me; or shall I put it off to the eternal world when my repentance will be my punishment?

SAMUEL DAVIES

[2722]
What the work of Christ requires is not our admiration or even gratitude, not our impressions or our thrills, but ourselves and our shame.

P. T. FORSYTH

[2723]
Amendment is repentance.

THOMAS FULLER

[2724]
A lady used to go to church with a pitchfork. When the preacher was declaiming about sin, she said to herself, "Oh, that sounds good. That's good for Brother Brown," and she pitched a load toward him. A little later she said, "That's good for Sister Sophie," and again she used the pitchfork. Then one day the Gospel reached her heart and she exchanged her pitchfork for a rake. Then when she went to church she said, "Yes, Lord, that's for me. That's for me. I receive it on faith."

HOWARD O. JONES

[2725]
There is no Christianity without repentance of some kind.

ADDISON H. LEITCH

[2726]
To do so no more is the truest repentance.

MARTIN LUTHER

[2727]
Sometimes we speak as if all that is needed for deliverance from sin is repentance toward God. But can repentance, can even remorse ever of itself abolish the guilt and curse of sin? If [the Savior's] final coming in might and judgment is postponed, it is because he wants first to meet every man at the cross, there to release him from his sin and guilt, there to ask of him the love of his heart, and there to remake him as God's dear child.

WILLIAM MANSON

[2728]
Jesus came into Galilee, preaching the gospel of God, and saying, "The time is fulfilled, and the kingdom of God is at hand; repent, and believe in the gospel."

MARK 1:14–15 (RSV)

[2729]
Our Lord has laid down most emphatically that a man must repent of his sins, and particularly of his critical and independent attitude toward God, or he cannot begin to live the Christian life.

LEITH SAMUEL

REPUTATION

[2730]
There are two modes of establishing our reputation: to be praised by honest men and to be abused by rogues. It is best to secure the former because it will invariably be accompanied by the latter.

CHARLES C. COLTON

[2731]
What people say behind your back is your standing in the community in which you live.

E. W. HOWE

[2732]
Good will, like a good name, is got by many actions, and lost by one.

FRANCIS JEFFREY

[2733]
Reputation is what folks think you are. Personality is what you seem to be. Character is what you really are.

ALFRED ARMAND MONTAPERT

[2734]
Character is what you possess when you leave, but reputation is what you have when you arrive.

W. A. "DUB" NANCE

[2735]
A good name is to be chosen rather than great riches.

PROVERBS 22:1 (RSV)

[2736]
[A bishop] must have a good reputation with the non-Christian public, so that he may not be exposed to scandal and get caught in the devil's snare.

1 TIMOTHY 3:7 (NEB)

[2737]
A proper self-regard becomes improper as soon as we begin to value reputation more than real character.

RESPONSIBILITY

[2738]
Our main business is not to see what lies dimly at a distance, but to do what lies clearly at hand.

THOMAS CARLYLE

[2739]
We are Goddes stewardes all, noughte of our owne we bare.

THOMAS CHATTERTON

[2740]
There can be no stable and balanced development of the mind apart from the assumption of responsibility.

JOHN DEWEY

[2741]
The vast majority of persons of our race have a natural tendency to shrink from the responsibility of standing and acting alone.

FRANCIS GALTON

[2742]
No matter how lofty you are in your department, the responsibility for what your lowliest assistant is doing is yours.

BESSIE R. JAMES
AND MARY WATERSTREET

[2743]
Unto whomsoever much is given, of him shall be much required.

LUKE 12:48 (KJV)

[2744]
I believe that every right implies a responsibility; every opportunity, an obligation; every possession, a duty.

JOHN D. ROCKEFELLER

[2745]
Man must cease attributing his problems to his environment, and learn again to exercise his will—his personal responsibility in the realm of faith and morals.

ALBERT SCHWEITZER

[2746]
Liberty means responsibility. That is
why most men dread it.
GEORGE BERNARD SHAW

[2747]
The ability to accept responsibility is
the measure of the man.
ROY L. SMITH

[2748]
The most important thought I ever had
was that of my individual responsibility
to God.
DANIEL WEBSTER

REST

[2749]
Desire hath no rest.
ROBERT BURTON

[2750]
Every morning I open the window for
my King's grace, and every evening I
sleep upon the pillow of his love and
care.
CELTIC SAINT

[2751]
There is no rest for a messenger till the
message is delivered.
JOSEPH CONRAD

[2752]
Absence of occupation is not rest.
WILLIAM COWPER
"Retirement"

[2753]
Rest is not quitting the busy career; /
Rest is the fitting of self to its sphere.
JOHN S. DWIGHT
"True Rest"

[2754]
The Reverend Evan Hopkins used to
teach the three positions: struggling,
clinging, and resting. The illustration
he used was of a shipwreck when people are thrown into the sea. In the *struggling* position they are in the water,
fighting with the waves, and are in need
of help themselves. In the *clinging* position they are holding on to the boat;
they are quite safe themselves, but cannot help anyone else, because both
their hands are occupied. In the *resting*
position they are sitting in the boat
with both hands free to help others.
The place of deliverance was always
when they got to the resting faith.
NORMAN P. GRUBB

[2755]
There remains a sabbath rest for the
people of God; for whoever enters
God's rest also ceases from his labors
as God did from his.
HEBREWS 4:9–10 (RSV)

[2756]
In the Christian warfare there is an inward relaxation even in the midst of
action which God gives to those who
trust him wholly.
PHILIP E. HOWARD, JR.

[2757]
If I rest, I rust.
MARTIN LUTHER

[2758]
Come to me, all who labor and are
heavy-laden, and I will give you rest.
MATTHEW 11:28 (RSV)

[2759]
We have been seeking everywhere for
[rest] but where there is a prospect of
finding it; and that is, within ourselves,
in a meek and lowly disposition of
heart.
LAURENCE STERNE

[2760]
Sunday is nature's law as well as God's.
                    DANIEL WEBSTER

[2761]
Thank God if you are dissatisfied with
wandering in the wilderness, with an
up-and-down kind of life, advancing a
little and then slipping back toward
Egypt [the old life]. The rest which
God comes to offer you through the
Scriptures is a realistic rest.
                    L. F. E. WILKINSON

[2762]
The paradox of faith is that the church
on fire is the church at rest.*

RESURRECTION

[2763]
I know of no one fact in the history of
mankind which is proved by better evidence of every sort, to the understanding of a fair inquirer, than the great
sign which God has given us that Christ
died and rose again from the dead.
                    THOMAS ARNOLD

[2764]
The stone at the tomb of Jesus was a
pebble to the Rock of Ages inside.
                    FRED BECK

[2765]
There is not a single pessimistic note
anywhere in the New Testament after
the resurrection.
                    ANDREW W. BLACKWOOD

[2766]
The door of the holy sepulcher is the
portal through which we enter the
Kingdom of God.
                    HERBERT F. GALLAGHER

[2767]
Whenever the church returns to Jesus
and begins to take him seriously, there
is always a resurrection.
                    T. R. GLOVER

[2768]
Our Lord has written the promise of
the resurrection, not in books alone,
but in every leaf in springtime.
                    MARTIN LUTHER

[2769]
The miracle of Christ's resurrection:
out of the grave into my heart.
                    DAVID J. NETZ

[2770]
The resurrection of Jesus stands fast as
a fact, unaffected by the waves of skep-
ticism that ceaselessly through the ages
beat themselves against it. It holds
within it the vastest hope for time and
eternity that humanity can ever know.
                    JAMES ORR

[2771]
The resurrection is a fact of history
without which history does not make
sense.
                    CLARK H. PINNOCK

[2772]
When I look over beyond the line and
beyond death to the laughing side of
the world, I triumph, and ride upon the
high places of Jacob; otherwise I am a
faint, dead-hearted, cowardly man, oft
borne down and hungry in waiting for
the marriage supper of the Lamb. Nevertheless I think it is the Lord's wise
love that feeds us with hunger and
makes us fat with wants and desertion.
                    SAMUEL RUTHERFORD

[2773]
The biggest fact about Joseph's tomb
was that it wasn't a tomb at all—it was
a room for a transient. Jesus stopped
there a night or two on his way back to
glory.
                    HERBERT BOOTH SMITH

[2774]
If Christ be not risen, the dreadful
consequence is not that death ends life,
but that we are still in our sins.
                    G. A. STUDDERT KENNEDY

[2775]
There are mysteries around this resurrection of the body which I can't explain. There are some things, however,
that we do know about the resurrected
body. It will be a glorious body. The
body as we now see it is but a skeleton
compared to what it would have been
had it not been marred by sin. It will be
an immortal body, a powerful body,
never tired, unconquerable forever.
Oh, blessed hope!
                    T. DeWITT TALMAGE

[2776]
Never was there as great an imposture
put upon the world as Christianity, if
Christ be yet in the grave.
                    JOHN TRAPP

[2777]
Taking all the evidence together, it is
not too much to say that there is no
single historic incident better or more
variously supported than the resurrection of Christ.
                    BROOKE FOSS WESTCOTT

[2778]
The Gospels do not explain the resurrection; the resurrection explains the
Gospels. Belief in the resurrection is
not an appendage to the Christian
faith; it is the Christian faith.
                    JOHN S. WHALE

REVELATION

[2779]
The knowledge of man is as the waters,
some descending from above, and
some springing up from beneath; the
one informed by the light of nature, the
other inspired by divine revelation.
                    FRANCIS BACON

[2780]
Man cannot cover what God would reveal.
                    THOMAS CAMPBELL

[2781]
Human beings cannot probe the mind
of God by asking themselves what they
would do if they were God. They are
men and not God. And if they are virtuous men, they will wait for God to reveal himself under conditions of his
own choosing.
                    EDWARD JOHN CARNELL

[2782]
What Christ did had to be done, or we
should never have had forgiveness; we
should never have known God. But he,
by taking on himself our responsibili-
ties and by dying our death, has so revealed God to us as to put forgiveness
within our reach.
                    JAMES DENNEY

[2783]
Unless the church has a message from
beyond the world, it will not move the
world by one hairsbreadth.
                    LESSLIE NEWBIGIN

[2784]
After reading the doctrines of Plato,
Socrates or Aristotle, we feel the specific difference between their words
and Christ's is the difference between
an inquiry and a revelation.
                    JOSEPH PARKER

REVIVAL

[2785]
The next great awakening will bring forth mighty men of God who will do something more than stir a local interest or excite a transient enthusiasm. Aided by all the modern devices of transportation and communication they will be able to extend their influence as the revivalists in former times could not.

WARREN A. CANDLER

[2786]
It is said that revival occurs for one of two reasons: to save a nation from the judgment of God, or to prepare the church for that judgment.

GORDON E. DIRKS

[2787]
Revival is nothing else than a new beginning of obedience to God.

CHARLES G. FINNEY

[2788]
If we were up to the New Testament normal we would not need revival. Revival is not the normal. The New Testament presents the normal. The reason—and as far as I am concerned, the only reason—that we need revival is to get back to the normal New Testament Christian life, as Christ offered it, as the disciples apprehended it, as the early church lived it.

ARMIN GESSWEIN

[2789]
Revival comes when, upon God's altar, our lives in consecration are *laid up,* our differences with each other are *made up,* our concerns for the lost souls of others are *prayed up,* and our tithes and debts to God are *paid up.*

WILBERT DONALD GOUGH

[2790]
Revivals are supernatural demonstrations of God's power.

P. V. JENNESS

[2791]
What [the Reformers] never tire of repeating is that they wish to introduce nothing new into the church of their time; that their sole interest is the revival of New Testament Christianity.

HUGH T. KERR, JR.

[2792]
Revival is a sovereign act of God upon the church whereby he intervenes to lift the situation completely out of human hands and works in extraordinary power.

GEOFFREY R. KING

[2793]
Revival is God's finger pointed right at me.

WILBERT L. MCLEOD

[2794]
The revival which is to be permanent in the life of a nation must be associated with the life of the churches.

G. CAMPBELL MORGAN

[2795]
Revival is God manifesting himself through human life, his redeeming power bursting forth in fruits of righteousness and holiness, in the constitution of his church, the reproduction of spiritual life, a fresh incarnation of the gladness, the rapture of the Gospel of the Galilean fields.

G. J. MORGAN

[2796]
The call to revival is given not to the unbelieving but to the family of God.

ROBERT BOYD MUNGER

[2797]
Revival is that strange and sovereign work of God in which he visits his own people, restoring, reanimating and releasing them into the fulness of his blessing.

STEPHEN F. OLFORD

[2798]
The best definition of revival is "times of refreshing . . . from the presence of the Lord."

J. EDWIN ORR

[2799]
Revival is the inrush of the Spirit into a body that threatens to become a corpse.

D. M. PANTON

[2800]
Wilt thou not revive us again, that thy people may rejoice in thee?

PSALM 85:6 (RSV)

[2801]
Evangelism affects the other fellow; revival affects me.

LEONARD RAVENHILL

[2802]
There have been great and glorious days of the Gospel in this land; but they have been small in comparison to what shall be.

JAMES RENWICK

[2803]
In the hydraulics of evangelism, narrowness builds up pressure; that is to say, revivalism is still bringing in the sheaves.

GEORGE E. SWEAZEY

[2804]
Revival is divine intervention in the normal course of spiritual things. It is God revealing himself to man in awful holiness and irresistible power. . . . If we find a revival that is not spoken against, we had better look again to ensure that it is a revival.

ARTHUR WALLIS

[2805]
Revival is a renewing and a reformation of the church for action.

MAX WARREN

REVOLUTION

[2806]
Inferiors revolt that they may be equal, and equals that they may be superior. Such is the state of mind which creates revolutions.

ARISTOTLE

[2807]
Jesus called for radical change and revolution, for an absolutely new beginning. He still does. He demands repentance, faith and obedience. This Revolutionary is calling you to a revolutionary experience with himself.

RALPH S. BELL

[2808]
A reform is a correction of abuses; a revolution is a transfer of power.

E. G. BULWER-LYTTON

[2809]
The scrupulous and the just, the noble, humane and devoted natures; the unselfish and the intelligent may begin a movement—but it passes away from them. They are not the leaders of a revolution. They are its victims.

JOSEPH CONRAD

[2810]
I'm strong for any revolution that isn't going to happen in my day.
FINLEY PETER DUNNE
Mr. Dooley Remembers

[2811]
Revolutions do not always establish freedom.
MILLARD FILLMORE

[2812]
What has evangelism to do with revolution? Just this: Christ's work never goes on in a vacuum, and today the Christian church is being called to evangelize people caught up in cataclysmic change.
LEIGHTON FORD

[2813]
[The American Revolution] was a vindication of liberties inherited and possessed. It was a conservative revolution.
WILLIAM E. GLADSTONE

[2814]
Certainly no revolution that has ever taken place in society can be compared to that which has been produced by the words of Jesus Christ.
MARK HOPKINS

[2815]
This country, with its institutions, belongs to the people who inhabit it. Whenever they shall grow weary of the existing government they can exercise their constitutional right of amending it, or their revolutionary right to dismember or overthrow it.
ABRAHAM LINCOLN

[2816]
When the [Communist] revolution came . . . he decided that this was the fulfillment of his dream. . . . Instead of that, he found he had only exchanged the old oppression of the czarist state for the new, much harsher yoke of the revolutionary superstate.
BORIS PASTERNAK
Dr. Zhivago

[2817]
Revolutions have never lightened the burden of tyranny: they have only shifted it to another shoulder.
GEORGE BERNARD SHAW

[2818]
Every revolution by force only puts more violent means of enslavement into the hands of the person in power.
LEO TOLSTOY

[2819]
Repression is the seed of revolution.
DANIEL WEBSTER

RIGHT

[2820]
One may go wrong in many different ways, but right only in one.
ARISTOTLE

[2821]
I prefer to do right and get no thanks, rather than to do wrong and get no punishment.
CATO THE ELDER

[2822]
Be sure you are right; then go ahead.
DAVID CROCKETT

[2823]
Shall not the Judge of all the earth do right?
GENESIS 18:25 (RSV)

[2824]
Don't take the wrong side of an argument just because your opponent has
taken the right side.

GRACIÁN

[2825]
Let us have faith that right makes
might, and in that faith let us to the end
dare to do our duty as we understand
it.

ABRAHAM LINCOLN

[2826]
Before you can help make the world
right, you must be made right within.

JOHN MILLER

[2827]
Every man has a right to become a
child of God, and therefore to become
God's heir. God gave to every man the
right to the washing of regeneration if
he will but repent and believe.

WILLIAM R. NEWELL

[2828]
No man has a right to do as he pleases,
except when he pleases to do right.

CHARLES SIMMONS

[2829]
Never, with the Bible in our hands, can
we deny rights to another, which, under the same circumstances, we would
claim for ourselves.

GARDINER SPRING

[2830]
The greatest discovery I made in life
was that God was probably right when
I thought him to be wrong.

R. A. TORREY

[2831]
To be right with God has often meant
to be in trouble with men.

A. W. TOZER

[2832]
No question is ever settled until it is
settled right.

ELLA WHEELER WILCOX

RIGHTEOUSNESS

[2833]
Let justice roll down like waters, and
righteousness like an everflowing
stream.

AMOS 5:24 (RSV)

[2834]
Christ came to reveal what righteousness really is, for nothing will do except
righteousness, and no other conception of righteousness will do except
Christ's conception of it—his method
and secret.

MATTHEW ARNOLD

[2835]
The ground of justification can be
found only in the perfect righteousness
of Jesus Christ, which is imputed to the
sinner in justification.

LOUIS BERKHOF

[2836]
The humblest citizen of all the land,
when clad in the armor of a righteous
cause, is stronger than all the hosts of
error.

WILLIAM JENNINGS BRYAN

[2837]
Be not righteous overmuch.

ECCLESIASTES 7:16 (RSV)

[2838]
If there be ground for you to trust in
your own righteousness, then all that
Christ did to purchase salvation, and
all that God did to prepare the way for
it, is in vain.

JONATHAN EDWARDS

[2839]
If righteousness were possible under the Law then Christ died for nothing!
GALATIANS 2:21
(Phillips)

[2840]
Righteousness is obedience to law, observance of duty, and fidelity to conscience.
J. P. HOPPS

[2841]
People wrap themselves up in the flimsy garments of their own righteousness and then complain of the cold.

SACRIFICE

[2842]
When the love of Christ comes into a human life it is the greatest uplifting and ennobling power of which the world has any knowledge. It brings new birth, for it brings Christ himself. For it no sacrifice is too great, no piece of service too humble.
HOWARD W. GUINNESS

[2843]
Was anything real ever gained without sacrifice of some kind?
ARTHUR HELPS

[2844]
For I desire steadfast love and not sacrifice, the knowledge of God rather than burnt offerings.
HOSEA 6:6 (RSV)

[2845]
It is only through the mystery of self-sacrifice that a man may find himself anew.
CARL GUSTAV JUNG

[2846]
Love's strength standeth in love's sacrifice.
HARRIET ELEANOR KING

[2847]
I never made a sacrifice. We ought not to talk of "sacrifice" when we remember the great sacrifice which he made who left his Father's throne on high to give himself for us.
DAVID LIVINGSTONE

[2848]
All profound affection admits a sacrifice.
LUC DE CLAPIERS VAUVENARGUES

[2849]
When men grow virtuous in their old age, they only make a sacrifice to God of the devil's leavings.
ALEXANDER POPE

[2850]
So then, my brothers, because of God's many mercies to us, I make this appeal to you: Offer yourselves as a living sacrifice to God, dedicated to his service and pleasing to him.
ROMANS 12:1
(Good News for Modern Man)

[2851]
Has the Lord as great delight in burnt offerings and sacrifices, as in obeying the voice of the Lord? Behold, to obey is better than sacrifice.
1 SAMUEL 15:22 (RSV)

SAINTS

[2852]
A saint is never consciously a saint; a saint is consciously dependent on God.
OSWALD CHAMBERS

[2853]
A saint is one who makes it easy to believe in Jesus.
                    RUTH BELL GRAHAM

[2854]
Those Saints, which God loves best, /
The devil tempts not least.
                    ROBERT HERRICK
                        "Temptation"

[2855]
A saint is one who makes goodness at-
tractive.
                    LAURENCE HOUSMAN

[2856]
God creates out of nothing. Wonderful, you say. Yes, to be sure, but he
does what is still more wonderful: he
makes saints out of sinners.
                    SØREN KIERKEGAARD

[2857]
To make a saint it must indeed be by
Grace; and whoever doubts this does
not know what a saint is, or a man.
                    BLAISE PASCAL

[2858]
Precious in the sight of the Lord is the
death of his saints.
                    PSALM 116:15 (RSV)

[2859]
A sad saint is a poor saint.
                    H. D. RANNS

[2860]
A saint is a person who has learned
how to get out of God's way.
                    MARGARET C. ROMANES

[2861]
Saints are persons who make it easier
for others to believe in God.
                    NATHAN SÖDERBLOM

SALVATION

[2862]
He is no fool who gives what he cannot
keep to gain what he cannot lose.
                    JIM ELLIOT

[2863]
I am conscious that for me my only
hope of salvation in this world lies in
Christ.
                    WILFRED T. GRENFELL

[2864]
God did not save you to be a sensation.
He saved you to be a servant.
                    JOHN E. HUNTER

[2865]
The "vision" of salvation and of sanctification may be sincerely grasped
both intellectually and spiritually, and
then fade because not expressed in action.
                    D. W. LAMBERT

[2866]
The salvation of a single soul is more
important than the production or preservation of all the epics and tragedies
in the world.
                    C. S. LEWIS

[2867]
If Christ had been too proud to die, he
could not have helped us whose basic
sin is pride. So Paul and others argue
that by giving himself up without pride,
Christ makes up for Adam's sin of arro-
gance. If all this is true, it comprises
certainly the most momentous fact of
human existence. Christ the free therapist for humanity, bringing us salvation
as a gift of grace—that indeed is a daring postulate.
                    ROLLO MAY

[2868]
To know Christ is not to speculate
about the mode of his incarnation, but
to know his saving benefits.
                    PHILIP MELANCHTHON

[2869]
That there is a great split today in
Christendom nobody would deny; but
the line of the cleavage does not run
between Catholic and Protestant or between Conformist and Nonconformist.
It runs, as it ran sixteen centuries ago,
between Athanasius and Arius—between those who believe that salvation
is of God and those who believe that
salvation is of man.
                    DOROTHY L. SAYERS

[2870]
It won't save your soul if your wife is a
Christian. You have got to be something more than a brother-in-law to the
church.
                    BILLY SUNDAY

[2871]
You don't "cab" into the Jesus Motel.*

SARCASM

[2872]
At the best, sarcasms, bitter irony,
scathing wit, are a sort of sword-play of
the mind.
                    CHRISTIAN NESTELL BOVEE

[2873]
Sarcasm I now see to be, in general, the
language of the devil.
                    THOMAS CARLYLE

[2874]
Sarcasm that scorns and slander that
sears: the Lord Jesus knew them both,
not so much from sardonic scribes and
Sadducees as from fellow citizens of his
own country. And what was his response? No offense taken.
                    V. RAYMOND EDMAN

[2875]
The arrows of sarcasm are barbed with
contempt.
                    WASHINGTON GLADDEN

[2876]
"You'll have to shout louder than
that," [Elijah] scoffed [to the prophets
of Baal], "to catch the attention of your
god! Perhaps he is talking to someone,
or is out sitting on the toilet, or maybe
he is away on a trip, or is asleep and
needs to be wakened!"
                    1 KINGS 18:27
                    (The Living Bible)

SATAN

[2877]
The devil's most devilish when respectable.
                    ELIZABETH BARRETT BROWNING

[2878]
The one concern of the devil is to keep
Christians from praying.
                    SAMUEL CHADWICK

[2879]
If you marry a son of the devil, you can
expect plenty of trouble from your
father-in-law.
                    ROY GUSTAFSON

[2880]
Satan rocks the cradle when we sleep at
our devotions.
                    JOSEPH HALL

[2881]
The best way to drive out the devil, if
he will not yield to texts of Scripture, is
to jeer and flout him, for he cannot
bear scorn.
MARTIN LUTHER

[2882]
Satan deals with confusion and lies. Put
the truth in front of him and he is gone.
PAUL MATLOCK

[2883]
The devil is the top hidden persuader
—the master of subliminal motivation.
JESS C. MOODY

[2884]
God is not dead, but neither is Satan.
CLATE A. RISLEY

[2885]
When I doubt there is an Evil One, I
have only to look into myself. There he
is.
JOHN SPONG

[2886]
Most of the methods that Satan uses to
confuse and tempt can be very beautiful and very alert. He seems to be not
the enemy of God, but the uplifter and
edifier of man.

SCIENCE

[2887]
We have too many men of science, too
few men of God. We have grasped the
mystery of the atom, and rejected the
Sermon on the Mount. The world has
achieved brilliance without wisdom,
power without conscience. Ours is a
world of nuclear giants and ethical in-
fants. We know more about war than
we do about peace, more about killing
than we do about living.
OMAR BRADLEY

[2888]
I find it as difficult to understand a
scientist who does not acknowledge
the presence of a superior rationality
behind the existence of the universe as
it is to comprehend a theologian who
would deny the advances of science.
And there is certainly no scientific reason why God cannot retain the same
position in our modern world that he
held before we began probing his creation with telescope and cyclotron.
WERNHER VON BRAUN

[2889]
There is something in man which your
science cannot satisfy.
THOMAS CARLYLE

[2890]
Science has not accounted for morality,
truth, beauty, individual responsibility
or self-awareness; and many people
hold that, from its nature, it can never
do so.
DAVID LACK

[2891]
Our scientific efforts to make things
right sometimes seem like rearranging
the deck chairs on the *Titanic*.
W. NORMAN MACFARLANE

[2892]
The man who leaves no room for mystery in the universe is not only not
representing the point of view of
science, but will soon be unable to understand it.
J. W. N. SULLIVAN

[2893]
One can search the brain with a micro-
scope and not find the mind, and can
search the stars with a telescope and
not find God.
J. GUSTAV WHITE

SCRIPTURE

[2894]
As in Paradise, God walks in the Holy Scriptures, seeking man.

AMBROSE OF MILAN

[2895]
If in these books I meet anything which seems contrary to truth I shall not hesitate to conclude that the text is faulty, or that the translator has not expressed the meaning of the passage, or that I myself do not understand.

AUGUSTINE OF HIPPO

[2896]
I am fully assured that God does not, and therefore that men should not, require any more of any man than this: to believe the Scripture to be God's Word, to endeavor to find the true sense of it, and to live according to it.

WILLIAM CHILLINGWORTH

[2897]
It is a great thing, this reading of the Scriptures! For it is not possible ever to exhaust the mind of the Scriptures. It is a well that has no bottom.

JOHN CHRYSOSTOM

[2898]
Explain the Scriptures by the Scriptures.

CLEMENT OF ALEXANDRIA

[2899]
I utterly dissent from those who are unwilling that the sacred Scriptures should be read by the unlearned translated into their vulgar tongue, as though Christ had taught such subtleties that can scarcely be understood even by a few theologians, or as though the strength of Christianity consisted in men's ignorance of it.

DESIDERIUS ERASMUS

[2900]
You search the scriptures, because you think that in them you have eternal life; and it is they that bear witness to me.

JOHN 5:39 (RSV)

[2901]
This great Book . . . is the best gift God has given to man. . . . But for it we could not know right from wrong.

ABRAHAM LINCOLN

[2902]
The Spirit is needed for the understanding of Scripture and every part of Scripture.

MARTIN LUTHER

[2903]
No prophecy recorded in Scripture was ever thought up by the prophet himself. It was the Holy Spirit within these godly men who gave them true messages from God.

2 PETER 1:20–21
(The Living Bible)

[2904]
The Bible is not only the foundation of modern English literature; it is the foundation of Anglo-Saxon civilization.

WILLIAM LYON PHELPS

[2905]
The archaeological discoveries of the last thirty years have, with hardly an exception, been dead against the most confident decisions of the mere literary critic, and in favor of the trustworthiness of our records.

A. H. SAYCE

[2906]
The devil can cite Scripture for his purpose.

SHAKESPEARE
The Merchant of Venice, I, iii

[2907]
All Scripture is inspired by God and is useful for teaching the truth, rebuking error, correcting faults, and giving instruction for right living, so that the man who serves God may be fully qualified and equipped to do every kind of good work.

2 TIMOTHY 3:16–17
(Good News for Modern Man)

[2908]
Most people are bothered by those passages of Scripture they don't understand, but for me I have always noticed that the passages that bother me are those I *do* understand.

MARK TWAIN

[2909]
The Bible is a book of faith and a book of doctrine and a book of morals and a book of religion, of especial revelation from God.

DANIEL WEBSTER

[2910]
The Bible is for the government of the people, by the people, and for the people.

JOHN WYCLIFFE

[2911]
You can only understand Scripture on your knees.

MAURICE ZUNDEL

SECOND ADVENT

[2912]
He may come any time. He's sure to come some time. Let's be ready when he does come.

ANDREW W. BLACKWOOD

[2913]
Whatever resistance we see today offered by almost all the world to the progress of the truth, we must not doubt that our Lord will come at last to break through all the undertakings of men and make a passage for his word.

JOHN CALVIN

[2914]
Our world is filled with fear, hate, lust, greed, war and utter despair. Surely the Second Coming of Jesus Christ is the only hope of replacing these depressing features with trust, love, universal peace and prosperity. For it the world wittingly or inadvertently waits.

BILLY GRAHAM

[2915]
Christ designed that the day of his coming should be hid from us, that being in suspense, we might be as it were upon the watch.

MARTIN LUTHER

[2916]
The primitive church thought more about the Second Coming of Jesus Christ than about death or about heaven. The early Christians were looking not for a cleft in the ground called a grave, but for a cleavage in the sky called Glory. They were watching not for the "undertaker" but for the "Uppertaker."

ALEXANDER MACLAREN

[2917]
We are not a postwar generation, but a pre-peace generation. Jesus is coming.

CORRIE TEN BOOM

[2918]
The Second Advent is possible any day, impossible no day.

RICHARD TRENCH

SECULARISM

[2919]
The obvious secularist solution for muddle is to subordinate everything to political power. . . . It is only in a society with a religious basis—which is not the same thing as an ecclesiastical despotism—that you can get the proper harmony and tension for the individual or for the community.
T. S. ELIOT

[2920]
Our world has been fooling around with secularism and with the idea that people can make it without God: The time has come to get with the Lord and to go with him.
OSWALD C. J. HOFFMANN

[2921]
[Secularism is] a form of opinion which concerns itself only with questions, the issues of which can be tested by the experience of this life.
G. J. HOLYOAKE

[2922]
Man displays an inability to cope with life on the basis of secular presuppositions.
CLARK H. PINNOCK

SELF

[2923]
He who knows himself best esteems himself least.
H. G. BOHN

[2924]
Oh, wad some power the giftie gie us / To see oursels as others see us! / It wad frae mony a blunder free us, / And foolish notion.
ROBERT BURNS
"To a Louse"

[2925]
Nothing is so easy as to deceive one's self.
DEMOSTHENES

[2926]
If you want to be respected by others the great thing is to respect yourself.
FYODOR DOSTOEVSKY

[2927]
Men are not against you; they are merely for themselves.
GENE FOWLER

[2928]
He who falls in love with himself will have no rivals.
BENJAMIN FRANKLIN

[2929]
You shall love your neighbor as yourself.
GALATIANS 5:14 (RSV)

[2930]
Many could forego heavy meals, a full wardrobe, a fine house; it is the ego that they cannot forego.
MOHANDAS K. GANDHI

[2931]
It is not the self which must be destroyed, but the Satanic spirit of egoism in the self.
NORMAN P. GRUBB

[2932]
The first step to self-knowledge is self-distrust.
J. C. AND A. W. HARE

[2933]
The first lesson in Christ's school is self-denial.
MATTHEW HENRY

[2934]
He that praiseth himself spattereth himself.
GEORGE HERBERT

[2935]
The very act of faith by which we receive Christ is an act of utter renunciation of self and all its works, as a ground of salvation.

MARK HOPKINS

[2936]
They that deny themselves for Christ shall enjoy themselves in Christ.

JOHN MASON

[2937]
If anyone wants to be a follower of mine, let him deny himself and take up his cross and follow me.

MATTHEW 16:24
(The Living Bible)

[2938]
God defend me from myself.

MICHEL DE MONTAIGNE

[2939]
You can always tell when a man is a great way from God: when he is always talking about himself, how good he is.

DWIGHT L. MOODY

[2940]
Jesus was not merely selfless; he was without self. He came "not to be ministered unto, but to minister." Jesus was selfless and therefore he was restful, because an adjustment to life that asks nothing for self always brings that happy result.

G. H. MORLING

[2941]
Too liberal self-accusations are generally but so many traps for acquittal with applause.

SAMUEL RICHARDSON

[2942]
When a man is all wrapped up in himself he makes a pretty small package.

JOHN RUSKIN

[2943]
Self-discipline never means giving up anything, for giving up is a loss. Our Lord did not ask us to give up the things of earth, but to exchange them for better things.

FULTON J. SHEEN

[2944]
The greatest burden we have to carry in life is self; the most difficult thing we have to manage is self.

HANNAH WHITALL SMITH

[2945]
To have a respect for ourselves guides our morals, and to have a deference for others governs our manners.

LAURENCE STERNE

[2946]
It is a great grace of God to practice self-examination; but too much is as bad as too little.

TERESA OF AVILA

[2947]
Everybody thinks of changing humanity and nobody thinks of changing himself.

LEO TOLSTOY

[2948]
He that has no government of himself has no enjoyment of himself.

BENJAMIN WHICHCOTE

[2949]
Self-preservation is the first law of nature, but self-sacrifice is the highest rule of grace.

SELFISHNESS

[2950]
Let me have my own way exactly in everything, and a sunnier and pleasanter creature does not exist.

THOMAS CARLYLE

[2951]
It is against himself that everybody sins.

LATIN PROVERB

[2952]
Nine-tenths of our unhappiness is selfishness, and is an insult cast in the face of God.

G. H. MORRISON

[2953]
No man is born unto himself alone; who lives unto himself, he lives to none.

FRANCIS QUARLES

[2954]
God defend me from myself.

SPANISH PROVERB

[2955]
Seldom is anyone so spiritual as to strip himself entirely of self-love.

THOMAS À KEMPIS

[2956]
Selfishness is the only real atheism.

ISRAEL ZANGWILL

SEPARATION

[2957]
Absence is to love what wind is to fire; it extinguishes the small, it enkindles the great.

ROGER DE BUSSY-RABUTIN

[2958]
Let us not confuse separation from the world with isolation from the world.

MAL COUCH

[2959]
Hell is eternal separation from the presence of the Lord.

V. RAYMOND EDMAN

[2960]
Death, to the Christian, means a separation from the victorious life in Christ. This separation man makes when by wilful sin he dissociates himself from Christ.

EVELYN FROST

[2961]
Whatever Jesus meant by hell, essentially it is the separation of the soul from God as the culmination of man's spiritual death.

BILLY GRAHAM

[2962]
The essence of hell is complete separation from God, and that is the ultimate disaster.

W. R. MATTHEWS

[2963]
Attachment to Christ results in detachment from the world.

MIRMER

[2964]
If you were not strangers here, the hounds of the world would not bark at you.

SAMUEL RUTHERFORD

[2965]
Separation equips the Christian with the weapons of his warfare. Instead of getting him out of the world, it gets him into the world more effectively. The sharper the separation, the greater the dependence upon Christ and the more fruitful the involvement.*

SERENITY

[2966]
Cheerfulness keeps up a kind of daylight in the mind, and fills it with a steady and perpetual serenity.

JOSEPH ADDISON

[2967]
For the man sound in body and serene of mind there is no such thing as bad weather.

GEORGE GISSING

[2968]
The Christian must be friends with every day.

DORA GREENWELL

[2969]
Serenity comes not alone by removing the outward causes and occasions of fear, but by the discovery of inward reservoirs to draw upon.

RUFUS M. JONES

[2970]
Order and the beauty of peace go together. The fair flower of peace does not grow among the weeds of an ill-regulated life. The radiance of a deep inner serenity is the product of disciplining both in the heart and in outward affairs.

G. H. MORLING

[2971]
It is impossible to have the feeling of peace and serenity without being at rest with God.

DOROTHY H. PENTECOST

[2972]
Serenity depends on a certain mental attitude—an attitude which accepts. We have to train ourselves to appreciate the good gifts of God, material, mental and spiritual. Among all God's gifts there is none greater than Christ himself.

GORDON POWELL

SERMONS

[2973]
He that has but one word of God before him, and out of that word cannot make a sermon, can never be a preacher.

MARTIN LUTHER

[2974]
A Scottish minister took considerable trouble in preparing and preaching a series of evening sermons under the title "Questions Folk Are Asking." After each address John, the beadle, helped him to take off his gown. After the final address had been delivered, the minister asked John what he had thought of the series. "Interesting," said John, "but those are no' the questions folk are asking!"

GEORGE F. MACLEOD

[2975]
Sermons may be divided into three classes: first, those you can listen to; second, those you can't listen to; and third, those you can't help listening to.

WILLIAM CONNOR MAGEE

[2976]
Some clergy prepare their sermons; others prepare themselves.

SAMUEL WILBERFORCE

[2977]
An optimist is a person who drops $1 in the collection plate and expects a $50 sermon.

SERVICE

[2978]
Take that gift God has entrusted to you, and use it in the service of Christ and your fellow men. He will make it glow and shine like the very stars of heaven.

JOHN SUTHERLAND BONNELL

[2979]
All service ranks the same with God.

ROBERT BROWNING
"Pippa Passes"

[2980]
No one gives himself freely and willingly to God's service unless, having tasted his Fatherly love, he is drawn to love and worship him in return.

JOHN CALVIN

[2981]
A man should be encouraged to do what the Maker of him has intended by the making of him, according as the gifts have been bestowed on him for that purpose.

THOMAS CARLYLE

[2982]
If one were in a rapture like St. Paul, and there was a sick man needing help, I think it would be best to throw off the rapture and show love by service to the needy.

MEISTER ECKHART

[2983]
A Christian man is the most free lord of all, and subject to none; a Christian man is the most dutiful servant of all, and subject to everyone.

MARTIN LUTHER

[2984]
They also serve who only stand and wait.

JOHN MILTON
"On His Blindness"

[2985]
It is not the possession of extraordinary gifts that makes extraordinary usefulness, but the dedication of what we have to the service of God.

F. W. ROBERTSON

[2986]
To serve God and my church and to love all human beings is my creed.

MARY G. ROEBLING

[2987]
The object of love is to serve, not to win.

WOODROW WILSON

[2988]
Service is the rent we pay for the space we occupy.

SEX

[2989]
Modern man refuses to recognize that God has set certain standards, certain absolutes for sex, as he has for behavior generally. To be ignorant of these absolutes, or to deny them or rationalize them, in no way invalidates them.

L. NELSON BELL

[2990]
Sexual information without relation to values is intellectually irresponsible.

PETER A. BERTOCCI

[2991]
Human sexuality is too noble and beautiful a thing, too profound a form of experience, to turn into a mere technique of physical relief, or a foolish and irrelevant pastime.

J. V. L. CASSERLEY

[2992]
There is a tendency to think of sex as something degrading; it is not, it is magnificent, an enormous privilege, but because of that the rules are tremendously strict and severe.

FRANCIS DEVAS

[2993]
The sexes were made for each other, and only in the wise and loving union of the two is the fulness of health and duty and happiness to be expected.

WILLIAM HALL

[2994]
Protestantism has contributed an obstacle to the fulfillment of legitimate sexual satisfaction whenever it has implied if not that sex is inherently evil, that it is at least repugnant and earthy.

CARL F. H. HENRY

[2995]
I find that the three major administrative problems on a campus are sex for the students, athletics for the alumni, and parking for the faculty.

CLARK KERR

[2996]
Love may or may not include sexual attraction. It may express itself in sexual desire. But sexual desire is not love. Desire is quite compatible with personal hatred, or contempt, or indifference.

JOHN MACMURRAY

[2997]
All this humorless document [the Kinsey report] really proves is: (a) that all men lie when they are asked about their adventures in amour, and (b) that pedagogues are singularly naive and credulous creatures.

H. L. MENCKEN

[2998]
We pray that the young men and women of today and tomorrow will grow up with the realization that sex is a beautiful flame they carry in the lantern of their bodies.

DEMETRIUS MONOUSOS

[2999]
When sex is divided from love there is a feeling that one has been stopped at the vestibule of the castle of pleasure.

FULTON J. SHEEN

[3000]
A person who despises or undervalues or neglects the opposite sex will soon need humanizing.

CHARLES SIMMONS

[3001]
Continence is the only guarantee of an undefiled spirit, and the best protection against the promiscuity that cheapens and finally kills the power to love.

GENE TUNNEY
(in a message to youth)

SILENCE

[3002]
One man keeps silence because he has nothing to say; another keeps silence because he knows it is the time for it.

ECCLESIASTICUS 20:6
(Goodspeed)

[3003]
How can you expect God to speak in that gentle and inward voice which melts the soul, when you are making so much noise with your rapid reflections? Be silent, and God will speak again.

FRANÇOIS DE LA MOTHE FÉNELON

[3004]
Sometimes silence is not golden but yellow.
WILBERT DONALD GOUGH

[3005]
There is another kind of silence besides that of the tongue. I mean silence as regards oneself—restraining the imagination, not permitting it to dwell overmuch on what we have heard or said, not indulging in the phantasmagoria of picture-thoughts, whether of the past or future.
JEAN NICOLAS GROU

[3006]
The activity-riddled atmosphere which coils around the Christian even in his prayer room is probably due largely to the atomic age to which he has been conditioned. This climate of bustle even penetrates Christian worship services. How can one experience this aspect of prayer—silent waiting before the Lord?
KAY GUDNASON

[3007]
Oh, please be quiet! That would be your highest wisdom.
JOB 13:5
(The Living Bible)

SIMPLICITY

[3008]
The seal of truth is simplicity.
HERMANN BOERHAAVE

[3009]
All great things are simple, and many can be expressed in a single word: freedom; justice; honor; duty; mercy; hope.
WINSTON S. CHURCHILL

[3010]
The greatest truths are the simplest, and so are the greatest men.
AUGUST W. HARE

[3011]
It's about time we gave up all this theological grand opera and went back to practicing the scales.
VANCE HAVNER

[3012]
Simplicity of character is no hindrance to subtlety of intellect.
JOHN VISCOUNT MORLEY

[3013]
Affected simplicity is a subtle form of imposture.
FRANÇOIS DE LA ROCHEFOUCAULD

[3014]
In character, in manners, in style, in all things, the supreme excellence is simplicity.
HENRY WADSWORTH LONGFELLOW

[3015]
Simplicity, of all things, is the hardest to be copied.
RICHARD STEELE

[3016]
Blissful are the simple, for they shall have much peace.
THOMAS À KEMPIS

[3017]
As people become wise in their own eyes . . . customs rise up from the spirit of this world . . . till a departure from the simplicity that there is in Christ becomes as distinguishable as light from darkness, to such who are crucified to the world.
JOHN WOOLMAN

SIN

[3018]
Sin is energy in the wrong channel.

AUGUSTINE OF HIPPO

[3019]
There are three things which the true Christian desires in respect to sin: justification, that it may not condemn; sanctification, that it may not reign; and glorification, that it may not be.

RICHARD CECIL

[3020]
To sin is human; but to persevere in sin is not human but altogether satanic.

JOHN CHRYSOSTOM

[3021]
Sin is the purposeful disobedience of a creature to the known will of God.

F. L. CROSS

[3022]
Surely there is not a righteous man on earth who does good and never sins.

ECCLESIASTES 7:20 (RSV)

[3023]
Don't try to deal with sin, for you are sure to lose. Deal with Christ; let him deal with your sin and you are sure to win.

ARTHUR H. ELFSTRAND

[3024]
Sin is not hurtful because it is forbidden, but sin is forbidden because it is hurtful.

BENJAMIN FRANKLIN

[3025]
Sin is no part of the true constitution of any member of the human race.

EVELYN FROST

[3026]
Esau sold his birthright for a bowl of chili.

BILLY GRAHAM

[3027]
Sin has many tools, but a lie is the handle which fits them all.

OLIVER WENDELL HOLMES

[3028]
Every one who commits sin is a slave to sin.

JOHN 8:34 (RSV)

[3029]
The sin they do by two and two they must pay for one by one.

RUDYARD KIPLING

[3030]
He does not cleanse himself of his sins who denies them.

LATIN PROVERB

[3031]
The suddenness of the provocation does not make me an ill-tempered man; it only shows me what an ill-tempered man I am.

C. S. LEWIS

[3032]
The measure of God's anger against sin is the measure of the love that is prepared to forgive the sinner and to love him in spite of his sin.

DAVID MARTYN LLOYD-JONES

[3033]
The ultimate proof of the sinner is that he does not know his own sin.

MARTIN LUTHER

[3034]
When we say, "Something should be done about Skid Row," God is saying the same thing about us. That is why he sent his Son to help us.

J. VERNON MCGEE

[3035]
Sin has always been an ugly word, but it has been made so in a new sense over the last half-century. It has been made not only ugly but passé. People are no longer sinful, they are only immature or underprivileged or frightened or, more particularly, sick.
PHYLLIS McGINLEY

[3036]
Sin is inevitable but not necessary.
REINHOLD NIEBUHR

[3037]
He that hath slight thought of sin never had great thoughts of God.
JOHN OWEN

[3038]
There are only two kinds of men: the righteous who believe themselves sinners, and the rest, sinners who believe themselves righteous.
BLAISE PASCAL

[3039]
Man did not sin because there was a bug in the factory. He sinned because there was external solicitation.
BERNARD RAMM

[3040]
I hate the sin, but I love the sinner.
THOMAS BUCHANAN READ

[3041]
Sin explained is sin defended.
E. G. ROBINSON

[3042]
Sinners can do nothing but make wounds that Christ may heal them; and make debts that he may pay them; and make falls that he may raise them; and make deaths that he may quicken them; and spin out and dig hells to themselves that he may ransom them. But it is neither shame nor pride for a drowning man to swim to a rock, nor for a ship-broken soul to run himself ashore upon Christ.
SAMUEL RUTHERFORD

[3043]
Some psychological and sociological conditioning occurs in every man's life and this affects the decisions he makes. But we must resist the modern concept that all sin can be explained merely on the basis of conditioning.
FRANCIS A. SCHAEFFER

[3044]
The first step toward the soul's recovery is the knowledge of the sin committed.
SENECA

[3045]
To call themselves "miserable sinners" is with many people a kind of religious good manners, just as a man inscribes himself "your humble servant."
J. A. SPENDER

[3046]
Sin is sovereign till sovereign grace dethrones it.
CHARLES H. SPURGEON

[3047]
One reason sin flourishes is that it is treated like a cream puff instead of a rattlesnake.
BILLY SUNDAY

[3048]
No sin is small. No grain of sand is small in the mechanism of a watch.
JEREMY TAYLOR

[3049]
God loves me even while I sin. But it cannot be said too strongly that there is a wrath of God against me as sinning; God's will is set one way and mine is set against it. And therefore, though he longs to forgive, he cannot do so unless either my will is turned from its sinful direction into conformity with his, or else there is at work some power which is capable of effecting that change in me.
WILLIAM TEMPLE

[3050]
It is absolutely certain that if a man sins, his own sin will dog him, that it will keep on his track night and day, like a bloodhound, and never quit until it catches him and brings him to book.
R. A. TORREY

[3051]
Sin may be clasped so close we cannot see its face.
RICHARD CHENEVIX TRENCH

[3052]
"Sin" is a seldom-used word today. But whether the word turns us on or off doesn't matter; it does not alter the truth, whatever we think. If my hang-ups and negatives are called "sin" by our Lord, then sin it is.
BOB TURNBULL

[3053]
Whatever weakens your reason, impairs the tenderness of your conscience, obscures your sense of God, or takes away the relish of spiritual things; in short, whatever increases the strength and authority of your body over your mind—that thing is sin to you.
SUSANNAH WESLEY

[3054]
Sin is any want of conformity to or transgression of the law of God.
WESTMINSTER CONFESSION OF FAITH

[3055]
We shall never understand anything of our Lord's preaching and ministry unless we continually keep in mind what exactly and exclusively his errand was in this world. Sin was his errand in this world, and it was his only errand. He would never have been in this world, either preaching or doing anything else, but for sin. He could have done everything else for us without coming down into this world at all; everything else but take away our sin.
ALEXANDER WHYTE

[3056]
Even in this age of inflation, the wages of sin remain the same.

SINCERITY

[3057]
Loss of sincerity is loss of vital power.
CHRISTIAN NESTELL BOVEE

[3058]
Sincerity is never ludicrous; it is always respectable.
CHARLOTTE BRONTË

[3059]
The sincere alone can recognize sincerity.

THOMAS CARLYLE

[3060]
Let us . . . celebrate the festival, not with the old leaven, the leaven of malice and evil, but with the unleavened bread of sincerity and truth.

1 CORINTHIANS 5:8 (RSV)

[3061]
The devil is sincere, but he is sincerely wrong.

BILLY GRAHAM

[3062]
You can be sincere and still be stupid.

CHARLES F. KETTERING

[3063]
Sincerity is an openness of heart; we find it in very few people.

FRANÇOIS DE LA ROCHEFOUCAULD

[3064]
Sincerity is impossible unless it pervade the whole being.

JAMES RUSSELL LOWELL

[3065]
If you take heed what you are within, you shall not reckon what men say of you. Man looks on the visage and God on the heart. Man considers the deeds and God praises the thoughts.

THOMAS A KEMPIS

[3066]
A corroding and deadening sin is professionalism, which shows itself in an affected tone of voice, a studied manner, a use of conventional phrases, and an unholy familiarity with spiritual things.

JOHN WATSON

SOCIETY

[3067]
The "permissive" society can be singularly intolerant to opinions which it deprecates. Often enough it is only permissive in regard to the values which the individuals or groups concerned themselves embrace, and seeks to eliminate contrary views not by persuasion but by suppression.

J. N. D. ANDERSON

[3068]
Man was formed for society, and is neither capable of living alone, nor has the courage to do it.

WILLIAM BLACKSTONE

[3069]
Human beings and human societies are not structures that are built or machines that are forged. They are plants that grow and must be tended as such.

WINSTON S. CHURCHILL

[3070]
Society is no longer satisfied to have scientific knowledge in books and brains alone. The quality of life, including the quality of the environment, has emerged as one of the critical social issues of our time. . . . If Christians withdraw from society because of the bewildering nature of its problems, they will soon lose the right to be heard on either scientific or religious topics.

GARY R. COLLINS AND JAMES F. JEKEL

[3071]
It is the religious impulse which supplies the cohesive force which unifies society and a culture.

CHRISTOPHER DAWSON

[3072]
A society has not ceased to be Christian until it has become positively something else. It is my contention that we have today a culture which is mainly negative, but which, so far as it is positive, is still Christian. . . . I believe that the choice before us is between the formation of a new Christian culture, and the acceptance of a pagan one.

T. S. ELIOT

[3073]
The final decision as to what the future of a society shall be depends not on how near its organization is to perfection, but on the degree of worthiness in its individual members.

ALBERT SCHWEITZER

[3074]
The life history of any society is an incessant fluctuation between periods of comparative well-being and those of calamity.

PITIRIM A. SOROKIN

SORROW

[3075]
No sorrow touches man until it has been filtered through the heart of God.

JOSEPH D. BLINCO

[3076]
You cannot prevent the birds of sorrow from flying over your head, but you can prevent them from building nests in your hair.

CHINESE PROVERB

[3077]
Sorrow is better than laughter, for by sadness of countenance the heart is made glad.

ECCLESIASTES 7:3 (RSV)

[3078]
He was . . . a man of sorrows, and acquainted with grief.

ISAIAH 53:3 (RSV)

[3079]
This world is so full of care and sorrow that it is a gracious debt we owe to one another to discover the bright crystals of delight hidden in somber circumstances and irksome tasks.

HELEN KELLER

[3080]
It is sorrow and failure which forces me to believe that there is One who heareth prayer.

CHARLES KINGSLEY

[3081]
The great thing with unhappy times is to take them bit by bit, hour by hour, like an illness. It is seldom the *present,* the exact present, that is unbearable.

C. S. LEWIS

[3082]
The happiest, sweetest, tenderest homes are not those where there has been no sorrow, but those which have been overshadowed with grief, and where Christ's comfort was accepted.

J. R. MILLER

[3083]
Sorrows remembered sweeten present joy.

ROBERT POLLOK

SOUL

[3084]
The first string that the musician usually touches is the bass, when he intends to put all in tune. God also plays upon this string first when he sets the soul in tune for himself.

JOHN BUNYAN
The Pilgrim's Progress

[3085]
One can hardly think too little of oneself. One can hardly think too much of one's soul.

G. K. CHESTERTON

[3086]
Either we have an immortal soul or we have not. If we have not, we are beasts; the first and wisest of beasts it may be; but still beasts. We differ only in degree and not in kind; just as the elephant differs from the slug.

SAMUEL TAYLOR COLERIDGE

[3087]
The soul is not where it lives but where it loves.

THOMAS FULLER

[3088]
We take excellent care of our bodies, which we have for only a lifetime; yet we let our souls shrivel, which we will have for eternity.

BILLY GRAHAM

[3089]
It is the natural yearning of the human soul touched by the Holy Spirit to pray.

LADY JULIAN OF NORWICH

[3090]
It was in the recognition that there is in each man a final essence, that is to say an immortal soul which only God can judge, that a limit was set upon the dominion of men over men.

WALTER LIPPMANN

[3091]
What is a man profited, if he shall gain the whole world, and lose his own soul? or what shall a man give in exchange for his soul?

MATTHEW 16:26 (KJV)

[3092]
As the flower turns to the sun, or the dog to his master, so the soul turns to God.

WILLIAM TEMPLE

[3093]
My soul is like a mirror in which the glory of God is reflected, but sin, however insignificant, covers the mirror with smoke.

TERESA OF AVILA

SOVEREIGNTY

[3094]
He who does not believe that God is above all is either a fool or has no experience of life.

STATIUS CAECILIUS

[3095]
What do we mean by this expression, "the sovereignty of God"? We mean the supremacy of God, the kingship of God, the godhood of God. To say that God is sovereign is to declare that God is God. He is the Most High, doing according to his will, so that none can stay his hand, defeat his counsels, or thwart his purpose.

ARTHUR W. PINK

[3096]
We need to reaffirm our stand on principles that have strongly motivated the conduct of our people throughout their history. The first principle is our recognition of the sovereignty of God. We need to reemphasize that man is not the center of the universe. It is Providence that is sovereign and gives the ultimate objectives and goals to mankind.

HERBERT V. PROCHNOW

[3097]
The Spirit's agency is sovereign, like the wind blowing where it will.
GEORGE SMEATON

SPACE

[3098]
I am willing to predict that because of space travel, by the end of the century, our churches will be full again. When we move out into the mystery and loneliness of space, when we begin to discover that we really are three billion lonely people on a small world, I think it's going to draw us much closer together.

RAY BRADBURY

[3099]
One reason why God made the moon was that it would be a "sign," a manifestation of himself. It bears testimony to the fact of a supreme intelligence behind all things that exist. It speaks eloquently of both the magnitude and the magnificence of the God who put it there.

Editorial, *Christianity Today*

[3100]
The God I worship is too big for space to contain.
JOHN H. GLENN

[3101]
I felt God's presence on the moon more than I have ever felt it here on earth.
JAMES B. IRWIN

[3102]
If you can be with God on earth, you can be with God in space as well.
JAMES McDIVITT

SPIRITUALITY

[3103]
In thirty years I have treated many patients. Among all my patients in the second half of life, every one of them fell ill because he had lost that which the living religions of every age had given their followers, and none of them was really healed who did not regain his religious outlook.
CARL GUSTAV JUNG

[3104]
Wherever God dwells he hides himself. . . . Men expect the Kingdom of God to come with observation; they know not that it is a hidden mystery, to be received only as God makes himself known in hearts surrendered and prepared for him. . . . Even when I cannot see the least evidence of the Holy Spirit's working, I am quietly and reverently to believe that he dwells in me.
ANDREW MURRAY

[3105]
The peace of the spiritual Christian is that of Christ's presence. . . . The spiritual man lives habitually under the dominating control of the Holy Spirit who indwells him. . . . It is a life of winsome holiness.
RUTH PAXSON

[3106]
It matters not how spiritual a church may profess to be, if souls are not saved something is radically wrong, and the professed spirituality is simply a false experience, a delusion of the devil. People who are satisfied to meet together simply to have a good time among themselves are far away from God. Real spirituality always has an outcome. There will be a yearning and a love for souls.
OSWALD J. SMITH

[3107]
Spiritual power is a force which history clearly teaches has been the greatest force in the development of man. Yet we have been merely playing with it and never really studied it as we have the physical forces.

CHARLES P. STEINMETZ

[3108]
It is usually not so much the greatness of our trouble as the littleness of our spirit which makes us complain.

JEREMY TAYLOR

[3109]
In the present dispensation every believer is indwelt by the Holy Spirit, and therefore experiential righteousness can be produced in any believer. This is the doctrine of spirituality.

ROBERT B. THIEME

STEWARDSHIP

[3110]
Stewardship is your commitment: the asking of God to take you back to himself—all that you have and all that you are.

LAWRENCE L. DURGIN

[3111]
More important than length of life is how we spend each day.

MARIA A. FURTADO

[3112]
Stewardship is what a man does after he says, "I believe."

W. H. GREEVER

[3113]
Stewardship is the acceptance from God of personal responsibility for all of life and life's affairs.

ROSWELL C. LONG

[3114]
Stewardship is not leaving a tip on God's tablecloth; it is the confession of an unpayable debt at God's Calvary.

PAUL S. REES

[3115]
God's work done in God's way will never lack God's supplies.

J. HUDSON TAYLOR

[3116]
Christian stewardship places emphasis upon tithing as a practical and historic measure of giving which is available for any person who seeks to be faithful in sharing his goods.

G. ERNEST THOMAS

[3117]
Stewardship is not a classroom exercise in fractions. It is a homework assignment in total living.

KENNETH L. WILSON

[3118]
Man is bound in stewardship to take care of this earth until he gets a better one.*

STRENGTH

[3119]
Lord, either lighten my burden or strengthen my back.

THOMAS FULLER

[3120]
When God wants to move a mountain, he does not take a bar of iron, but he takes a little worm. The fact is, we have too much strength. We are not weak enough. It is not our strength that we want. One drop of God's strength is worth more than all the world.

DWIGHT L. MOODY

[3121]
Life is a hard fight, a struggle, a wrestling with the Principle of Evil, hand to hand, foot to foot. Every inch of the way must be disputed. The night is given us to take breath, to pray, to drink deep at the fountain of power. The day, to use the strength which has been given us, to go forth to work with it till the evening.

FLORENCE NIGHTINGALE

[3122]
"They that wait upon the Lord shall renew their strength." They that wait upon men often dissipate their energies.

LEONARD RAVENHILL

[3123]
I have learned that assistance given to the weak makes the one who gives it strong, and that oppression of the unfortunate makes one weak.

BOOKER T. WASHINGTON

SUCCESS

[3124]
To find his place and fill it is success for a man.

PHILLIPS BROOKS

[3125]
The secret of success is constancy to purpose.

BENJAMIN DISRAELI

[3126]
I look on that man as happy who, when there is a question of success, looks into his work for a reply.

RALPH WALDO EMERSON

[3127]
A successful man cannot realize how hard an unsuccessful man finds life.

EDGAR W. HOWE

[3128]
Success is neither fame, wealth nor power; rather it is seeking, knowing, loving and obeying God. If you seek, you will know; if you know, you will love; if you love, you will obey.

CHARLES MALIK

[3129]
By success I mean the development of mature and constructive personality.

NORMAN VINCENT PEALE

[3130]
Physicians of all men are most happy; what good success soever they have, the world proclaimeth, and what faults they commit, the earth covereth.

FRANCIS QUARLES

[3131]
Out of every fruition of success, no matter what, comes forth something to make a new effort necessary.

WALT WHITMAN

SUFFERING

[3132]
There are comforts and compensations that one who has not suffered knows nothing of—like the lamps that nobody sees till the tunnel comes.

R. W. BARBOUR

[3133]
What is unbearable is not to suffer but
to be afraid of suffering. To endure a
precise pain, a definite loss, a hunger
for something one knows—this it is
possible to bear. One can live with this
pain. But in fear there is all the suffering of the world: to dread suffering is to
suffer an infinite pain since one sup-
poses it unbearable; it is to revolt
against the universe, to lose one's place
and one's rights in it, to become vul-
nerable over the whole extent of one's
being.
                              LOUIS EVELY

[3134]
The chief pang of most trials is not so
much the actual suffering itself as our
own spirit of resistance to it.
                    JEAN NICOLAS GROU

[3135]
If suffering is accepted and lived
through, not fought against and
refused, then it is completed and
becomes transmuted. It is absorbed,
and having accomplished its work, it
ceases to exist as suffering, and
becomes part of our growing self.
                      E. GRAHAM HOWE
               AND L. LE MESURIER

[3136]
It is suffering and then glory. Not to
have the suffering means not to have
the glory.
                    ROBERT C. MCQUILKIN

[3137]
Suffering is nature's way of indicating a
mistaken attitude or way of behavior,
and to the nonegocentric person every
moment of suffering is the opportunity
for growth. People should rejoice in
suffering, strange as it sounds, for this
is a sign of the availability of energy to
transform their characters.
                              ROLLO MAY

[3138]
You are never at any time nearer to
God than when under tribulation,
which he permits for the purification
and beautifying of your soul.
                    MIGUEL DE MOLINOS

[3139]
My mind is absorbed with the sufferings of man. Since I was twenty-four
there never [has been] any vagueness
in my plans or ideas as to what God's
work was for me.
                  FLORENCE NIGHTINGALE

[3140]
The self-centered suffer when others
disappoint them. The Christ-centered
suffer when they disappoint others.
                    LEONARD RAVENHILL

SUPERNATURAL

[3141]
The Christian life is something wholly
different from the best that the non-
Christian world can produce. It is
unique. It is frankly supernatural; that
is to say, it is lived by the grace of God.
Trusting in Christ, we do that which is
naturally impossible: we set out to live
a supernatural life.
         MARK RUDOLPH CARPENTER-GARNIER

[3142]
Science points unmistakably to the existence of a Creator of vast intelligence,
of limitless power and wisdom, and yet
personal in the fullest sense. It shows
us, moreover, that the Creator is not a
part of nature, but beyond nature and
therefore supernatural—since by
working intelligently upon nature he
causes supernatural events to take
place contrary to physical laws.
                    ROBERT E. D. CLARK

[3143]
Learn of the philosophers always to look for natural causes in extraordinary events; and when such natural causes are wanting, recur to God.

COUNT DE GABALIS

[3144]
The supernatural is the native air of Christianity.

DORA GREENWELL

[3145]
Victory in service is to be expected from supernaturally born men who are supernaturally delivered, supernaturally sustained and supernaturally directed. We are thus supernaturally created for a supernatural work which is supernaturally prepared and is to be supernaturally performed.

L. L. LEGTERS

[3146]
A supernatural event is one that takes place by the immediate, as distinguished from the medial power of God. . . . It presupposes the existence of a personal God, and the existence of a real order of nature.

J. GRESHAM MACHEN

[3147]
The supernaturalism of Christianity rests distinctly and solidly upon the supernaturalism of its founder, Jesus Christ.

WILBUR M. SMITH

SURRENDER

[3148]
God can make you anything you want to be, but you have to put everything in his hands.

MAHALIA JACKSON

[3149]
Whether it be something tremendously important in our eyes or the greatest triviality, nothing, nothing may be so put between ourselves and Christ that it becomes a condition. For in such a case we cannot surrender ourselves to him. The surrender must be unconditional; then—and this is a different thing from making prior conditions— we can pray for ourselves that our burden may not be too heavy.

SØREN KIERKEGAARD

[3150]
I have held many things in my hands, and I have lost them all; but whatever I have placed in God's hands, that I still possess.

MARTIN LUTHER

[3151]
To take all that we are and have and hand it over to God may not be easy; but it can be done, and when it is done, the world has in it one less candidate for misery.

PAUL E. SCHERER

SYMPATHY

[3152]
Needs there groan a world in anguish just to teach us sympathy?

ROBERT BROWNING

[3153]
Next to love, sympathy is the divinest passion of the human heart.

EDMUND BURKE

[3154]
It is better to be generous than just. It is sometimes better to sympathize instead of trying to understand.

PIERRE LeCOMTE DU NOüY

[3155]
Sympathy is never wasted except when you give it to yourself.

J. W. RAPER

[3156]
Rejoice with those who rejoice, weep with those who weep.

ROMANS 12:15 (RSV)

TAXES

[3157]
It is against the franchises of the land for freemen to be taxed [except] by their consent in Parliament.

EDWARD COKE

[3158]
It was as true, said Mr. Barkis, as taxes is. And nothing's truer than them.

CHARLES DICKENS
David Copperfield

[3159]
In this world nothing is sure but death and taxes.

BENJAMIN FRANKLIN

[3160]
Taxes and gruel will continually grow thicker.

HINDU PROVERB

[3161]
He who feels the advantage ought also to feel the expense.

LATIN LEGAL PROVERB

[3162]
The power to tax involves the power to destroy.

JOHN MARSHALL

[3163]
Cf: The power to tax is not the power to destroy while this court sits.

OLIVER WENDELL HOLMES, JR.

[3164]
Taxation without representation is tyranny.

JAMES OTIS

[3165]
One difference between death and taxes is that death doesn't get worse every time Congress meets.

ROY L. SCHAEFER

[3166]
Taxation is the legitimate support of government.

LOUIS ADOLPHE THIERS

[3167]
The income tax evader soon finds it would have been better to give than to deceive.

TEMPTATION

[3168]
No temptation has overtaken you that is not common to man. God is faithful, and he will not let you be tempted beyond your strength, but with the temptation will also provide the way of escape, that you may be able to endure it.

1 CORINTHIANS 10:13 (RSV)

[3169]
Do not say, "It was because of the Lord that I fell away," for he will not do things that he hates. Do not say, "It was he that led me astray," for he has no need of a sinner.

ECCLESIASTICUS 15:11–12
(Goodspeed)

[3170]
When we do ill, the devil tempteth us; when we do nothing, we tempt him.

THOMAS FULLER

[3171]
Temptation is Satan's opening wedge
into a man's being. He does not want to
stop there. If a man will obey demonic
promptings to do evil, Satan will do
worse with him by far than merely to
tempt him.
                    McCandlish Phillips

TENSION

[3172]
How can there be such a sweet flavor in
the bitter fruit we pluck from life—with
all its groans, tears, sighs, and wail-
ings? Does the sweetness come from
the hope that you [God] will hear us?
. . . Or is it that weeping is a bitter thing
that gives us pleasure only because it
relieves the tension created by sorrow?
                    Augustine of Hippo

[3173]
There is a sense in which modern psychiatry should be included with the
world religions, for . . . the same raw
material is taken—man with his storm
and stress, his tension and anxiety—
and the same result sought, namely, release, not by supernatural means, but
by natural ones. But one may ask, does
that release provide man with the objective foundations of Gospel truth?
Does it rightly relate him to God?
                    Robert O. Ferm

[3174]
Nervous tensions do not exist within a
vacuum. They do not exist exclusively
within the nervous system. They exist
within all of the organs of the body.
                    David Harold Fink

[3175]
Much is said today of the tensions of
modern life, and how to overcome
them. Tension is deep-seated, and cannot be cured by man-made remedies.
The source of man's trouble lies far-
ther back—in his heart. It is there that
the cure must begin. God invites us to
cast all our care on him.
                    Philip E. Howard, Jr.

[3176]
Tension, to a very large degree, may be
called the prevailing malady of the
American people.
                    Norman Vincent Peale

[3177]
Horizontal tensions pull an individual
apart; vertical tensions pull him together.
                    Fred Smith

TESTIMONY

[3178]
When revelation is described as testimony, it becomes that which is hu-
manly heard, believed and written
down. When testimony is described as
revelation, [it becomes] the self-tes-
timony of the sovereign God . . . ultimately transcendent and independent
of any human witness or support.
                    James M. Boice

[3179]
I cannot give a successful pastor's testimony, but I can give a sinner's testimony.
                    Roy Hession

[3180]
So long as our personal testimony exalts the glory and all-sufficiency of Christ as Savior, rather than our character either before or after conversion, it will be helpful. A Spirit-led worker will know how to use this instrument.

J. C. MACAULAY
AND ROBERT H. BELTON

[3181]
Confidence in others' honesty is not light testimony to one's own integrity.

MICHEL DE MONTAIGNE

[3182]
It is one thing to testify in a church service surrounded by people who agree and appreciate the testimony; but it is an entirely different matter to testify to the person outside Christ who is ignorant of the Gospel or in opposition to its truth.

LORA LEE PARROTT

[3183]
Is your Christianity ancient history or current events?

SAMUEL M. SHOEMAKER

TESTING

[3184]
In this world of ours, that which matters most is not what happens to the outside of things, but what happens to the inside of people.

WALTER RUSSELL BOWIE

[3185]
When God wants to make a man, he puts him into some storm.

LETTIE COWMAN

[3186]
No pain, no palm; no thorns, no throne; no gall, no glory; no cross, no crown.

WILLIAM PENN

[3187]
God does not offer us a way out of the testings of life. He offers us a way through, and that makes all the difference.

W. T. PURKISER

[3188]
There is no circumstance, no trouble, no testing, that can ever touch me until, first of all, it has gone past God and past Christ, right through to me. If it has come that far, it has come with a great purpose, which I may not understand at the moment. But I refuse to become panicky, as I lift up my eyes to him and accept it as coming from the throne of God for some great purpose of blessing to my own heart.

ALAN REDPATH

[3189]
Christians are like tea bags. You never know what kind you are until you are in hot water.

ELEANOR SEARLE WHITNEY

THANKFULNESS

[3190]
No duty is more urgent than that of returning thanks.

AMBROSE OF MILAN

[3191]
A thankful heart is not only the greatest virtue, but the parent of all other virtues.

CICERO

[3192]
One distinguishing mark of an unregenerate man is ingratitude.

E. J. CONRAD

[3193]
Every virtue divorced from thankfulness is maimed and limps along the spiritual road.

JOHN HENRY JOWETT

[3194]
For three things I thank God every day of my life: thanks that he has vouchsafed me knowledge of his works; deep thanks that he has set in my darkness the lamp of faith; deep, deepest thanks that I have another life to look forward to—a life joyous with light and flowers and heavenly song.

HELEN KELLER

[3195]
To be thankful for what I have received, and for what my Lord has prepared, is the surest way to receive more.

ANDREW MURRAY

[3196]
[Imagine being] in this glorious world with grateful hearts—and no one to thank.

CHRISTINA GEORGINA ROSSETTI

[3197]
This is the finest measure of thanksgiving: a thankfulness which springs from love.

WILLIAM C. SKEATH

[3198]
The atheist's most embarrassing moment is when he feels profoundly thankful for something but can't think of anybody to thank for it.

MARY ANN VINCENT

[3199]
Every misery that I miss is a new mercy.

IZAAK WALTON

[3200]
Three things for which thanks are due: an invitation, a gift and a warning.

WELSH PROVERB

THANKSGIVING

[3201]
Giving thanks is one course from which we never graduate.

VALERIE ANDERS

[3202]
For the ability to be of service to a fellow creature, we ought to give thanks, not demand it.

W. J. CAMERON

[3203]
Let all of us . . . give thanks to God and prayerful contemplation to those eternal truths and universal principles of Holy Scripture which have inspired such measure of true greatness as this nation has achieved.

DWIGHT D. EISENHOWER
Thanksgiving Proclamation, 1956

[3204]
No matter how great his trials may be, every saved sinner can always find reason for thanksgiving.

PHILIP E. HOWARD, JR.

[3205]
Let us . . . give thanks to God for his graciousness and generosity to us—pledge to him our everlasting devotion—beseech his divine guidance and the wisdom and strength to recognize and follow that guidance.

LYNDON B. JOHNSON
Thanksgiving Proclamation, 1964

[3206]
Let us observe this day with reverence and with prayer that will rekindle in us the will and show us the way not only to preserve our blessings, but also to extend them to the four corners of the earth.

JOHN F. KENNEDY
Thanksgiving Proclamation, 1961

240 THEOLOGY

[3207]
It has seemed to me fit and proper that [the gifts of God] should be solemnly, reverently, and gratefully acknowledged with one heart and one voice by the whole American people. I do, therefore, invite my fellow citizens . . . to set apart and observe the last Thursday of November next as a day of thanksgiving and praise to our beneficent Father who dwelleth in the heavens.

ABRAHAM LINCOLN
Thanksgiving Proclamation, 1863

[3208]
I thank my God in all my remembrance of you.

PHILIPPIANS 1:3 (RSV)

[3209]
There are three kinds of giving: grudge giving, duty giving, and thanksgiving.

ROBERT N. RODENMAYER

[3210]
We should be thankful for our tears; they prepare our eyes for a clearer vision of God.

WILLIAM A. WARD

[3211]
[Let us thank God] for his kind care and protection of the people of this country previous to their becoming a nation . . . for the great degree of tranquility, union and plenty which we have enjoyed . . . for the peaceable and rational manner in which we have been enabled to establish constitutions of government for our safety and happiness.

GEORGE WASHINGTON
Thanksgiving Proclamation, 1789

THEOLOGY

[3212]
All my theology is reduced to this narrow compass, "Jesus Christ came into the world to save sinners."

ARCHIBALD ALEXANDER

[3213]
Theology is that which is thought and said concerning God. Any theology which draws its materials from the Bible and attempts to be faithful to the Biblical norm is a Biblical theology.

GEOFFREY W. BROMILEY

[3214]
Any theology which attempts to speak to an age in its own language runs the danger of compromising the eternal message of the Gospel with the temporarily plausible conviction of the time.

KENNETH CAUTHEN

[3215]
None but a theology that came out of eternity can carry you and me safely to and through eternity.

THEODORE L. CUYLER

[3216]
I have always admired Mrs. Grote's saying that politics and theology were the only two really great subjects.

WILLIAM E. GLADSTONE

[3217]
It is the heart that makes the theologian.

MARCUS FABIUS QUINTILIAN

[3218]
The reason why the churches are discredited today is not that they are too bigoted about theology, but that they have run away from theology.

DOROTHY L. SAYERS

[3219]
The publican stood afar off and beat
his breast and said, "God, be merciful
to me, a sinner." I tell you that man had
the finest theology of any man in all
England.

CHARLES H. SPURGEON

THOUGHT

[3220]
If you would voyage Godward, you
must see to it that the rudder of
thought is right.

W. J. DAWSON

[3221]
We cannot by taking thought add a cu-
bit to our mental stature. What we can
do, however, is to make the most of the
capacity that is ours.

LINDSAY DEWAR

[3222]
Thoughts are toll-free, but not hell-
free.

GERMAN PROVERB

[3223]
The Word that God speaks . . . exposes
the very thoughts and motives of a
man's heart.

HEBREWS 4:12
(Phillips)

[3224]
My thoughts are not your thoughts,
neither are your ways my ways, says the
Lord. For as the heavens are higher
than the earth, so are my ways higher
than your ways and my thoughts than
your thoughts.

ISAIAH 55:8–9 (RSV)

[3225]
Thinking is essentially purposive, directed and controlled . . . by the conscious exercise of will, and set in motion by . . . the existence of a problem
demanding solution.

R. W. JEPSON

[3226]
The universe is one of God's thoughts.

JOHANN FRIEDRICH VON SCHILLER

[3227]
They are never alone that are accompanied with noble thoughts.

PHILIP SIDNEY

[3228]
Everything that can be thought at all
can be thought clearly. Everything that
can be said can be said clearly.

LUDWIG WITTGENSTEIN

TIME

[3229]
Time never takes time off.

AUGUSTINE OF HIPPO

[3230]
Whenever I attempt to frame a simple
idea of time, abstracted from the
succession of ideas in my mind, which
flows uniformly, and is participated by
all beings, I am lost and embrangled in
inextricable difficulties.

GEORGE BERKELEY

[3231]
If a man has no time or only a short
time for seeing people, you can be
fairly sure that he is neither very important nor very busy.

JOHN SPENCER CHURCHILL

[3232]
Right now God is ready to welcome
you. Today he is ready to save you.
2 CORINTHIANS 6:2
(*The Living Bible*)

[3233]
The two ideas that most clearly eluci-
date the New Testament conception of
time are those usually expressed by
kairos ("a point of time"), and *aion*
("age"). The characteristic thing about
kairos is that it has to do with a definite
point of time which has a fixed content,
while *aion* designates a *duration* of time.
A divine decision makes this or that
date a *kairos*, a point of time that has a
special place in the execution of God's
plan of salvation.
OSCAR CULLMANN

[3234]
For everything there is a season, and a
time for every matter under heaven.
ECCLESIASTES 3:1 (RSV)

[3235]
Time and tide wait for no man.
ENGLISH PROVERB

[3236]
We all find time to do what we really
want to do.
WILLIAM FEATHER

[3237]
There is no mortar that time will not
loose.
FRENCH PROVERB

[3238]
There is one thing stronger than all the
armies in the world: an idea whose
hour is come.
VICTOR HUGO

[3239]
Throughout the whole [New Testa-
ment] there runs the conviction that
the time looked forward to by the
prophets has in fact arrived in history
with the advent of Jesus Christ. . . . The
time of Jesus is *kairos*—a time of opportunity. To embrace the opportunity
means salvation; to neglect it, disaster.
There is no third course.
JOHN MARSH

[3240]
These three will be effaced by time: a
debt, a sore, and a stain.
SANSKRIT PROVERB

[3241]
Time heals what reason cannot.
SENECA

[3242]
Great men never complain about the
lack of time. Alexander the Great and
John Wesley accomplished everything
they did in twenty-four-hour days.
FRED SMITH

[3243]
Enjoy the blessings of this day, if God
sends them; and the evils of it bear patiently and sweetly: for this day only is
ours, we are dead to yesterday, and we
are not yet born to the morrow.
JEREMY TAYLOR

TRANSCENDENCE

[3244]
Worship is transcendent wonder.
THOMAS CARLYLE

[3245]
On the assumption that modern knowledge renders unintelligible the scriptural formulation of the Gospel, the secular theologians eliminate the invisible, transcendent, absolute God of the Bible. . . . The most obvious defect of this contemporary theological faddism is its mislocation of the problem of modern man. . . . The modern problem is not the transcendent God but rebellious man—not modern man in some peculiar way but man as fallen.
CARL F. H. HENRY

[3246]
The man who weighs the importance of his rational faculties is in some sense more than "reason," and has capacities which transcend the ability to form general concepts. . . . If one . . . asks whether life is worth living, the very character of the question reveals that the questioner must in some sense be able to stand outside of, and to transcend, the life which is thus judged and estimated. . . . [This is man's] capacity for self-transcendence.
REINHOLD NIEBUHR

[3247]
The characteristic difference between the Old Testament teaching concerning God and the conception of God among the other Oriental peoples is the absolute transcendence of God's Being.
THEODORUS C. VRIEZEN

TRANSFORMATION

[3248]
We were chaff, now we are wheat; we were dross, now we are gold; we were ravens, now we are doves; we were goats, now we are sheep; we were thorns, now we are grapes; we were thistles, now we are lilies; we were strangers, now we are citizens; we were harlots, now we are virgins; hell was our inheritance, now heaven is our possession; we were children of wrath, now we are sons of mercy; we were bondslaves to Satan, now we are heirs of God and co-heirs with Jesus Christ.
JAMES BISSE

[3249]
The transformation of personality, through the decisive act of faith, wrought in the individual by the ministry of the Spirit of God, is termed salvation. This moral and spiritual change is also known as the new birth.
ROBERT O. FERM

[3250]
When you come to Christ, the Holy Spirit takes up residence in your heart. Something new is added to your life supernaturally. You are transformed by the renewing of your mind. A new power, a new dimension, a new ability to love, a new joy, a new peace—the Holy Spirit comes in and lives the Christian life through you.
BILLY GRAHAM

[3251]
Do not be conformed to this world but be transformed by the renewal of your mind.
ROMANS 12:2 (RSV)

TRIALS

[3252]
So far you have faced no trial beyond what man can bear. God keeps faith, and he will not allow you to be tested above your powers, but when the test comes he will at the same time provide a way out, by enabling you to sustain it.

1 CORINTHIANS 10:13 (NEB)

[3253]
There are three ways that prepare us for life's trials. One is the Spartan way that says, "I have strength within me to do it, I am the captain of my soul. With the courage and will that is mine, I will be master when the struggle comes." Another way is the spirit of Socrates, who affirmed that we have minds, reason and judgment to evaluate and help us cope with the enigmas and struggles of life. The Christian way is the third approach. It doesn't exclude the other two, but it adds, "You don't begin with yourself, your will or your reason. You begin with God, who is the beginning and the end."

LOWELL R. DITZEN

[3254]
Trial is God's alchemy by which the dross is left in the crucible, the baser metals are transmuted, and the character is enriched with gold.

WILLIAM MORLEY PUNSHON

[3255]
God helps us to do what we can, and endure what we must, even in the darkest hour. But more, he wants to teach us that there are no rainbows without storm clouds and there are no diamonds without heavy pressure and enormous heat.

W. T. PURKISER

[3256]
The fack can't be no longer disgised that a Krysis is onto us.

ARTEMUS WARD

TROUBLE

[3257]
In all troublous events we may find comfort, though it be only in the negative admission that things might have been worse.

AMELIA BARR

[3258]
There are people who are always anticipating trouble, and in this way they manage to enjoy many sorrows that never really happen to them.

JOSH BILLINGS

[3259]
The way to the soul's final greatness lies through its misery rather than through its success.

P. T. FORSYTH

[3260]
He that seeks trouble never misses.

GEORGE HERBERT

[3261]
Man is born to trouble as the sparks fly upward.

JOB 5:7 (RSV)

[3262]
Outward attacks and troubles rather fix than unsettle the Christian, as tempests from without only serve to root the oak faster.

HANNAH MORE

[3263]
It is distrust of God to be troubled about what is to come; impatience against God to be troubled with what is present; and anger at God to be troubled for what is past.

SIMON PATRICK

[3264]
This poor man cried, and the Lord heard him, and saved him out of all his troubles.

PSALM 34:6 (RSV)

[3265]
God is our refuge and strength, a very present help in trouble.

PSALM 46:1 (RSV)

[3266]
Trouble is a marvelous mortifier of pride and an effectual restrainer of self-will.

WILLIAM MORLEY PUNSHON

[3267]
It is not the will of God to give us more troubles than will bring us to live by faith in him.

WILLIAM ROMAINE

[3268]
You must learn to make your evils your great good and to spin comforts, peace, joy, communion with Christ, out of your troubles. They are Christ's wooers, sent to speak on your behalf to himself.

SAMUEL RUTHERFORD

[3269]
If you tell your troubles to God, you put them into the grave; if you roll your burden somewhere else, it will roll back again like the stone of Sisyphus.

CHARLES H. SPURGEON

[3270]
Trouble has done it, Bilgewater, trouble has done it; trouble has brung these gray hairs and this premature balditude.

MARK TWAIN

TRUST

[3271]
What does a child do whose mother or father allows something to be done which it cannot understand? There is only one way of peace. The loving child trusts.

AMY CARMICHAEL

[3272]
For God to explain a trial would be to destroy its object, which is that of calling forth simple faith and implicit obedience.

ALFRED EDERSHEIM

[3273]
If the basis of peace is God, the secret of peace is trust.

JOHN BENJAMIN FIGGIS

[3274]
When you cannot trust God you cannot trust anything; and when you cannot trust anything you get the condition of the world as it is today.

BASIL KING

[3275]
We must not close with Christ because we feel him, but because God has said it. We must take God's Word even in the dark.

ROBERT MURRAY MCCHEYNE

[3276]
Trusting means looking forward to getting something we don't yet have—for a man who already has something doesn't need to hope and trust that he will get it.

ROMANS 8:24
(*The Living Bible*)

[3277]
Christ never was in a hurry. There was no rushing forward, no anticipating, no fretting over what might be. Each day's duties were done as each day brought them, and the rest was left with God.

MARY SLESSOR

[3278]
Be it ours, when we cannot see the face of God, to trust under the shadow of his wings.

CHARLES H. SPURGEON

[3279]
The highest pinnacle of the spiritual life is not joy in unbroken sunshine, but absolute and undoubting trust in the love of God.

A. W. THOROLD

[3280]
He who trusts men will make fewer mistakes than he who distrusts them.

TRUTH

[3281]
The New Testament does not say, "You shall know the rules, and by them you shall be bound," but, "You shall know the truth, and the truth shall make you free."

JOHN BAILLIE

[3282]
A truth that's told with bad intent /
Beats all the lies you can invent.

WILLIAM BLAKE

[3283]
A half-truth is a dangerous thing, especially if you have got hold of the wrong half.

MYRON F. BOYD

[3284]
To exaggerate invariably weakens the point of what we have to say.

FRENCH PROVERB

[3285]
Before I ever saw Jerusalem, I knew that Christ was Very God. I knew that God was born of a virgin before I saw Bethlehem's stable. I believed in the Lord's resurrection before I looked upon the church built upon its memory.

GREGORY OF NYSSA

[3286]
Our world is so exceedingly rich in delusions that a truth is priceless.

CARL GUSTAV JUNG

[3287]
Christianity founds its whole system of truths upon the existence of God. The first word of Christianity is God. The solution of the problems of existence is to be found in God. The truth which we need and seek is God—the living, personal God. This is the truth which is the foundation of the Christian view of the universe.

CHRISTOPH ERNST LUTHARDT

[3288]
If a man will not think about Christian truth he will not have the blessedness of Christian possession of God. There is no mystery about the road to the sweetness and holiness and power that may belong to a Christian. The only way to win them is to be occupied with the plain truths of God's revelation in Jesus Christ.

ALEXANDER MACLAREN

[3289]
The Bible cannot at the same time be unbelievable history and evangelical truth.

A. H. MJORUD

[3290]
I felt like a child playing with pebbles on the shore when the ocean of truth lay all about me.

ISAAC NEWTON
(on discovering the law of gravitation)

[3291]
It is senseless to pay tuition to educate a rebel who has no heart for truth.

PROVERBS 17:16
(*The Living Bible*)

[3292]
Christianity is not a drug which suits some complaints and not others. It is either sheer illusion or else it is the Truth. But if it is the Truth, if the universe happens to be constituted in this way, the question is not whether the God of Christianity suits us, but whether we suit him.

WILLIAM TEMPLE

TYRANNY

[3293]
Rebellion to tyrants is obedience to God.

JOHN BRADSHAW
Epitaph quoted in Randall's
Life of Jefferson

[3294]
No intervals of good humor, no starts of bounty, will atone for tyranny and oppression.

JEREMY COLLIER

[3295]
Nature has left this tincture in the blood, / That all men would be tyrants if they could.

DANIEL DEFOE
"The Kentish Petition"

[3296]
Of all plagues with which mankind are curst, / Ecclesiastic tyranny's the worst.

DANIEL DEFOE
"The True-Born Englishman"

[3297]
I have sworn upon the altar of God eternal hostility against every form of tyranny over the mind of man.

THOMAS JEFFERSON

[3298]
The accumulation of all powers, legislative, executive and judiciary, in the same hands, whether of one, a few or many, and whether hereditary, self-appointed or elective, may justly be pronounced the very definition of tyranny.

JAMES MADISON

[3299]
Men must be governed by God or they will be ruled by tyrants.

WILLIAM PENN

[3300]
Where law ends, tyranny begins.

WILLIAM PITT

[3301]
Nothing is more abhorrent to the tyrant than the service of Christ.

GIROLAMO SAVONAROLA

UNDERSTANDING

[3302]
Understanding is the reward of faith.

AUGUSTINE OF HIPPO

[3303]
When I was a child I spoke and thought
and reasoned as a child does. But when
I became a man my thoughts grew far
beyond those of my childhood, and
now I have put away the childish
things.
1 CORINTHIANS 13:11
(*The Living Bible*)

[3304]
If you see a man of understanding, go
to him early, and let your feet wear out
his doorstep.
ECCLESIASTICUS 6:36
(Goodspeed)

[3305]
Our Lord opened the understanding of
his disciples. He sought entrance for
truth by that avenue. He does so still.
T. C. HAMMOND

[3306]
What is most necessary for under-
standing divine things is prayer.
ORIGEN

[3307]
The peace of God, which passes all understanding, will keep your hearts and
your minds in Christ Jesus.
PHILIPPIANS 4:7 (RSV)

[3308]
Wisdom is the principal thing; therefore get wisdom: and with all thy getting get understanding.
PROVERBS 4:7 (KJV)

[3309]
I believe in order that I may under-
stand.
TERTULLIAN

[3310]
Comprehension must be the soil in
which grow all the fruits of friendship.
WOODROW WILSON

[3311]
The more we learn about the wonders
of our universe, the more clearly we are
going to perceive the hand of God.
FRANK BORMAN

[3312]
I don't pretend to understand the universe—it's a great deal bigger than I
am.
THOMAS CARLYLE

[3313]
The new physics does not regard the
universe as atomic chaos but . . . has
found strong evidence pointing to the
existence of "a directive intelligence."
ARTHUR H. COMPTON

[3314]
How could anyone observe the mighty
order with which our God governs the
universe without feeling himself inclined . . . to the practice of all virtues,
and to the beholding of the Creator
himself, the source of all goodness, in
all things and before all things?
COPERNICUS

[3315]
The beginning [of the universe] seems
to present insuperable difficulties unless we agree to look on it as frankly
supernatural.
ARTHUR S. EDDINGTON

[3316]
Did the atoms take counsel together
and devise a common plan and work it
out? That hypothesis is . . . rational in
comparison with the notion that . . .
chance produced such a universe as
that in which we live.
ROBERT FLINT

[3317]
Man is not born to solve the problems of the universe, but to find out where the problems begin, and then to take his stand within the limits of the intelligible.

JOHANN WOLFGANG VON GOETHE

[3318]
The universe can be best pictured, though still very imperfectly and inadequately, as consisting of pure thought, the thought of what we must describe as a mathematical thinker.

JAMES H. JEANS

[3319]
God showed me a little thing the size of a hazelnut in the palm of my hand, and it was as round as a ball. I thought, "What may this be?" and was answered thus: "It is the universe."

LADY JULIAN OF NORWICH

[3320]
If the universe is so bad, or even half so bad, how on earth did human beings ever come to attribute it to the activity of a wise and good Creator?

C. S. LEWIS

[3321]
The Engineer of the universe has made me part of his whole design.

LEIGH NYGARD

[3322]
The universe is a thought of God.

JOHANN FRIEDRICH VON SCHILLER

[3323]
Wonderful and vast as is the universe, man is greater. The universe does not know that it exists; man does. The universe is not free to act; man is.

MARTIN J. SCOTT

[3324]
When I view the universe as a whole, I admit that it is a marvelous structure; and what is more, I insist that it is of what I may call an intelligent design.

WILLIAM FRANCIS GRAY SWANN

[3325]
That the universe was formed by a fortuitous concourse of atoms, I will no more believe than that the accidental jumbling of the alphabet would fall into a most ingenious treatise of philosophy.

JONATHAN SWIFT

VICTORY

[3326]
True triumphs are God's triumphs over us. His defeats of us are our real victories.

HENRY ALFORD

[3327]
"O death, where is thy victory? O death, where is thy sting?" The sting of death is sin, and the power of sin is the law. But thanks be to God, who gives us the victory through our Lord Jesus Christ.

1 CORINTHIANS 15:55–57 (RSV)

[3328]
The way to get the most out of a victory is to follow it up with another which makes it look small.

HENRY S. HASKINS

[3329]
This is the victory that overcomes the world, our faith.

1 JOHN 5:4 (RSV)

[3330]
God has never lost a game and has never tied one.

BILL KRISHER

[3331]
Peace hath her victories / No less renowned than War.
JOHN MILTON
"To the Lord General Cromwell"

[3332]
The first step on the way to victory is to recognize the enemy.
CORRIE TEN BOOM

[3333]
Remember, the triumphant Christian does not fight for victory; he celebrates a victory already won. The victorious life is Christ's business, not yours.
REGINALD WALLIS

VIOLENCE

[3334]
Mainstream Christianity distinguishes between force and violence. Force is the power wielded to make and keep human life truly human. Violence is useless, indiscriminate, and absurd.
VERNON C. GROUNDS

[3335]
Violence defeats its own ends.
WILLIAM HAZLITT

[3336]
Pride is unwilling to believe the necessity of assigning any other reason than her own will; and would rather maintain the most equitable claims by violence and penalties than descend from the dignity of command to dispute and expostulation.
SAMUEL JOHNSON

[3337]
It is well known that firearms go off by themselves if only enough of them are together.
CARL GUSTAV JUNG

[3338]
Perseverance is more prevailing than violence.
PLUTARCH

[3339]
Violent delights have violent ends.
SHAKESPEARE
Romeo and Juliet, III, vi

[3340]
Let us not forget that violence does not have its own separate existence and is, in fact, incapable of having it: it is invariably interwoven with the lie. They have the closest of kinship, the most profound natural tie: violence has nothing with which to cover itself except the lie, and the lie has nothing to stand on other than violence.
ALEKSANDR I. SOLZHENITSYN

[3341]
A good portion of the evils that afflict mankind is due to the erroneous belief that life can be made secure by violence.
LEO TOLSTOY

[3342]
The right to resist oppression by violence is beyond doubt. But its exerciser would be unwise unless the suppression of free thought, free speech, and a free press were enforced so stringently that all other means of throwing it off had become hopeless.
BENJAMIN R. TUCKER

VOCATION

[3343]
The Christian community has a specific task in just this field: to work out a concrete doctrine of vocation through its lay members who know the jobs and their threat to working morale, and to demand and create such technical and psychological conditions as are necessary to regain the lost sense of work as a divine calling.

EMIL BRUNNER

[3344]
I quit drawing my unemployment check and signed on as a fisherman.

CAROLYN P. ELLIS

[3345]
Walk worthy of the vocation wherewith ye are called.

EPHESIANS 4:1 (KJV)

[3346]
A sense of mission is to a man's soul the sustaining thing that food is to the body. [Yet] there is nothing in the whole world so dangerous as a sense of vocation without a belief in God.

W. R. FORRESTER

[3347]
Heaven is his vocation, and therefore he counts all earthly employments as avocations.

THOMAS FULLER

[3348]
My dear Miss Florence, it would be unusual, and in England whatever is unusual is thought to be unsuitable; but I may say to you . . . if you have a vocation for that way of life, act up to your inspiration and you will find there is never anything unbecoming . . . in doing your duty for the good of others. Choose, go on with it, wherever it may lead you and God be with you.

DR. WARD HOWE
(to Florence Nightingale)

[3349]
Momentous, cardinal decision—the choice of one's work in the world; of one's career. . . . First requirement—an honest and determined effort to discover and understand oneself.

J. C. W. REITH

[3350]
I ask that work should be looked upon, not as a necessary drudgery to be undergone for the purpose of making money, but as a way of life in which the nature of man should find its proper exercise and delight and so fulfil itself to the glory of God.

DOROTHY L. SAYERS

[3351]
The vocation of every man and woman is to serve other people.

LEO TOLSTOY

[3352]
Luther taught the Christian to serve God in his vocation (in vocatione), Calvin through his vocation (per vocationem).

HUGH WATT

[3353]
Vocation is witnessing to Jesus Christ in and through one's function in the social order.*

WAR

[3354]
In peace the sons bury their fathers and in war the fathers bury their sons.

FRANCIS BACON

[3355]
There are many things worse than war. Slavery is worse than war. Dishonor is worse than war.

WINSTON S. CHURCHILL

[3356]
As never before, the essence of war is fire, famine and pestilence. They contribute to its outbreak; they are among its weapons; and they become its consequences.

DWIGHT D. EISENHOWER

[3357]
The wars that rage within the world are a reflection of the wars that rage inside people.

LEIGHTON FORD

[3358]
There never was a good war or a bad peace.

BENJAMIN FRANKLIN

[3359]
What we need to discover in the social realm is the moral equivalent of war: something heroic that will speak to men as universally as war does, and yet will be compatible with their spiritual selves as war has proved itself to be incompatible.

WILLIAM JAMES

[3360]
In modern warfare there are no victors; there are only survivors.

LYNDON B. JOHNSON

[3361]
Cannons and firearms are cruel and damnable machines; I believe them to have been the direct suggestion of the devil. If Adam had seen in a vision the horrible instruments his children were to invent, he would have died of grief.

MARTIN LUTHER

[3362]
War is an ugly thing, but not the ugliest of things: the decayed and degraded state of moral and patriotic feeling which thinks nothing worth a war is worse.

JOHN STUART MILL

[3363]
It is always easy to begin a war, but very difficult to stop one, since its beginning and end are not under the control of the same man.

SALLUST

[3364]
It becomes a wise man to try negotiation before arms.

TERENCE

[3365]
To be prepared for war is one of the most effectual means of preserving peace.

GEORGE WASHINGTON

[3366]
Take my word for it: if you had seen but one day of war you would pray to Almighty God that you might never see such again.

ARTHUR WELLESLEY

[3367]
War is indeed hell, and we cannot pray it pure.

KENNETH L. WILSON

[3368]
Many men have served God and country well in arms; they have been valorous in battle, magnanimous in victory, patient in defeat and capture, and faithful in death.*

WEAKNESS

[3369]
God purposely chose . . . what the world considers weak in order to put powerful men to shame.

1 CORINTHIANS 1:27
(Good News for Modern Man)

[3370]
He said to me, "My grace is sufficient for you, for my power is made perfect in weakness." I will all the more gladly boast of my weaknesses, that the power of Christ may rest upon me. For the sake of Christ, then, I am content with weaknesses . . . for when I am weak, then I am strong.

2 CORINTHIANS 12:9–10 (RSV)

[3371]
Weak things united become strong.

THOMAS FULLER

[3372]
There are two kinds of weakness, that which breaks and that which bends.

JAMES RUSSELL LOWELL

[3373]
When God delivered Israel out of Egypt, he didn't send an army. We would have sent an army or an orator! But God sent a man who had been in the desert forty years, and had an impediment in his speech. It is weakness that God wants! Nothing is small when God handles it.

DWIGHT L. MOODY

[3374]
In all our weaknesses we have one element of strength if we recognize it: knowledge of danger is often the best means of safety.

EDWARD P. ROE

[3375]
Christ can triumph in a weaker man than I am, if there be any such.

SAMUEL RUTHERFORD

[3376]
The acknowledgment of our weakness is the first step toward repairing our loss.

THOMAS À KEMPIS

WHOLENESS

[3377]
The church has thought about the matter of wholeness, or holiness (the words have a common meaning), too moralistically. Holiness does not mean just the avoidance of certain habits; it is related to the wholeness of life. God's therapy is at the level of persons. His purpose is to make men and women whole in a broken world, to produce men and women [who] can demonstrate convincingly to our society what God really intends for man.

MYRON S. AUGSBURGER

[3378]
Disobedience consists in the fact that it is not possible for man to be one thing and then another; that it is lack of wholeness, it is the divided heart. God does not wish to have my obedience as something which is valuable in itself. He wants me, my whole personality, in the totality of all my actions, both inward and outward.

EMIL BRUNNER

[3379]
In conversion, whether it comes gradually or suddenly, the whole self comes under the power of a new master sentiment whose force is of total personality significance.
ROBERT O. FERM

[3380]
Christian healing is not mere negation of disease but a ministry of life to the whole personality.
EVELYN FROST

[3381]
The harder a man tries to be himself without being right with God, the less like himself he becomes and the more like everyone else he is. Man was made to have fellowship with God, and man is never himself until he submits to this divine rule. Not your talent first, or your money, or your time, or your service, but the complete "you" is what God requests and requires—not that he might make you into a slave, but that he might emancipate you.
RICHARD C. HALVERSON

[3382]
If a man's Bible is coming apart, it is an indication that he himself is fairly well put together.
JAMES E. JENNINGS

[3383]
Man is not truly man until he is God's man.
JOHN A. MACKAY

[3384]
When we set ourselves to the work of collecting or re-collecting the scattered pieces of ourselves, we begin a task which, if carried to its natural conclusion, ultimately becomes prayer.
WILLIAM SADLER

[3385]
The highest value for the religious man may be called unity. He seeks to comprehend the cosmos as a whole, to relate himself to its embracing totality.
EDWARD SPRANGER

[3386]
Whenever the soul comes to itself and attains something of its natural soundness, it speaks of God.
TERTULLIAN

[3387]
Something must really change in the world, and this can come only through men who themselves are changed. But when a man is changed under the influence of grace, then not only the state of his soul, but also his whole comportment, is changed. He is suddenly free from the old habits which kept him imprisoned, free from the rancor and remorse that consumed him. [He has] become whole in a broken world.
PAUL TOURNIER

WILL

[3388]
When I vacillated about my decision to serve the Lord my God, it was I who willed and I who willed not, and nobody else. I was fighting against myself. . . . All you asked was that I cease to want what I willed, and begin to want what you willed.
AUGUSTINE OF HIPPO

[3389]
When the will is ready the feet are light.
GEORGE HERBERT

[3390]
Not only in works, but also in faith, God has given man freedom of the will.
IRENAEUS

[3391]
God never burglarizes the human will.
He may long to come in and help, but
he will never cross the picket line of our
unwillingness.

JAMES JAUNCEY

[3392]
All theory is against the freedom of the
will; all experience for it.

SAMUEL JOHNSON

[3393]
Our wills are ours, we know not how; /
Our wills are ours, to make them
Thine.

ALFRED TENNYSON
"In Memoriam"

[3394]
He is a fool who thinks by force or skill
/ To turn the current of a woman's will.

SAMUEL TUKE
"Adventures of Five Hours"

WISDOM

[3395]
A wise judge will instruct his people,
and the rule of a man of understanding
is well ordered.

ECCLESIASTICUS 10:1
(Goodspeed)

[3396]
Knowledge is horizontal. Wisdom is
vertical—it comes down from above.

BILLY GRAHAM

[3397]
It is not the old that are wise, nor the
aged that understand what is right.

JOB 32:9 (RSV)

[3398]
That wisdom must sometimes refuse
what ignorance may quite innocently
ask seems to be self-evident.

C. S. LEWIS

[3399]
The days that make us happy make us
wise.

JOHN MASEFIELD

[3400]
Without wise leadership, a nation is in
trouble; but with good counselors
there is safety.

PROVERBS 11:14
(The Living Bible)

[3401]
Even a fool, when he holds his peace,
is counted wise.

PROVERBS 17:28 (KJV)

[3402]
There can be no wisdom disjoined
from goodness.

RICHARD C. TRENCH

WITNESSING

[3403]
A young RAF pilot said to a Christian,
"Don't try to help me or tell me what
I ought to think yet. Don't work for my
salvation—show me yours, show me it
is possible, and the knowledge that
something works will give me courage
and belief."

FLORENCE ALLSHORN

[3404]
The real witnessing Christian does not
talk about people he has "converted."
Witnessing is hard work unless it is
done in the Spirit, and then we can't
brag about it.

WILLIAM R. BRIGHT

[3405]
We do not argue about worldliness; we witness. We do not discuss philosophy; we preach the Gospel. We do not speculate about the destiny of sinners; we pluck them as brands from the burning.

SAMUEL CHADWICK

[3406]
A Christian is not one who withdraws but one who infiltrates.

BILL GLASS

[3407]
He who can tell men what God has done for his soul is the likeliest to bring their souls to God.

ROBERT LEIGHTON

[3408]
Your theology is what you are when the talking stops and the action starts.

COLIN MORRIS

[3409]
A multitude of laymen are in serious danger. It is positively perilous for them to hear more sermons, attend more Bible classes and read more religious and ethical works, unless accompanying it all there be afforded day by day an adequate outlet for their new-found truth.

JOHN R. MOTT

[3410]
It is more effective to spend time talking to Christ about a man than talking to a man about Christ, because if you are talking to Christ about a man earnestly, trustingly, in the course of time you cannot help talking to the man effectively about Christ.

ROBERT BOYD MUNGER

[3411]
Cf: I am seeing so-and-so; I could help him more if I set apart the hour in which I would have seen him to pray for him.

FORBES ROBINSON

[3412]
Tell what Christ did for you today or yesterday. If you have to go back twenty years to find something that happened in your life, it is fatal.

WESLEY NELSON

[3413]
If Christ lives in us, controlling our personalities, we will leave glorious marks on the lives we touch. Not because of our lovely characters, but because of his.

EUGENIA PRICE

[3414]
I am convinced that many converts who turn back to their old way of life do so because they fail to bear witness to the change that has taken place. Thus they become easy prey for the tempter. They lose their joy and peace and the assurance that they are children of God. If you have accepted Christ and the salvation he offers, then confess him, no matter what it costs, and God will give you an assurance of which neither the world nor the devil can rob you.

ERIK AUGUST SKOGSBERGH

[3415]
To be a witness does not consist of engaging in propaganda or in stirring people up. It means to live in such a way that one's life would not make sense if God did not exist.

EMMANUEL SUHARD

[3416]
The great thing we can learn from missionary churches is that they inform the new convert he is responsible to tell the Gospel to his family.
CLYDE W. TAYLOR

[3417]
Our task as laymen is to live our personal communion with Christ with such intensity as to make it contagious.
PAUL TOURNIER

[3418]
We do not stand in the world bearing witness to Christ; we stand in Christ bearing witness to the world.
RALPH L. WILLIAMS

[3419]
Lighthouses don't fire guns or ring bells to call attention to their light, they just shine.

WOMAN

[3420]
Next to God we are indebted to women, first for life itself, and then for making it worth having.
CHRISTIAN NESTELL BOVEE

[3421]
There is something in a woman beyond all human delights: a magnetic virtue, a charming quality, an occult and powerful motive.
ROBERT BURTON

[3422]
God, when he made the first woman
. . . made her not of the head of Adam, for she should not climb to great lordship . . . also, certes, God made not woman of the foot of Adam, for she should not be holden too low . . . but God made woman of the rib of Adam, for woman should be fellow unto man.
GEOFFREY CHAUCER
The Parson's Tale

[3423]
Cf.: The woman was formed out of man—not out of his head to rule over him; not out of his feet to be trod upon by him; but out of his side to be his equal, from beneath his arm to be protected, and from near his heart to be loved.
MATTHEW HENRY

[3424]
Man's sin is that he has not had enough humility; woman's that she has had too much of it. It is as if, by letting women carry the burden of being humble and pious for them, men have got rid of any need to appropriate these virtues for themselves and so have felt free to visit aggression on the world.
SHEILA D. COLLINS

[3425]
There is a woman at the beginning of all great things.
ALPHONSE DE LAMARTINE

[3426]
I'm not denying the women are foolish: God Almighty made 'em to match the men.
GEORGE ELIOT

[3427]
The society of women is the foundation of good manners.
JOHANN WOLFGANG VON GOETHE

[3428]
It was Christ who discovered and emphasized the worth of woman. It was Christ who lifted her into equality with man. It was Christ who gave woman her chance, who saw her possibilities, who discovered her value.
ARTHUR JOHN GOSSIP

[3429]
A beautiful and chaste woman is the perfect workmanship of God and the sole wonder of the world.
GEORG HERMES

[3430]
Man has his will, but woman has her way.
OLIVER WENDELL HOLMES

[3431]
When I see the elaborate study and ingenuity displayed by women in the pursuit of trifles, I feel no doubt of their capacity for the most herculean undertakings.
JULIA WARD HOWE

[3432]
A hearth is no hearth unless a woman sit by it.
RICHARD JEFFERIES

[3433]
Nature intended that woman should be her masterpiece.
GOTTHOLD EPHRAIM LESSING

[3434]
When you educate a man you educate an individual; when you educate a woman you educate a whole family.
CHARLES D. MCIVER

[3435]
Who can tell how many of the most original thoughts put forth by male writers belong to a woman by suggestion? If I may judge by my own case, a very large proportion indeed.
JOHN STUART MILL

[3436]
Women are not altogether in the wrong when they refuse the rules of life prescribed to the world, for men only have established them and without their consent.
MICHEL DE MONTAIGNE

[3437]
The best woman has always somewhat of a man's strength, and the noblest man of a woman's gentleness.
DINAH MARIA MULOCK

[3438]
With more and more women of our day there is an urge to creativeness which lies underneath and deeper, above and beyond the begetting of children. These women have a contract with life itself.
LAURENS VAN DER POST

[3439]
A good wife who can find? She is far more precious than jewels.
PROVERBS 31:10 (RSV)

[3440]
Many people entertain the idea that a woman does not achieve acceptance, respect, dignity and status unless or until she becomes a wife and mother. Jesus Christ does not make such distinctions. He confers no second-class citizenship. In Christ all men and women are set free to seek the abundant life. They need only to acknowledge his Lordship.
MAVIS R. SANDERS

[3441]
God save us all from wives who are angels in the street, saints in the church, and devils at home.
CHARLES H. SPURGEON

[3442]
Whatever women do, they must do twice as well as men to be thought half as good. Luckily, this is not difficult.

CHARLOTTE WHITTON

[3443]
Of course it's a man's world. A woman would surely be too sensible to want it.

WONDER

[3444]
Wonder . . . is the seed of knowledge.

FRANCIS BACON

[3445]
If you accept this Gospel and become Christ's man, you will stumble on wonder upon wonder, and every wonder true.

BRENDAN TO KING BRUDE

[3446]
I would sooner live in a cottage and wonder at everything than live in a castle and wonder at nothing.

JOAN WINMILL BROWN

[3447]
The first wonder is the offspring of ignorance, the last is the parent of adoration.

SAMUEL TAYLOR COLERIDGE

[3448]
Wonder is reverence for the infinite values and meaning of life, and marveling over God's purpose and patience in it all.

GEORGE WALTER FISKE

[3449]
Wonder connected with a principle of rational curiosity is the source of all knowledge and discovery . . . but wonder which ends in wonder and is satisfied with wonder is the quality of an idiot.

SAMUEL HORSLEY

WORK

[3450]
In time you may perhaps find that most of the work of the world is done by people who aren't feeling very well.

LE BARON RUSSELL BRIGGS

[3451]
I considered all that my hands had done and the toil I had spent in doing it, and behold, all was vanity and a striving after wind, and there was nothing to be gained under the sun.

ECCLESIASTES 2:11 (RSV)

[3452]
Work won't kill, but worry will.

ENGLISH PROVERB

[3453]
God give me work till my life shall end, and life till my work is done.

WINIFRED HOLTBY

[3454]
It's no credit to anyone to work too hard.

EDGAR W. HOWE

[3455]
Nothing is work unless you would rather be doing something else.

WILLIAM JAMES

[3456]
A dairymaid can milk cows to the glory of God.

MARTIN LUTHER

[3457]
It is our best work that he wants, not the dregs of our exhaustion. I think he must prefer quality to quantity.

GEORGE MACDONALD

[3458]
If people knew how hard I work to get my mastery it wouldn't seem so wonderful after all.

MICHELANGELO

[3459]
Our self-centered and subjective-minded generation tends to think that work is justified only if it "assists in the development of personality.". . . The ready acceptance and faithful performance of work because it is socially necessary will develop the only kind of personality worth developing.

ALEXANDER MILLER

[3460]
I look back on my life like a good day's work.

GRANDMA MOSES

[3461]
I have learned to place myself before God every day as a vessel to be filled with his Holy Spirit. He has given me the blessed assurance that he, as the everlasting God, has guaranteed his own work in me.

ANDREW MURRAY

[3462]
Work expands so as to fill the time available for its completion. The thing to be done swells in importance and complexity in a direct ratio with the time to be spent.

C. NORTHCOTE PARKINSON

[3463]
Work is the natural exercise and function of man. . . . Work is not primarily a thing one does to live, but the thing one lives to do. It is, or should be, the full expression of the worker's faculties, the thing in which he finds spiritual, mental and bodily satisfaction, and the medium in which he offers himself to God.

DOROTHY L. SAYERS

[3464]
God buries his workmen but carries on his work.

CHARLES WESLEY

[3465]
Everybody wants to harvest, but nobody wants to plow.

[3466]
When the load feels heavy, it's a sign you're climbing.

WORKS

[3467]
Serving Christ is not overwork but overflow.

CURTIS B. AKENSON

[3468]
Good works must be done, not to merit thereby eternal life, which is a free gift of God, nor for ostentation or from selfishness, which the Lord rejects, but for the glory of God.

HENRY BULLINGER

[3469]
We are saved not by works, yet not without works.

JOHN CALVIN

[3470]
The greatest competitor of devotion to Jesus is service for him.

OSWALD CHAMBERS

[3471]
In contemplation you serve only yourselves. In good works you serve many
people.
                            MEISTER ECKHART

[3472]
Many a man preaches Christ but gets in
front of him by the multiplicity of his
own works. It will be your ruin if you
do! Christ can do without your works,
what he wants is you. Yet if he really
has you he will have all your works.
. . . It is possible to be so active in the
service of Christ as to forget to love
him.
                                P. T. FORSYTH

[3473]
I expect to pass through the world but
once. Any good therefore that I can do,
or any kindness that I can show to any
fellow creature, let me do it now. Let
me not defer it or neglect it, for I shall
not pass this way again.
                        STEPHEN GRELLET (attr.)

[3474]
Teach us, O gracious Lord, to begin
our works with a reverent spirit, to go
on with obedience, and to finish them
in love, and then to wait patiently in
hope, and with cheerful confidence to
look up to Thee, whose promises are
faithful and rewards infinite, through
Jesus Christ our Lord.
                            GEORGE HICKES

[3475]
As the body apart from the spirit is
dead, so faith apart from works is dead.
                            JAMES 2:26 (RSV)

[3476]
The greatest pleasure I know is to do a
good action by stealth, and to have it
found out by accident.
                            CHARLES LAMB

[3477]
Our faith in Christ does not free us
from works but from false opinions
concerning works, that is, from the
foolish presumption that justification is
acquired by works.
                            MARTIN LUTHER

[3478]
Let your good deeds glow for all to see,
so that they will praise your heavenly
Father.
                            MATTHEW 5:16
                            (The Living Bible)

[3479]
I desire you to insist on these things, so
that those who have believed in God
may be careful to apply themselves to
good deeds; these are excellent and
profitable to men.
                            TITUS 3:8 (RSV)

[3480]
Do all the good you can, by all the
means you can, in all the ways you can,
in all the places you can, at all the times
you can, to all the people you can, as
long as ever you can.
                            JOHN WESLEY

[3481]
A do-gooder is a person trying to live
beyond his spiritual income.
                            H. A. WILLIAMS

WORLD

[3482]
The world is like a board with holes in
it, and the square men have got into the
round holes, and the round into the
square.
                            GEORGE BERKELEY

[3483]
O Lord, support us all the day long,
until the shadows lengthen and the
evening comes, and the busy world is
hushed, and the fever of life is over,
and our work is done. Then in Thy
mercy grant us a safe lodging, and a
holy rest, and peace at the last.

BOOK OF COMMON PRAYER

[3484]
I am a citizen of the world.

DIOGENES

[3485]
The end of God's creating the world
was to prepare a kingdom for his Son.

JONATHAN EDWARDS

[3486]
It is not a world out of joint that makes
our problem, but the shipwrecked soul
in it. It is Hamlet, not his world, that is
wrong.

P. T. FORSYTH

[3487]
The world has a lot of glitter, but it
doesn't have the glow.

BILL FRYE

[3488]
The world is charged with the grandeur of God.

GERARD MANLEY HOPKINS
"God's Grandeur"

[3489]
God loved the world so much that he
gave his only Son so that anyone who
believes in him shall not perish but
have eternal life.

JOHN 3:16
(The Living Bible)

[3490]
It is five minutes to twelve on the clock
of the world's history.

ADOLPH KELLER

[3491]
What the soul is in the body, this the
Christians are in the world. Christians
hold the world together.

Letter to Diognetus

[3492]
The sons of this world are wiser in their
own generation than the sons of light.

LUKE 16:8 (RSV)

[3493]
The view we entertain of God will determine our view of the world.

CHRISTOPH ERNST LUTHARDT

[3494]
The world has become a global village.

MARSHALL McLUHAN

[3495]
The unrest of this weary world is its
unvoiced cry after God.

THEODORE T. MUNGER

[3496]
I look upon all the world as my parish.

JOHN WESLEY

[3497]
The world hopes for the best but Jesus
Christ offers the best hope.

JOHN WESLEY WHITE

[3498]
The ship's place is in the sea, but God
pity the ship when the sea gets into it.
The Christian's place is in the world,
but God pity the Christian if the world
gets the best of him.

WORRY

[3499]
We would worry less about what others
think of us if we realized how seldom
they do.

ETHEL BARRETT

[3500]
There are two days in the week about which I never worry. Two carefree days, kept sacredly free from fear and apprehension. One of these days is yesterday—and the other is tomorrow.
ROBERT BURDETTE

[3501]
Are you looking unto Jesus now, in the immediate matter that is pressing, and receiving from him peace? If so, he will be a gracious benediction of peace in and through you. But if you try to worry it out, you obliterate him and deserve all you get.
OSWALD CHAMBERS

[3502]
Worry is interest paid on trouble before it becomes due.
WILLIAM R. INGE

[3503]
Worry and trust cannot live in the same house. When worry is allowed to come in one door, trust walks out the other door; and worry stays until trust is invited in again, whereupon worry walks out.
ROBERT G. LETOURNEAU

[3504]
Worry does not empty tomorrow of its sorrow; it empties today of its strength.
CORRIE TEN BOOM

[3505]
Ulcers are something you get from mountain-climbing over molehills.

[3506]
Why worry about things you cannot control? Why not get busy controlling the things that depend on you?

[3507]
You can't change the past, but you can ruin a perfectly good present by worrying about the future.

WORSHIP

[3508]
O my Lord! If I worship Thee from fear of hell, burn me in hell, and if I worship Thee from hope of Paradise, exclude me from it; but if I worship Thee for Thine own sake, then withhold not from me Thine Eternal Beauty.
RABIA AL-ADAWIYYA

[3509]
It is only when men begin to worship that they begin to grow.
CALVIN COOLIDGE

[3510]
As you worship, so you serve.
THOMAS L. JOHNS

[3511]
Worship depends not upon our own activities, but upon the activities which God brings to bear upon us; to them we are forced to react as worshipers.
KENNETH E. KIRK

[3512]
Every act of worship is its own justification. It is rendering to God that of which he is worthy.
ERIC L. MASCALL

[3513]
We are the true circumcision, who worship God in spirit, and glory in Christ Jesus, and put no confidence in the flesh.
PHILIPPIANS 3:3 (RSV)

[3514]
If the order of your worship service is so rigid that it can't be changed, it had better be changed.
THEODORE A. RAEDEKE

[3515]
When Christian worship is dull and joyless, Jesus Christ has been left outside—that is the only possible explanation.

JAMES S. STEWART

[3516]
The true inner life is no strange or new thing; it is the ancient and true worship of God, the Christian life in its beauty and in its own peculiar form. Wherever there is a man who fears God and lives the good life, in any country under the sun, God is there, loving him, and so I love him too.

GERHARD TERSTEEGEN

WRITING

[3517]
To write well, express yourself like the common people, but think like a wise man.

ARISTOTLE

[3518]
Writers should use a rifle rather than a shotgun.

JOSEPH BAYLY

[3519]
Men have lost sight of distant horizons. Nobody writes of humanity, for civilization; they write for their country, their sect; to amuse their friends or annoy their enemies.

NORMAN DOUGLAS

[3520]
Any man who will look into his heart and honestly write what he sees there will find plenty of readers.

EDGAR W. HOWE

[3521]
What is written without effort is in general read without pleasure.

SAMUEL JOHNSON

[3522]
Writing is like a "lust," or like "scratching when you itch."

C. S. LEWIS

[3523]
The mark of a really great writer is that he gives expression to what the masses of mankind think or feel without knowing it. The mediocre writer simply writes what everyone would have said.

G. C. LICHTENBERG

[3524]
What I like in a good author is not what he says, but what he whispers.

LOGAN PEARSALL SMITH

[3525]
There ain't nothing more to write about, and I am rotten glad of it, because if I'd a knowed what a trouble it was to make a book I wouldn't a tackled it, and ain't a-going to no more.

MARK TWAIN
Huckleberry Finn

YOUTH

[3526]
Young men soon give and soon forget affronts; old age is slow in both.

JOSEPH ADDISON

[3527]
Young men are fitter to invent than to judge; fitter for execution than for counsel; and fitter for new projects than for settled business.

FRANCIS BACON

[3528]
Oh, youth! The strength of it, the faith of it, the imagination of it! To me she was not an old rattletrap carting about the world a lot of coal for a freight—to me she was the endeavor, the test, the trial of life.

JOSEPH CONRAD

[3529]
Almost everything that is great has been done by youth.
BENJAMIN DISRAELI

[3530]
Remember also your Creator in the days of your youth.
ECCLESIASTES 12:1 (RSV)

[3531]
Young people will respond if the challenge is tough enough and hard enough. Youth wants a master and a controller. Young people were built for God, and without God as the center of their lives they become frustrated and confused, desperately grasping for and searching for security.
BILLY GRAHAM

[3532]
Youth is pre-eminently the forming, fixing period, the spring season of disposition and habit; and it is during this season, more than any other, that the character assumes its permanent shape and color, and the young are wont to take their course for time and for eternity.
JOEL HAWES

[3533]
At almost every step in life we meet with young men from whom we anticipate wonderful things, but of whom, after careful inquiry, we never hear another word. Like certain chintzes, calicoes and ginghams, they show finely on their first newness, but cannot stand the sun and rain, and assume a very sober aspect after washing-day.
NATHANIEL HAWTHORNE

[3534]
There is a feeling of eternity in youth.
WILLIAM HAZLITT

[3535]
The sins of youth are paid for in old age.
LATIN PROVERB

[3536]
When we are out of sympathy with the young, then I think our work in this world is over.
GEORGE MACDONALD

[3537]
The glory of young men is their strength.
PROVERBS 20:29 (RSV)

[3538]
Let no one despise your youth, but set the believers an example in speech and conduct, in love, in faith, in purity.
1 TIMOTHY 4:12 (RSV)

ZEAL

[3539]
Fire is the chosen symbol of heaven for moral passion. God is love; God is fire. The two are one. The Holy Spirit baptizes in fire. Spirit-filled souls are ablaze for God. They love with a love that glows. They believe with a faith that kindles. They serve with a devotion that consumes. They hate sin with a fierceness that burns. They rejoice with a joy that radiates. Love is perfected in the fire of God.
SAMUEL CHADWICK

[3540]
The joy of catching a soul is unspeakable! When we have got one soul we become possessed by the passion for souls. Get one and you will want a crowd. Why should a man apologize for leading his fellows to the running waters and the bracing air of the open moor? Ours is the Pentecostal inheritance. Let us assume the Pentecostal attitude of zealous and hungry reception.

JOHN HENRY JOWETT

[3541]
It was a Saturday, toward noon, in the month of July of 1903. The "preparation" service of an old-time Scottish Communion season was being held in the open air among the hills, in the Highland parish of Rogart, in Sutherlandshire. A minister was preaching from a wooden pulpit, traditionally called "the tent," to some hundreds of people seated on benches and on the ground, in the shade of some large trees, in the glen. I cannot recall anything that the minister said. But something, someone, said within me with overwhelming power that I, too, must preach, that I must stand where that man stood.

JOHN A. MACKAY

[3542]
[Church] reunion lies in all of us becoming responsive to the perennial Reformation that is the work of the Holy Spirit speaking to each successive age. . . . When, in obedience, we all get back to find again the Gospel principles of fellowship and worship that are never old, the temper of our respective zeals will rise again to white heat.

GEORGE F. MACLEOD

[3543]
The true zealot whom God approveth [is] he whose spirit is in fervency and not in show.

MEDE

[3544]
Misplaced zeal is zeal for God rather than zeal of God.

WILLIAM L. PETTINGILL

[3545]
The zeal of thine house hath eaten me up.

PSALM 69:9 (KJV)

[3546]
I bear them record that they have a zeal of God, but not according to knowledge.

ROMANS 10:2 (KJV)

[3547]
Take away everything I have, but do not take away the sweetness of walking and talking with the King of Glory!

JOHN STAM (martyr)

[3548]
Have therefore first zeal to thyself, and then mayest thou have zeal to thy neighbor.

THOMAS À KEMPIS

[3549]
Zeal is like fire; it needs both feeding and watching.

Index of Authors

Numbers in this index correspond to numbers placed serially in the left-hand margin throughout the book.

Sanders, J. Oswald, 2449
Sanders, Mavis R., 3440
Sanderson, John, 316
Sangster, W. E., 232
Sanskrit Proverb, 3240
Santayana, George, 74, 740
Sarnoff, David, 2329
Savonarola, Girolamo, 3301
Sayce, A. H., 2905
Sayers, Dorothy L., 261, 981, 1779, 2869, 3218, 3350, 3463
Schachtel, Hyman Judah, 2048
Schaefer, Roy L., 3166
Schaeffer, Francis A., 92, 467, 489, 2018, 2612, 3043
Scharper, Philip, 963
Scherer, Paul E., 233, 1079, 3151
Schiller, Johann Friedrich von, 747, 2594, 3226, 3322
Schleiermacher, Friedrich, 1093
Schlesinger, Arthur M., Jr., 2637
Schlink, M. Basilea, 1145
Schmidt, Henry J., 2053
Scholtes, Peter, 824
Schopenhauer, Arthur, 490, 1346
Schrödinger, Erwin, 2089
Schroeder, Johann Hieronymus, 1267
Schwab, Charles M., 871
Schweitzer, Albert, 2745, 3073
Scots Confession, 1206
Scott, Martin J., 3323
Scott, Walter, 1642, 2680
Scottish Proverb, 1463, 1529
Scroggie, W. Graham, 614
Secker, Thomas, 98
Second Vatican Council, 825
Seeberg, Reinhold, 1760
Selden, John, 75
Seneca, 99, 1329, 1929, 3044, 3241
Senn, J. P., 76
Sewall, Samuel, 958
Seward, William H., 1307
Shakespeare, William, 38, 77, 317, 1207, 1330, 2189, 2595, 2906, 3339
Sharp, William, 1970
Shaw, Geoffrey, 2054
Shaw, George Bernard, 305, 427, 714, 1474, 1649, 1654, 2274, 2746, 2817
Shedd, John A., 1687
Sheen, Fulton J., 318, 388, 615, 1072, 2308, 2943, 2999
Sheppard, R. H. L. (Dick), 192
Shoemaker, Samuel M., 1016, 1816, 2379, 2707, 3183
Sidney, Philip, 715, 3227
Silone, Ignazio, 137
Simmons, Charles, 2828, 3000
Simpson, A. B., 2517

Singh, Sadhu Sundar, 1424, 1791
Sioux Indian Saying, 861
Sizoo, Joseph, 2685
Skeath, William C., 3197
Skinner, Tom, 2309, 2659
Skinsnes, Olaf, 2111
Skogsbergh, Erik August, 3414
Slessor, Mary, 209, 756, 3277
Sloan, Steve, 193
Small, Dwight, 2027
Small, R. Leonard, 1817
Smeaton, George, 3097
Smedes, Lewis B., 144
Smith, Alexander, 389
Smith, Dorothy Cameron, 390
Smith, Estelle, 1573
Smith, Fred, 349, 1701, 1873, 2367, 3177, 3242
Smith, George L., 939
Smith, Hannah Whitall, 370, 2944
Smith, Herbert Booth, 2773
Smith, J. E., 194
Smith, Logan Pearsall, 3524
Smith, O. E., 1017
Smith, Oswald J., 3106
Smith, Roy L., 119, 587, 1030, 1908, 2132, 2526, 2747
Smith, Sydney, 2352
Smith, Wilbur M., 1437, 3147
Sockman, Ralph W., 391
Söderblom, Nathan, 2861
Solzhenitsyn, Aleksandr I., 3340
Sorokin, Pitirim A., 3074
South, Robert, 2708
Southcott, Ernest, 410
Southern Prayer, 1464
Spanish Proverb, 1296, 1887, 2123, 2954
Spender, J. A., 3045
Spong, John, 2885
Spranger, Edward, 3385
Sprat, Thomas, 319
Spring, Gardiner, 2829
Spurgeon, Charles H., 51, 65, 110, 648, 958, 1232, 1452, 1732, 1749, 2233, 2479, 2509, 2510, 2518, 2539, 2709, 3047, 3219, 3269, 3278, 3441
Stam, John, 3547
Steele, Richard, 2282, 3015
Steinmetz, Charles P., 848, 3107
Sterne, Laurence, 2596, 2759, 2945
Sterner, Robert L., 284
Stevenson, Robert Louis, 253, 320, 1268, 1322, 1369, 1818, 2112
Stewart, James S., 273, 350, 877, 1283, 1356, 1548, 1630, 2113, 2456, 3515
Stolz, Karl Ruf, 1733
Stott, John R. W., 1505, 1783
Strachan, Susan B., 1734

Strecker, Edward S., 509, 2606
Strong, Augustus Hopkins, 2597
Strumsky, Simeon, 686
Studdert Kennedy, G. A., 2774
Suhard, Emmanuel, 3415
Sullivan, A. M., 924
Sullivan, Harry Stack, 1996
Sullivan, J. W. N., 2892
Sunday, Billy, 321, 795, 914, 1137, 1284, 1598, 2155, 2353, 2392, 2613, 2870, 3047
Swann, William Francis Gray, 3324
Sweazey, George E., 2803
Sweet, W. W., 940
Swift, Jonathan, 78, 908, 2710, 3325
Swope, Herbert Bayard, 993
Symington, William, 2467
Syrus, Publilius, 1537, 1851, 1948, 2049, 2275

Tacitus, 1909, 2256
Talmadge, T. DeWitt, 1409, 2775
Tatian, 1409
Tauler, Johannes, 716
Taylor, Clyde W., 2114, 3416
Taylor, F. J., 2671
Taylor, H. G., 1735
Taylor, J. Hudson, 1239, 2115, 3115
Taylor, Jeremy, 336, 725, 1031, 1233, 1438, 1949, 2078, 3048, 3108, 3243
Temple, Frederick, 810
Temple, William, 411, 564, 616, 925, 1224, 1702, 1761, 3049, 3092, 3292
Ten Boom, Betsie, 1256
Ten Boom, Corrie, 52, 285, 872, 1114, 1357, 2099, 2623, 2917, 3332, 3504
Tenney, Merrill C., 617
Tennyson, Alfred, 1101, 2283, 3393
Terence, 1558, 3364
Teresa of Avila, 1997, 2205, 2450, 2642, 2946, 3093
Teresa of Calcutta, 2408
Tersteegen, Gerhard, 3516
Tertullian, 1643, 1762, 2035, 2133, 3309, 3386
Thackeray, William Makepeace, 898, 2156, 2341
Theologia Germanica, 706, 1453
Thielicke, Helmut, 695, 1240, 1506, 1998, 2206
Thieme, Robert B., 3109
Thiers, Louis Adolphe, 3166
Thiessen, Evelyn A., 243, 306
Thomas à Kempis, 626, 640, 1146, 1198, 1384, 1819, 2164, 2267, 2955, 3016, 3065, 3376, 3548
Thomas, G. Ernest, 3116
Thomas, Ian, 1792
Thomas, Nancy, 1767

Thompson, Francis, 1138
Thompson, T. H., 1852
Thoreau, Henry David, 472, 726, 959, 2147, 2165, 2575
Thornwell, J. H., 1147, 1490
Thorold, A. W., 3279
Tingson, Gregorio, 2213
Tolstoy, Leo, 307, 1033, 2818, 2947, 3341, 3351
Tooher, Thomas V., 687
Topsell, Edward, 120
Torrey, R. A., 145, 234, 2830, 3050
Tournier, Paul, 7, 497, 1018, 1046, 1054, 1828, 2544, 3387, 3417
Tourville, Henri de, 1999
Toynbee, Arnold J., 293, 428
Tozer, A. W., 235, 337, 351, 429, 649, 769, 1250, 1507, 1874, 2831
Trapp, John, 2776
Trench, Richard Chenevix, 2480, 2918, 3051, 3402
Trotman, Dawson, 1793
Trotter, I. Lilias, 1491
Troutt, Margaret, 826
Trueblood, Elton, 688, 964, 982, 2576
Tucker, Benjamin R., 1650, 3342
Tuke, Samuel, 3394
Tunney, Gene, 3001
Turkish Proverb, 2598
Turnbull, Bob, 3052
Turnbull, Ralph G., 576, 707
Tusser, Thomas, 2225
Twain, Mark, 983, 1331, 1583, 2226, 2409, 2908, 3270, 3525
Tyndale, William, 1285
Tyndall, Thomas, 1410

Ullmann, Hermann, 1475
Unamuno, Miguel de, 116, 1176, 1665, 1910, 2000
Underhill, Evelyn, 362, 969, 2036
Unger, Merrill F., 1213
Unknown, 16, 17, 18, 41, 42, 55, 56, 66, 79, 80, 154, 155, 197, 198, 199, 210, 238, 276, 288, 322, 323, 338, 339, 353, 354, 396, 397, 398, 399, 412, 474, 491, 511, 538, 580, 581, 582, 629, 757, 770, 774, 789, 801, 899, 944, 945, 946, 984, 995, 1020, 1021, 1055, 1088, 1179, 1199, 1200, 1241, 1257, 1298, 1358, 1391, 1425, 1439, 1575, 1585, 1651, 1688, 1689, 1690, 1705, 1853, 1912, 1957, 1973, 2004, 2028, 2050, 2080, 2117, 2135, 2208, 2215, 2234, 2330, 2331, 2410, 2411, 2412, 2468, 2520, 2529, 2545, 2546, 2607, 2615, 2625, 2643, 2666, 2737, 2841, 2886, 2949, 2977, 2988, 3056, 3167,

Index of Topics

The subtopics listed under each topic heading are cross references which may be found alphabetically listed in this volume.